Feasting in a Famine of the Word

Feasting in a Famine of the Word

Lutheran Preaching in the Twenty-First Century

Edited by
MARK W. BIRKHOLZ
JACOB CORZINE
and JONATHAN MUMME

Foreword by Jonathan Fisk

☙PICKWICK *Publications* · Eugene, Oregon

FEASTING IN A FAMINE OF THE WORD
Lutheran Preaching in the Twenty-First Century

Copyright © 2016 Wipf and Stock Publishers. All rights reserved. Except for brief quotations in critical publications or reviews, no part of this book may be reproduced in any manner without prior written permission from the publisher. Write: Permissions, Wipf and Stock Publishers, 199 W. 8th Ave., Suite 3, Eugene, OR 97401.

Pickwick Publications
An Imprint of Wipf and Stock Publishers
199 W. 8th Ave., Suite 3
Eugene, OR 97401

Unless otherwise indicated, all Scripture quotations are from the ESV® Bible (The Holy Bible, English Standard Version®), copyright © 2001 by Crossway, a publishing ministry of Good News Publishers. Used by permission. All rights reserved.

www.wipfandstock.com

PAPERBACK ISBN 13: 978-1-4982-0316-6
HARDCOVER ISBN 13: 978-1-4982-0318-0

Cataloguing-in-Publication data:

Feasting in a famine of the word : Lutheran preaching in the twenty-first century / edited by Mark W. Birkholz, Jacob Corzine, and Jonathan Mumme.

xxiv + 300 pp. ; 23 cm. Includes bibliographical references.

ISBN: 978-1-4982-0316-6 (paperback) | ISBN: 978-1-4982-0318-0 (hardback)

1. Preaching 2. Lutheran Church—Doctrines 3. Luther, Martin, 1483–1546 I. Birkholz, Mark W. II. Corzine, Jacob. III. Mumme, Jonathan. IV. Title

BT 764.3 F111 2016

Manufactured in the U.S.A. 02/16/2016

Contents

Foreword: Filled to Starving | vii
 —Jonathan Fisk

Contributors | xi
Abbreviations | xiii
Introduction | xvi

1. Is There a Text in This Sermon? A Lutheran Survey of Contemporary Preaching Methods | 1
 —John Bombaro

2. Certainty in the Sermon: Patterns of Preaching from Peter and Pentecost | 30
 —Mark W. Birkholz

3. The Israel of God in the Sermon: Connecting Old Testament Texts to New Testament People | 45
 —Paul M. C. Elliott

4. Nicholas of Cusa and the Reformation of Preaching | 63
 —Richard J. Serina Jr.

5. Systematic Theology and Preaching in the Thought of Johann Gerhard | 78
 —Roy Axel Coats

6. Assuring the Faithful: On Faith and Doubt in Lutheran Preaching | 98
 —Jacob Corzine

7. The Difference of Differentiating Address: The "We," "I," and "You," of Preaching, and the Gospel as the Gospel | 117
 —Jonathan Mumme

8   Preaching as Foolishness | 140
    —Steven Paulson

9   Paraenesis in Preaching: Some Systematic-Theological Considerations for a Homiletical Problem | 157
    —Hans-Jörg Voigt

10 Liturgical Preaching: The Pitfalls and the Promise | 166
    —John T. Pless

11 The Real Presence and Liturgical Preaching | 179
    —John W. Kleinig

12 The Preacher's Tongue and the Hearer's Ear: Compelled by the Spirit | 192
    —David Petersen

13 Gloomy Revelations or Comforting Doctrines? | 210
    —Esko Murto

14 Learning to Lament: Preaching to Suffering in the Lament Psalms | 225
    —Jeremiah Johnson

15 The Preacher as Physician for the Sick in Spirit | 241
    —Jakob Appell

16 Present Preaching | 257
    —Daniel J. Schmidt

17 The Path from the Text to the Sermon: A German Preacher Takes Stock of Methods from America | 277
    —Gottfried Martens

Foreword
Filled to Starving

—Jonathan Fisk

Water is what we seek. Food. Sustenance. Something to propitiate the pain.

Day in and day out we give our lives to the filling of our bellies. By the sweat of our brows and the callouses on our hands, in gray and dwindling days we busy ourselves with the unhappy work God has given to the children of fallen man, constantly trying to fool ourselves with saccharine lies.

If only the meaninglessness could be its own meaning! If only the vanity could not be so futile! If only our folly could somehow become great and precious—even godly! If only our evil could be turned into something good!

The root of this malnourished state is not the starvation of our bodies. It is the atrophy of our souls. Destroying humanity one life at a time, the bent inward hunger of our race believes from conception that "I" is the greatest spiritual feast, confesses with every thought that "myself" is the ultimate source of satisfaction.

It is killing us.

It was a well-fed man in a garden designed for perfect joy who first chose to shackle us to the consignment of "me."

It was a starving man in a desert who finally had the essential qualities to call it all the lie that it is.

"Man shall not live by bread alone." (Matt 3:4a)

Thus preached Jesus of Nazareth.

"Man lives on every word that comes from the mouth of God." (Matt 3:4b, alt.)

If there was any great insight, any divine spark, in the mind of Dr. Martin Luther, the man who catalyzed the Reformation of the catholic church, it was this preaching. Yes, "grace alone." Yes, "faith alone." But the gospel of these truths exists because the foundational doctrine on which every "for you!" and "your forgiveness!" rings out is *Scripture alone*. For the Reformer, this was no new law from Moses. This is greatest promise of the saving God: the actual, audible, even physical, words of the living, Creator God have actually been written down for sinful men to inwardly digest and so be saved from sin, death and the devil. Eternal words have been written down for our reading, for our marking, and for our learning. But more than any of these, they have been written down for our *hearing*.

"So faith comes from hearing, and hearing through the word of Christ." (Rom 10:17)

Luther understood, perhaps as no other church father before him, that in Adam's sin, the first man reduced all men to mean beggars in the most particular of ways. That thing for which all people must beg, that thing for lack of which men, women, and children alike are starving, is not the fruit of peace or patience or kindness. It is the food on which branches that bear fruit must feed: God's mouth.

Empty sacks of arrogance and death as we are, worthy of nothing but to be cast into endless flames along with all evil that sets itself against the good, our root of wickedness, our core of evil, stems not first from pride, but from a rejection of God's own spoken word *as* God's own spoken eternal Word. With nothing to believe, our faith dies, and so with it our souls. Luther understood this, as well as the magnificent counteraction of the God who chose to speak again, in spite of our deaf ears, and even for the sake of healing them. "The Lord! the Lord! A God merciful and gracious!" (Exod 34:6)

In his unfathomable steadfastness, and particularly (even scandalously!) against all human reason, God looked down upon the wretchedness wrought on mankind by mankind, and spoke that the fact it would not be so. The Word went forth from his mouth against our void, the begotten Son hurtling toward the now-too-quiet planet for the express purpose of a voice crying in the wilderness once more. From the cross, the Christ spoke seven words, and in every direction through all of history, back and back, even to the garden where the promise of a Seed was first prophesied, forward and more so, even to this moment where you and I hear, believe and confess, the atoning goodness of Jesus preaches, preached and will preach.

Against the lies.
Against the vanity.
Against the wisdom and strength of men.
"Be still, and know that I am God." (Ps 46:10a)
Gospel!
"I am the God who wills it that you not to die!"

This was Luther's insight. This is why Luther preached. This is what so many heard. Believed. Preached and confessed themselves.

With this hidden power of the living God, the Reformation shattered the dark and twisted peace of Babylon's quiet captivity of the church. There, in the little town of Wittenberg God ended the famine with a great and marvelous feast.

But today we live in different times.

It has happened more than once. It will no doubt happen again if our Lord should tarry. It is always a well-fed man who is least hungry. The belly filled with many things burps up apathy when offered the one thing needful. The cares and pleasures of finer life rise up and distract. Satiated on the delicacies of the flesh, men cannot bear another bite, and so choke on the precious texts of Holy Scripture. They are too difficult, to tasteless, to tiresome to swallow.

"Feed my sheep." (John 21:17b)

Many charged to be great chefs, do the same. Seeing that the people are not hungry enough, they bring out of their pantries anything they can find that might sweeten the meal they have been sent to serve. Mixing a porridge of spiced poisons and leavened platitudes, they dole out to foolish children food which gorges the palate but does not fill, until at last the bellies ache and the people cast about for even a drop of pure water to moisten their now parched and burning tongues. By then it is too late.

All the more, the chefs preach not, nor trust the Scripture's plain text. A bitter herb will not avail us now! Instead, they open a jar of dreams, and purchase the fine flavor of power from the markets of the world. While the people starve, the air is filled with hot and lofty words, the babble of possibilities, pretentions and empty promises. The sheep grow lean and weary. The lambs are pushed aside by stronger goats who smell a morsel. The flock wanders and the heard scatters, driven by need and despair for any hint, any scent of real food.

Wolves always prowl.

But.

But. The words of that starving man in the desert are still written down. The words of that teacher who had no place to reset his head still remain for our reading. The words of that God who died on the cross can yet be preached into the face of the growing storm.

"I will build my church," Jesus said. (Matt 16:18)

He told us beforehand so that we might understand when these things took place. Nothing is new. Nothing has changed. There is no postmodern need which is not common to the children of men. The devil, the world and our flesh are hardly so creative as that. What the Everlasting Man has instituted cannot be broken. He who neither slumbers nor sleeps shall not stop preaching from the beginning of history to the end of the world and beyond.

"If anyone loves me, he will keep my word." (John 14:23a)

While the pews grow more empty year by year, as the callous and willful ignore this fact, as the vainglorious maintain the system, or the building, or call for a new day, a new man, or a new song, blind men lead the blind, and the body of the western church staggers, drunk with the euphoria of starvation. The pit looms before us all. Judgment is not sleeping. Night soon comes when no man can work, and a voice from heaven says, "Cry!"

What shall we cry?

It is in the humiliated and weak contemplation of our poor estate that, as children of the Reformer, we offer this collection of essays to the catholic church of gray and latter days. It is in surreal awareness of our hunger that we have pondered, struggled, studied, and discussed. It is painfully keen awareness of our poverty that, as beggars, we return to the clay from which our Reformation was first formed by the hand of God and seek to dredge from its witness a morsel that might enliven our age once again.

When the pews sit empty, with our generation coming of age only to frolic like Israel before the calf of gold, hearing the world with scornful wonder mock, watching congregations destroy their pastors and shepherds feed on their own sheep, we know this much: it is only a fool who can look out upon the vacancy of faith in which we together are dying and fail to ask, "Might it not be that there is a problem with our preaching?"

> "There is no more terrible disaster with which the wrath of God can afflict men than a famine of the hearing of his word."
>
> Dr. Martin Luther, *Treatise on Christian Liberty*.

Contributors

Jakob Appell, Assistant Pastor of the Kvillebäcken Congregation of the Mission Province and Chaplain of the Lutheran School of Theology, Gothenburg, Sweden.

Mark Birkholz, Pastor of Faith Evangelical Lutheran Church, Oak Lawn, IL.

John Bombaro, Senior Pastor of Grace Lutheran Church, Lecturer in the Department of Theology and Religious Studies at the University of San Diego, and Chaplain, LT of the United States Navy Reserves, San Diego, CA.

Roy Axel Coats, Pastor of the Lutheran Church of the Redeemer, Baltimore, MD.

Jacob Corzine, Lutheran Campus Minister, University of Pretoria, Pretoria, South Africa and ThD Candidate, Humboldt University, Berlin, Germany.

Paul M. C. Elliott, PhD Candidate at Hebrew Union College-Jewish Institute of Religion, Cincinnati, OH and Assistant Pastor of St. John Lutheran Church, Aurora, IN.

Jonathan Fisk, Pastor of St. John's Lutheran Church, Oakes, ND.

Jeremiah Johnson, Pastor of Glory of Christ Lutheran Church, Plymouth, MN

John Kleinig, Emeritus Lecturer and Sessional Lecturer at Australian Lutheran College, Adelaide, Australia.

Gottfried Martens, Pastor of Trinity Evangelical Lutheran Church, Berlin (Steglitz), Germany.

Jonathan Mumme, Assistant Professor of Theology at Concordia University Wisconsin, Mequon, WI.

Esko Murto, Pastor of St. Mark's Lutheran Congregation, Mission Diocese, Helsinki, Finland.

Steven Paulson, Professor of Systematic Theology at Luther Seminary, St. Paul, MN.

David Petersen, Senior Pastor at Redeemer Lutheran Church, Fort Wayne, IN.

John T. Pless, Assistant Professor of Pastoral Ministry and Missions at Concordia Theological Seminary, Fort Wayne, IN.

Daniel Schmidt, Pastor of Immanuel Lutheran Church, Groß Oesingen, Germany.

Richard J. Serina, Jr., Pastor of Christ the King Lutheran Church, Ringwood, NJ and Guest Lecturer in Historical Theology, Concordia Seminary, St. Louis, MO.

Hans-Jörg Voigt, Bishop of the Independent Evangelical Lutheran Church of Germany (*Selbstständige Evangelisch-Lutherische Kirche—SELK*), Hannover, Germany.

Abbreviations

REFERENCE WORKS

BDAG   Danker, Frederick W., et al. *A Greek-English Lexicon of the New Testament and other Early Christian Literature*. 3rd ed. Chicago: University of Chicago Press, 2000.

DTIB   Vanhoozer, Kevin J., et al., eds. *Dictionary for Theological Interpretation of the Bible*. Grand Rapids: Baker, 2005.

EC   Fahlbusch, Erwin, and Geoffrey W. Bromiley, et al. *The Encyclopedia of Christianity*. 5 vols. Grand Rapids: Eerdmans, 2005.

LSB   The Commission on Worship of The Lutheran Church—Missouri Synod. *Lutheran Service Book*. St. Louis: Concordia, 2006.

LW   Pelikan, Jaroslav and Helmut Lehman, eds. *Luther's Works*. American Edition. 55 vols. Philadelphia: Muhlenberg and Fortress and St. Louis: Concordia, 1955–1986.

RPP   Betz, Hans Dieter, et al. *Religion Past & Present: Encyclopedia of Theology and Religion*. 6 vols. Leiden: Brill, 2009.

TDNT   Kittel, G. and G. Friedrich, eds. *Theological Dictionary of the New Testament*. Translated by G. W. Bromiley. 10 vols. Grand Rapids: Eerdmans, 1964–1976.

TLH   The Evangelical Lutheran Synodical Conference of North America. *The Lutheran Hymnal*. St. Louis: Concordia, 1941.

WA   Luther, Martin. *D. Martin Luthers Werke, kritische Gesamtausgabe*. 120 vols. Weimar: H. Böhlaus, 1883–2009.

LUTHERAN CONFESSIONS

Works within the Book of Concord are abbreviated as follows:

AC	The Augsburg Confession
AP	The Apology to the Augsburg Confession
FC EP	The Epitome of the Formula of Concord
FC SD	The Solid Declaration of the Formula of Concord
LC	The Large Catechism
SA	The Smalcald Articles
SC	The Small Catechism

Editions and translations of the Book of Concord are referenced as follows:

BSLK   *Die Bekenntnisschriften der evangelish-lutherischen Kirche.* Göttingen: Vandenhoeck & Ruprecht, 1930

KW   Kolb, Robert and Timothy Wengert, eds. *The Book of Concord: The Confessions of the Evangelical Lutheran Church.* Translated by Charles Arand, et al. Minneapolis: Fortress, 2000

Tappert   Tappert, Theodore G., et al eds. *The Book of Concord: The Confessions of the Evangelical Lutheran Church.* Philadelphia: Fortress, 1959.

JOURNALS AND SERIES OF PUBLICATIONS

AB	The Anchor Bible
AJL	*Australian Journal of Liturgy*
BTB	*Biblical Theology Bulletin*
CBQ	*Catholic Biblical Quarterly*
CJ	*Concordia Journal*
CT	*Christianity Today*
CTM	*Concordia Theological Monthly*
EKKNT	*Evangelisch-katholischer Kommentar zum Neuen Testament*
FSÖTh	*Forschungen zur systematischen und ökumenischen Theologie*
ICC	International Critical Commentary
JSOT	*Journal for the Study of the Old Testament*
JSSR	*Journal for the Scientific Study of Religion*
LCL	Loeb Classical Library

LTJ	*Lutheran Theological Journal*
LTK	*Lutherische Theologie und Kirche*
NeoT	*Neotestamentica*
NIGTC	New International Greek Testament Commentary
NICNT	New International Commentary on the New Testament
NovT	*Novum Testamentum*
NTS	*New Testament Studies*
SNTS	Society for New Testament Studies Monograph Series
SP	Sacra Pagina
ZNW	*Zeitschrift für die Neutestamentliche Wissenschaft*

Introduction[1]

THE COLLECTION OF ESSAYS brought together in this volume is concerned with preaching, with the sermon, and with preaching as carried out and sermons as delivered by Lutherans. It presumes that a renewed and theologically reflective emphasis on preaching is one of the hallmarks of the Reformation and therefore also of the Lutheran church. But the volume is motivated by the concern that the contemporary Lutheran sermon falls short of that moniker: "hallmark." Thus the title of the collection, *Famine to Feast*. The editors and authors are united in their conviction that Lutheran preaching is both in need and worthy of rehabilitation, and the essays reflect their attempt to contribute to this task. A close look will reveal a body of young theologians and pastors contributing, and may call up accusation of youthful idealism. Doubtless some truth lies therein. But the pastors, seminary professors, and church leaders also contributing may ease the reader's skepticism. The intention of this volume is not to replace old with new, but to learn from theologians, pastors, bishops, and apostles who have gone before—to learn from past preachers and present gifts for the perennial task of preaching as it plays out in our day, challenges included. The Lutheran understanding of the sermon as proclamation of the judgment and the promise is a common denominator in all the essays. The consideration of this task from exegetical, historical, systematic, and practical perspective forms their substance.

Setting the stage for the context in which modern preachers, at least in America, are given to work and contemplate their task is the essay from John Bombaro. "Is there a Text in This Sermon? A Lutheran Survey of Contemporary Preaching Methods" takes stock of current homiletical methods in America. Bombaro argues that consumerism forms the backdrop against which a sea of new, mixed, and hybrid homiletical forms must be understood; this ideology affects, though does not necessarily determine,

---

1. Contributed by Jacob Corzine and Jonathan Mumme.

all modern homiletical methodologies. He offers tools for navigating waters that may be foreign to many preachers and can be outright dangerous for any. Firstly, categories of sermon structures as propounded by the Lutheran homiletician, David Schmitt, provide a serviceable guide to the changing landscape. Secondly, a Lutheran homiletical distinctive of proclamation as primary discourse applied to hearers, wherein the gospel is properly distinguished from the law, anchors preachers at the center of their identity and task. So equipped, preachers setting out to faithfully preach the gospel from the biblical text may make use of virtually any type of sermon structure born of this plethora of modern methodologies.

Mark Birkholz's exegetical inquiry into the Lukan prologue and Peter's Pentecost sermon (Acts 2), "Pentecost and Peter: Patterns for Preaching," asks the question of the ground of certainty in New Testament preaching. The author deftly addresses exegetical questions while leading the reader in a clear direction, namely toward the place of such certainty in sermons today. He identifies two key aspects of this preaching which serve certainty: the reliability of the scriptural witness to speak to the events of salvation, and the ability of the hearers today to testify to the reality of God's working. These form two important components (fulfillment and witness) of apostolic preaching, both of which can be relevantly employed today. The author finally makes some remarks about the implications of these conclusions for contemporary preaching, encouraging the preacher to draw on Old Testament texts and to trace the fulfillment of biblical passages not only to the New Testament, but also to the lives of the hearers. In this way, today's preacher can provide certainty to hearers in a manner in line with the preaching of the apostles.

In his essay "The Israel of God in the Sermon," Paul Elliott addresses the question of interpreting the Old Testament faithfully and in a manner fruitful for application in the Christian sermon. He argues for a typological approach, which has both scriptural attestation and historical precedent in the Lutheran church. In particular, he develops the typological connection between Israel and the church. This connection is impossible without Jesus Christ as the link, for the people of Israel believing in him, for the prayers of Israel which are prayed by him, and for the institutions of Israel which point toward him. Elliott converses capably with modern understandings of typological exegesis, and even as he contends that his approach is particularly Lutheran, his frequent citation of ancient church authors makes a case for catholicity.

In a volume of essays by Lutheran authors with much to say about Lutheran preaching, the historically oriented piece by Richard J. Serina, Jr., "Nicolas of Cusa and the Reformation of Preaching," provides sober and insightful restraint for any possible homiletical hubris of this Reformation tradition. Preaching and the reform of its problems are not simply the cares of Protestant reformers and their historical progeny. Preaching was also a concern of medieval reform, and in "Nicholas of Cusa and the Reformation of Preaching," Serina demonstrates by the example of Cusanus that rehabilitation of preaching in the middle ages is actually a byproduct of other, somewhat mundane, though strikingly perennial factors, such as education, theological competency, proximity to one's flock, and the commitment to the care of these souls. Reformation of preaching does not begin with the formation of sermons; it is a byproduct of something else, namely (re)formation of the clergy.

Turning to the Reformation and post-Reformation era, Roy Axel Coats enquires into preaching's place in the larger discipline of theology or the vocation of a minister. In "Systematic Theology and Preaching in the Thought of Johann Gerhard," the author comes at the question of preaching's relationship to systematic theology by way of the classical Lutheran dogmatician, Johann Gerhard, drawing not only on his famous *Loci Communes* but also on his *Methodus Studii Theologici*. In what feels like a breath of fresh orthodoxy, Gerhard pleads for ordered, clear, and concise preaching drawn from systematic theology. This saves the preaching of ecclesiastical ministers from bondage to popular, conversational colloquialism or people's lower passions and emotions. More surprising, however, is Gerhard's conviction that the proper end of systematic theology, the goal to which it is ordered, is preaching. Thus systematic theology is actualized in teaching, reproving, correcting, training in righteousness (cf. 2 Tim 3:16), and comforting. Putting the old dogmatician's work under a new heading, one might say that Gerhard offers a theologically holistic way of looking at preaching.

As "faith comes by hearing" (Rom 10:17), it is preaching that awakens faith, but how does a preacher preach to those who already believe? In his essay, "Assuring the Faithful: On Faith and Doubt in Lutheran Preaching," Jacob Corzine takes up the question of how one preaches to believers who are struggling to believe (cf. Mark 9:24), taking seriously their doubt and *Anfechtung*, whilst recognizing it as theirs—namely as the doubt and struggle of believers. Toward this end "double faith" (*fides duplex/duplicia*) is examined through the reformer, Johannes Brenz's commentary on his own catechism (there as *fides visibilis/invisibilis* and *fides revelata/abscondita*), and through categories of Lutheran dogmaticians (there as *fides directa/reflexa*). Drawing on their distinctions, Corzine suggests how a preacher preaches to those believers who doubt their own faith and thus themselves as believers. By specifying the preaching of the law as a reproof of unbelief circumscribed by the gospel in the "controlled situation" of the sermon, he maintains salvation and the status of believers as realities defined by faith alone (*sola fide*) yet delivered to and therefore looked to as realities that obtain beyond them (*extra nos*) and indeed in the face of what they may not be able to see or affirm of their own faith in moments of doubt and times of trial.

In his contribution "The Difference in Differentiating Address," Jonathan Mumme addresses the question of how the preacher speaks. He parses the difference between the preacher identifying himself with those receiving his proclamation (saying "we"), or differentiating himself from them (saying "I" and "you"). His analysis of St. Paul's manner of speaking in 1 and 2 Corinthians draws out the point of departure of a "differentiating address," that is, the preaching does not legitimate the preacher's authority, but rather flows from that authority, which is God-given. In further addressing Martin Luther's preaching, the author appropriates to the preacher a proper confidence that, when he speaks, Christ speaks. This confidence, he argues, has immediate bearing for the evangelical confidence of the hearer. Mumme makes the case that this decision on the part of the preacher is pivotal for how he understands the proclamation of the gospel and thus of no little importance for one's understanding of the very nature of the gospel and of salvation.

Continuing in a systematic-theological vein, Steven Paulson argues against a readily accepted definition of theology as pertaining to thinking or understanding. Instead, theology is for proclamation, i.e. for preaching. In his article, "Preaching as Foolishness," he presents preaching as a *verbum reale* or *efficax* and thus not a word about a higher reality or a statement of an already existing fact, but rather as a creating word that gives and does what it says. This understanding of preaching stands against preaching conceived of as persuasion or as instruction toward formation (as demonstrated in the medieval classic, *The Seventh Ring*, by Alan of Lille and reflected in modern estimations of preaching). Instead, Paulson claims, "the first truth of preaching is folly." In an exposition of 1 Cor 1–4, he presents preaching as a word of which no wisdom could conceive, namely as a faithful word of divine promise, in which is fully given all that God there vouches, leaving nothing in want.

In his essay "Paraenesis in Preaching," Bishop Hans-Jörg Voigt (SELK, Germany) examines the relationship between paraenesis, law, and gospel. This systematic-theological question, he contends, cannot be answered without the practice of preaching and the applied care of souls in view. As an example of the question's complexity, he calls to attention not only the phenomenon of law–gospel "now let us" sermons, but also discrepancies between C. F. W. Walther's theses on the proper distinction between law and gospel and Walther's own preaching. Via a close reading of the Formula of Concord's relevant articles Voigt offers insights for preaching and pastoral care by which neither paraenesis nor the gospel come up short.

John Pless's article, "Liturgical Preaching: The Pitfalls and the Promise," addresses a recognized trend in twentieth century preaching and seeks to attend to the proper way to understand and implement preaching within the context of the liturgy. He surveys twentieth century liturgical preaching movement, and then looks critically to several Lutheran theologians (Hermann Sasse, Gerhard Forde, Peter Brunner, Oswald Bayer) for their critiques and appropriations of it. Pless addresses in particular the relationship of the sermon to the sacraments of baptism and the Lord's Supper and contends for an understanding of the sermon itself as sacramental. In the second part of his essay he makes a case, supported by a remark from Martin Luther about the relationship between the catechism and the divine service, for Luther's Small Catechism guiding the preacher. In so doing, Pless stakes out his position in opposition to "fanciful exegesis" and "impressionistic preaching," preferring the approach he sees in the catechism's answers, which "draw us to the promise" and "deliver the goods of the promise" instead of getting "lost in analogies to washings and meals." Pless sees the liturgy as also focused on delivery of this promise, and sees it serving as context and reinforcement for such (liturgical) preaching.

Likewise concerned with the liturgy, Australian professor John Kleinig's essay, "The Real Presence and Liturgical Preaching," addresses the location of the sermon. He expounds on the implications of preachers carrying out their office "in Christ," "in the presence of God" (2 Cor 2:17). Instead of promoting "a kind of practical Christological atheism" by speaking and acting as if the work of worship was theirs, preachers operating in the confidence of being Christ's instruments and standing in his presence may say what they say and do what they do in him and with him. The location of this speaking and acting is the liturgy, where heaven meets and is indeed brought to earth. Taking preachers into his use, in the liturgy Christ not only speaks words that bind sin and open heaven, he also delivers all that he promises by making himself present, in body and blood in the Lord's Supper. "When we preach," he says, "we do so under an open heaven."

A third run suggests a trend. David Petersen likewise enquires into the place of preaching in the Mass and in the Lutheran tradition. Implied is also a question of the relationship of preaching and preacher to the Holy Scriptures and the Holy Supper. In "The Preacher's Tongue and the Hearer's Ear: Compelled by the Spirit," the author engages not only a high view of the Holy Scriptures typical to Lutheranism, but also a high view the Holy Supper's place in the divine service, which has at times been less prominent in this tradition. In view of the holiness of Scripture and the holiness of the supper, why, he asks, would one even bother to preach? Working from the Augsburg Confession, Romans 10, and texts from Martin Luther, Petersen shows preaching to be holy speech, given and used by the Holy Spirit to create and sustain faith, and preachers to be endowed with an authority of which they need not be ashamed. For these reasons preaching is absolutely and unavoidably central, even, and precisely where the Scriptures and the supper are held in holy esteem.

In his essay, "Gloomy Revelations or Comforting Doctrines," Finnish pastor Esko Murto addresses the practicality of the supposedly unpreachable doctrines of election, the bondage of the will, and original sin. He concedes the difficulty many modern Christians have in accepting the reality of each of these doctrines, but argues that the solution to this lies not in banning them from the pulpit. Instead, he shows how a deepened understanding of these three teachings—as is present in the Lutheran tradition—in fact places them among the most useful tools available to the pastor in preaching and pastoral care. Election does not make preaching unnecessary, but is rather the very thing that happens in preaching. The bondage of the will does not reduce the sermon hearer to the status of a rock or log, but does direct him in times of anguish of faith to look to the gospel and not his own strength. Finally, the teaching of original sin affirms the worth of the individual as someone responsible to God even as it removes the impossible demand for perfect contrition. Without these teachings, Murto argues, the pastor remains little more than a pompous Bible salesman.

The conviction that preaching is an art of applied pastoral care underlies Jeremiah Johnson's article, "Learning to Lament: Preaching to Suffering in the Lament Psalms." He shows that not only in a pragmatic American culture, but also in the church, suffering is seen as an obstacle to be overcome rather than a reality to be acknowledged and borne. In the lament psalms Johnson finds a divine but foreign grammar, in which Christians need tutoring—something, he argues, which begins at the pulpit. Taking up Thomas Long's images of preacher as herald and pastor through the christological lens of the threefold office of Christ, the author shows that it is not only proper for preachers to act according to Christ's prophetic office, but also to demonstrate his priestly office. "Intercessory preaching" exhibits prayers, specifically those of lament, being brought before God. In a christological and homiletical appropriation of the lament psalms, the preacher takes suffering seriously whilst instilling confidence in God and his deliverance, which confidence, along with suffering, is of the essence of lament.

Swedish pastor Jakob Appell explores the analogy of the preaching pastor as physician in his essay, "The Preacher as Physician for the Sick in

Spirit." He orients himself closely on the understanding of a physician as one who is licensed by an authority, acts on behalf of that authority, and possesses both knowledge and skill in application. Appell zeroes in on the preaching task as that of diagnosis, prognosis, and medication. He draws out the challenges of diagnosing without intimate knowledge of the sermon-hearers and commends, among other things, the pastor's own self-diagnosis as a tool to this end. In prognosis, he draws on the concept of *ordo salutis* to depict different responses the patient may have at different times during treatment. The preaching task here is to encourage persistence in following the prescription. The medicines available for prescription are baptism, absolution, and Holy Communion. Like a physician, it is incumbent upon a pastor to prescribe the proper medication at the proper time. Appell notes the limits of the analogy, but values it nevertheless, regarding it as underestimated.

German Pastor Daniel Schmidt, a long-time missionary in Botswana, shows his interest and expertise in twentieth-century North American homiletics while asking the very practical question of what makes a sermon a good sermon. His title, "Present Preaching," is a play on words, referring both to the presence of God in the sermon and to the task of preaching in the present tense to the people who are present. In two sections, he evaluates these two challenges within the context of North American homiletics. Though he is critical of most approaches, he is equally inclined to glean an insight or a valuable method from the same. For Schmidt there is no magic bullet, but many methods can be put into the service of God communicating himself to the hearer (presence) and of the hearer as sinner being addressed with the word of forgiveness (present situation). A good sermon is not judged chiefly by its content or delivery, but theologically by its foundation, that it is the living God who speaks in the sermon, and his Holy Spirit who assures that it accomplishes that for which it is intended.

German pastor Gottfried Martens also takes up North American homiletical methods. As any preacher knows, in preaching there is a text, there is a preacher in a pulpit, and there is the space in between. In a treatment both systematic and immanently practical Gottfried Martens asks the question of how a preacher traverses "The Path from Text to Sermon" according to homiletical methods either exported from or directly learned in America. Martens offers a theological and practical critique of the so-called "new homiletic" whilst delivering a plea both compelling and alluring for a classic among Lutheran methods, namely a form of Richard Caemmerer's "Goal, Malady, Means" approach, augmented by insights from Manfred Seitz and Gerhard Aho, and refined by parish experience. Walking the reader through steps and pointing out a host of pitfalls between exegetical textual study and delivery, the path here directed aims to enhance the coherence, continuity, and hear-ability of sermons and to ensure the proclamation of the gospel by honing the preparation process on the grindstone of properly distinguishing the gospel from the law.

Looking over this array of essays, one may note the international and otherwise variegated backgrounds of the contributors. Of the seventeen essays, three are contributed by Germans, and one each from Swedish, Finnish, and Australian theologians. Of the eleven American contributors, one is located in South Africa, another has studied in Germany and taught in England, others have studied in Australia and England. Although most of the American contributors belong to The Lutheran Church—Missouri Synod, one (Paulson) is a theologian of The Evangelical Lutheran Church in America. Six of the contributors teach at a university or seminary, a seventh has, at the time of writing, received a call to teach, an eighth and ninth have taught in the past. Two of the contributors are serving or have served in overseas missions, at least two more in domestic missionary settings. We, as editors, regard this as one of the chief strengths of the volume.

Regardless, however, of the strengths they perceive, the editors commend the following collection of essays to the judgment of the reader and the glory of God in the preaching of Jesus Christ. It is our hope that this volume serves the preaching of the gospel, making contribution to those who read and being met with the charity by preachers able to see our shortcomings and further the common efforts of all those who would faithfully proclaim Christ.

1

Is There a Text in This Sermon?
A Lutheran Survey of Contemporary Preaching Methods

—John Bombaro

ORIENTATION

In a thoughtful critique of contemporary hermeneutics, Kevin Vanhoozer challenged his readers beginning with a postmodern wordplay for a title to his book asking, *Is There a Meaning in This Text?*[1] By sampling the more popular (i.e., downloaded, podcast, viewed and broadcast) preachers in the United States en route to a survey of contemporary preaching methods[2]

---

1. Vanhoozer, *Meaning*.
2. The groundwork for this article is a sampling of three sermons from 100 individual preachers, representing various ecclesiastical and theological traditions. Denominational selections were proportioned to their demographic representation of Christianity in the United States with, of course, representation from non-denominational churches and associations. Major denominations were handled as non-factional, inclusive entities and consisted of ten general headings, viz., Roman Catholic, Lutheran, Episcopal/Anglican, Presbyterian/Reformed, Southern Baptist, Methodist/Wesleyan, Anabaptist, Pentecostal, Congregational (United Church of Christ), and Orthodox. With more than 28,000 Modern Protestant non-denominational ecclesial associations (denominations, if you will) present in the USA, sampling was limited to the sixty largest bodies of this kind as delineated by the Hartford Institute for Religion Research at Hartford

from a Lutheran perspective, I found myself frequently asking a similar question, "Is there a text in this sermon?" and sometimes even, "Is there gospel in this sermon?"

Much discussed and critiqued have been the sermons of contemporary preachers Robert Schuler, T. D. Jakes, Bill Hybels, Joyce Meyer, and Charles Stanley for their lack of exposition and gospel proclamation, their tenuous identification with Christian orthodoxy, sentimentalism and anthropocentrism. Perhaps America's foremost celebrity preacher, Joel Osteen, pastor of Lakewood Church in Houston, offers the clearest example of text-less, gospel-less preaching in America. His February 2014 homily "Removing Negative Labels"[3] typifies both his method and content. Having imbibed the warm and informal delivery forged throughout the megachurch enclaves of Willow Creek and Saddleback, but with the evangelical familiarity of Calvary Chapel, Osteen proclaims "finding your champion within" by "removing the negative labels people put on you." No text serves so much as a foil for his victorious life theme. In his anthropocentric address, there is not a single reference to the life, death, resurrection, ascension of Christ, or to the rule of God in him. The triune name is not invoked and even the name of Jesus finds no utterance. Instead, it is the sanguine report, "The same God who can help you get a 'C' can help you get an 'A' in life." There is no redemption heralded because there is no condemnation of sin or, indeed, no identification of sinners; just tips and techniques on how to "remove the negative labels" and "start wearing good ones." Yet even without the gospel Osteen remains an iconic example of American preaching, celebrated as an effective preacher to be emulated in style and content throughout the country *because* of his commercial, numerical success.[4] And emulated he is—sometimes in part, sometimes in toto.

To be sure, a sermon with no biblical text is a problem. But without gospel proclamation whatever takes place in a pulpit cannot be called an evangelical sermon. If for Bo Giertz there is "No liturgy without a sermon" then for Gerhard Forde there is no sermon without proclaiming the gospel

---

Theological Seminary: "Fast Facts about American Religion," 15 June 2014, www.hirr.hartsem.edu, corroborated by data from the Religious Congregations Membership Study, 15 June 2014, www.rcms2010.org (accessed Feb. 13, 2014); and Hadaway and Marler, "How Many Americans Attend Worship Each Week?," 307–22. These would include recognizable associations such as Calvary Chapel, Vineyard, Evangelical Free, Christian and Missionary Alliance, and the like. Sermons were accessed via media sources (mentioned above) save for sixteen witnessed in person in various locations across the nation. Lutheran sermons accounted for eighteen of the 300.

3. Osteen, "Labels."

4. Gallo, "Joel Osteen"; Good Morning America, "Preaching Success."

of Christ,[5] echoing sentiments from Martin Luther and Philip Melanchthon. For the Wittenberg reformers, a sermon was not of the new covenant if the gospel was not preached.[6] Gospel proclamation properly distinguished from the law, always informed by and conventionally exegeted from Scripture, constituted Lutheran distinctives. These distinctives need to resurface in fresh way for contemporary hearers.

Disconcertingly, then, Osteen-*esque* sermons (i.e., gospel-less, text-less, and moralistic and motivational in content and style) are more the norm than the exception in the most popular of American preaching. With gospel proclamation as the *sine qua non* of the new covenant sermon, then what is being heralded from pulpits and podiums of America, on the whole and even in what were once strongholds of the Reformation tradition, now better reflects the intersection of Christian *values* with existential consumerist concerns than the theological message of divine reconciliation and kingdom rule through Christ's crucifixion, resurrection, and the giving of the Holy Spirit. In the broad spectrum of popular American preaching, rarely are sermons as egregious as Osteen's. At the same time, in terms of theological and methodological taxonomy, their classification as "Protestant" would be generous, "Reformational" exaggerated, and "evangelical" generally unwarranted. What, then, has happened to the bulk of contemporary preaching?

The root of gospel-less or text-less sermons (if they may be so designated) is not simply methodology, though methodology undoubtedly plays a role. Instead, the principal factor in these sermons being (and not being) what they are is *ideological*. Ideological frameworks provide the hermeneutical engine that drives both interpretative approaches to the biblical text and the teleology of homiletics. Stated differently, the means and ends of contemporary preaching are resultant of prior ideological commitments that provide the lenses through which preachers understand, engage and interpret the world. In turn, these worldview lenses set the parameters and purposes for preaching and, indeed, what is actually preached because they bespeak a theology that is itself the result of ideological commitments. In America the ideological antecedent that rules even over sentimentalism, pragmatism, and romanticism, is *consumerism*.[7]

---

5. Giertz, "The Meaning and Task," 133; Forde, *Theology*, 60.

6. Cf. Forde, *Where God Meets Man*, 65–67; and Wengert, *Reading the Bible*, 58–68.

7. See the brilliant analysis of the church and contemporary culture in Clavier, *Rescuing the Church*; but also Cavanaugh, *Being Consumed*. Miles sees consumerism as bearing all the traits of a religion in *Consumerism*, 1, *ad passim*; and Friedman terminates individuality and identity in consumerist ideas of "freedom" in *Free to Choose*.

In a culture effectively reconceived in economic terms, market desires determine product or, often in this case, what the preacher delivers. No preacher is exempt from the pervasive and paradigmatic hold of market concerns on Western social, economic, intellectual and religious life. Mark Clavier explains the connection between consumerism and Christianity:

> Consumerism has [the] capacity to introduce an alien culture into local communities in a way that transforms how the members of those communities understand themselves and their world. But consumerism is far more adaptable to different circumstances and cultures: once people begin to think of themselves as consumers, they are free to believe almost anything else they want. Consumerism can import almost any religion, ideology, culture or philosophy and transform it into mere lifestyle choices.[8]

Consumerism *is* alien to the Christian community, but it has undeniably transformed how Christians conceive of themselves: primarily as *consumers* and only thereafter as baptized disciples. Once consumerism situated itself in the human condition and imported the Christian narrative of salvation and sanctification, it recast them "within the overarching narrative of desire, self-invention and identity; beginning with the cradle we imbibe the idea that we pursue happiness and identity through the purchase of products."[9] The American Christian draws identity less from a dyadic understanding of the self ensconced within the sacred community (the "social-self")[10] and more individualistically by way of personal choice (now the essence of "freedom"). We call this personalized and largely aesthetic volitional existence a *lifestyle*. Classified lifestyles, drawing from a combination of secularism, economics, and psychology, are marketed behavioral patterns that facilitate the self-creation of people through consumption of products emblematic for those "cultural" lifestyles. Christianity, demographically divided into marketing niches, has been reconceived in America as a spectrum of religious brands facilitating self-invention. Lutheranism can be seen as one such brand. The market drives the product, even when what is on offer is redemption and sanctification, because the starting point of one's identity and place in the world is as a *consumer*. And the promise of the product is sanctified sentimentalism: happiness. That's the gospel according

---

8. Clavier, *Rescuing the Church*, 3.
9. Ibid., 4.
10. See Malina, *The New Testament World*, 67–73.

to consumerism and, as a plethora of research has evidenced, it has found a fertile market in American churches.[11]

The impact of a consumerist plausibility structure falls directly upon theology and, inasmuch as "theology is for proclamation,"[12] forcefully on preaching itself, reshaping the homiletical discipline. When pre-modern Christology and soteriology routinely find themselves subservient to modernity's consumerist ways, then the cart is put before the horse: practical theology governs dogmatics, but with a twist. Homiletics becomes a marketing medium for a commodified Christianity poised to attract customers (converts) and retain brand loyalty (membership). Osteen is merely symptomatic. Even in confessional Lutheran circles where orthodoxy usually remains of paramount concern, compromise can be readily found at the points of catechesis, liturgics, youth ministry and especially homiletics (frequently the first point of contact). Pulpits are underutilized; vestments go unworn; commentaries lay unconsulted; sermons are delivered unpolished with undemanding content. Hardly distinguishable is the Lutheran Church sometimes from the Calvary Chapel down the street. It is a familiar scene that was not too long ago unfamiliar. It fits the lowest-common-denominator consumerist mold, just like the marketing medium of pop culture. In 1968, the World Council of Churches ironically iterated this compromising spirit with their slogan, "The World Sets the Agenda." Forty-five years later it may be more accurately reiterated by saying, "The market sets the agenda."[13] With the market pragmatically managing the message there has been a notable alteration to the way traditional theological cultures engage contemporary preaching methods, impacting sermon content, style and goals. The same applies to theologically liberal Mainline denominations. One notes theological and methodological discontinuity from previous generations as a result of today's preachers imbibing market-driven methods.[14] This discontinuity may also account for the ever-expanding spectrum

---

11. See Smith, *Souls in Transition:* and *Soul Searching*; Dean, *Almost Christian*; MacDonald, *Thieves in the Temple*; Twitchell, *Lead Us Into Temptation*; Miller, *Consuming Religion*; and Breen, "Celebrity, Consumerism & Competition."

12. Forde, *Theology*.

13. Gordon in "Why Johnny Can't Preach" claims that the "media has shaped the messengers"; that is, the world we live in and the way our understanding of speaking and communicating has changed, has had its effect on preachers. When "pop culture" is recognized as a marketing medium, then the effect on preachers and auditors can be seen as all the more acute. Perhaps the reasons behind the changes in preaching are not necessarily conscious and theologically motivated, but rather the consequence of a Western culture that has changed/is changing, and with that our way of speaking and listening has changed as well.

14. Indeed, Joel Osteen confesses that he could not do "old school" theology and

of homiletical methods to broaden marketability by giving consumeristic auditors what they desire to hear *as* Christianity (a negative implication); but also such methodological discontinuity carries the potential to accommodate modern auditors in common parlance (a positive implication). Confessional Lutherans must learn to navigate the former and exploit the possibilities of the latter without compromising the proclaimed God.

There are new market-sensitive methods for a new consumerist agenda that challenges the necessity of the conjunction of the word and the Spirit formerly ubiquitous in "old school" theologically conservative Evangelicalism and confessional Protestantism.[15] That "old school" was demanding and entailed theological familiarity, rigor and wholesale dependence upon the Spirit to work through the real voice of God in his word and real presence of God in his sacraments. The new school, on the other hand, operates by economic principles factored to maximize appeal, accessibility and convenience. This paradigm shift may have started with Charles G. Finney's unabashed Pelagianism in the Second Great Awakening, which championed his "new methods" of homiletical salesmanship, but since 1958 consumerism has been *the* plausibility structure of American Christianity and it is clearly reflected in today's sermonic content, delivery and goals. Consequently, a disproportionate percentage of contemporary sermons share constitutive ideological principles: the appeal to human desire, personal taste, sentimentality, fashion, and philosophical voluntarism.[16] In contrast, Lutherans in the past were taught that "preaching" is a transitive verb—Lutherans preach *on* a person and *on* that person's objective work, usually from a biblical text. Lutherans do not preach a sermon. Today's Lutherans then, along with others, could stand a reminder that other prepositions cannot be permitted to creep in if the proclamation is to be *sola gratia, sola fide, solus Christus*.

Within America's nearly inescapable and comprehensible consumerist paradigm, sermons now characteristically connect individuals emotionally and ideologically with their consumption of a "Christian lifestyle" by offering pre-packaged Christian lifestyles, replete with nook music, generational clothing, accessories, literature, conventions, retreats, paraphernalia,

---

preaching like his father, John Osteen. Instead of "expounding the books of Ephesians and Colossians" as his father had done, Joel focuses on his gift of preaching prosperity. "And I've said it 1,000 times," exclaims Osteen, "it's being healthy, it's having great children, it's having peace of mind. Money is part of it; and yes, I believe God wants us to excel . . . to be blessed so we can be a bigger blessing to others" (Menzie, "Joel Osteen").

15. Mumme, "The Spirit," 18–22.

16. Marsden, *Fundamentalism*, 27–25, 45–54, 79–87; and Clavier, *Rescuing the Church*, 4. "Voluntarism" is the doctrine that the uncoerced will is the dominate factor in the individual above rational and emotional powers.

celebrity speakers, and product promoters that fit their consumer demographic and implicitly if not explicitly justify one's preferred lifestyle within which Christianity plays a part. The tendency of preaching to gravitate to what auditors *want* to hear verses what they *need* to hear is undeniable.[17] In that tendency, I would argue, *the* problem with contemporary preaching may be found: most preaching has been commandeered by an antecedent ideology that is at the same time the plausibility structure of American society. A consumerist approach to preaching overshadows homiletical methodologies and can render preaching itself a mere lifestyle advertisement—an infomercial on self-creation through "Christianity." Osteen happens to be the most successful marketer, possessing the widest shelf space in the current climate of religious consumption. Others (competitors) struggle with covetousness, a temptation to which Lutheran preachers are not immune.

This assessment, of course, is working with broad observations. Even in a climate dominated by a consumerist ideology there are many faithful preachers delivering exemplary sermons, and this is reflected below, too. And as "old school" theology has considered and engaged modernity's consumerist culture, its homiletical repertoire has become more nuanced and winsome, as David Schmitt's commendable guide to sermon structures exhibits through its multimedia examples.[18] But even these homileticians "live and move and have their being" in the land of consumerism. No one is immune—Lutherans, Baptists, Calvinists and Catholics all must address their auditors making conscious decisions about the task of the preacher and purpose of proclamation vis-à-vis consumerism and the conditioned expectations of auditors. It is here that the Lutheran distinctives of always preaching on the gospel of Christ and making a distinction between it and the law, and doing so as primary discourse, offers a unifying antidote to consumerist purposes, no matter what type of sermon structure may be employed.

This brings us back to the issue of antecedent ideological frameworks. In juxtaposition to the felt needs of expectant auditors, economic needs of congregations, and endemic "moralistic, therapeutic deism" that seems to determine the *telos* of preaching within American Christianity,[19] this survey of today's methodological spectrum will use Luther and Melanchthon's litmus test for bona fide evangelical preaching (i.e., the New Testament's mandated gospel proclamation of God's grace and rule through Jesus Christ

17. See, e.g., Witten, *All Is Forgiven*; Barna, *Marketing*; and Horton, *Christless Christianity*.

18. Schmitt, "Sermon Structures."

19. "Moralistic, therapeutic, deism" is a term introduced by Smith in *Soul Searching* to describe the common religious beliefs among American youth.

crucified for our salvation and resurrected for our justification) to appraise the suitability of contemporary preaching methods for confessional Lutherans.

We open with (1) observations from the survey, then (2) present the survey itself organized under the preferred headings of David Schmitt's "Sermon Structures," then (3) move to the task of the preaching according to select Lutheran thinkers, and (4) conclude with some thoughts on past and present Lutheran homiletical distinctives and their importance for the curacy of the Holy Gospel amidst our consumerist milieu.

OBSERVATIONS

The challenge of contemporary preaching appears compounded by the fact that evangelical America effectively operates without a lectionary, leaving it all the more susceptible to consumeristic intrusions. Curiously, a growing number of Lutherans have adopted this characteristic, too. So sometimes expounding "the word" does not necessarily mean *God's* prescribed word, much less the word of the *gospel*,[20] since neither the liturgical calendar nor a purposeful set of Scripture lessons from both testaments is essential. In a consumerist framework, the inspiration for the sermon is as likely to come from a movie, book, sentiment, current event, socio-economic aspiration, motivational vignette or a combination of these, and frequently does. Moreover, my sampling of sermons[21] concluded that rarely was such preaching grounded by a homiletical touchstone of a biblical text either within a lectionary or ordered textual system or ecumenical creed (allowing for freedom and experimentation) save in certain Reformed, Lutheran and Anglican enclaves, but not always. On the whole, thematic "proof texting"[22] and extemporaneous oration were preferred over traditional methodological exposition of the biblical text, implicitly portraying the preacher as sovereign over text and message. In arenas evidencing overt consumerist

---

20. Lutherans traditionally have understood the nature and use of Scripture differently than Protestants in that a "canon within a canon" is acknowledged, holding the gospel as God's highest authority and final word. See Wengert, *Reading the Bible*, 54.

21. See n2 above.

22. "Prooftexting" is a methodological approach to and use of the Bible whereby a person appeals to a biblical text—invoking its authority—to prove or justify a position (thematic, theological, or otherwise) without regard for the context or authorial intention of the passage they cite. See Treier, "Proof Text," 622–24; and Reese, "Pitfalls," 121–23. *Nave's Topical Bible* remains a bestseller for Zondervan, serving as a regular resource for prooftexting thematic homilies.

commitments,[23] distinctive methods were less identifiable. This phenomenon of methodological libertarianism *in relation to the text* (be it scriptural or creedal) is increasingly characteristic of lectionary traditions too. Presbyterian, Lutheran, Roman Catholic, Anglican and Methodist preachers increasingly resort to intentionally brief, thematic sermons or impromptu addresses evocative of fireside chats (at best) or motivational seminars (at worst) with minimal regard for appointed texts or seasons. It seems *a* word is just as good as *the* word. Investigation into preparatory techniques (precluded from the scope of this survey) would yield more specific results into this and other phenomena signaling an abandonment of text-based gospel proclamation.

Relatedly, where the gospel is recognizably preached from a biblical (or creedal or catechetical) text, standardized methods generally give way to methodological mixture. This makes a precise survey of current homiletical methods somewhat elusive. Identifying preaching methodologies and their associated techniques requires constant updating, decoding, and the fundamental recognition that categories standardized perhaps a generation ago are fluid today. The reason for this may be a combination of factors, such as: (i) the ever-evolving and frequently devolving nature of the discipline of preaching, (ii) the fickle and impatient dispositions of contemporary preachers and auditors molded by consumerist expectations, (iii) shifting cultural and ecclesial agendas due to ideological conditioning and, consequently, (iv) homiletical goals.

So, while identifiable traits of historic preaching methods can be identified (e.g., textual, thematic, textual-topical, systematic expositional, creedal/catechetical, and lectionary) definitive categorization is now a futile exercise. One must describe structures *within* a sermon rather a sermon's classification per se. On the whole homileticians today preach hybrid-style. Indeed, even the most consistent homileticians (e.g., John Piper, Philip G. Ryken, David Jackman) rarely stay within the boundaries of their preferred or inherited method, opting for more of a cafeteria-style approach to constructing and delivering sermons, borrowing here, augmenting there. Preaching has gone postmodern in its attempt to reach auditors. This observation notes the need for variety in an age of near-ubiquitous entertainment, shorter attention spans, and theological unfamiliarity. "Sermons that are habitual and predictable soon become trite and boring."[24] True, indeed. Amal-

---

23. "Consumerist commitments" would include performance-entertainment orientation, radical informality, dependence upon technological multimedia, preoccupation with contemporary comforts and conveniences, stimulation and sentiment, along with sacramental, liturgical, and iconographic minimalism.

24. Killinger, *Fundamentals*, 177.

gamating and alternating methods is a likely and commendable necessity in all circumstances and traditions because, in fact, times have changed.

Notwithstanding the fact of hybrid methodologies, if we permit that historically identifiable preaching methods still offer general parameters (albeit with requisite flexibility yielding cross-germinated methodological sermons) then a survey is possible, especially when utilizing three general headings suggested by David Schmitt. Schmitt advances the methodological conversation by considering *sermon structures* as denominations of homiletical methodologies. So while observation is made complex by the lack of lectionaries (etc.) and by the common phenomenon of hybrid and fluid methodologies, David Schmitt's categories of sermon structures provide a serviceable framework for a survey of contemporary preaching methodologies. According to Schmitt, a sermon structure is "the purposeful ordering of ideas and experiences in the sermon . . . [which] helps the preacher identify what material will be included in the sermon and organize that material into purposeful proclamation."[25] For Schmitt, there are three general categories of sermon structures: *textual*, *thematic*, and *dynamic*. These three are sufficient to envelop a growing spectrum of homiletical methods and forms.

SURVEY OF IDENTIFIABLE CONTEMPORARY PREACHING METHODS

The current landscape of preaching methods consists more of undulating hills rather than a topography dominated by peaks. And there are new hills emerging, with ridgelines blending hills together.

Given the developing topography of preaching methodologies, David Schmitt's sermon structure designations capture former categories that have evolved or now seem redundant and give them place. For example, *the developmental sermon*[26] no longer seems to stand on its own as a major category, but now fits within Schmitt's *textual* heading as a *storied discourse structure* or the *dynamic* heading as a *relational structure*. The same is true of the dated *synthetic* and *analytic* models, and others. The following represents Schmitt's major branches:[27]

---

25. Schmitt, "Sermon Structures."

26. Defined by Killinger as having "a central idea or controlling purpose that is worked out through a series of two or more progressive stages in which the idea grows to its climax" (*Fundamentals*, 59–60).

27. Schmitt, "Sermon Structures." "Textual and Thematic" have been transposed for this study.

Aside from the up-to-date nature of these headings, they are flexible and easily cobbled, making the task of surveying a more plausible endeavor. Nouveau proposals (e.g., *organic, discursive, impressionistic*) also find place in Schmitt's schema but so do classic designations like *expository* preaching, making his "Sermon Structures" a comprehensive and satisfactory classification system for contemporary preaching methodologies.

Textual Structures	Thematic Structures	Dynamic Structures
Text-Application	Analogy	Law/Gospel Structure
Verse-by-Verse	Cause/Effect	Proverbial Structure
Genre	Classical Argument	Narrative Structures
Storied Discourse Structures	Classification	Lowry Loop
Biblical Story Interrupted	Comparison/Contrast	Epic Form
Story Whole Structures	Definition	Multiple Perspectives
Biblical Story Told	Paradox Maintained	Relational Structure
Framing the Biblical Story	Problem/Solution	Imagistic Structure
Multiple Story Structure	Process	Central Image
	Question Answered	Frame and Refrain
		Image Delayed
		Multiple Image
		Dialogical Structures
		Metaphorical Movement

Textual Structures and Expository Preaching

"Systematic exposition," commonly known as "expository preaching," is a method or form of preaching that expounds more than exegetes texts chosen consecutively from a unit of Scripture.[28] The structure of the sermon will be governed by how the preacher desires to unfold the biblical text (hence, its *textual* designation) while its content and delivery would be *expository*. Until late modernity, it was *the* endorsed method of sermon preparation and delivery, finding its authorization in the New Testament (e.g., Acts 2:14–40) and, supremely from Jesus himself who, "beginning with Moses and all the Prophets . . . interpreted to them in all the Scriptures the things concerning himself" (Luke 24:27; cf. 24:44). The general heading of *textual*

---

28. On the whole, expository preaching, as modern a cultural phenomenon, has precluded catechetical preaching.

allows for interpretations in which preaching may be done verse-by-verse, by text-application, genre, and/or storied structures.

In keeping with its etymology from the Latin *expositio*, expository preaching intends a detailed explanation of *Scripture*. To be sure, grammatical exposition bespeckles such sermons with technical philological declension of nouns and parsing of verbs, but this broadly defined method requires no specified amount of proper exegesis. By "proper" I mean thoroughgoing: preachers have been observed to wax and wane in exegetical consistency, departing from exegesis for thematic exposition or polemical enterprises and rightly so: the Scriptures are to bear witness to the all-authoritative Christ who lives and reigns outside the pages of the Bible and can also be proclaimed from the gospel-suffused creeds, liturgy, catechisms and confessions of Christendom. In the early church, however, rhetoric quickly eclipsed genuine exposition of the text and remained the hallmark of preaching until the Reformation. John Killinger notes that the Renaissance *ad fontes* approach to scholarship signaled a paradigm shift in preaching methodologies impacting systematic exposition by reviving Scripture's prominence.[29]

Over the last century classic exposition of the text became standardized through the works of Martin Lloyd-Jones (Westminster Chapel) and John Stott (All Souls, London) Donald Grey Barnhouse and James Montgomery Boice (successive voices of *The Bible Study Hour* radio program) and among Baptists through J. Vernon McGee, John MacAurther, Haddon Robinson, to name a few. Christian radio, evangelical commentary series, and organizations such as The Proclamation Trust, Banner of Truth Trust, and Dallas Theological Seminary, forged a revival of expository preaching that mandated the systematic expositional method as the only legitimate form of preaching among conservative and biblicist seminarians until the 1990s. Although undergoing decline due to the rise of hybrid-homiletics, the survey shows that it retains clout among non-denominational evangelicals and especially the Calvinist-Puritan tradition (both Reformed Baptist and Presbyterian) given its biblical approbation and pedigree.[30]

29. Killinger: "Rhetorical sermons, which paid homage to many biblical texts but derived their main thrust from a battery of devices intended to convince the hearer by the application of philosophical reason, thus became the staple of Christendom until the Reformation, when Martin Luther, Huldrich Zwingli, John Calvin, and others returned to a more biblical emphasis in preaching, intentionally permitting texts to speak for themselves" (*Fundamentals*, 57).

30. Neh 8:1-8 (esp. v. 8) recounts how Ezra and the priests "read from the book, from the Torah of God, paragraph by paragraph, and they gave the sense, so that the people understood the reading" (my translation). This may have given rise to or, alternatively, instantiated a Jewish tradition of the priest, scribe, or rabbi offering *Dvar*

The appropriateness of expositional preaching receives buttressing by the aforementioned traditions by juxtaposing favorable *direct* exposition of the text with unfavorable *indirect* usage. "To use a text for the goal for which it was originally written or spoken has been termed the direct method of using a text. . . . To utilize an idea in a text toward a goal for which the text was not originally written is then termed the indirect method," explains Richard Caemmerer.[31] Thus, *systematic exposition* garners, at times, confessional boundaries or at least interpretations respected and preserved by approved commentators, evidenced by expanding commentary series with imprints from Zondervan, Baker, Concordia, IVP, Eerdmans, Hendrickson, P&R, WJK, etc.

Textual structures encase both direct and indirect expository preaching classifications. Subdivisions ensue. Beneath the umbrella of *textual structures* one finds a variety of approaches: *text-application, verses-by-verse,* and *genre* (with its own branching: *storied discourse structures, biblical story interrupted, story whole structures* and *multiple story structure*). One structure cannot be judged better or more correct than another, so long as established hermeneutics govern exegesis, exposition, and proclamation. Schmitt's structures manifest how confusticated methodological classifications may be, since even within an identifiable structure like the *textual*, there may be substructures within a single sermon, to say nothing of potential movements between *textual, thematic,* and *dynamic* elements. Nearly all the sermons surveyed that fall under this general classification evidenced dynamic and thematic structural influences (approx. 90 of 300). Again, straightforward and thoroughly consistent adherence to a fixed structure seems neither necessary nor plausible amidst an age of biblical (and theological) illiteracy.[32] Various structures are frequently necessary to adapt content for auditor relatability and to achieve homiletical goals. Other factors conditioning *textual* preaching were theological-hermetical traditions (covenantal theology, historical-redemptive, literal-historical) and the interplay between proclamation and systematics. The abundance of purposeful *textual* preaching is encouraging no matter how the text may be derived, particularly because many Protestant associations do not have gospel-suffused subordinate (confessional and catechetical) standards, divine liturgy or ecumenical creeds. From the perspective of the survey, *textual* preaching appears more resistant to consumeristic accommodations.

Torah, an interpretation of a biblical text during the services of prayer.

31. Caemmerer, *Preaching*, 69.
32. See Burge, "Greatest Story," 45–49.

The selection of a text for exposition may differ entirely from, say, thematic preaching, due to the source(s) from which it may arise. Texts are usually selected from the following:

1. a one-year lectionary or three-year lectionary (e.g., *Revised Common Lectionary*);[33]

2. a *lectio continua*;[34]

3. an individual selection of a biblical book (also known as the "individual choice method");

4. a genre.

Each has its merits and, encouragingly, each was represented in the survey among Mainline, Catholic and Confessional denominations. It should be noted that the Revised Common Lectionary is perhaps entirely unused and frequently unknown among American evangelicals who typically employ the *individual choice method*.[35] None of the sixty non-Mainline Protestant homileticians surveyed referenced prescribed lectionary texts. Not surprisingly, this same group also represented nearly every recorded instance of text-less sermons, lending credence to the notion that the debate over so-called "traditional" and "free" or "contemporary" forms of worship may be a substantive contest over theology not style. Having a text to preach within the complex of liturgical worship seemed to be the simplest way to ensure that the Scriptures remained the source of the message being heralded and, indeed, that it *is* the gospel message.

The *lectionary method* (sometimes, the *liturgical method*)[36] in its varied manifestations, evidenced the advantage of theological arrangement around an efficient church calendar, the life/ministry cycle of Christ, and the drama of redemption (loosely based on the chronology of Jesus' life/ministry).

---

33. See http://lectionary.library.vanderbilt.edu/faq2.php for more on the *Revised Common Lectionary* and http://catholic-resources.org/Lectionary/1998USL.htm for a comprehensive explanation of the contents and history of the Roman Catholic three-year lectionary.

34. There are variations to this tradition, e.g., *lectio semi-continua* skips passages in the reading sequence, while *lectio selecta* follows a selected sequence of passages in a predetermined order. See West, "Readings," 491–92.

35 *The Revised Common Lectionary* is only endorsed in Mainline Protestant churches, the LCMS, the Mormon Community of Christ enclave, the Moravian Church in America, and among the Unitarian Universalist Christian Fellowship.

36. Sometimes the "lectionary method" is anything but synonymous with the "liturgical method." Lectionary use does not necessitate employment of a standardized Eucharist liturgy but, for the sake of classification, liturgical employment almost invariably utilizes lectionary lessons: hence the association. For an interesting collection of essays on liturgical preaching, see, Grime and Nadasdy, *Liturgical Preaching*.

It provides an annual and seasonal rhythm to the Christian life through which the full scope of the biblical metanarrative and gospel narratives are rehearsed.[37] Additionally, distinct genres of Scripture were thematically linked to the gospel pericope, underscoring the covenantal or testamental unity of the Bible and thus its Christocentricity and the internal universality of its Christological themes. Those adjudicated "liturgical preachers" made regular use of the purposeful pairings of lectionary texts, further displaying a conscious correlation between the sermon and its liturgical setting. Where lectionary readings were preached they also liturgically linked churches of different geographic locations in an effective fashion by fostering common expectations, celebrations and movements, and by underscoring catholicity. To hear and see the same text preached on opposing coasts amidst the same Eucharistic liturgy minimized the sense of ecclesial detachment or isolation. Current appraisals of pan-Lutheran practices approximate eighty percent of churches using the lectionary settings and, still, a very high regard for the liturgical calendar. Lutherans, on the whole, preach lectionary texts, as do Roman Catholics, Anglicans, and Episcopalians (though the preaching is not necessarily expository). The Methodists and Wesleyans surveyed in Southern California evidenced no lectionary adherence, though it remains denominationally endorsed.[38]

The *lectio continua*, on the other hand, affords a systematic approach to preaching the Bible in keeping with its canonical arrangement and it does so at the individual expositor's rate of progression.[39] The process is usually greatly accelerated and, truly, the *lectio continua* abandoned for an epochal or generalized rendering. Mark Dever's two-volume set, *The Message of the Old Testament: Promises Made* and *The Message of the New Testament: Promises Kept*, is a recent Southern Baptist example of summating what the *lectio continua* would otherwise yield if expounded in minutia.[40]

---

37. Gieschen, "Preaching," 84–87.

38. Even among those devoted to liturgical preaching, complaints surface about important passages omitted from the lectionary cycles or their lack of consistency in progressing contiguously through a given text. Consequently, it is becoming commonplace to find a suspended use of the lectionary during Lent or Advent for catechetical preaching and/or enacting the *individual choice method* during summer months.

39. Even the seventeen-year continuous preaching efforts of W. A. Criswell (First Baptist Church, Dallas, TX) was not a verse-by-verse exposition per se. Likewise, radio broadcaster of *Through the Bible*, J. Vernon McGee, in his five-year cycling through the Bible omits substantial portions of the text. These may be among the closest examples.

40. *The Message of the Old Testament*. Mark Dever, a pastor of the Southern Baptist Convention, originally preached these Bible overview sermons through sixty-nine individual messages, corresponding to the sixty-six books of the Bible, plus three introductions. A drawback to the *lectio continua* method is the rate of progression itself. The

The systematic expository example of Tenth Presbyterian Church of Philadelphia warrants special mention in relation to *individual book selection*. To be sure, of those churches and preachers still given to the traditional method of systematic expository preaching, the *individual book selection/individual choice method* appears axiomatic.[41] Of many good examples, Tenth is perhaps the most exemplary. Beginning with Donald Grey Barnhouse (1895–1960) and continuing through the legendary preaching of James Montgomery Boice (1938–2000) and his protege, Philip Graham Ryken (1966–) Tenth's book by book systematic exposition, broadcast over *The Bible Study Hour* radio program and reproduced in dozens of expository commentaries, has been a highly replicated model throughout conservative evangelical and Reformed communities. Tenth's preachers were never without a text even though they were without a lectionary. In this way, Tenth provides an alternative model of text-commitment that also resists a consumeristic agenda.[42]

Selecting a text by way of *genre* allows the text to influence the form and function of the sermon. Apocalyptic texts fundamentally differ from war chronicles, which essentially differ from proverbial passages. Surprisingly, genre profoundly and routinely affected the homiletical task. For the most part, prophesy was respected as prophesy and, of the four sermons on the book of Revelation and several on the Psalms to which I was exposed, deference was given to genre that in turn influenced exposition. While content may not always rule supreme, the genre of text frequently did.

Thematic or Topical Preaching Method

Thematic structures and preaching is the preferred and most pervasive method of preaching today. Nearly sixty-five percent of the sermons surveyed for this study were topical or thematic, with representation evenly

---

1,189 chapters of the Bible would take nearly twenty-three years of Sundays to preach if expounded one chapter following another. The forest can easily be lost for the trees, and parishioners no doubt would quickly tire of such an approach, which is why only one of a hundred preachers surveyed was found attempting it.

41. http://sharefaith.com provides evangelical expository fare through hundreds of PowerPoint™ based sermons.

42. But even at Tenth the expository preaching—*individual choice* method also could be described as intermittent. Systematic exposition of, say, an epistle would give way to a topical series about *The Doctrines of Grace* or *Renewing Your Mind in a Mindless World*. Dozens of such sermon series emerged and were set to print for popular consumption. The individual choice method utilized to facilitate a topical sermon series really had an ulterior motive—fulfilling contractual obligations for publishers.

distributed among denominations and associations. The method permits the homiletician to use multiple texts from one or more books of the Bible or biblical authors to speak on an issue, doctrine or practice. Thus, it is synthetic in structure in the attempt to coherently unify content. The texts may or may not be related in terms of their biblical context. Sermons typifying this method may range from "Biblical Patriarchs" to "Biblical Marriage" to "Business Principles." They may be a single topical sermon (an excursus for those employing the lectionary or individual selection method) or a thematic series (e.g., "The Last Week," "Apologetics 101," "Six Chief Parts of the Catechism," etc.).

Thematic preaching readily converts into other formats and media (E.g., slides, videos) for dissemination and distribution. Significantly, there exists a cottage industry profiting from the sale of topical/thematic sermons and series. Prepackaged sermons may be acquired via the Internet and downloaded into PowerPoint™ presentations or manuscripts. I could not determine the number of purchased sermons, but four sermons were unmistakably identical in outline and verbiage, indicating a common purchase and raising ethical questions as well as confirming consumerism's strength of presence. Be that as it may, there are several advantages to the thematic method. For example, thematic preaching (i) allows a preacher to trace a theme through multiple books of the Bible, which shows consistency; (ii) provides the ability to address questions and controversies that arise; and (iii) allows for a preacher to select the most appropriate verse from Scripture on a given topic in light of his/her perceived needs or goals.

Criticisms of thematic preaching are legion. Sermons of this nature routinely abandon *gospel proclamation* for *thematic explanation* resulting in moralizing or patronizing. The justification for such gospel-less homiletics appear to emerge directly from biblicist hermeneutical principles, which espouse the following features:

> Total Representation: The Bible represents the totality of God's communication to and will for humanity, both in containing all that God has to say to humans and in being the exclusive mode of God's true communication. . . . Complete Coverage: The divine will about all of the issues relevant to Christian belief and life are contained in the Bible. . . . Internal Harmony: All related passages of the Bible on any given subject fit together almost like puzzle pieces into single, unified, internally consistent bodies of instruction about right and wrong beliefs and behaviors. . . . Inductive Method: All matters of Christian belief and practice can

be learned by sitting down with the Bible and piecing together through careful study the clear "biblical" truths that it teaches.[43]

A full two-thirds of the sermons surveyed posit divinely authoritative answers on any topic upon which the inspired, infallible and inerrant Bible touched, ranging from moral reformation, friendships, economics and medicine to the physical sciences, politics, business principles, romance and more. Nowhere was the presence of consumer demand and preacher supply more clearly evident than here. Even among liberal Mainline denominations biblicist principles were employed to justify thematic agendas no less than among fundamentalists. Where the former thematically vindicated, for example, homosexuality, the other denounced the same through an identical piecemeal of authoritative passages. At the same time, excellent thematic sermons were found on propitiation, the doctrine of representation, and Holy Baptism. Worthy of consideration, then, is the relationship between a consumerist hermeneutical framework and the production of sermons that are *thematic* as opposed to, say, *dynamic* (e.g., *law/gospel structure* or *imagistic structures*). Such considerations, sadly, were beyond the scope of this study.

A Textual-Thematic Hybrid

Under the heading "Textual preaching," a certain expository-thematic hybrid method can also be classified. The method consists of selecting one section or perhaps one pericope of Scripture from within a book of the Bible and expounding a/the principle theme of that section through a series of sermons. In the 1500s William Perkins did this with his famous compilation of homilies expounding Jesus' "Sermon in the Mount."[44] In the twentieth century Arthur W. Pink produced *The Seven Sayings of the Savior on the Cross*[45] utilizing a textual preaching method. So, too, there are numerous sermon series currently in print on the texts from Handel's "Messiah" to the biblical canticles.

This method is enjoying something of a revival because it (i) straddles the line between expository and thematic methodologies; (ii) employs the analogy of faith, whereby the internal consistency of the Scriptures is evidenced thematically; (iii) facilitates short sermon series to keep truncated attention spans engaged by militating against boredom and saturation; (iv)

---

43. Smith, *The Bible*, 4–5.
44. Perkins, "Sermon on the Mount, 226–34.
45. Pink, *Seven Sayings*.

permits flexibility in focus so that problematic texts can be navigated; and (v) accommodates the thematic elements present in the church calendar.

Dynamic Methodologies

Coming under the auspices of *dynamic structures*, the *narrative preaching style* is the rising star across all denominations and non-denominations. Narrative preaching employs the concept of storytelling indicative of the business community[46] and, likewise, may imbibe more from our consumerist culture than herald the contents of Scripture, especially since many portions of the biblical text are not narrative. Nevertheless stories could be told about one's experience of the text or, as the *dynamic* would have it, the auditors' effectual experience of the *use* of the text. Schmitt says of *dynamic structures* that they emphasize the experience of the hearers:

> Understanding the sermon as an event in time, the preacher structures the sermon by ordering the sequence of experiences on the part of the hearers. This sequence mirrors a particular spiritual or cultural way of knowing. For example, recognizing the centrality of daily repentance as an experience of the faith, the preacher might organize the sermon as a movement from the experience of law (leading to the confession of sin) to the experience of gospel (leading to trust in God's gracious work in Christ). In some cases, dynamic structures can use the rhetorical experiences of a culture in service of the proclamation of the gospel and thereby be quite accessible for contemporary hearers. The sermon structure helps the preacher identify the dynamics of a particular cultural experience (i.e., the contemporary cultural experience of images) and then creatively appropriates those dynamics for proclamation of the faith (i.e., helping hearers approach the faith through the experience of images).[47]

Curiously, *dynamic structures* were the survey's least represented method. This may be due to their relative sophistication requiring additional explanation, but in part due to their confusion with the *organic form theory*. Organic form theory of Romanticism has assisted preachers to free themselves from potentially constricting norms and rules of form. Sometimes called "the new homiletic," its progenitors (Samuel T. Coleridge and Henry G. Davis) prompt preachers to express their individual voices

---

46. See, for example, O'Conner, "Storied Business," 36–54; Clarke and Holt, "Entrepreneur," 69–83; and Fenton and Langley, "Strategy," 1171–96.

47. Schmitt, "Sermon Structures."

and create their own authentic forms by offering innovative methods to creatively imitate, blend, and mix a wide variety of sermon forms.[48] Perhaps less a methodology than an observation, organic forms substantiate the reality of hybrid methodological approaches indicative of all preaching but do not characterize truly identifiable *dynamic* methodologies.

Homiletics is in a state of flux, permitting perhaps like at no other time methodological freedom and experimentation. Hybrid-structures are normative and arguably necessary, so adjudicating one method or structure better than another is unwarranted, although manifest deficiencies were present in text-less sermons. In an expanding milieu of text-less and gospel-less sermons, the ideology of consumerism pervades and must be recognized as the factor that supersedes all observations about sermon methodology, since it conditions and alters the preacher's task.

THE PREACHER'S TASK

Just as with apologetics and liturgics, so too with homiletics: the goal is the *edification* of the auditor "Let all things be done for edification," writes Paul to the Corinthians (1 Cor 14:26, RSV). Edification in homiletics may be to help persons stand in their justification or, alternatively, enter into the justified state. In his second epistle to the Corinthians, Paul summarizes the vocational enterprise and edifying message of the preacher:

> All this is from God, who through Christ reconciled us to himself and gave us the ministry of reconciliation; that is, in Christ God was reconciling the world to himself, not counting their trespasses against them, and entrusting to us the message of reconciliation. Therefore, we are ambassadors for Christ, God making his appeal through us. We implore you on behalf of Christ, be reconciled to God. (5:18–20)

Johann Michael Reu explores the mandate to edify both the congregation and the individual through a consideration of Bible's metaphorical use of "edifice."[49] He depicts the church as an edifice or house or, better, as a temple of the Lord built upon the reconciliatory foundation of the apostles' gospel, where Christ Jesus himself is the cornerstone (Eph 2:19–22):

---

48. Park, *Organic Homiletic*.

49. Reu reasons: "If edification is the purpose of the Christian service, the sermon must have the same purpose in view." *Homiletics*, 98. See also Penner's Kierkegaardian critique of rationalistic apologetics in *The End of Apologetics*.

> Upon this foundation the individual Christians, as they are added to the church, are built up (edified) as living stones (1 Pet 2:5). But these same Christians, built up once for all upon this foundation, are again described as being built up or edified, so that what took place once for all is to be constantly repeated, and they are to become more completely that which they already are.[50]

In this light, edification involves two things: first, the church must have constantly refreshed "her consciousness of what God has done and is still doing for her and of what she has become by the grace of God, of what God and faith in him and his word mean to her, so that she may rejoice in her faith and Christian life and learn to cherish her communion with God as the chief of all her blessings."[51] With this is closely connected the second aspect of edification. "The sermon must bring the congregation to the realization of that which, on the basis of what she is through the grace of God, she must now become."[52]

The sermon, then, is a principle means by which God ingathers his elect and sanctifies his saints through the dual proclamation of law and gospel. The sermon must set before the church *God's* idea of his church, as Reu puts it, but also "awaken in the hearts of her members an earnest desire to reach this goal, and move them to a ceaseless struggle with sin and to the faithful imitation of Christ."[53] Here then we find Luther's theological ("second") use of the law, but especially the power of the gospel to actually save and sanctify. For the preacher of the biblical text, distinguishing law and gospel is simply a matter of successively telling two truths: the one about the human condition (law) and the other about God in Christ (gospel). And it is the latter truth that the Holy Spirit uses in the forum of salvation (*theatrum salutis*) established by preaching to forgive and revivicate.

For the execution of the preacher's task, the mode of address stands at the fore. A combination of both *primary* and *secondary* discourse is necessary, with *secondary* serving the purposes of *primary*. The difference between the two, explains Forde, approximates the distinction between proclaiming and explaining. "Explaining, talking, and writing about God and things theological is secondary discourse.... [It is] generally third-person, past-tense discourse." But proclamation "belongs to the proper discourse of the church.... [It is] first- to second-person, present-tense, unconditional

---

50. Reu, *Homiletics*, 103.
51. Ibid.
52. Ibid.
53. Ibid., 104.

address."⁵⁴ Primary discourse constitutes the efficacy of the liturgy and sacraments because it conveys a *divine performative speech act*. Proclamation is verbal action from God where, by his divine authority, his word achieves a new state of affairs.

> The most helpful analogy to this difference between primary and secondary discourse is that of the difference between the language *of* love and language *about* love. One might compare it to writing a book about love, or giving a lecture on the essence of love, or the art of loving or some such thing, and actually saying "I love you" to one's beloved. It ought to be obvious that one should make a proper distinction between these two types of discourse. There is a place for both.⁵⁵

Also important for understanding the preacher's task is the nature of the preacher's commissioning. Behind the preacher's ordination as an ambassador of Christ is the intertestamental Jewish concept of שלוחים (*shelichim*) where the rabbinic proverb "the messenger of a man is as the man himself" obtains. Persons commissioned as a שליח (*shaliach*, singular) were endowed with authority to legally and morally represent their commissioner. Significantly, the Septuagint translates the Hebrew word שליח (to send) with the Greek ἀποστέλλω, sustaining the emphasis of sending someone with a commission to represent another with corresponding authority. This is why the rabbis of Jesus' day considered Moses, Elijah, Elisha, and Ezekiel שלוחים, authorized messengers of God who represented Yahweh in their office as prophet. As Robert Scudieri notes, "When the *shelichim* went on a mission, they were actually considered to be the person or group who sent them."⁵⁶ But there was a caveat: the active representation of another availed only for a specific mission. There was no extension of conferred authority beyond the parameters of the commissioning specifications. Once the mission was completed שליח representation expired. "The *shaliach* is a progenitor of the New Testament apostle. Jesus did not invent the word *apostle*, he assumed it. There was already in God's plan a well-known system within which Jewish apostles were operating, a system Jesus accepted and used."⁵⁷ This concept of authoritative personal representation is brought directly into the New Testament understanding of the great commission (Matt 28:16–20) but with two important innovations by Jesus: first, he commissioned apostles for missional endeavors also to the Gentiles, whereas the

---

54. Forde, "Whatever Happened to God," 45.
55. Ibid., 46.
56. Scudieri, *Apostolic Church*, 9.
57. Ibid., 11.

שליח never eclipsed the boundaries of the Jewish community; and second, the power of the commissioner (viz. the Holy Spirit sent by the Father and the Son) would actually be present with the commissioned to achieve the that which is commissioned and only that.

By way of a preacher's commissioning and conferred authority we come to the performative nature of divine primary speech acts in the proclamation of law and gospel. The preacher can engage in *secondary* discourse, but always in a way that serves the *primary* discursive proclamation—the very message of God in Christ, the gospel. Thus, the task of the preacher may be delineated as

1. to herald the gospel of Christ, to wit: that God has been reconciled to treasonous humanity through the Christ, Jesus, and that the same Christ is presently ruling through grace and mercy in the power of the Holy Spirit or, which is to say the same thing, that God's kingdom has come (though not fully);

2. to do said heralding of the gospel *in persona Christi* with apostolic authority derived from the gospel of Christ in *primary discourse*;

3. to endeavor to remove "every human artifice out of the way of the Word of God in Christ;"[58]

4. to articulate Jesus the Christ as the consummation of God's signature work in and through Israel, as the Old Testament foretold;

5. and to express the divine missional concern for humanity to be redeemed in Christ and sanctified/edified in him.

It is in view of his task to engender faith and hope in Christ Jesus that the preacher then approaches and deliberates homiletical methodologies for the purpose of facilitating the proclamation of the truth about humanity and God in Christ through primary divine speech acts (direct proclamation) augmented by secondary discourse (exegesis and explanation).

Historically, Lutheran ministers have embraced a high view of the Office of Holy Ministry and eschewed a functionalist perspective on the priesthood. The pastor's representative role as *Christ present* amidst his people has been inseparably bound to three Lutheran homiletical distinctions: (i) properly distinguishing the law from the gospel for a clear proclamation of the latter, perceivably from the biblical text; (ii) doing so utilizing primary discourse as a divine speech-act; and (iii) understanding that the *use* of the gospel upon an auditor took precedence over the auditor's propositional understanding. In these ways, Lutherans forged their characteristic homiletical

---

58. Caemmerer, *Preaching*, 7.

traits.[59] Where they have been retained, they continue to serve as a clarion call to preachers to recover the purity of text-based gospel proclamation, regardless of methodological preferences, and thus serve as a bulwark to the intrusion of consumeristic principles upon preaching.

It is important to note that the Lutheran distinctive of the law-and-gospel dynamic is not necessarily a two-part sermon structure. The law-and-gospel is a *mode* of discourse rather than a sermon *model* or type of structure. Simply put: *the* Lutheran distinctive in preaching is the living dynamic of law and gospel *applied* to hearers (as primary discourse) which discursive and living dynamic can make use of virtually any type of sermon *structure* (including dynamic *structures*) toward the proclamation and application of law-and-gospel.

Again, the dynamic of law-and-gospel concerns not so much genre or relative position in the Bible as what this sort of proclamation *does* to its auditors, that is, how hearers experience God's application of law and gospel to them. "When the Reformers used the words *law* and *gospel*, they were actually observing how God's word works on hearers or, even better, how God uses commands and promises on us."[60] Telling the truth about the human condition and God's remedy in Christ through direct speech (primary discourse) is the heart of a distinctly Lutheran homiletic.

> At its heart, the law/gospel sermon structure is divided into two parts, law proclamation and gospel proclamation, with greater attention preferably devoted to the gospel proclamation. In each section, the preacher references both the text and the lives of the hearers.... The first portion focuses upon law proclamation: it depicts the sin or trouble that is present both in the life situation of the text and in the contemporary lives of the hearers. The second portion focuses upon gospel proclamation: it depicts God's gracious intervention to forgive people their sins both in the life situation of the text and in the contemporary lives of the hearers.[61]

Though Schmitt speaks of "two parts" the dynamic does not and need not fall into two "parts," "sections," or "portions," but can, in fact, pervade and permeate all parts, sections, or portions of a sermon; or it can fall across its overarching structure in a way other than a law-section followed by a

---

59. "Preaching with proper distinction the law and the gospel," writes Wengert, "is the central concept from the Reformation that distinguished these early Lutheran biblical interpreters from all the other exegetes of the period" (*Reading the Bible*, 29).

60. Ibid., 31.

61. Schmitt, "Sermon Structures."

gospel-section. While already employing a general *textual* structure, for example, Lutherans may exhibit considerable creativity within the domains of *dynamic* and *thematic* structures to articulate the law and the gospel such that their commanding and promising may be subject to divine use upon the hearers. Here are but four models of general sermon structures in which the law/gospel dynamic could be implemented.

1. From C.F.W. Walther and J. Michael Reu[62] (Lutherans)

    A. Law as Demand > How Christ has met the Demand (gospel)

    B. Law as Threat > Gospel as Protection/Shelter

2. Textual Structure using a Plotline-Antitheses Model:

    A. Expulsion from Eden to the New Jerusalem

    B. Exodus to Promised Land

    C. Good Friday to Easter

    D. Slaves to Free Men

    E. Orphans to Children of the Father

    F. Dirty to Clean / Darkness to Light

3. A Model from Richard Lischer (Lutheran) Law and Gospel as Deep Grammar[63]

    A. Chaos to Order

    B. Bondage to Deliverance

    C. Rebellion to Vindication

    D. Wrath to Love

    E. Defeat to Victory

4. A Model from Herman Stuempfle (Lutheran) Vertical and Horizontal Access[64]

    A. Judgment to Forgiveness

    B. Alienation to Reconciliation

    C. Anxiety to Certitude

    D. Despair to Hope

---

62. Walther, *Proper Distinction* and Reu, *Homiletics*. I am indebted to Brian Thomas for allowing me to use these examples, which he compiled.

63. Lischer, *Theology*.

64. Stuempfle, *Preaching*.

E. Transience to Homecoming

Telling the truth about humanity (law) and telling the truth about God (gospel) categorically militates against ideological consumerism and any hold it may have on either the preacher or auditor. This is because, while the law is about us, as it were, the gospel is not. The gospel, writes Timothy Wengert, "always and only puts God as the subject of the theological sentence."[65] Still, both law and gospel are *used* by the Spirit to actuate divine purposes. They are not "used" or "consumed" by those who hear the proclamation; they are used by God *for* us. There is nothing to consume; there is only to be acted upon by another and to receive by faith. Just the same, Lutherans do well to revisit the task of the preacher to herald a specific bipartite message (law-and-gospel) in primary discourse, before committing to any fixed structure, especially thematic structures. Structures or models are meant to facilitate the primary discourse of God's word to us and for us, not vice versa.

CONCLUSION

Consumerism stands as *the* major obstacle to genuine theological proclamation. Too frequently moralism is identified as the problem of contemporary preaching. Certainly, moralism commits a basic hermeneutical error, from the Lutheran point of view, by making law the gospel and the gospel the law. But moralistic preaching is really the result of a consumerist framework, whereby preachers give people what they want, if not expect: a self-contentment or happiness that comes from the justification of one's lifestyle, whatever lifestyle that may be. Consumerism and Lutheranism are a clash of orthodoxies precisely at the point of justification. Lutheranism, however, is at home in the church as the church, while consumerism must remain alien to the church if the law and gospel are to be efficaciously preached and "the whole counsel of God" broadcast. Nothing, therefore, is more important to a Lutheran curacy of the gospel than for Lutherans to fastidiously retain their distinctive of proclaiming law and proclaiming gospel for divine use upon hearers. With this priority, the spectrum of sermon structures with its various homiletical methodologies comes once again into the service of Christ's mandate.

The task of the Lutheran preacher, indeed of all preachers, begins with a recognition of the authority of Jesus Christ and his mandate to edify individuals and congregations through gospel proclamation. How that task

---

65. Wengert, *Reading the Bible*, 45.

should be faithfully accomplished is safeguarded by his giving preachers a canonical text that stands outside ourselves and bears true witness to him; a text corroborated by other, derived, gospel-infused authoritative texts, such as the Ecumenical Creeds, Augsburg Confession, and Luther's Small Catechism. The possibility of being illumined by the truth concerning humankind (law) and the truth about God in Christ (gospel) is left to the work of the Holy Spirit. That work belongs to the "sword of the Spirit" not to the preacher. Herein, then, is the bedrock of the Lutheran homiletical distinctive: the gospel is proclaimed from the inherited textual-tradition of Holy Scripture, creeds, catechisms and confessions, being distinguished from the proclaimed law, so that *God* may save and sanctify sinners through *his* performative speech-activity. With that as the Christ-mandated starting point for all preachers, the Lutheran homiletician has considerable liberty outside the inefficacious expectations of the consumeristic agenda to be methodologically hybrid-textual and hybrid-structural since the dynamic is at play in the texts themselves.

What is missing from compromised Lutheran preaching is the very heritage of Lutheranism—theological proclamation. In that twofold proclamation is made manifest the life of the world, and that makes it a matter of the highest conceivable importance. What can be done about its recovery, preservation, and proliferation? Remembering the place of the sermon within the divine liturgy would do much to dispel tendencies to compromise with ideological consumerism and foster the recovery, preservation and proliferation of the gospel by keeping out notions of the "contemporary" and of "style." The sermon cannot hold the same place in the Lutheran mass as it does in the Calvinist or evangelical gathering, for its rightful place is to bridge together the words of the King preserved in Holy Scripture (his real voice) and the self-giving of the King in the Eucharist (his real presence) through explicit primary speech and secondary discourse explaining precisely who it is present and how he is so *for* them.

BIBLIOGRAPHY

Barna, George. *Marketing the Church: What They Never Told You about Church Growth.* Colorado Springs: Nav, 1998.
Breen, Mike. "How Celebrity, Consumerism & Competition are Killing the Church." 3 Sep. 2013." http://www.vergenetwork.org/2013/09/03/how-celebrity-consumerism-competition-are-killing-the-church (accessed 30 Dec. 2015).
Burge, Gary. "The Greatest Story Never Read." *CT* 43, no. 9 (1999) 45–49.
Caemmerer, Richard R. *Preaching for the Church.* St. Louis: Concordia, 1959.

Cavanaugh, William T. *Being Consumed: Economics and Christian Desire.* Grand Rapids: Eerdmans, 2008.

Clarke, Jean, and Robin Holt. "The Mature Entrepreneur: A Narrative Approach to Entrepreneurial Goals." *Journal of Management Inquiry* 19 (2010) 69–83.

Clavier, Mark. *Rescuing the Church from Consumerism.* London: SPCK, 2013.

Dean, Kenda Creasy. *Almost Christian: What the Faith of Our Teenagers is Telling the American Church.* New York: Oxford University Press, 2010.

Dever, Mark. *The Message of the Old Testament: Promises Made.* Wheaton, IL: Crossway 2006.

———. *The Message of the New Testament: Promises Kept.* Wheaton, IL: Crossway 2005.

Fenton Christopher, and Ann Langley. "Strategy as Practice and Narrative Turn." *Organizational Studies* 32 (2011) 1171–96.

Forde, Gerhard. *Theology Is for Proclamation.* Minneapolis: Augsburg, 1990.

———. "Whatever Happened to God? God Not Preached." In *The Preached God: Proclamation in Word and Sacrament*, edited by Mark C. Mattes and Steven D. Paulson, 33–55. Grand Rapids: Eerdmans, 2007.

———. *Where God Meets Man: Luther's Down-to-Earth Approach to the Gospel.* Minneapolis: Augsburg, 1972.

Friedman, Milton. *Free to Choose.* New York: Avon, 1980.

Gallo, Carmine. "Joel Osteen: 7 Keys to Successful Public Speaking." 1 Sep 2012. http://www.forbes.com/sites/carminegallo/2012/01/09/joel-osteen-7-keys-to-successful-public-speaking/ (accessed 30 Dec. 2015).

Giertz, Bo. "The Meaning and Task of the Sermon in the Framework of the Liturgy." In *The Unity of the Church: A Symposium*, 133–42. Minneapolis: Augsburg, 1957.

Gieschen, Charles A. "Preaching Through the Seasons of the Church." In *Liturgical Preaching: Contemporary Essays*, edited by Paul J. Grime and Dean W. Nadasdy, 84–87. St. Louis: Concordia.

Good Morning America. "Preaching Success: Joel Osteen Teaches Positivity." 15 Oct. 2007. http://abcnews.go.com/GMA/TenWays/story?id=3730401 (accessed 30 Dec. 2015).

Gordon, T. David. *Why Johnny Can't Preach.* Philipsburg, NJ: P. & R., 2009.

Grime, Paul J., and Dean W. Nadasdy, eds. *Liturgical Preaching: Contemporary Essays.* St. Louis: Concordia, 2001.

Hadaway, Kirk, and Penny Long Marler. "How Many Americans Attend Worship Each Week? An Alternative Approach to Measurement." *JSSR* 44 (2005) 307–22.

Horton, Michael S. *Christless Christianity: The Alternative Gospel of the American Church* Grand Rapids: Baker, 2009.

Killinger, John. *Fundamentals of Preaching.* Minneapolis: Fortress, 1996.

Lischer, Richard. *A Theology of Preaching: The Dynamics of the Gospel.* Eugene, OR: Wipf and Stock, 2001.

Malina, Bruce J. *The New Testament World: Insights from Cultural Anthropology.* Rev. ed. Louisville: Westminster John Knox, 1993.

MacDonald, Jeffrey. *Thieves in the Temple: The Christian Church and the Selling of the American Soul.* New York: Basic, 2010.

Marsden, George. *Fundamentalism and American Culture: The Shaping of Twentieth Century Evangelicalism 1870–1925.* New York: Oxford University Press, 1980.

Menzie, Nicola. "Joel Osteen Talks Biggest Preaching Mistake, 'Owning the Room.'" 25 Apr. 2013. http://www.christianpost.com/news/joel-osteen-talks-biggest-preaching-mistake-owning-the-room-94667 (accessed 30 Dec. 2015).

Miles, Steven. *Consumerism—as a Way of Life*. London: Sage, 1998.

Miller, Vincent J. *Consuming Religion: Religious Belief and Practice in a Consumer Culture*. New York: Continuum, 2005.

Mumme, Jonathan. "The Spirit, the Spirits, and the Letter: Martin Luther on the Holy Spirit and the Holy Scriptures." *Modern Reformation* 19, no. 6 (2010) 18–22.

O'Conner, Ellen. "Storied Business: Typology, Intertextuality, and Traffic in Entrepreneurial Narrative." *Journal of Business of Communication* 39 (2002) 36–54.

Osteen, Joel. "Removing Negative Labels." iTBN. 22 Dec. 2013. http://www.itbn.org/index/detail/ec/hob2d2aTpRnVlBgJXy2j9UIkEXv57q_p#ooid=hob2d2aTpRnVl BgJXy2j9UIkEXv57q_p (accessed 30 Dec. 2015).

Park, Richard Hee-Chun. *Organic Homiletic: Samuel T. Coleridge, Henry G. Davis, and the New Homiletic*. American University Studies. Series VII. Theology and Religion. New York: Lang, 2006.

Penner, Myron B. *The End of Apologetics*. Grand Rapids: Baker Academic, 2013.

Perkins, William. "Christ's Sermon on the Mount." In *The Workes of That Famous and Worthy Minister of Christ in the Universitie of Cambridge, M. William Perkins*, 3:226–34. London, 1613.

Pink, Arthur W. *The Seven Sayings of the Savior on the Cross*. Grand Rapids: Baker, 1976.

Reese, J. "Pitfalls of Proof-Texting." *BibTB* 13 (1983) 121–23.

Reu, M. *Homiletics: A Manual of the Theory and Practice of Preaching*. Grand Rapids: Baker, 1967.

Schmitt, David. "Sermon Structures." 2011. http://www.concordiatheology.org/sermon-structs (accessed 30 Dec. 2015).

Scudieri, Robert J. *The Apostolic Church: One, Holy, Catholic and Missionary*. Chino, CA: Lutheran Society for Missiology, 1995.

Smith, Christian. *The Bible Made Impossible: Why Biblicism Is Not a Truly Evangelical Reading of Scripture*. Grand Rapids: Brazos, 2011.

———. *Souls in Transition: The Religious and Spiritual Lives of Emerging Adults*. New York: Oxford University Press, 2009.

———. *Soul Searching: The Religious and Spiritual Lives of American Teenagers*. New York: Oxford University Press, 2009.

Stuempfle, Herman G. *Preaching Law and Gospel*. 2nd ed. Mifflintown, PA: Sigler, 1991.

Treier, Daniel. "Proof Text." In *DTIB*, 622–24.

Twitchell, James B. *Lead Us into Temptation: The Triumph of American Materialism*. New York: Columbia University Press, 2000.

Vanhoozer, Kevin. *Is There a Meaning in This Text? The Bible, the Reader, and the Morality of Literary Knowledge*. Grand Rapids: Zondervan, 2009.

Walther, C. F. W. *The Proper Distinction between Law and Gospel*. St. Louis: Concordia, 1986.

Wengert, Timothy. *Reading the Bible with Martin Luther*. Grand Rapids: Baker Academic, 2013.

West, Fritz. "Readings, Scripture." In *EC* 4:491–96.

Witten, Marsha. *All Is Forgiven: The Secular Message in American Protestantism*. Princeton: Princeton University Press, 1993.

2

Certainty in the Sermon
Patterns of Preaching from Peter and Pentecost

—Mark W. Birkholz

INTRODUCTION

"Therefore let the whole house of Israel know for certain that God has made this Jesus, whom you crucified, both Lord and Christ."[1] (Acts 2:36) This is the conclusion to the first Christian sermon, Peter's address at Pentecost.[2] Peter's claim of certainty may seem odd in post-modern ears, and yet it is consistent with the stated purpose of the author's composition of Luke-Acts, "in order that you may know the certainty of the things which you have been taught." (Luke 1:4)[3]

In order to explore this topic further, a more detailed examination of the prologue of Luke will be helpful. The fruits of this study will then be applied to the specific example of Peter's Pentecost sermon. Finally, applications will be made for a manner of proclamation of the gospel today that will

---

1. All translations are the author's.

2. For the purposes of this paper, the term "sermon" will be used loosely to denote any proclamation of the good news of Jesus Christ as applied to a group of hearers. In the book of Acts, these speeches are typically found in the context of evangelism rather than that of Christian congregations.

3. For more on the unity of Luke and Acts, see note 13 below.

similarly provide certainty to those who hear. In the course of this study two particular components will be brought to the fore as contributing towards the establishment of certainty. The first is an emphasis on fulfillment, not only on the fulfillment of the OT in the person and life of Jesus, but also the ongoing fulfillment of Jesus' own words today. The second is the reliability of the transmission of witness of these fulfillments, again in both biblical and contemporary contexts. Taken together, the preacher's presentation of God's work of salvation as having been and still being fulfilled, and that this message has been and is still being delivered by witnesses to these events, will contribute towards the establishment of certainty consistent with the manner in which this theme is developed in Luke –Acts.

CERTAINTY IN LUKE'S PROLOGUE

Structure of the Prologue

The key term in the conclusion of Peter's Pentecost address is ἀσφαλῶς, the adverbial form of ἀσφάλεια ("certainty"). This word points the reader back to the prologue of Luke itself, where Luke explains to Theophilus his purpose in writing.[4] In the final clause of the prologue, Luke states that he is writing "in order that you may know the certainty of the things which you have been taught" (ἵνα ἐπιγνῷς περὶ ὧν κατηχήθης λόγων τὴν ἀσφάλειαν). The term ἀσφάλεια and its cognates are rarely used in the NT. It conveys a sense of security, and can be used quite literally to refer to securely locked prison doors as in Acts 5:23. It is used elsewhere in Acts in contexts where a government official needs to establish the certainty or truth of an account in the midst of confusion or conflicting stories (21:34; 22:30; 25:26) When Luke attempts to establish certainty, it is noteworthy that he does not present logical argumentation in the form of a bare systematic theology. Instead, he uses the form of a story, including major sections of dialogue, to impart this certainty to Theophilus.[5]

---

4. The traditional ascription of the authorship of the Third Gospel as well as the Acts of the Apostles to Luke will be assumed throughout. For a defense of this position, see Keener, *Acts* 1:410–14.

5. The precise identity of Theophilus is uncertain and not critical to the study at hand. It is noteworthy, however, that he is called a catechumen, one who has been instructed. Although this could mean that he is merely familiar with these events, it is most likely that he is one in the formative stages of joining the Christian community (cf. Fitzmyer, *Luke*, 1:301; Johnson, *Luke*, 28).

Luke's prologue is considered by many to have the highest literary quality of any passage in the NT.[6] It is comprised of a single periodic sentence, containing five clauses. Four adverbial clauses enclose the single independent clause, formed by the impersonal verb ἔδοξε ("it seemed good") and the supplementary infinitive γράψαι ("to write"). The key thought expressed in this sentence, therefore, is that it seemed good for Luke to write. The other four clauses explain both why it seemed good for Luke to write, and how he planned to compose his account.

The precise meaning of nearly every term in the prologue is disputed, and so a complete analysis of this text is not possible here. A few features will be briefly examined, however, that have direct bearing on Peter's Pentecost sermon.

The first clause of the prologue (Ἐπειδήπερ πολλοὶ ἐπεχείρησαν ἀνατάξασθαι διήγησιν περὶ τῶν πεπληροφορημένων ἐν ἡμῖν πραγμάτων, "Inasmuch as many have set their hands to compile an account concerning the things that have been fulfilled among us") explains Luke's reason for writing this account. His mention of other writers ("many") is not meant to demean the previously written accounts, but to establish the topic as important based on the attention that it has already received.[7] For the purposes of this study, the most notable term in this clause is πεπληροφορημένων. Although some scholars assert that this term merely refers to events that have "happened," it is best, in view of Luke's usage of πληρόω in this sense throughout the text of Luke-Acts, to understand it as a reference to fulfillment in the narrow sense.[8]

With the second clause (καθὼς παρέδοσαν ἡμῖν οἱ ἀπ' ἀρχῆς αὐτόπται καὶ ὑπηρέται γενόμενοι τοῦ λόγου, "just as the eyewitnesses from the beginning who were made ministers of the word handed down to us") Luke indicates how he will be writing, namely in a manner faithful to how it has been handed down to him. Here Luke refers to the eyewitnesses who have become ministers of the word.[9] Luke is not claiming a new or innovative approach, but merely an accurate recounting based on the testimony of those

---

6. E.g., Bovon, *Lukas*, 17; Blass and Debrunner, *Greek Grammar*, § 464; Fitzmyer, *Luke*, 1:287–88.

7. Green, *Luke*, 38; Marshall, *Luke*, 41; Plummer, *St. Luke*, 4.

8. Fitzmyer, *Luke* 1:292–94; Green, *Luke*, 39–40; Marshall, *Luke* 41; Trocmé, Le "livre des Actes," 46.

9. It is best to take these as dual descriptions of the same group of people. The use of the single article and verb point in this direction, as well as Paul's own self-designation as a minister and witness (Acts 26:16; see also Bovon, *Lukas*, 1:21; Green, *Luke*, 41; Marshall, *Luke*, 42).

who have experienced these events firsthand and have been made servants to the message of Jesus.

There is certainly much more that could be said about the prologue, but it is these two features that are most critical or this analysis. Luke understands the events about which he is writing to be a fulfillment, and he places a high value on the importance of faithful transmission through eyewitnesses. In the following section these two topics will be explored at further length, but first a few comments regarding the applicability of the prologue to the remainder of the text of Luke-Acts are in order.

Applicability of the Prologue to Luke-Acts

Generally speaking, there are two schools of thought regarding the applicability of the prologue to the text of Luke-Acts. The first, and most prevalent, is that Luke lays out his plan for composing and editing his text in these opening verses.[10] The other view, and one that is gathering some scholarly following, is that the prologue has no bearing on the text of Luke-Acts per se, and is only written as a generic preface following the example of other scientific manuals of Luke's day.[11]

Although most scholars still accept a connection between the prologue and the text of Luke, the applicability to Acts is more disputed. Much of this debate centers on the question of the relationship of these two books to each other. While common authorship is nearly undisputed, a question remains as to whether the books were composed at the same time or on separate occasions. The resumptive prologue to Acts (Acts 1:1–2) with its close parallels to similar resumptive prologues in contemporary literature, seems to point to a unified composition.[12] The other key factor is the use of the prepositional phrase ἐν ἡμῖν ("among us") in Luke 1:1. The only events to which Luke himself was a witness are those described in the book of Acts, and so if this pronoun is taking in the narrowest sense, the events of Acts must be in view. It is possible, though, that the term is being used here more loosely to talk about the Christian community in general. Even if, however, Acts was not written at the same time as the third gospel, one would expect the author to have a similar approach to the topic.

---

10. Klein, "Lukas 1.1–4," 193–216; van Unnik, "Once More," 26n79; du Plessis, "Once More," 271.

11. Alexander, *Preface*, 13.

12. Josephus, *Contra Apionem* 2.1; Polybius, *Histories* IV.1.1; Diodorus Siculus ii.1; Irenaeus, *Adv. Haer.* Ii.1; see also Jackson and Lake, "Internal Evidence," 133–35.

Usage of the Old Testament

Luke uses the OT extensively as he presents his account in Luke-Acts. Generally speaking, there are three ways in which it is utilized. First, and easiest to identify, are the direct quotations from the OT. Second are the general statements of fulfillment without any specific quotation. Finally, there are allusions to OT texts and patterns.

Luke's quotation of the OT occurs most often in the course of the narratives as various characters apply the OT to their situation.[13] The OT is quoted not only by major protagonists, such as Jesus, Peter, Stephen, Philip, and Paul, but also by the Sadducees and even Satan itself. Even when the use of the OT is not in direct fulfillment, its quotation indicates its continuing importance within the text. At each major point in the story, the OT is used to support the assertions of the text. These include Jesus' ministry, Jesus' identity, Jesus' rejection by the Jewish leadership, Jesus' sacrificial death, Jesus' resurrection, and the mission to the Gentiles.[14] Even when a specific OT text is not quoted, Luke frequently notes that certain events took place to fulfill the Scriptures. Again, these are found in a variety of contexts.[15]

Finally, there are instances in which the text includes an allusion to an OT text or concept. These are much more difficult to identify with certainty and would need to be analyzed on an individual basis.[16] The most frequently identified OT concept in Luke-Acts is the journey motif, drawing from the story of the Exodus as well as the return from exile.[17] In general, it can be said that Luke's use of the OT, particularly to indicate its fulfillment, is a complex phenomenon, going beyond the use of simple quotations.

The concept of fulfillment in Luke-Acts extends beyond the use of the OT, to intratextual fulfillment as well. There are many instances where a prophecy or prediction is made at one point of the narrative and fulfilled in another. These intratextual fulfillments are found throughout the narrative,

---

13. There are a few instances of OT quotation by the narrator, e.g., Luke 2:23–24 and 3:4–6.

14. See Birkholz, "Certainty," 76–90.

15. E.g., Luke 1:70; 18:31; 24:25–27, 44–49; Acts 3:18, 24; 13:27, 29; 26:6–7, 22–23, 27–28.

16. The work of Hays is a helpful starting point (*Echoes*) taking into account the critique of Beker regarding the determination of authorial intentionality with the use of allusions and echoes ("Echoes," 64–65). See also Longenecker, *Exegesis*; and Bock, *Proclamation*.

17. E.g., Borgman, *The Way*; Pao, *Acts*.

including statements relative to Jesus' birth, death, and resurrection, as well as to the expansion of the Gentile mission.[18]

This demonstrates that the reader of Luke-Acts will expect Peter's Pentecost sermon to highlight the fulfillment of the OT as it moves forward to establish certainty regarding the actions and identity of Jesus and their enduring significance.

Eyewitness Testimony

The testimony of eyewitnesses is also a critical feature, not only of the prologue, but of the entire text of Luke-Acts. This is fitting with the expectations created by other ancient historians. Beginning with Herodotus, historians were expected to have visited the sites about which they wrote, if not to have participated in the events themselves.[19] The most reliable accounts were written by those who took part in the historical events. Both Thucydides and Josephus emphasize their roles and firsthand knowledge of the various battles in the wars about which they write.[20] If an author was not personally involved, he was at least expected to have personally interviewed the eyewitnesses in order to judge the veracity of their statements. It was helpful if he had had similar experiences to guide his judgments. The least reliable sources were the written records of others, as the authors of these accounts were not available for interrogation.

Throughout Luke-Acts, Luke emphasizes the importance of witnesses and the faithful transmission of their accounts. This includes incidents in the infancy narratives, in the ministry of Jesus, and especially in the account of his death and resurrection.[21] The identification of the apostles as witnesses to the deeds of Jesus drives the narrative in the book of Acts.[22] When Saul/Paul is introduced, his reliability is based on his personal encounter with Jesus on the road to Damascus, a point that he emphasizes repeatedly in the later accounts of his various trials.[23]

The role of witnesses is not limited to the authorized witness of the apostles to Jesus' death and resurrection. It also includes the ongoing

---

18. Jesus predicts his death in Luke 9:18–22; 9:44; and 18:31–34. These predictions are fulfilled in chaps. 22–23. He speaks of the Gentile mission in Luke 24:46–49 and Acts 1:8, which is fulfilled in the book of Acts as a whole.

19. Schepens, "History," 1:43.

20. Thucydides, *Histories* 1.22; Josephus, *Contra Apionem* 1.47–49.

21. E.g., Luke 2:15–18; 7:22; 24:48.

22. Acts 1:8, 22; 2:32; 3:15; 5:32; 10:39–41; 13:31.

23. Acts 22:15; 26:16.

witness of God's people to his continued activity among them.[24] In this way even those who are not firsthand witnesses to Jesus' death and resurrection are still able to speak about what had done for them.

CERTAINTY IN PETER'S PENTECOST SERMON

These two factors, fulfillment and transmission, are vitally important for Luke as he sets out to impart certainty to Theophilus regarding what he has already been taught. But how do these factors influence Peter's address at Pentecost? Does Luke faithfully reproduce Peter's sermon, or is it his own creation? Since there are no other records of this address, there are no points of comparison for discerning Luke's editorial work on this or any of the speeches in Acts. To gain further insight, we will first turn to Luke's contemporaries and then to the text of Luke-Acts itself.

Speeches were an expected element of any ancient history. They gave the author an opportunity to interpret the events through the voice of a main character and demonstrate his rhetorical flair.[25] These speeches were expected to be suitable to the occasion. Aristotle went so far as to say that speeches that were suitable but entirely created by the author may be preferable to what was actually said.[26] This is not to say that the ancients had no regard for accuracy. Some historians were criticized for taking liberty with speeches.[27]

In the case of the speeches found in Acts, it appears as though the addresses have been shortened significantly for inclusion within the narrative. Luke has chosen to highlight the content that he deems to be particularly significant for the themes that he is developing. With regard to the Pentecost sermon, Luke himself notes, "And with many other words, [Peter] was bearing witness and exhorting . . ."[28] Here Luke indicates that he is not including the entirety of Peter's address. It makes sense that Luke would include the portions that he considered most crucial to the development of the story and achievement of his stated purpose. With regard to the portions that are included, Luke makes the claim in his prologue that he will be giving an accurate (ἀκριβῶς) account. Peter's address was given publicly to a large audience. It is likely that Luke would have had an opportunity to speak with

---

24. This is particularly evident in the use of the first person plural in Luke 1:1.
25. Fornara, *The Nature of History*, 142; Marincola, "Speeches," 1:118–32.
26. *Poet.* 25.
27. Lucian, *On the Writing of History*, §§ 7–12.
28. Acts 2:40a. The use of the imperfect forms διεμαρτύρατο and παρεκάλει ("he was witnessing" and "he was exhorting") emphasize the ongoing nature of Peter's address.

one or more witnesses to this event and to create an accurate representation of what Peter actually said.

Fulfillment in Peter's Sermon

Peter quotes the OT at three distinct points in his sermon as recounted by Luke. First, he uses Joel 2:28–32 to provide an interpretative context for the events of the day and to introduce Jesus to the crowd.[29] Second, he quotes from Psalm 16 to establish Jesus' identity as Christ. Lastly, he draws from Psalm 110 to point to Jesus as Lord. These three texts taken together in the way that Peter interprets them leads to his conclusion that Jesus is both Lord and Christ.

After gaining the attention of the gathering crowd, Peter quotes from Joel 2 to interpret what the crowd is seeing and hearing. His application of this text is a possible example of pesher ("this is that") technique and has parallels with the interpretative methods of the Qumran community.[30] He is stating in the boldest possible terms that what the crowd is experiencing is the fulfillment of Joel's prophecy.

As Barnabas Lindars so helpfully demonstrates, NT quotations often have a larger OT textual context in view.[31] The larger literary context of the quote given by Peter is helpful in understanding its application. Joel 2 opens with a dire prediction of the impending judgment on the Day of the Lord (Joel 2:1–11). The expected response is one of repentance and return to the Lord (Joel 2:12–17). The chapter concludes with a collection of expected blessings from the Lord in terms of abundant food, peace, and a removal of their shame (Joel 2:18–27). Peter quotes the conclusion of the oracle, which promises that the Lord will pour out his spirit, give signs in nature, and save those who call upon his name.

The outpouring of God's spirit was reserved for specific prophets in the OT.[32] There are a few prophets who did predict that all Israel would one day receive the spirit.[33] Joel specifically enumerates that all people, regardless of gender, age, or social status, would receive the spirit on the Day of the Lord. This prophecy is fulfilled first through the apostles, but then later as

---

29. These verses are typically numbered as Joel 3:1–5 in the Hebrew text. The English numbering system will be used in the discussion that follows.

30. Evans, "The Prophetic Setting," 149; Keener, *Acts*, 1:873–74.

31. *New Testament Apologetic*.

32. Num 11:16–25; 1 Sam 10:6; 19:10; 1 Chr 12:18; 2 Chr 15:1; 20:14; 24:20; Ezek 2:2; Mic 3:8; Zech 7:12.

33. Isa 32:15; 44:3; Ezek 39:29; Zech 12:10.

the hearers receive the Holy Spirit at their baptism. This outpouring of the Holy Spirit is evidence that the Day of the Lord has come.

This outpouring is connected to visible signs in nature. It is not immediately clear to what this is being applied in this context. It could be the noise and the fire that accompanied the speaking in tongues that day. It could also be a reference to the darkening of the sky and the earthquake when Jesus was crucified (Luke 23:44–45). Later in the sermon Peter uses these same terms to refer to Jesus' miracles (Acts 2:22) so this appears to be the connection Peter is intending. Although these specific signs are not present among the miracles of Jesus per se, they still demonstrate Jesus' authority over the natural forces. Finally, this could simply be a portion of the prophecy that remains unfilled at this time, although this is unlikely.

Finally, the quotation from Joel concludes with the promise that everyone who calls on the name of the Lord will be saved. This terminology is a common reference to saving faith expressed through prayer.[34] The important point made here is the extension of salvation to all people, including the Gentiles. Although there is no indication that the people present at Pentecost included Gentiles, the wide array of nations represented indicate this broadening to include a wide geographic distribution. Further fulfillment is found again at the conclusion of Peter's address, when he states, "For this promise is for you and for your children and for all who are far off, whomever our Lord God will call." (Acts 2:39)

Joel 2, therefore, has a dual fulfillment. First, it is fulfilled in the events of Pentecost itself, but it is further fulfilled in the ensuing action as those assembled also receive the Holy Spirit and the gift of salvation. This indicates that fulfillment is not a punctilliar event with a definite terminus ad quem, but rather one that continues through the whole narrative.[35]

Following the quotation of Joel 2, Peter addresses the crowd again. He uses the reference to "signs and wonders" to connect with the story of Jesus. From there, he uses Psalm 16 connected to the resurrection of Jesus as the centerpiece in his argument that Jesus is the Christ.

After giving evidence to the death and resurrection of Jesus (see below) Peter quotes Psalm 16 and makes a common sense argument to the assembled crowd. Since David refers to a "Holy One" who will not see decay, and since David died but Jesus is alive, Jesus must be this Holy One to whom David refers. Peter also connects this passage to God's promise to David that

---

34. E.g., Gen 4:26; 12:8; 13:4; 21:33; 26:25; 1 Kgs 18:24; 2 Kgs 5:11; Pss 80:18; 99:6; Isa 64:7; Jer 10:25; Lam 3:55; Zeph 3:9; cf. Keener, *Acts* 1:920.

35. One could certainly see further fulfillment of Joel 3 in the further outpourings of the Holy Spirit, signs and miracles carried out by the apostles, and ongoing mission activity in the Book of Acts.

one of his descendants would remain on the throne forever.³⁶ David then applies the title of "Christ" to the one to whom David here refers, namely, Jesus.

Psalm 110 is the final text used by Peter in his address. This is the most widely quoted OT passage in the NT.³⁷ It is used by Jesus himself in his dispute with the Pharisees (Luke 20:41–44). This is the climax of the sermon, where Peter identifies Jesus not only as the Christ, but also as the Lord.

Again, Peter uses a quotation from the Psalms and shows why it cannot apply directly to David himself. The link between his citation of Psalm 16 and Psalm 110 is the common term "right hand" made by use of *gezerah schevah*.³⁸

Since Jesus is at God's right hand by virtue of his exaltation and ascension, the quotation of Psalm 110 establishes him as Lord. It is only from heaven that he would be able to send the Holy Spirit and the accompanying signs and wonders. The evidence of the working of the Holy Spirit is given as proof of Jesus' ascension and therefore also of his lordship.

Peter concludes chiastically by naming Jesus as both Lord (on the basis of his ascension and Psalm 110) and Christ (on the basis of his resurrection and Psalm 16). This is something that can be known for certain by any true Israelite, since they have both the texts and witnesses to prove it.

Transmission in Peter's Sermon

Throughout Peter's address, he emphasizes the importance of personal witness on two different levels. First there is the witness of the apostles. They are the ones who have personally seen and heard Jesus both pre- and post-resurrection. But equally important is the witness of the assembled crowd to what Jesus is continuing to do among them in their presence.

The most important role of the apostles is their role as witnesses to the resurrection. This point is made multiple times by Jesus and throughout the rest of the narrative of Luke-Acts. It is an important component to choosing the successor to Judas and is emphasized in the continuing confrontations between the apostles and the Jewish leadership.

When Peter refers to the signs and miracles done by Jesus, he assumes that these are common knowledge to the assembled crowd (Acts 2:22). But when he turns to the resurrection, he indicates that the company of apostles

---

36. 2 Sam 7:12–13; 1 Kgs 3:6; Ps 132:12.

37. Matt 22:44; Mark 12:36; Luke 20:42–43; Acts 2:34–35; Heb 1:13; 5:6; 7:17.

38. This Rabbinic interpretative technique links two passages through the useage of a similar term found in both. Cf. Juel, "Social Dimensions," 546; Keener, *Acts*, 1:944.

are the witnesses to this event (Acts 2:32). The reference to "we" refers most likely to Peter and the eleven (Acts 2:14), but it could also include the entire group upon whom the Holy Spirit came (Acts 2:1). In either case, they are well in excess of the two or three witnesses required by the law.[39]

Not only the apostles, but also all those who are seeing and hearing the events of that day (Acts 2:33) are witnesses. The combination of seeing and hearing is often used by Luke in the context of witnesses to important events.[40] What Peter is saying is this, "Even if you do not believe us, you can see and hear for yourselves the proof of what God is doing."

Although there is much more that can be said about this sermon, these two aspects, used by Peter and drawn out by Luke, come to the fore. The authoritative interpretation of the events not only of the past, but also of the present, is found in the Scriptures, and the reality of the events themselves can be established both on the basis of the testimony of the apostles as well as the hearers. These two factors, in particular, lead to certainty in the conclusions drawn by Peter and to the response of faith in repentance, baptism, reception of the Holy Spirit, and inclusion in the community.

CERTAINTY IN PREACHING TODAY

So what relevance does the foregoing have for those who preach today? In the present context, many would say that doubt is the only certainty, and unqualified assertions of truth are quickly dismissed. Could Peter speak the same words of certainty to hearers today as he did on Pentecost?

Before proceeding, it is necessary once more to remember the words of AC V, that faith is created by the Holy Spirit "where and when he wills."[41] There is no guaranteed procedure or method to create faith automatically. Faith is a gift and by nature rejectable. This rejection is apparent throughout the ministry of Jesus, and that of the apostles as well. The book of Acts concludes with the rejection of Paul by the Jewish community in Rome.

The message of the gospel is certain, whether it is received by faith or not. The truth and the reliability of Jesus' person and work do not depend on their reception. The preacher's words are certain, even if they are not judged to be so by the hearers. The certainty of the message of Jesus is testified to by its coherence with the preceding word of God (fulfillment) and by the witness of those who have seen and heard the events of salvation. This

---

39. Deut 17:6; 19:15.
40. Luke 2:20; 7:22; Acts 4:20; 22:15.
41. KW 40–41 = *BSLK* 58.

fulfillment and witness is ongoing in the church as God continues to act to save his people.

The goal of this essay is not to provide a set of principles to apply to preaching that will make their preaching more effective, but to describe these two components of apostolic preaching, as presented by Luke, so that preachers are faithful in following the approach to preaching demonstrated by the apostles. For example, the use of parables has a long history, both in the preaching of the OT prophets and the preaching of Jesus. For centuries, preachers have utilized appropriate stories in their preaching not because stories are guaranteed to create faith, but because this is often how the gospel is presented in Holy Scripture. Similarly, those who preach will utilize OT (and NT) citations appropriately and make direct reference to the witness of both the apostles and the hearers as these components are present in apostolic preaching. As the preacher weaves together both ancient authoritative texts and the present experience of the work of God, he is following the pattern of preaching laid down by Peter and the apostles. This allows him to declare the certainty of his message with confidence.

For Peter and the authors of the NT, their written Scriptures were the OT. There is some evidence of awareness of other NT writings, but in general these were not yet widely known.[42] The OT has continuing relevance throughout the NT, and its importance in the book of Acts points to its vital position in Christian preaching today. Preachers will do well to utilize the OT as well as the NT in showing fulfillment, not just in the person and life of Jesus, but also in the current life of their hearers, similar to how Peter applied Joel 2 to the crowds at Pentecost. Here the prophetic writings themselves will bear much fruit, but also the more indirect patterns and allusions found in the NT.

The key to interpreting and applying the words of the OT in a Christian context is to see them as first fulfilled in Jesus. This is Jesus' own hermeneutic, as he explains to his disciples.[43] The OT texts apply to contemporary hearers as they are fulfilled first in Christ and then in his body, the church. Much more can be said about the hermeneutics of the OT in preaching. The essays by Paul Elliot and Jeremiah Johnson in this volume both speak to this issue.[44] In general, it may be said that a Christian preacher who stands in line with Jesus and the apostles will present the story of salvation as a whole, and emphasize the continuity between the OT and the NT. In doing this,

---

42. Luke 1:1; 2 Pet 3:15–16.
43. Luke 24:27, 44.
44. See also Greidanus, *Preaching Christ*; Hummel, "How to Preach."

he uses Jesus as the interpretive key, as modeled by Peter in the Pentecost address treated at length above.

Preachers will also give testimony to the reliability of the events occurring of which they speak. Although much time has passed since the days of Jesus and the apostles, preachers should be able to assert with confidence that the miracles, death, and resurrection of Jesus are historic events that actually took place. Apart from these events, Christianity can easily drift into a Gnosticism of knowledge or float into the Platonic realm of the idea. In order to impart certainty, Luke tells a story that can be verified by eyewitnesses. Although Luke and his witnesses, along with the apostles, have all died, their common account has been accurately preserved to this day. Although it might be more appropriate for a Bible class than in a sermon, preachers must be able to demonstrate how the OT and NT texts have been preserved in the church and are a reliable record of the events they describe. They must also be able to speak with authority regarding issues of manuscript traditions and textual criticism. With the proliferation of modern translations comes further confusion regarding the text of Scripture. Although he may not be able to prove it to the satisfaction of all, the preacher must be prepared to argue for the plausibility that the Scriptures accurately preserve eyewitness accounts of the events which they record.

Further, preachers will not only focus on the witness of what happened in the life of Jesus and the early church, but also on what God is doing in the lives of the hearers today. Peter spoke very directly to his audience and called their attention to the events of that day. They could see and hear the miraculous events and become witnesses themselves. He then pointed them to the work that God would do in them as he poured out the Holy Spirit on them through baptism.

It is important, then, to make application to the work of God in giving his Holy Spirit to the hearers in word and sacrament. The sermon not only draws attention to what God has done in the past, but also to what he is doing in the present and what he has promised to do in the future. The preacher will encourage the hearers to weigh his words on the basis of their own experience of the work of God in their lives, as God continues to fulfill his word in his people.

Along with Peter (and with Luke) preachers today can boldly assert that the message of salvation in Jesus Christ is certain. It is certain because it is grounded in the events of the life of Jesus and in the life of the church as God fulfilled his word and continues to do so. It is certain because Jesus has provided witnesses to his words and deeds not only among the apostles, but also still today. In an uncertain world, preachers can provide certainty to their hearers as they follow the pattern of preaching found at Pentecost and throughout Luke-Acts.

BIBLIOGRAPHY

Alexander, Loveday C. A. *The Preface to St. Luke's Gospel: Literary Convention and Social Context in Luke 1.1-4 and Acts 1.* SNTS 78. Cambridge: Cambridge University Press, 1993.

Aristotle, *Poetics*. Translated by Stephen Halliwell. LCL 199. Cambridge, MA: Harvard University Press, 1995.

Beker, J. Christaan. "Echoes and Intertextuality: On the Role of Scripture in Paul's Theology." In *Paul and the Scriptures of Israel*, edited by Craig A. Evans and James A. Sanders, 64-65. Sheffield: JSOT, 1993.

Birkholz, Mark. "Certainty in Luke-Acts: Fulfillment, Transmission, and Order." PhD diss., Trinity Evangelical Divinity School, 2013.

Blass, Friedrich, and Albert Debrunner. *A Greek Grammar of the New Testament and other Early Christian Literature*. Translated by. Robert W. Funk. Chicago: University of Chicago Press, 1961.

Bock, Darrell L. *Proclamation from Prophecy and Pattern: Lucan Old Testament Christology*. JSOTSupp 12. Sheffield: JSOT, 1987.

Borgman, Paul. *The Way according to Luke: Hearing the Whole Story of Luke-Acts*. Grand Rapids: Eerdmans, 2006.

Bovon, François. *Das Evangelium nach Lukas*. 3 vols. EKKNT 3. Zürich: Benziger, 1989-2001.

Diodorus of Sicily. *Library of History*. Translated by C. H. Oldfather. 12 vols. LCL 279, 303, 340, 375, 377, 384, 389-90, 399, 409, 422. Cambridge, MA: Harvard University Press, 1960.

Du Plessis, I. I. "Once More: The Purpose of Luke's Prologue (Lk 1:1-4)" *NovT* 16 (1974) 259-71.

Evans, Craig A. "The Prophetic Setting of the Pentecost Sermon." *ZNW* 74 (1984) 148-50.

Fitzmyer, Joseph A. *The Gospel according to Luke: Introduction, Translation, and Notes*. 2 vols. AB 28. Garden City, NY: Doubleday, 1981-1985.

Fornara, Charles W. *The Nature of History in Ancient Greece and Rome*. Eidos. Berkeley: University of California Press, 1983.

Green, Joel B. *The Gospel of Luke*. NICNT. Grand Rapids: Eerdmans, 1997.

Greidanus, Sidney. *Preaching Christ from the Old Testament: A Contemporary Hermeneutical Method*. Grand Rapids: Eerdmans, 1999.

Hays, Richard. *Echoes of Scripture in the Letters of Paul*. New Haven: Yale University Press, 1989.

Hummel, Horace D. "How to Preach The Old Testament." In *Concordia Pulpit 1986*, 1-23. St. Louis: Concordia, 1985

Irenaeus of Lyon. *Contre les Hérésies*. 5 vols. Sources Chrétiennes 100, 152, 153, 210, 211, 263, 264, 293, 294. Edited by Adelin Rousseau. Paris: Cerf, 1965-1982.

Jackson, F. J. Foakes, and Kirsopp Lake. "Internal Evidence of Acts." In *Prolegomena II: Criticism*, vol. 2 of *The Beginnings of Christianity, Part I: The Acts of the Apostles*, edited by F. J. Foakes Jackson and Kirsopp Lake, 121–204. London: MacMillan, 1922.

Johnson, Luke T. *The Gospel of Luke*. SP 3. Collegeville, MN: Liturgical, 1991.

Josephus. Translated by H. St. J. Thackeray et al. 10 vols. LCL. Cambridge, MA.: Harvard University Press, 1930–65.

Juel, Donald H. "Social Dimensions of Exegesis: The Use of Psalm 16 in Acts 2." *CBQ* 43 (1981) 543–56.

Keener, Craig S. *Acts: An Exegetical Commentary: Introduction and 1:1—2:47*. Grand Rapids: Baker, 2012.

Klein, Günther. "Lukas 1.1–4 als theologische Programm." In *Zeit und Geschichte: Dankesgabe an Rudolf Bultmann zum 80. Geburtstag*, edited by Erich Dinkler and Hartwig Thyen, 193–216. Tübingen: Mohr, 1964.

Lindars, Barnabas. *New Testament Apologetic: The Doctrinal Significance of the Old Testament Quotations*. Philadelphia: Westminster, 1961.

Longenecker, Richard N. *Biblical Exegesis in the Apostolic Period*. Grand Rapids: Eerdmans, 1999.

Lucian of Samosata. *How to Write History*. Translated by K. Kilburn. LCL 430. Cambridge, MA: Harvard University Press, 1959.

Marincola, John. "Speeches in Classical Historiography." In *A Companion to Greek and Roman Historiography*, edited by John Marincola, 1:118–32. Blackwell Companions to the Ancient World. Malden, MA: Blackwell, 2007.

Marshall, I. Howard. *The Gospel of Luke: A Commentary on the Greek Text*. NIGTC; Grand Rapids: Eerdmans, 1978.

Pao, David W. *Acts and the Isaianic New Exodus*. Grand Rapids: Baker Academic, 2002.

Plummer, Alfred. *A Critical and Exegetical Commentary on the Gospel According to St. Luke*. ICC 28. Edinburgh: T. & T. Clark, 1922.

Polybius. *The Histories*. Translated by W. R. Paton. 6 vols. LCL 128, 137, 138, 159–61. Cambridge, MA: Harvard University Press, 1922–1927.

Schepens, Guido. "History and *Historia*: Inquiry in the Greek Historians." In *A Companion to Greek and Roman Historiography*, edited by John Marincol, 1:35–59. Blackwell Companions to the Ancient World. Malden, MA: Blackwell, 2007.

Trocmé, Étienne. *Le "livre des Actes" et l'histoire*. Paris: Presses Universitaires de France, 1957.

Unnik, Willem C. van. "Once More St. Luke's Prologue," *NeoT* (1973) 7–26.

3

The Israel of God in the Sermon
Connecting Old Testament Texts to New Testament People

—Paul M. C. Elliott

One of the great deficiencies in Christian preaching in recent times has been the general neglect of preaching from the Old Testament.[1] Many factors surely contribute,[2] but a major part of the problem is hermeneutical—it is simply difficult to interpret the Old Testament for application to congregational life. Given the enormity of the pastoral task, it is often easier for preachers simply to ignore the Old Testament and spend their precious time preparing sermons on the parts of Scripture that are most comfortable, such as the Gospels and the Pauline Epistles. On the few occasions when the subject of the Old Testament is broached, it is in texts that have a crystal clear prophecy-fulfillment relationship with the New Testament. This response is understandable, but it comes at the expense of the largest portion of the canonical writings. If the Church is not to become functionally Marcionite,

---

1. Greidanus, *Preaching Christ*, 15, estimates that less than 20 percent (and maybe even less than 10 percent) of Christian sermons are preached on Old Testament texts. He admits that statistics are hard to come by, and his data was out-of-date even when he cited it in 1999. Nonetheless, his numbers conform to experience.

2. For example, most pastors are better trained and more comfortable working in Greek than in Hebrew. Seminary education tends to focus on New Testament interpretation.

then we must find ways to encourage the beleaguered preacher to preach from the Old Testament.

It is a fundamental belief of the New Testament writers that there is continuity between the Old Testament and the New Testament. That is not to say that nascent Christianity did not see the coming of Christ as something radically new in God's relationship with humanity. God was "doing a new thing" (Isa 43:19); however, it was still the same God who was doing it, and the new thing that he was doing was foretold in ancient Scriptures and spoken of in the theological language of the Old Testament.[3] There are those who tried to resolve the tension, such as Marcion (c. 85–160) who denied any sort of continuity, or some branches of Judaeo-Christianity which denied any sort of discontinuity.[4] However, the New Testament writers and the Church Fathers maintained this paradox of continuity and discontinuity between the Testaments, a tension which Luther and his successors maintained. There are numerous ways in which the relationship between the Testaments can be and has been handled hermeneutically over the centuries, but one distinctively Lutheran approach has been typology. This study will take an approach that is typological and Christocentric, in order to provide some tools to help the preacher successfully connect Old Testament texts to New Testament realities. By finding Christ in the Hebrew Scriptures, the preacher will also be able to find the church there.

WHAT IS TYPOLOGY?

The definition of typology is still divisive in scholarship to a large degree. In one of the most exhaustive recent works on the topic, Richard M. Davidson concludes, "Despite the prodigious amount of literature on the subject of biblical typology that has appeared in previous centuries, and particularly in recent decades, still almost every area of typological interpretation is as yet unsettled."[5]

One of the first attempts to rigorously define typology can be found in the works of the post-Reformation Lutherans who defined typology in relation to other well-known approaches, such as allegory and symbolism. Johann Gerhard wrote, "Typology consists in the comparison of facts. Allegory is not concerned with facts but with the words from which it draws out useful and hidden doctrines."[6] Salomo Glassius, a student of Gerhard,

---

3. Goppelt, *Typos*, 16–17.
4. Greidanus, *Preaching Christ*, 18–19.
5. Davidson, *Typology*, 112.
6. Johann Gerhard, *Loci Theologici* 1. 69, cited by Goppelt, *Typos*, 7.

further built up the definition, "It is an allegory when the Holy Spirit intends that the historical events of Scripture refer to a mystery or some spiritual doctrine. It is a type when hidden things, whether present or future, are presented under the external events or prophetic visions, when events in the Old Testament prefigure or foreshadow events in the New Testament. It is a parable when something or event is related to or applied to some other spiritual entity."[7]

This basic definition still finds traction in the twentieth century, especially in Leonhard Goppelt's classic work from 1939. Goppelt further characterizes typology as necessarily involving a heightening or escalation (*Steigerung*) between type and antitype.[8] It is not sufficient for the fulfillment to be a restatement of the type—it must be far greater, which in Goppelt's sense usually means that it is Christological and/or eschatological.

Another useful revision of the definition of typology can be found in the dissertation of Davidson. He argues that past attempts at a definition have failed because they were based on *a priori* assumptions rather than the Scriptures' self-testimony about typology. He attempts to backwards-engineer the New Testament rules of typological interpretation by studying all of the texts in which the *typos*-word group is used in a technical exegetical sense (of which there are six occurrences in five New Testament texts).[9] This criterion is far too limiting, but Davidson's results are still a helpful contribution to the field. He characterizes the New Testament typological structures as historical (types are assumed to be historical reality, and the correspondence of type and antitype involves historical details), eschato-

---

7. Goppelt, *Typos*, 6, quotes this passage without precise citation. Goppelt (ibid, 18n55) goes on to illustrate this definition with a very useful example about various ancient interpretations of the bronze serpent in Num 21. When the apocryphal book *Wisdom of Solomon* (16:8) interprets the account of the bronze serpent, it gives a symbolic interpretation: the bronze serpent symbolizes that God is a helper in every emergency. Thus, a historical event is connected directly to a general truth. Philo of Alexandria gives an allegorical interpretation of the bronze serpent, "If the mind (i.e. Israel) when bitten by pleasure, the serpent of Eve, shall have succeeded in beholding in soul the beauty of self-mastery, the serpent of Moses, and through beholding this, beholds God himself, he shall live." Note that the literal sense of the text is of no consequence to the allegorical interpretation. The figures in the story are transformed through various techniques into a general psychological observation. By contrast, the interpretation of the bronze serpent given in John 3:14 is typological—the lifting up of the bronze serpent for temporal salvation foreshadowed the far greater lifting up of the Christ for eternal salvation. Typology connects a real, historic entity—whether that thing is a person, institution, event, etc.—and connects it to another real, historic entity.

8. Ibid, 18. Cf. Goppelt, "Τυπος, Αντιτυπος, Τυπικος, Ὑποτυπωσις," 252. Baker, "Typology," 152, disagrees, considering something a type even if it is on the same plane as its antitype.

9. 1 Cor 10:1–13 ; Rom 5:12–21; 1 Pet 3:18–22; Heb 8 and 9.

logical (types are intensified in their fulfillment at the "end of the ages"), Christological-soteriological (types find their *telos* in the saving work of Christ), ecclesiological (types involve the corporate, individual, and sacramental dimensions of God's people), and prophetic (types have elements of prefiguration, divine design, and necessity).[10]

Furthermore, Davidson finds many implications in the New Testament use of typology. First, Old Testament types are historical realities, and their legitimacy is dependent on their historicity.[11] Second, Old Testament types are scriptural realities, that is to say, based on what was written down (cf. 1 Cor 10:11) in Scripture and not on extra-biblical material.[12] Third, correspondences between Old Testament types and New Testament antitypes involve specific details (e.g., in 1 Cor 10, the parting of the Red Sea is connected to baptism not just in the sense that both are salvation-events but also in the detail of the watery element) but they do not involve trivial or insignificant details.[13] Fourth, a historical, eschatological escalation (*Steigerung*) exists in the movement from type to antitype.[14] Fifth, types can be events, people, or institutions.[15] Sixth, the typological nature is inherent in the events themselves and not imposed upon them by the interpreter.[16] Lastly, typology can be horizontal (i.e. between one historical reality and another) or vertical (i.e. between a historical reality and a spiritual reality).[17] Davidson's work remains the best attempt to systematically observe how the New Testament authors themselves used typology.

---

10. Davidson, *Typology*, 416–19.

11. Ibid., 293, demonstrates that the arguments of the New Testament authors would make little sense if the Old Testament types were not actual historical events. Goppelt, *Typos*, 229–33, hedges on this issue in deference to the higher critical scholarship of his day. By arguing that New Testament antitypes are valid even if the Old Testament types are historically inaccurate, Goppelt enervates his entire argument in favor of typological interpretation.

12. Davidson, *Typology*, 293–94.

13. Ibid., 294.

14. Ibid., 295, 416–17.

15. Ibid., 295, contra Friederichsen, who argues that typology is only valid in relation to the rituals and cultus of Israel. Ibid., 47–48.

16. Ibid., 295–96.

17. In fact, the Epistle to the Hebrews argues that vertical typology is already present in the Old Testament, offering the example of Exod 25:40. Ibid., 363–67.

WHY TYPOLOGY?

Why then is the typological approach used here as a distinctively Lutheran way of interpreting and applying the Old Testament? It is neither possible nor profitable to give a complete treatment of the debate surrounding typology in this short article, but there are two criteria that underlie the choice for typology. First of all, typology is consistent with foundational Lutheran principles. Chief among these is Luther's hermeneutic of *sola scriptura* and "Scripture interprets Scripture." In short, the Bible provides the hermeneutical keys for interpreting itself.[18] It is not a controversial statement to say that New Testament authors used typology in making use of the Old Testament. Goppelt would even go so far as to say that typology is the primary and most distinctive hermeneutic of the apostles.[19] Perhaps this is even the method which Jesus taught his disciples on the road to Emmaus and in other post-Easter accounts, when "beginning with Moses and all the Prophets, he interpreted to them in all the Scriptures the things concerning himself." (Luke 24:27) Moreover, there is evidence that early Christianity inherited this approach from the Old Testament itself.[20] For example, Jeremiah interprets the exodus from Egypt as being a type of the return from the Babylonian exile (Jer 16:14–15). In fact, the prophet predicts that the return from exile shall be so great, that it will entirely overshadow its type, the exodus. A further example would be the texts which provide David as the type of the eschatological savior-king.[21] In all of these cases, the earlier event in Old Testament history is the shadow, which is only truly fulfilled in the antitype. Thus, typology is an exegetical method founded in Scripture's self-testimony, which the Lutheran exegete can feel free to appropriate.[22]

---

18. Origen (hardly a Lutheran, but sounding much like one on this point) used the example of the Bible being like a house full of locked rooms. In front of each door is a key, but not for that room. Each key opens one of the other rooms. By this, Origen means that each text can only be understood by finding its hermeneutical key in another text. It is also worth knowing that Origen claimed that this hermeneutic was not his original idea but came from a Jewish source. Origen, *Philocalia* 2.3.

19. Goppelt, *Typos*, provides the most comprehensive compiling of all of the New Testament passages which could be understood as examples of typological interpretation, devoting the majority of his volume to the task.

20. Ibid., 38–41, n99.

21. Especially Ezek 34:23–34; 37:24–25; Hos 3:5.

22. Even though the fact that the New Testament uses typology is not especially controversial, there has been a recent debate about whether New Testament exegesis is meant to be normative. That is to say, are Christians today meant to imitate the apostles in their typological approach? Longenecker, *Biblical Exegesis*, argues that the doctrinal conclusions of the apostles are normative, but their exegetical methods were culturally conditioned and unnecessary to reproduce. He argues that, just as Scriptures

A second, though less significant, criterion in support of typology is that it has been the practice of both historic and contemporary Lutheranism. Typology has been a major component of the hermeneutics of a large number of Lutheran thinkers over the centuries.[23] Martin Luther, who rejected medieval four-fold allegorical interpretation, revived the ancient method of typology.[24] Luther's successors appropriated typological interpretation as being inherent to the Lutheran proclamation of the gospel. Particularly rich

---

were expressed in the imperfect languages of Hebrew and Greek, so the apostles used the imperfect exegetical methods of their contemporaries to reach divinely inspired conclusions. In other words, they did not draw a meaning from the Old Testament but rather supplied a new meaning to the text under divine inspiration. A number of scholars have opposed Longenecker and given a rationale for imitating apostolic exegesis. For instance, Hays, *Echoes*, 178–92, has argued that Paul included his exegetical methods in his statement in 1 Cor 4:16: "Become imitators of me." Beale, *Handbook*, 25, points out that the typological method pervades the Old Testament itself and that the wider context of the types in the Old Testament shows that they were meant to be read typologically. Therefore, the typological method is good grammatical-historical exegesis, taking in the full canonical context. Beale also finds Longenecker's explanation troubling, "If a radical hiatus exists between the interpretive method of the NT and our method today, then the study of the relationship of the OT and the NT from the apostolic perspective is something to which the church has little access. Furthermore, if Jesus and the apostles were impoverished in their exegetical and theological method, and if only divine inspiration salvaged their conclusions, then the intellectual and apologetic foundation of our faith is seriously eroded" (ibid., 26).

23. This statement comes with a few caveats. First of all, typology, while distinctively Lutheran, is not exclusively Lutheran. In fact, there is wide consensus that typological interpretation goes back to the New Testament era or earlier, and it has influenced many other modern branches of Christian thought. Secondly, typology is not the only Lutheran approach to the Old Testament. Historical-grammatical exegesis, prophecy-fulfillment structures, and others can be used. However, typology will be given the focus here, both because of its prominence in the literature and in its usefulness to answer the questions being posed. Thirdly, the use of typology is not unanimously accepted among those who go by the name of Lutheran. With that said, it will be asserted that typology remains the most distinctively Lutheran approach for interpreting and applying the Old Testament.

24. In adopting typology as an exegetical tool, Luther was not merely repeating the tradition that he had received. The predominant form of Old Testament interpretation in his day had been the four-fold method of allegorical medieval exegesis, the *quadriga*. Luther firmly rejected the *quadriga* and insisted on the literal sense alone. However, Luther identified the literal sense with the christological interpretation of the Old Testament, making use of typology to draw out the christological meaning of the Hebrew Scriptures. At times Luther was not entirely free of the "old leaven of the Papacy," as he himself admits; thus, his typological interpretations may sometimes stray into allegory. However, these lapses represent mistakes and should not be considered indicative of Luther's hermeneutics. Luther was a pioneer in his reestablishment of the typological method, but he was not the first to use it. The typological interpretations of Luther can be traced to the New Testament itself and to the church fathers. Cf. Goppelt, *Typos*, 6; Greidanus, *Preaching Christ*, 11–126; Davidson, *Typology*, 27–30.

examples of post-Reformation Lutheran typologizing can be found in the works of David Chytraeus (1530–1600) and Johann Gerhard (1582–1637).[25] Although the use of typology faded with the rise of biblical higher criticism in the nineteenth century,[26] scholarly interest has resurged, especially since the mid-twentieth century and especially among conservative Lutheran exegetes.[27]

WHAT IS A VALID TYPE?

While it is a foundational apostolic belief that Christ is to be found in the Old Testament, various schools of thought have developed over the centuries concerning the limitations that one places on where Christ is to be found. At one extreme end of the spectrum stands Herbert Marsh (1757–1839)

---

25. Unfortunately, the works of the post-Reformation theologians are not always accessible to the English reader. A couple good examples of typological interpretation that are available in translation include the following: Johann Gerhard, *Explanation*; Chytraeus, *On Sacrifice*.

26. The modern critics of typology have fallen into two major camps. The one denied predictive prophecy and the unity of Scripture while championing grammatical-historical exegesis alone. Thus, they severed Old Testament and New Testament studies and saw typology as being nothing more than an example of early Christians imposing alien meanings on the ancient texts. The other source of opposition to typology came from the anti-allegorists, who did not believe that it was possible to distinguish between typology and allegory, with all of its attendant subjectivity and caprice. However, both of these objections are based on assumptions that contradict historic Lutheran thought. The higher critical assumptions against the notion of predictive prophecy and the unity of Scripture are antithetical to the thought of Luther and his successors. As regards the anti-allegorists, they do provide an important caution against unrestrained use of typology. However, the misuse of an exegetical technique does not invalidate its proper use. Davidson, *Typology*, 46–93, provides a wonderful history of scholarship, especially of the nineteenth and twentieth centuries.

27. It is not possible to give a complete listing of contemporary Lutheran scholars who are using typology in one form or another. The method has become deeply imbedded in Lutheran exegetical thought, at least in the Lutheran Church—Missouri Synod. Typology has been used in official statements from the Commission on Theology and Church Relations of the Lutheran Church—Missouri Synod, such as in their document "The End Times: A Study on Eschatology and Millennialism," September 1989. The typological method has been crucial to many of the authors of the ongoing Concordia Commentary series. Good discussions on typology in this series include the following (not exhaustive) Mitchell, *Song of Songs*, 69–97; Gibbs, *Matthew 1:1—11:1*, 139–45; Kleinig, *Leviticus*, 24–30; Lessing, *Jonah*, 11–13, 207–8; Lessing, *Isaiah 40–55*, 79–83. Typology is also supported in the current standard textbook on Lutheran hermeneutics, Voelz, *What Does This Mean?* Typology is also presupposed in many Lutheran homiletics resources, such as Schurb, *The Old Testament Collection*; Hummel, "How to Preach The Old Testament," 1–23. See the bibliography for further examples.

who rejected any types which were not explicitly mentioned in the New Testament.[28] While this may seem like a sober-minded way to approach the text, it is founded on the assumption that the New Testament's exegesis of Old Testament texts is exhaustive. As a possible counter-example, the New Testament never explicitly presents Joshua as a type of Christ, and so Bishop Marsh would not have considered Joshua as a Christ-type. Nonetheless, it is not difficult to find shadows of Christ in the work of Joshua, who faithfully led his people into the Promised Land and triumphed over every enemy. Should the New Testament's silence concerning Joshua be understood as indicating that Joshua was not intended to be a type of the Messiah? If one answers in the negative, then the assumption is that the New Testament is providing the model for Christian biblical interpretation, and thus Christians can in good faith extrapolate from the data found there to find types beyond those unambiguously given by the apostles. At the other extreme end of the spectrum stands Johannes Cocceius (1603–1669) who found Christ in every minor character and every miniscule detail of the text. For example, Cocceius claimed that the event in which Samson encounters a lion was a type for Christ meeting Saul on the road to Damascus.[29] For the Cocceians, typology was actually used as an excuse to create elaborate allegories, with all the subjectivity and capriciousness associated with that technique. However, while the typological method may produce some irresponsible exegesis at times, allowing the preacher some freedom in seeking out Christ-types is not a bad thing—the loose typologist is something like a young man who is so deeply in love that he sees his lover's face in every crowd. The fervently infatuated lover of Christ might find the Savior's face in every text, even those which were not intended to do so. The preacher should not feel paralyzed by the fear of seeing Christ too much.

At this point, it would be useful to lay out a few guidelines for determining when it is valid to seek types beyond those which are given in the New Testament. There is a sort of hierarchy of certainty when presenting such types. The types that stand on absolutely firm bedrock are those which are identified in the New Testament, especially those which actually use the

---

28. Davidson, *Typology*, 36–37. The Antiochene exegete Theodore of Mopsuestia also called for greater restraint in seeking out types and messianic texts in the Old Testament. He argued that a typological interpretation is only possible in texts that are undeniably messianic, and so he only accepted that Pss 2, 8, 44, and 110 were typical of Christ. Theodore bases his interpretation on the fact that these four psalms are connected with Christ in the New Testament and that they were already regarded as messianic among the Jews in the time before Christ. Simonetti, *Biblical Interpretation*, 69–70.

29. Davidson, *Typology*, 33–36.

typos word-group to identify them.³⁰ After these, there are also types which are highly probable but are open to some debate. One grouping that would fit in this secondary category would be those Old Testament figures which are themselves typologically related to a known Christ-type.³¹ For example, Joshua is not explicitly identified as a Christ-type in the New Testament, but Moses is. However, Joshua is also presented as a "new Moses" in the book that bears his name, i.e. he is the antitype of Moses. Thus if Moses is a type of Joshua (implicitly, according to Old Testament) and Moses is a type of Christ (explicitly, according to the New Testament) then Joshua is also a type of Christ.

Another group of highly probable types would include statements in the Old Testament which are heavily hyperbolic when referred to an Old Testament referent. This concept was identified by the Antiochene exegete Theodore of Mopsuestia (350–428) who was known for his sober-minded use of typology.³² According to Theodore, if the statement is too great to apply literally to its near-in-time referent, then the statement must be applied to Christ. The implication is that the author of the original text knew that the Old Testament referent only worked metaphorically and in shadows; the text cries out for an antitype that would fulfill it literally and fully. For example, the statement of divine sonship in Ps 110:1 is hyperbolic when referring to David or one of the other kings of Judah, but it is literally true when applied to Jesus Christ. St. Peter in his Pentecost sermon in Acts 2 demonstrates that the things said of David foreshadowed his much greater son Jesus, in whom all of the things said of David would become true in the fullest sense.

One more group of probable types includes those redemptive-historical events which are part of the biblical pattern of divine action in history.³³ The grand paradigm for God's redemptive acts is found in the exodus from Egypt, which Paul interprets with very clear and explicit *typos*-structures in 1 Cor 10:1–13.³⁴ If the exodus is a Christ-type, can other Old Testament historical events be viewed in the same way, even when not explicitly identified as such in the New Testament? The key here is the pattern of God's actions vis-à-vis his people. The exodus is the grandest paradigm of how God acts— that he saves by his pure grace alone in unexpected and marvelous ways. The return from the Babylonian captivity conforms to the same paradigm,

---

30. 1 Cor 10:1–13; Rom 5:12–21; 1 Pet 3:18–22; Heb 8 and 9.
31. Beale, *Handbook*, 21. Hugenberger, "Introductory Notes," 341.
32. Simonetti, *Biblical Interpretation*, 69.
33. Beale, *Handbook*, 22–23.
34. Davidson, *Typology*, 291–97.

as is made explicit in Jer 16:14–15. However, these are not the only examples of the pattern in the Old Testament. Numerous other events—for example, the call of Abram, the conquest of the land under Joshua, the deliverance of Israel under judges like Gideon, the deliverance of Hezekiah's Jerusalem from Assyria, and many others—build up this consistent pattern of God's continued faithfulness to his people and his continued acts of unexpected and marvelous grace. Thus, the preacher would benefit from showing how an event of Old Testament history fits into this pattern, how it conforms to the way in which God always acts faithfully to his people in all generations. Then, one can move typologically from this point-of-view on history to the ultimate and complete example of God's actions towards humanity in Jesus Christ. His death and resurrection are prefigured in every act of divine deliverance.[35]

Beyond these, there are also debatable types that may be part of some other biblical pattern. For instance, Johann Gerhard finds a Christ-type in every Old Testament figure that suffered innocently—such as Joseph, Noah, or Job.[36] It is important when seeking out such types to use restraint, focusing on the pattern and not on extraneous details of these individuals' lives that are irrelevant to the pattern. Also, one should beware of stretching the facts in order to force more examples to fit into a biblical pattern.

FINDING THE CHURCH IN THE NATION OF ISRAEL

Having addressed where Christ is to be found in the Old Testament, the question remains: how can we apply these texts to New Testament realities, specifically to modern congregational life? What does a typological reading say about the relationship between Old Testament Israel and the New Testament church? The question raises the need for further definition: what is "Israel" and what is the "church"? Both terms have been used in a plethora of senses, and this situation has produced more than a little confusion. For the purposes of this study, both terms refer to God's people, whom he has

---

35. This approach guards against some spurious attempts at typology. The theological "charge" or orientation (i.e., whether a thing is portrayed in the Old Testament in a positive, negative, or neutral light) of an Old Testament event is the same as that of its New Testament antitype. For example, only positive events in the scope of redemptive history, such as acts of deliverance, can be types of Christ's great deliverance. Likewise, only negative events, such as reports of Israel's unfaithfulness, can be types of the rejection of Christ. Events that are "neutral" with regard to salvation history (like Samson meeting a lion, which Cocceius claimed was a type of Christ meeting Saul on the road to Damascus) are most likely not valid Christ-types.

36. Gerhard, *Explanation*, 30.

chosen and called and redeemed. Israel is God's Old Testament people, starting with the patriarchs and continuing until the coming of Christ. The church refers to God's New Testament people, starting with the calling of the twelve disciples and continuing into the present. An essential continuity exists between Israel and the church; in fact, Paul refers to the church as the "Israel of God" in Gal 6:16. However, it is not a one-to-one correspondence. Thus, it would be foolish to simply rewrite an Old Testament text by substituting "the church" for "Israel" in all of its occurrences. First of all, this would do violence to the historical context of the Old Testament, which was written in a specific language by specific authors to a specific people group at a specific time of history. Even worse, a direct equation of Israel and the church would ignore the sweep of salvation history with its grand climax in the person and work of Jesus Christ. However, it would equally be an error to say that the Old Testament knows nothing of the church. The church was always essential to God's plan, and therefore it was taught in the Old Testament in a typological and proleptic sense.[37]

To illustrate this from the New Testament, when Jesus called the disciples, he chose twelve men. Just as the Lord had directly called the patriarchs to be his people, culminating in the twelve sons of Israel, so the Lord Jesus personally called these twelve to be a new Israel. This new people of God was not simply the remnant of the old people of God; rather, the twelve disciples are related to the twelve tribes by a common redemptive history and in a typological way.[38]

However, it is not sufficient to say merely that Israel is a type of the church, for Israel is first and foremost a type of Christ. Israel was called to be the Lord's faithful son,[39] even though the Israelites failed to live up to this high calling. In response to the sins of Israel, God winnowed the people down until only a remnant remained—the faithful and true Israel, called to be God's obedient son. Yet even the remnant was not sinless; they were only a shadow of the perfectly holy people that the Lord desired. If the Lord was to have a perfect Israel, then he would have to take matters into his own hands. He did this in Jesus Christ, who was in the truest sense God's Son and the faithful Israel. Jesus Christ was the perfect representative for Israel—Israel-reduced-to-one—who fulfilled God's will on behalf of the entire nation and suffered vicariously for their sake.[40] In this sense, all of the Old Testament texts about Israel which failed to find their fulfillment

37. LaRondelle, *The Israel of God*, 104–8.
38. Goppelt, *Typos*, 108.
39. Cf. Exod 4:22; Deut 32:9–12; Hos 11:1.
40. CTCR, "End Times," 13–14.

in the imperfect Israelite people are typologically fulfilled in Christ as the true representative of Israel. For example, when the prophets say that Israel will shine as a light to the nations (Isa 42:6, 49:6, 60:3) the Old Testament Israelites were a light to a limited few individual Gentiles, such as Rahab or Naaman. However, Jesus' enlightening message was *literally* extended to all nations, thus being the true antitype of which Israel was only a shadow (Luke 2:32).

Having become Israel-reduced-to-one, Jesus then called a new remnant, the twelve, to be the new people of God. These twelve disciples are Israel by virtue of being called by Jesus, the true Israel, the perfect antitype. In Pauline language, they are "in Christ" and thus faithful sons of God by virtue of being incorporated into the only perfectly faithful Son of God. From this remnant, the Lord would call people from all nations and languages and ethnicities to become the church, the Israel of God. The former Israel was a mere shadow of what God intended for his new people. This is made explicit in Peter's Pentecost sermon (Acts 2:16–24) in which he connects the church at Pentecost with the prophetic hope for a people who would know the Lord's will in their hearts (Joel 2:28–32). Moreover, the early Christians recognized that, while the Old Testament Israelites were a people group united by common descent from Abraham, Isaac, and Jacob, their true antitype—the true Israel—was related by a common faith in Christ and a common unity as his body. As St. Paul says, "In Christ Jesus you are all sons of God, through faith. For as many of you as were baptized into Christ have put on Christ. There is neither Jew nor Greek, there is neither slave nor free, there is neither male nor female, for you are all one in Christ Jesus. And if you are Christ's, then you are Abraham's offspring, heirs according to promise" (Gal 3:26–29).

However, it is important to remember in what sense that Israel is a type of the church. The church is the true Israel insofar as she has been grafted into Christ, as Paul draws out in Rom 11:11–24. The hermeneutical line from God's Old Testament people to God's New Testament people runs through the person and work of Christ. For this reason, it is not possible to relate Old Testament Israel to the New Testament church without proclaiming Christ, who is both the antitype/representative of Old Testament Israel and the type/head of the New Testament Church. Jesus Christ is himself the norm that should control our hermeneutics and prevent gross errors in preaching the Church from Old Testament texts.

One helpful guideline for making this hermeneutical move from Israel to Christ to the Church can be found in the works of a rather obscure theologian: Tyconius, a late fourth century Donatist clergyman from North Africa. Tyconius wrote a series of exegetical rules for the interpretation of

Revelation, titled the *Liber Regularum*.[41] This text would have fallen into complete obscurity had it not been recommended by so great a theologian as St. Augustine, who adapted the material from Tyconius in his own landmark treatment of hermeneutics, *De Doctrina Christiana*. Augustine applied these exegetical rules not only to the Book of Revelation but also to the Scriptures in general, including the Old Testament. The first rule of Tyconius is that, whenever Scripture refers to Christ, it also may refer to Christ's body (that is, the church) and vice versa. In other words, insofar as the church is in Christ, texts which refer to Christ or to Christ-types may be applied to the church. In fact, this guideline expressed by Tyconius and Augustine is no different than the typological-Christocentric interpretation suggested above, merely arrived at from a different direction. These ancient Fathers would agree that the necessary link between Israel and the church can only be found in Jesus Christ, who is both Israel's antitype and the church's head. Therefore, before searching for the church in the Old Testament, first seek Christ there.

Another way of coming at this same conclusion from a different line of thought can be found in Christopher Mitchell's commentary on Song of Songs. After acknowledging the more traditionally typological approach to Song of Songs (i.e. that the marriage of Solomon and the Shulamite is a type of the spiritual marriage of the Lord and his people)[42] Mitchell also presents what he terms an analogical approach. In short, the marriage of Solomon and the Shulamite is connected by analogy to the marriage of Christ and the church. Likewise, the marriage of Christ and the church is connected by analogy to the Christian marriage of any man and woman, according to Eph 5. Mitchell then completes the triangle, by saying that, because these two analogies exist, there is also a relationship between Solomon's marriage and a Christian marriage, but only by virtue of their mutual analogy with Christ. Through the lens of Christ, Solomon's marriage as described in Song of Songs can serve as a model for a Christian marriage.[43] What Mitchell posits as an analogical relationship, this study would regard as a different category of typology. Thus, Mitchell's triangle with Christ in the center is equivalent to the double-typology with Christ in the center as shown above.

---

41. Simonetti, *Biblical Interpretation*, 95.
42. Mitchell, *Song of Songs*, 91–92.
43. Ibid., 92–97.

FINDING THE CHURCH IN THE SPEAKER OF THE PSALMS

The Psalms have historically been claimed as the prayer book of the church, which presents some unique hermeneutical challenges, given the Psalms' historical context. The first special preaching challenge presented by the Psalter is to identify who the speaker of the Psalms is. In a sense, this can be given a historic answer. Various psalms are attributed to David, Asaph, the sons of Korah, and other authors. However, the New Testament provides another perspective on the speaker of the Psalms. In Peter's Pentecost sermon, he indicates that David spoke as a prophet and that the Psalms speak of the Christ (Acts 2:30). Furthermore, the New Testament writers place several of the psalms in the mouth of Christ, such as in Heb 2:12 and 10:5. In the Gospels, Christ himself directly quotes Ps 22 as being his own statement of suffering, and he states that the Psalter, alongside the Law and the Prophets, announced his own death and resurrection (Luke 24:44). Based on this evidence, Dietrich Bonhoeffer concludes, "The prayers of David were prayed also by Christ. Or better, Christ himself prayed them through his forerunner David."[44] Martin Luther refers to this phenomenon as the *sensus Christus* of the Psalter, which he regards as its only true sense.[45] In other words, the historical speaker of the Psalms (i.e. David et al.) is the type of which Jesus Christ is the antitype. The words of the Psalter which were figuratively fulfilled in the life of David are literally and in a greater way fulfilled in the life of David's greater Son, Jesus Christ.

So, in what sense then is the church able to pray the Psalms? Certainly, it has been the practice of the church throughout its history to pray the Psalms in public worship, claiming them as the church's own prayer book. The key is, once again, found in Christ. Insofar as the church is "in Christ" as his own body, she is able to pray his prayers with her own lips. Bonhoeffer explains it more eloquently:

> How is it possible for a man and Jesus Christ to pray the Psalter together? It is the incarnate Son of God, who has borne every human weakness in his own flesh, who here pours out the heart of all humanity before God and who stands in our place and prays for us. He has known torment and pain, guilt and death more deeply than we. Therefore it is the prayer of the human nature assumed by him which comes here before God. It is really our prayer, but since he knows us better than we know ourselves

---

44. Bonhoeffer, *Psalms*, 19.
45. Greidanus, *Preaching Christ*, 115.

and since he himself was true man for our sakes, it is also really his prayer, and it can become our prayer only because it was his prayer. Who prays the Psalms? David (Solomon, Asaph, etc.) prays, Christ prays, we pray.[46]

As a practical case study, let us examine the way in which Ps 22 may be preached according to a typological-Christocentric reading of the Old Testament. First, one must acknowledge that the historical speaker of the Psalm, according to the attribution formula in the superscript, is David. The exact circumstances of David's life that would prompt so grievous a lament are not specified here, but they are clearly severe. However, the reader should note that the words only apply to David in a figurative sense. As one example, the words of v. 15 ("My strength is dried up like a potsherd, and my tongue sticks to my jaws; you lay me in the dust of death") describe the metaphoric death of David in his great suffering, not his physical death. This hyperbolic language gives some indication that the author of this psalm is speaking in a typological-prophetic manner.

That which was only figuratively true of the type is literally true of the antitype. Thus, David's metaphoric death points to the literal death of Jesus Christ, a connection which Jesus himself asserts by speaking these words on the cross. Christ is claiming the entire psalm as his own lament, as he suffers the fullness of all human suffering and dies in ignominy and shame. Even though he was sinless, he speaks as one who bears the guilt of intense sin. This is because Jesus speaks these words as the representative of all.

By the connection between the head and the body, his lamentation is the lamentation of all of those who suffer because of the brokenness of this fallen world. Moreover, his grief is also the grief of all sinners over the guilt of their sins. Thus, when the church prays Ps 22, she pours out her own lament and receives solace, knowing that she has a savior who empathizes with her sufferings and—even more so—knowing that her guilt has been borne by Christ on the cross. When this psalm is used in public worship, David laments, Christ laments, and the church laments, and in this mutual lamentation, one is led to the comfort of Christ's suffering as the representative of all sinners and as the one who takes away that suffering. A typological sermon on Ps 22 would capture each of these voices of lamentation, while driving the listener toward the comfort of the suffering Savior who bore our guilt.

---

46. Bonhoeffer, *Psalms*, 20–21.

FINDING THE CHURCH IN THE INSTITUTIONS OF ISRAEL

Another place to seek the church in the Old Testament text is through the institutions of national Israel. All of the institutions of Israel find their antitype in Christ. This is one of the primary themes of the Book of Hebrews—Christ is the true and greater fulfillment of the Israelite leadership (Heb 3:1–5) the land/Sabbath (3:7–4:13) the priesthood (4:14–5:10; 8:1–13) the tabernacle/temple (9:1–10) and the sacrificial system (10:1–18). To this list, we could add that Jesus is the true and greater fulfillment of kingship, the office of prophet, the annual festivals, the year of Jubilee, and many others. All of these things point forward to the person and work of Christ in both his first and second comings. Since the church is the Israel of God by virtue of being "in Christ," the institutions of Israel may be typical of the church in this derived sense. For example, the Mosaic sacrificial system is primarily a type of the once-for-all sacrifice of Christ on the cross, but it is also, by virtue of the church being the body of Christ, a type of the living sacrifices that each Christian presents to God (Rom 12:1). In the same manner, the temple is typical of Christ, who even referred to his own body as the temple (John 2:19) but it also finds its antitype in the congregation of New Testament believers, who are living stones built into a spiritual temple (1 Pet 2:5).

However, even though this typological connection can be drawn between Old Testament institutions and New Testament realities, there is not necessarily a one-to-one correspondence between them. That is to say, a single Old Testament institution does not always correspond to a single New Testament reality. For example, the Old Testament priesthood at times seems to be typical of the Office of the Holy Ministry, but at other times it seems to typify the priesthood of all believers. Likewise, a single New Testament reality is not necessarily foreshadowed in only one Old Testament institution. For instance, both the Old Testament office of priest and of prophet can be typical of the Holy Ministry.

Thus, it is sadly not possible simply to give a list of Old Testament institutions and their New Testament antitypes as an aid for the busy preacher. Nonetheless, a few guidelines can be put in place in order to make the interpretative move from one to the other. The most important thing to remember is that Jesus Christ is the center of this typological process. The New Testament realities are only connected to the Old Testament types because both are related to Jesus Christ. Therefore, the manner in which an institution is typical of Christ may give some indication as to how that same institution may be typical of the Church or one of its institutions. For example, the prophetic office is typical of Christ, in that both types and antitype faithfully speak the word of God and often face rejection. Likewise, the Office of the Holy Ministry, by virtue of Christ its Head, is related by analogy to the prophetic office specifically in those facets stated above—that they faithfully speak the word of God and often face rejection.[47] By contrast, the prophets also had ecstatic visions and wrote their prophecies in poetic form, but these are not meant as a model for the Holy Ministry, as they are not details that are typologically found in their antitype, Christ.

CONCLUSION

The church, the true Israel of God, is in Christ, who is the true representative of Israel. Therefore, in Christ, it is possible to forge an exegetical link between the world of the Old Testament and the world of contemporary hearers. However, the connection is made always through Christ and never without him. Using this typological hermeneutic, the church (and thus the context of a modern congregation) can be found in texts about the nation of Israel, in texts about Israel's institutions, and in the Psalms. This list is not exhaustive, but it is a starting point for preachers today who may be timid to write sermons on the Old Testament.

BIBLIOGRAPHY

Baker, David L. "Typology and the Christian Use of the Old Testament." *Scottish Journal of Theology* 29 (1976) 137–57.

Beale, G. K. *Handbook on the New Testament Use of the Old Testament: Exegesis and Interpretation*. Grand Rapids: Baker Academic, 2012.

Bonhoeffer, Dietrich. *Psalms: The Prayer Book of the Bible*. Minneapolis: Augsburg, 1970.

Chytraeus, David. *On Sacrifice: A Reformation Treatise in Biblical Theology*. Translated by John Warwick Montgomery. St. Louis: Concordia, 1962.

Commission on Theology and Church Relations of The Lutheran Church—Missouri Synod. "The End Times: A Study on Eschatology and Millennialism." Sept, 1989.

Davidson, Richard M. *Typology in Scripture: A Study of Hermeneutical Τυπος Structures*. Berrien Springs, MI: Andrews University Press, 1981.

Gerhard, Johann. *An Explanation of the History of the Suffering and Death of Our Lord Jesus Christ according to the Four Evangelists*. Edited by David O. Berger. Translated by Elmer M. Hohle. Malone, TX: Repristination, 1999.

Gibbs, Jeffrey A. *Matthew 1:1—11:1*. St. Louis: Concordia, 2006.

Goldsworthy, Graeme. *According to Plan: The Unfolding Revelation of God in the Bible*. Downers Grove, IL. InterVarsity, 2002.

---

47. Matt 10:24–25 reveals this same pattern: if the teacher is rejected, so is the disciple.

Goppelt, Leonhard. "Τύπος, Ἀντίτυπος, Τυπικός, Ὑποτύπωσις." In TDNT 4:246–59.
———. *Typos: The Typological Interpretation of the Old Testament in the New*. Grand Rapids: Eerdmans, 1982.
Greidanus, Sidney. *Preaching Christ from the Old Testament: A Contemporary Hermeneutical Method*. Grand Rapids: Eerdmans, 1999.
Hays, Richard B. *Echoes of Scripture in the Letters of Paul*. New Haven: Yale University Press, 1989.
Hugenberger, G. P. "Introductory Notes on Typology." In *The Right Doctrine from the Wrong Texts? Essays on the Use of the Old Testament in the New*, edited by G. K Beale, 331–41. Grand Rapids: Baker, 1994.
Hummel, Horace D. "How to Preach The Old Testament." In *Concordia Pulpit 1986*, 1–23. St. Louis: Concordia, 1985.
Kaiser, Walter C., et al. *Three Views on the New Testament Use of the Old Testament*. Edited by Kenneth Berding and Jonathan Lunde. Grand Rapids: Zondervan, 2008.
Kleinig, John W. *Leviticus*. St. Louis: Concordia, 2003.
LaRondelle, Hans K. *The Israel of God in Prophecy: Principles of Prophetic Interpretation*. Berrien Springs, MI. Andrews University Press, 1983.
Lessing, R. Reed. *Isaiah 40–55*. St. Louis: Concordia, 2011.
———. *Jonah*. St. Louis: Concordia, 2007.
Longenecker, Richard N. *Biblical Exegesis in the Apostolic Period*. Grand Rapids: Eerdmans, 1974.
Mitchell, Christopher Wright. *The Song of Songs*. St. Louis: Concordia, 2003.
Roehrs, Walter R. "The Typological Use of the Old Testament in the New Testament."*CJ* 10 (1984) 204–16.
Schurb, Ken. *The Old Testament Collection: Preaching Christ in the Old Testament during the Church Year*. Concordia Pulpit Resources. St. Louis: Concordia, 2010.
Simonetti, Manlio. *Biblical Interpretation in the Early Church: An Historical Introduction to Patristic Exegesis*. Edited by Anders Bergquist et al. Translated by John A Hughes. Edinburgh: T. & T. Clark, 1994.
Voelz, James W. *What Does This Mean? Principles of Biblical Interpretation in the Post-Modern World*. St. Louis: Concordia, 1997.
Wright, Christopher J. H. *Knowing Jesus through the Old Testament*. Downers Grove, IL: InterVarsity, 1995.

4

Nicholas of Cusa and the Reformation of Preaching

—Richard J. Serina Jr.

INTRODUCTION

A common approach in narrating the Protestant Reformation is to contrast Luther and his reforming successors with their predecessors in the Middle Ages. The resulting impression is that the Protestant Reformation set out to counteract what the medieval church had done, without any consideration of the dependencies the reformers had on their predecessors or the unique challenges their predecessors had which the reformers did not. This is particularly the case with preaching. As one critic of the medieval church puts it, the desire for popular preaching on the eve of the Reformation reflected "dissatisfaction with the irregularity and low quality of preaching of secular clergy" and was a "sign of failure on the part of the established parish clergy to fully satisfy the religious needs of the people."[1] Some of this is true, no doubt, but it is not the whole story, nor is it a fair one. It does not tell the tale of repeated medieval attempts to redress the inadequate quality and regularity of preaching. Nor does it detail the actual successes of the late medieval church in promoting better preaching among clergy. Nor still does it account for the debt the Protestant reformers owed the medieval church

---

1. Ozment, *Reformation in the Cities*, 40.

for fostering the conditions in which they might reform it, including the preaching of its clergy.²

The situation—then as now—is more complex than such a picture suggests. Poor preaching is a byproduct of something else, not a cause, and so consequently it is best also to see a reformation of preaching as a by-product of something else, too. This essay will attempt to contextualize that claim by examining the conditions which fostered both the weaknesses of medieval preaching and the attempts to improve it prior to the Reformation. After addressing several popular misconceptions about the period, it will argue that the fundamental problem in medieval preaching was the lack of competent, educated parish clergy who could deliver regular, orthodox sermons to the faithful. The remainder of the essay will use the example of one late medieval preacher, the fifteenth-century cardinal and bishop Nicholas of Cusa (1401–64) to illustrate the efforts at reforming preaching in the late Middle Ages, as well as how the similarities and differences between Cusa's preaching and Reformation preaching reveal the common issue facing both the Middle Ages and the Reformation (and I would hasten to add the contemporary church as well) the reform of preaching depends fundamentally upon the reform of the clergy through improved education, theological competence and commitment to pastoral care. Where those conditions remain impoverished, preaching is likely to follow.

PROBLEMS IN MEDIEVAL PREACHING— MISCONCEIVED AND REAL

In order to understand better what the problems were in medieval preaching, it is important to understand first what they were not. Several potential misconceptions about preaching can lead to a muddled picture. One such potential misconception is that there were no vernacular translations of Scripture from which to preach. On the contrary, numerous translations were available through the Middle Ages in English, French, Spanish, and Italian, among others.³ By the thirteenth century, even Pope Innocent III dictated that vernacular translations should be made available so rogue preachers could not manipulate the faithful. Another potential misconcep-

---

2. This point is made well by one commentator, who argues that the reformers "had in a sense turned against 'the church,' but they could and had to do so only because the church had educated them in their responsibilities and brought them to expect great things of it. For them, the church in the late Middle Ages had provided only too well," Duggan, "Unresponsiveness," 3–26.

3. See the several recent essays on medieval vernacular translations in Boynton and Reilly, *Practice of the Bible*.

tion is that there were no vernacular sermons preached in the Middle Ages. Here it is easy to be misled by the documents themselves since nearly all medieval sermons were published in Latin. But such edited sermon collections were originally preached in the vernacular save for those that were either never preached at all or preached for a university audience where Latin was the language of instruction and discourse. Vernacular sermons were predominant, though, and where a Latin transcript does exist it is the result of a notary recording the sermon in Latin or a version transcribed into Latin for dissemination amongst clerics who shared Latin competence in common.[4]

A more problematic misconception about medieval preaching, however, would be that there were no sermons preached on a regular basis in the medieval church. On the contrary, there was in certain respects too much preaching in the Middle Ages and the church had to take vigorous measures to counteract it. From the eleventh century onward, heretical preaching movements such as the Cathars in southern France or the Humiliati and Waldensians of northern Italy circumvented the standard channels of licensure for preaching and began to spread their theology in open contradiction to official church doctrine.[5] The popularity of these preachers, not to mention their lack of opposition from orthodox apologists, evoked a reaction.[6] In response to requests from bishops and apologists on the ground, popular preachers of an orthodox variety such as Dominic de Guzman, founder of the Dominicans (also known as the *Ordo Praedicatorum*, or "order of preachers") arose. Under Pope Innocent III, chiefly in his general council Lateran IV (1215) bishops were urged to preach orthodox doctrine, and if they could not they were required to find suitable preachers to do so. Orders such as the Dominicans and Franciscans were conscripted to defend the orthodox faith as apologists in lands overrun by popular heresies, and their chosen instrument of defense was the sermon. With this upsurge in preaching, new resources emanated from the universities in particular to aid the preacher in his task. Those included volumes of authoritative sayings (*florilegia*) he could quote in support of a point, compilations of analogies (*similitudines*) for use, model sermon collections he could adapt or simply preach verbatim, even manuals for preaching (*ars praedicandi*) that pro-

---

4. Spencer, *English Preaching*, 15–19.

5. On these heresies and their relationship with the ensuing ecclesiastical and monastic responses, see Grundmann, *Religious Movements*, 1–68, and Lambert, *Medieval Heresy*, 35–146. The latest treatment of Catharism and the ecclesiastical reaction to it is Moore, *The War on Heresy*.

6. For what follows, see especially Rouse and Rouse, *Preachers*, 43–64; and d'Avray, *Preaching*, 13–28.

vided rhetorical rules for sermons, outlines to structure them, and practical advice on their delivery.

Despite these notable advancements, medieval preaching still had its problems—not only from the perspective of the Reformation, but in the eyes of its subsequent medieval critics themselves. The chief problem was that it lacked competent priests who could deliver orthodox sermons on a regular basis. This resulted in the near complete absence of preaching in the ordinary Sunday liturgy. As one expert in medieval preaching put it, the problem was not demand, but supply.

The bishops were too few to meet the demand, and qualified candidates at the parish level were too sparse.[7] It might be helpful at this juncture to describe what medieval preaching and clerical practice looked like. The problem with such a description is that there in fact was no single medieval preaching or clerical practice common across the board, but instead regional and local diversity in nearly all matters of diocesan ecclesiastical organization. Nevertheless, it is fair to say that some relatively consistent structures existed throughout the majority of the Western church during this period.[8] Preaching at the Sunday mass was reserved for the bishop himself, but the fact that bishops often did not reside in their dioceses meant in turn that there was no one actually preaching on a weekly basis during the liturgy.[9] Where preaching occurred in much of the medieval church, it was usually done by mendicant preachers, either in more informal, public venues or more regularly in their monasteries. The priests were often elevated from within a diocese, though absent formal training. Examination of candidates for the priesthood was required, but often treated haphazardly by bishops because of the need in the parishes for clergy.[10] The priests themselves were largely present to say private masses, in part because their lack of

---

7. "Demand was great: the problem for the church was on the supply side. Preaching by the bishops could not begin to meet the demand. The general run of parish priest ... still lacked the training to do so adequately. A beginning had been made: already there were some successful popular preachers who had studied at Paris. Yet one wonders how many of those who trained in the Paris schools went on to a life of regular preaching. University clerics would tend to gravitate towards the higher echelons of ecclesiastical and secular administration. Educated and orthodox men devoted to pastoral work, below the episcopal level, remained in short supply" (d'Avray, *Preaching*, 28).

8. For the best (if somewhat dated) overviews of the state of the medieval clergy in their ecclesiastical, economic, and educational contexts, see Pantin, *English Church*; Barraclough, *Papal Provisions*; Hay, *Church in Italy*; and Hay, *Europe*, esp. 45–60. For a more recent monograph that qualifies this picture somewhat, see Salonen and Hanska, *Entering a Clerical Career*, especially 1–18.

9. This was apparently the case by the eleventh century. Rouse and Rouse, *Preachers*, 43.

10. Hay, *Church in Italy*, 53; and Duggan, "Unresponsiveness," 24.

education or competence would not harm the celebration of the Eucharist the way it might a sermon, in part because the role of the private mass in obtaining salvation for both the living and the dead led to an increase in endowed masses, thereby both necessitating more priests to celebrate the *missa solitaria* and establishing the financial means to provide for them.[11] In any event, regular parish clergy did not preach, nor were they expected to preach. If there was no bishop residing in the diocese, then there was likely no preaching in a liturgical context at the Sunday mass.

How did medieval preaching reach such a state? There were several interrelated reasons. One was economic. The medieval church was essentially founded on a feudal system, where the residential bishop received support from the local lord as patron of the church, in what came to be called a benefice.[12] As the economy in Western Europe began to shift toward a more mercantile, commercial system, so too did vocational opportunities and resources.[13] This was no different for the talented cleric, who increasingly made his way into a university, a cathedral chapter in a large city, the court of a secular ruler, or even the growing Roman (or Avignonese) curia. In his place, the great majority of churches were left to elevate a candidate locally with limited or no preparation.[14] A related cause for the lack of competent clergy was the shifting ecclesiastical structure of the day. This came in the form of absenteeism, where a bishop or priest would reside outside of his diocese, and pluralism, the holding of two or more positions in the church that could not both be carried out in the same place. Though canon law forbade pluralism, certain exemptions were granted in the case of exceptionally gifted clerics who might be of service elsewhere in the church or who were in need of further education.[15] Exemptions were common, however, and the consequence was a limited number of residential clergy present to preach on a regular basis. A final circumstance limiting the supply of qualified preachers was educational. Though the establishment of cathedral schools for the training of clergy was a goal of the ninth-century Carolingian reforms, it

---

11. On the role the medieval mass played in the community, see Bossy, "The Mass," 29–61; as well as the broader treatment in Swanson, *Religion and Devotion*.

12. For the origins of this system, see the extensively detailed Wood, *Proprietary Church*.

13. On these socioeconomic developments within Europe and their implications for the Western church, see Bartlett, *The Making of Europe*; Martines, *Power and Imagination*; and Moore, *The First European Revolution*.

14. Pantin, *English Church*, 27–29; and Hay, *Europe*, 53–54. He often received a pittance of a salary and found himself obtaining additional income only from tutoring or some other such employment outside of his clerical duties (Hay, *Church in Italy*, 52).

15. Pantin, *English Church*, 39.

went largely unfulfilled. Universities springing up in the twelfth century going forward were rare, expensive, and at too great a distance for most aspiring clergy to attend. When they did, it was typically funded through a benefice from the local parish, which in turn meant that the funding for a fully salaried candidate was being used elsewhere. This was a gambit on the part of the parish because they had no certainty the educated benefice holder would return to carry out his pastoral duties.[16]

The end product of this state of affairs was the lack of theologically and rhetorically trained clergy at the parish level. Bishops or more gifted clergy found better places to land than the common parish that most needed a preacher. Parishes themselves were loath to extend benefices or fund the education of clergy with the prospect of such a long vacancy before their return—or even that they might not return at all. Clergy posts were filled most often with uneducated laity trained in what amounted to an apprenticeship system, but without the competence to preach, and thus without the expectation from the faithful or the ecclesiastical hierarchy that they should do so. Though they did not always understand the causes, nor were they sympathetic to them when they did, clergy and laity in the late Middle Ages decried the result, and it led them to forge new ways forward.

NICHOLAS OF CUSA AND THE LATE MEDIEVAL REFORMATION OF PREACHING

Those ways forward went through a variety of movements one could easily call a *late-medieval* reformation of preaching. As the church of the twelfth and thirteenth centuries responded to the need for orthodox popular preaching, so too did many in the fifteenth century seek to correct the problem of an intellectually and rhetorically impoverished parish clergy unable to fulfill its task as preachers. Three may be cited in particular.[17] One

---

16. Duggan, "Unresponsiveness," 24. Such a candidate might find his way into another discipline like law or medicine or canon law while there, or his skills might attract the attention of a university master or secular ruler or ecclesiastical official who could find him better employment elsewhere. One recent monograph has studied the effects of a 1298 papal decree (Pope Boniface VII's *Cum ex eo*) urging parish priests to attend university for the purpose of a more educated clergy, and claims that the majority of those thusly educated did in fact return to their parishes—though the data is limited to a single diocese in England. See Logan, *University Education*.

17. A fourth could also be added: economic. In the wake of massive devastation of the fourteenth-century plague in Western Europe, population shrunk drastically, meaning labor and land opened up much employment for survivors as commerce recovered in the fifteenth century. Greater income in turn meant more available funding for university education, clerical education, and clerical appointments. On this

broad movement of consequence for the parish clergy and their preaching was the late medieval attempt at a "reform of head and members" amongst the church hierarchy, starting with the papacy and working its way down to the ordinary parish priest.[18] While such reform efforts were part and parcel of the Middle Ages, calls for reform increased exponentially during the conciliar controversy that followed the Western Schism (1378–1417). Various proposals throughout the fifteenth century urged the return of bishops to their dioceses where they could carry out the pastoral care they were charged with, and do it where they were charged to do so.[19] Though a more strict regulation of pluralism and absenteeism would have to wait for the Protestant and Catholic reformations, the goal of residential episcopal care—the *cura animarum* (care of souls)—remained a popular reform desideratum of the fifteenth century.

Another such trend was the humanist remedy for educational and rhetorical deficiencies. The humanist movement itself began out of a desire to reform education by restoring the classical ideals of grammar, rhetoric, poetry, history, and moral philosophy.[20] While this more classically influenced curriculum not only provided an alternative to the logic-heavy education of medieval scholasticism, it could not help but influence preaching. Along with their renewed interested in classical literature, Renaissance humanists found new examples for preaching in classical oratory. No longer was it sufficient for a sermon merely to instruct or entertain. On the contrary, it was to move the hearer affectively or to persuade the hearer to act.[21] These humanists also found new methods for preaching in the expository sermons delivered by the early church fathers, which were shorter and more practical in nature than the more extensive scholastic sermons. A final impetus toward improved preaching during this period came from the simple popular demand for sermons. Such popular desire often led to the contracting of preachers other than the local priest to deliver sermons, usually on Sunday evenings and most prevalently during penitential seasons of Advent and Lent. They were ordinarily contracted from local mendicant orders or universities, oftentimes even mendicant friars on university faculties.

---

development, see Rice and Grafton, *Foundations*, 45–76.

18. On this reform, particularly during the course of the conciliar controversy, see Bellitto, *Renewing Christianity*, 47–101; Oakley, *Western Church*, 213–60; and Stump, *Reforms*. The most comprehensive treatment, though as yet untranslated from the Italian, is Alberigo, *Chiesa Conciliare*.

19. See especially Stump, *Reforms*, 138–52.

20. The most concise statement of humanism as an educational-literary-rhetorical movement is Kristeller, "Humanist Movement," 3–23.

21. On Renaissance humanist preaching, see O'Malley, *Praise and Blame*, esp. 7–76.

By the end of the fifteenth century, these preachers were nearly ubiquitous throughout parts of Western church, numbering one per town in southwest Germany.[22]

While there are any number of preachers in the late Middle Ages who embody one or more of these movements, there are few more representative than Nicholas of Cusa (1401–64) ex-conciliarist, cardinal, papal legate, curial reformer, and bishop of Brixen (modern day Bressanone in the South Tyrol province of Italy).[23] Educated at humanist strongholds such as Deventer and Padua, Cusanus—as he came to be called by fellow conciliarist defector, Aeneas Sylvius Piccolomini (later Pope Pius II)—was a prolific writer, composing numerous influential philosophical, theological, even mathematical treatises. What makes him relevant for consideration, however, was his tenure as the residential bishop of Brixen over a six-year period, when he delivered just short of 170 sermons that reflect the exact inverse of the common medieval cleric: a theologically and rhetorically trained intellectual committed to the care of souls in his diocese which he exercises through the weekly task of preaching to his flock.

Nicholas of Cusa's episcopate synthesizes all three trends in late medieval preaching. Like the late medieval conciliar reformers who criticized clerics for failing to minister in the churches to which they were appointed, he spent six years as a residential bishop in his diocese. He set about the task reforming secular (parish) and regular (monastic) clergy, lay morality, diocesan finances, and church liturgies. He published reform documents, visited parishes and clergy, and preached on a regular basis. He held four diocesan synods in a diocese that had only convened three in the previous fifty years, delivering substantial homilies at each and at other meetings of his diocesan priests, monks, or parish visitors.[24] He would remain in Brixen despite much opposition until an attempt on his life was made, forcing him to retreat to a protected castle on the outskirts of the diocese. Like the late medieval preachers contracted to deliver regular sermons, Cusanus also committed himself to regular preaching in his diocese.[25] Over the six years of his residency, he delivered 167 sermons, 142 of them in his Brixen cathedral. He preached on average three sermons per month throughout his resi-

---

22. Moeller, "Piety," 62; Ozment, *Reformation*, 38–42; and generally Taylor, *Soldiers*, 15–36.

23. The most comprehensive English sources on Cusanus's life and career are Meuthen, *Nicholas of Cusa*; and Watanabe, *Nicholas of Cusa*. For contemporaries of Cusanus who shared some of the same criticisms and approaches, see Bellitto, *Nicholas de Clamanges*, 111–26; and Pascoe, *Jean Gerson*, 118–28.

24. On Cusanus's efforts at reform as bishop, see Pavlac, "Reform," 59–112.

25. On Cusanus's preaching in general, see Hundersmarck, "Preaching," 232–69.

dential episcopate, mostly on Sundays in his cathedral church or on festival days or visitations of other parish outposts. Though these sermons were collated and published in Latin, there were originally preached in the vernacular language (German dialect of the Mosel region). Finally, like the late medieval humanists, he was a well-educated thinker competent to the task of moving and persuading the people through diligently crafted homilies. Despite publishing numerous theological, philosophical, or mathematical tracts on a regular basis, he took a personally unprecedented four-year sabbatical from writing to concentrate his attention on his sermons. Though he was unafraid to speak of substantive theological or philosophical matters, Cusanus's sermons were not academic lectures or scholastic compositions. He ordinarily preached from the gospel lesson for the day and spent a significant amount of time interpreting it expositionally with ample references to other biblical texts or sermons. In this sense, his preaching reflected a late medieval move toward a more expositional, homiletic style modeled after patristic sermons (and referred to in that day as "ancient" preaching) rather than the medieval scholastic ("modern") sermon.[26]

Above all, Cusanus understood the sermon as the prime responsibility of the preacher and as a task fundamental for the salvation of the faithful. A few examples will suffice.[27] One early sermon, delivered well before his elevation to cardinal or bishop, acknowledges Christ's saying that man does not live by bread alone to suggest that the sermon then provides a "double nourishment" of both body and soul. Christ provides in the word the external bread given to the preacher, and then the preacher is a "baker or a cook of the refreshments who receives the word of God from the breadth of the Scriptures and crushes and stews them together for nourishment."[28] This word is distributed through the clergy, as Jesus commanded the apostles Phillip and Andrew in John 6 to do with the two fish and five loaves of bread, "Therefore let us strive, most beloved, we who are pastors of the flock of the Lord, to be like Jesus alone, who distributed the word of life, that we fisherman might put before the people bread for their cultivation."[29] Cusanus tells the laity of his Brixen congregation that the priesthood is given to them as teachers for the purpose of communicating the Scriptures. Consequently, the clergy attain their position in the church only through perfect-

---

26. On the ancient-medieval distinction, see Spencer, *English Preaching in the Late Middle Ages*, 228-68.

27. The critical edition of the sermons is found in the Heidelberg edition of Nicolas of Cusa's *Opera Omnia*. The 293 total sermons are collected in volumes 16-19. All translations are mine from the Latin.

28. *Sermo* 41.1.

29. *Sermo* 207.7.

ing their knowledge of the truth they must communicate to the faithful.[30] But he reminds the clergy that not all preachers are created equal, however. Whereas consecrating the Eucharist is the same for every clergyman, some preachers are better than others, "one might labor and bears fruit better than another."[31] Addressing a synod of diocesan clergy in his last months at Brixen, the bishop declares that above all it is the pastoral responsibility of the clergy as shepherds to *evangelizare Christum*—to preach Christ. They are entrusted with preaching Christ that they might make him known to the sheep and the sheep might receive salvation through faith in him.[32] In these and many other respects Cusanus was the fulfillment of the late medieval desire for a reformation of preaching.

NICHOLAS OF CUSA'S PREACHING AND THE PROTESTANT REFORMATION

The fact that Nicholas of Cusa was an educated, theologically competent, residential bishop committed to the task of regular preaching also makes him a harbinger of the prototypical minister of the sixteenth century reformations, both Protestant and Catholic.[33] More than just a matter of style, Cusanus's sermons also shared much in common with the ecclesiastical and theological concerns of later Protestant reformers. In his synodal sermons, he preaches the reform of the clergy with unblinking honesty. He exhorts the clergy to visit the parishes with no fear because they stood in the same place as their Lord when he tossed the moneychangers out of the temple. He condemns those who hear confession for pecuniary gain as thieves who reside not in dens, but "churches and altars."[34] His sermons for the laity have the same vigor and substance. He reproaches the licentiousness of their marriage customs, lack of concern for the poor, and usury.[35] He also delivers numerous catechetical sermons on the Creed and the Lord's Prayer.[36]

---

30. *Sermo* 223.13–14.

31. *Sermo* 152.10.

32. *Sermo* 280.12–15.

33. In this connection, it should be unsurprising that his sermons were first published by the French humanist and later Protestant reformer, Jacques Lefèvre d'Étaples in 1515 (Vansteenberghe, *Le Cardinal Nicolas de Cues*, 420).

34. *Sermo* 147.7.

35. *Sermo* 196.11–17.

36. By my count, he preaches four catechetical sermons on the Pater Noster (*Sermo* 18, *Sermo* 24, *Sermo* 76, *Sermo* 198) two sermons based on articles of the Nicene Creed (*Sermo* 225, *Sermo* 278) and one on the Athanasian Creed (*Sermo* 233).

Beyond practical concerns, his sermons speak in the theological idiom of many later Protestants. For instance, in one sermon he speaks in language eerily reminiscent of Luther's on vocation:

> Let us consider that for whomever is free and not enslaved it is necessary that he first notice how "every action of Christ is for our instruction," that we might ourselves know the freedom of the sons of God to follow [him], indeed that we might become followers of the Son of God. And since the body of the church has diverse members, it is necessary that everyone remains in his calling (*vocation*). Therefore, first it is necessary that you see, if the Spirit of Christ is in you, you will not believe him to be in you unless you discover him in your unique calling (*in singularis vocation tua*). For the life of Christ is the universal path by which nevertheless the diverse walk. Thus the Christian presbyter ought to bear being the Christian presbyter, and the religious the religious, and the duke the ducal, and the citizen the citizen, each one in his order, office and calling (*vocation*). There is no more of Christ in one than the other, as there is no single garment for the secular prince and the religious monk, but different kinds of garments are received from the same garment of the immaculate Lamb of God, and they ought to bear them. It is as the Lord desires. For he varies the surrounding clothing for the resplendence of his court, which is the church militant.[37]

Such remarks call to mind Luther's own discussions of vocation. Cusanus's preaching about faith in Christ likewise uses terms that evoke Luther. He denies that works of the law save, "For works of the law do not justify. For the one living (*existens*) apart from righteousness is not able to justify himself. And if he is able to be justified through works, then he can justify himself."[38] He says explicitly that "our works do not justify us without faith, but Christ justifies those who through grace follow him."[39]

None of this is to imply that Cusanus was somehow a "proto-Reformer" or a "reformer before the Reformation." He would have been at odds with his Protestant successors on issues such as the role of the will or works

---

37. *Sermo* 169.16.

38. *Sermo* 179.10, 37–40. The Roman Catholic Luther scholar Erwin Iserloh referred to such statements as "spontaniously leading us to think of Martin Luther" ("Reform," 71).

39. *Sermo* 280.18. In this, he puts into pastoral practice his own stated position in 1453's *De pace fidei* that "no living soul is justified in the sight of God by works, but through grace ... he is justified, since from faith alone he obtains the promise, for he believes God and expects God's word to be done." *De pace fidei* 55, in Biechler and Bond, *Nicholas of Cusa*, 52.

in salvation, the authority of the papacy, the doctrine of transubstantiation, among others. Caution is needed to avoid finding superficial agreement. For all the differences, however, Cusanus in both his work as a preacher and bishop and his ecclesiological thought shared a position that would lie at the root of the Protestant Reformation: any attempt to reform the church must begin with the reform of the clergy. As one account of the relationship between Cusanus and the Protestant Reformation put it:

> If the Protestant Reformation seemed to produce changes in the laity at a slower rate than the reformers wished, that delay was owing perhaps to the insufficient supply of new, well-trained clergy to serve their parishes. But without the production of such clergy, the original network of reformers would not have sustained an evangelical movement at all. Without question Cusanus would have preferred the reforms of the Catholic to those of the Protestant Reformation. In my view, however, neither reformation would have survived without its clergy, who were both the objects and the agents of reform. In that sense, the Protestant Reformation was also an actualizing, if not an incarnation, of Cusanus' vision.[40]

That vision for Cusanus entailed a thoroughgoing reform of clergy and laity consistent with much of the late Middle Ages. But whereas other reformers concerned themselves with changing the structures of the church in Rome, Cusanus directed his reforms at the local clergy. As described earlier, he held diocesan synods to instruct and reform the clergy and attendance was compulsory (even resulting in one instance of excommunication). He drafted instructions for visitations in his diocese, provided his clergy new rites for marriage, and urged their catechesis of the faithful.[41] He received a bull from Pope Nicholas V in 1451 authorizing the visitation and reform of monastic houses throughout Germany and the Low Countries, then another in 1453 to visit and reform orders within his Brixen diocese. After his residential tenure at Brixen came to an end, he went on to Rome and composed an important reform proposal, the 1459 *Reformatio Generalis*, which urged the pope to initiate reform of the church by first confirming himself to Christ that he might be an example for others. He did the same with the Roman Curia in the reform proposal, and on downward throughout the ecclesiastical hierarchy.[42]

40. Hendrix, "Ecclesiology," 124.
41. Some of these documents are found in Hürten, *Cusanus-Texte V*.
42. Many of Cusanus's writings and sermons on reform have been translated in Nicholas of Cusa, *Writings on Church and Reform*.

What Cusanus shared in common with the Protestant Reformation was a conviction that the reform of the church—including anything resembling a reformation of preaching—would prove impossible apart from the reform of the clergy. Without well educated, theologically competent ecclesiastics and pastors who can bring their competence to bear upon their responsibilities within the church, there is no hope for changing thought and practice in a healthy, productive fashion. Reformation begins with the clergy. This is what Cusanus aimed to do, not only in his preaching as a residential bishop, but in his philosophical and theological writings, reform tracts, episcopal visitations, and diocesan synods. It is also what the Lutheran reformers sought to do, whether in academic disputation or educational reform at Wittenberg, catechisms and handbooks on preaching designed for clergy use, visitations to assess the relative "success" or "failure" of their reform efforts, even new orders of the mass or the voluminous *Kirchenordnungen* filled with binding *Kirchenrechten* that gave clergy guidelines for governing ecclesiastical and civil life.

In the final analysis, this is the contribution Cusanus's preaching makes to any contemporary discussion of the topic. A reformation of preaching—medieval, late-medieval, Lutheran, or contemporary—is never finally about tweaking methods or formats or oratorical skill. It has to do rather with the theological competence of the clergy charged with preaching and with their understanding of the significance and goal of those sermons they deliver. In the Middle Ages, the problem was a lack of competent clergy to preach. In the late Middle Ages, as for Cusanus and in the Protestant Reformation, there was an attempt to renew preaching through the improved education of the clergy and increased commitment to their pastoral tasks. The situation is not entirely different today. The reform of preaching is not a goal, but a by-product of a clergy well educated, theologically competent, and pastorally committed to their tasks as *episcopi loci* charged with the *potestas ordinis*—preaching the gospel and administering the sacraments in accordance with their vocation. Where those conditions obtain, history tells us the likelihood of improved preaching will follow.

BIBLIOGRAPHY

Alberigo, Giuseppe. *Chiesa Conciliare: Identità e significato del conciliarismo*. Brescia: Paideia, 1981.

Barraclough, Geoffrey. *Papal Provisions: Aspects of Church History, Constitutional, Legal, and Administrative in the Later Middle Ages*. Oxford: Blackwell, 1935.

Bartlett, Robert. *The Making of Europe: Conquest, Colonization, and Cultural Change, 950–1350*. Princeton, NJ: Princeton University Press, 1993.

Bellitto, Christopher. *Nicholas de Clamanges: Spirituality, Personal Reform, and Pastoral Renewal on the Eve of the Reformations*. Washington, DC: Catholic University of America Press, 2001.

———. *Renewing Christianity: A History of Church Reform from Day One to Vatican II*. New York: Paulist, 2001.

Bossy, John. "The Mass as Social Institution, 1200–1700." *Past and Present* 100 (1983) 29–61.

Boynton, Susan, and Diane J. Reilly, eds. *The Practice of the Bible in the Middle Ages: Production, Reception, and Performance in Western Christianity*. New York: Columbia University Press, 2011.

d'Avray, D. L. *The Preaching of the Friars: Sermons Diffused from Paris before 1300*. Oxford: Clarendon, 1985.

Duggan, Lawrence. "The Unresponsiveness of the Late Medieval Church: A Reconsideration." *Sixteenth Century Journal* 9 (1978) 3–26.

Grundmann, Herbert. *Religious Movements in the Middle Ages*. Translated by Steven Rowan. South Bend, IN: University of Notre Dame Press: 1995.

———. *Europe in the Fourteenth and Fifteenth Centuries*. New York: Holt, Reinhard, and Winston, 1966.

Hay, Denys. *The Church in Italy in the Fifteenth Century*. Cambridge: Cambridge University Press, 1977.

Hendrix, Scott H. "Nicholas of Cusa's Ecclesiology between Reform and Reformation." In *Nicholas of Cusa on Christ and the Church*, edited by Gerald Christianson and Thomas M. Izbicki, 107–26. Leiden: Brill, 1996.

Hundersmarck, Lawrence F. "Preaching." In *Introducing Nicholas of Cusa: A Guide to a Renaissance Man*, edited by Christopher M. Bellitto et al., 232–69. New York: Paulist, 2004.

Hürten, Heinz, ed. *Cusanus-Texte V: Akten zur Reform des Bistums Brixen*. Heidelberg: Carl Winter Universitätsverlag, 1960.

Iserloh, Erwin. "Reform der Kirche bei Nikolaus von Kues." *Mitteilungen und Forschungsbeiträge der Cusanus-Gesellschaft* 4 (1964) 54–73.

Kristeller, Paul O. "The Humanist Movement." In *Renaissance Thought, 1: The Classic, Scholastic, and Humanist Strains*, edited by Paul O. Kristeller, 3–23. New York: Harper & Row, 1961.

Lambert, Malcolm. *Medieval Heresy: Popular Movements from the Gregorian Reform to the Reformation*. 3rd ed. Oxford: Wiley-Blackwell, 2002.

Logan, F. Donald. *University Education of the Parochial Clergy in Medieval England: The Lincoln Diocese, c. 1300–c. 1350*. Toronto: Pontifical Institute of Mediaeval Studies, 2014.

Martines, Lauro. *Power and Imagination: City-States in a Renaissance Italy*. Baltimore: Johns Hopkins, 2000.

Meuthen, Erich. *Nicholas of Cusa: A Sketch for a Biography*. Translated by David Crowder and Gerald Christianson. Washington, DC: Catholic University of America Press, 2010.

Moeller, Bernd. "Piety in Germany Around 1500." In *The Reformation in Medieval Perspective*, edited by Steven E. Ozment, 50–75. Chicago: Quadrangle, 1971.

Moore, R. I. *The First European Revolution, c. 970–1215*. Oxford: Blackwell, 2000.

———. *The War on Heresy*. Cambridge, MA: Belknap, 2012.

Nicolas of Cusa. *Opera Omnia*. 22 vols. Leipzig: Meiner, 1932–2005.

———. *Nicholas of Cusa on Interreligious Harmony: Text, Concordance and Translation of De Pace Fidei*. Edited and translated by James E. Biechler and H. Lawrence Bond. Lewiston, NY: Mellen, 1990.

———. *Writings on Church and Reform*. Edited and translated by Thomas M. Izbicki. Cambridge, MA: Harvard University Press, 2008.

Oakley, Francis. *The Western Church in the Later Middle Ages*. Ithaca, NY: Cornell University Press, 1979.

O'Malley, John. *Praise and Blame in Renaissance Rome: Rhetoric, Doctrine, and Reform in the Sacred Orators of the Papal Court, c. 1450–1521*. Durham, NC: Duke University Press, 1979.

Ozment, Stephen. *The Reformation in the Cities: The Appeal of Protestantism to Sixteenth-Century Germany and Switzerland*. New Haven: Yale University Press, 1975.

Pantin, William Abel. *The English Church in the Fourteenth Century*. Cambridge: Cambridge University Press, 1955.

Pascoe, Louis B. *Jean Gerson: Principles of Church Reform*. Leiden: Brill, 1973.

Pavlac, Brian A. "Reform." In *Introducing Nicholas of Cusa: A Guide to a Renaissance Man*, edited by Christopher M. Bellitto et al., 59–112. New York: Paulist, 2004.

Rice, Eugene F., and Anthony Grafton. *The Foundations of Early Modern Europe, 1460–1559*. 2nd ed. New York: Norton, 1994.

Rouse, Richard H., and Mary A. Rouse. *Preachers, Florilegia, and Sermons: Studies on the Manipulus Florum of Thomas of Ireland*. Toronto: Pontifical Instituted of Medieval Studies, 1979.

Salonen, Kirsi, and Jussi Hanska. *Entering a Clerical Career at the Roman Curia, 1458–1471*. Burlington, VT: Ashgate, 2013.

Spencer, H. Leith. *English Preaching in the Late Middle Ages*. Oxford: Clarendon, 1993.

Stump, Phillip H. *The Reforms of the Council of Constance (1414–1418)*. Leiden: Brill, 1994.

Swanson, R. N. *Religion and Devotion in Europe c. 1215–c.1515*. Cambridge: Cambridge University Press, 1995.

Taylor, Larissa. *Soldiers of Christ: Preaching in Late Medieval and Reformation France*. Oxford: Oxford University Press, 1992.

Vansteenberghe, Edmond. *Le Cardinal Nicolas de Cues (1401–1464) L'action–l'pensée*. Paris: Champion, 1920.

Watanabe, Morimichi. *Nicholas of Cusa: A Companion to His Life and Times*. Burlington, VT: Ashgate, 2011.

Wood, Susan. *The Proprietary Church in the Medieval West*. New York: Oxford University Press, 2006.

5

Systematic Theology and Preaching in the Thought of Johann Gerhard

—Roy Axel Coats

INTRODUCTION

Martin Luther writes concerning Phillip Melanchthon's *Loci Communes*, "By God's grace a great many systematic books now exist, among which the *Loci Communes* of Phillip excel, with which a theologian and a bishop can be beautifully and abundantly prepared to be mighty in preaching the doctrine of piety...."[1] Here Luther states that the purpose of systematic theology is to prepare bishops and pastors to preach in the church. This view is echoed by the fact that a couple of the first compendiums of theology were written specifically for the sake of preaching.[2] Therefore, well ordered, clear, and concise systematic theology is to be ordered to good preaching. Likewise, well ordered, clear, and concise preaching is to be drawn from systematic theology. In order to unfold the connection between systematics and preaching we will look at the writings of Johann Gerhard, considered

---

1. LW 34:327. This passage is quoted by Chemnitz, *Loci Theologici*, 12.

2. For example Urbanus Rhegius, *Formula quaedam caute*. This work was published in English as *Preaching the Reformation*. One could also look at official preaching manuals, such as the *Predigtanweisung* of the Duchy of Lüneburg, a predecessor to Rhegius's work.

to be one of the foremost of the dogmaticians of the age of Lutheran Orthodoxy.[3] We will look at both his systematic writings, namely his *Loci*, and his more practical writings, namely his *Methodus Studii Theologici*, and see how he grounds preaching in systematic theology and orders his systematic theology to preaching.

The question of how preaching and systematic theology are related is an important one for the church today. Where there is a disconnect between the two, where one allows there to be systematics that are ordered to an end other than preaching, the systematic endeavor seems to degrade into endless rational speculation, lacking the proper end. This type of false theology Gerhard would have called "philosophical."[4] Likewise, preaching that is not based on systematics would lack its source of true content and method for clarity and thus be based primarily on the lower passions and emotions of men. This type of false theology was called "vulgar."[5] If this is the case, then a divorce has been made between theology as an academic endeavor, as an objective science, and the pastoral act of preaching, as a subjective art.

In order to establish how Johann Gerhard relates systematic theology to the act of preaching, we will first analyze both systematic theology and preaching. Then we will be able to synthesize by way of comparison the similarities and differences between them and determine any causality between them. For the analysis we will first look at what systematic theology is and then preaching.

ANALYSIS

1. Systematic Theology

For Johann Gerhard systematic theology is not a branch or method of theology but the whole of theology taken abstractly. This is important to realize that unlike our day where systematic theology is generally taken in opposition to other branches of theology, such as historical or practical, Gerhard sees that all theology can be considered systematic when viewed abstractly.

---

3. See Preus, *Theology* 1:53. Johann Gerhard (1582–1637) was professor of Theology at the University of Jena from 1616 to 1637.

4. Gerhard, *Theological Commonplaces* Preface, 14, 32.

5. Ibid.

1.1. Division

In order to understand what Gerhard means by systematic theology we must then look at how he defines the genus, theology, and the difference, abstract. We will then divide systematic theology into its parts in order to understand as it is most proper to our topic.

1.1.1. Genus

For Gerhard, theology is a God-given (*theodosis*) wisdom about God; wisdom being the greatest and most exact of all modes of knowing.[6] It is rational discourse grounded on certain first principles. The object of this knowledge is simply God himself.

1.1.2. Difference

During the time of Gerhard, the distinction between the abstract and concrete is a basic logical one, drawn from the beginning of Aristotle's Organon, in *Categories* 1. It is developed from the *antepraedicamentum* of paronymous terms.[7] Paronymous terms are those that have similar names but which differing by some discrepancy of case. The meanings of these names are likewise similar but not the same. Paronymous terms are thus a median between homonyms and synonyms; these terms to do not have the same names and meanings nor completely diverse names and meanings. An example of these terms is sweet and sweetness. The relation between these terms is that of the denominator, sweetness, to and that which is denominated, sweet.[8] These terms stand for concepts that are considered either within a subject or in themselves, that is, as their own subject.[9] Examples of concepts presented in a subject is man, sweet, and grammarian. Examples of concepts presented without a subject is humanity, sweetness, and grammar. The former are called concrete, they are presented in a determined subject, while the latter are called abstract, that is separated from the determination

---

6. In these discussions Gerhard favors using the general term *gnosis* as opposed to *episteme*.

7. Martini, *Logicae Peripateticae* I.i.9; *Institutiones Logicae* 2.1. Jacob Martini (1570–1649) was a professor of Logic and Theology at Wittenberg from 1623 to 1646, at the same time that Gerhard was professor of Jena. His logical works were very popular and influential at that time.

8. Ibid., 2.1. It seems that terms can have either a concrete voice or an abstract voice, much like the active and passive for verbs.

9. Ibid., 2.1. The abstract term is substantial, the concrete term is adjectival.

of a subject. Thus when there is a discussion of the abstract and the concrete three things are to be distinguished: the abstract voice, as in "philosophy"; the concrete voice, as in "philosopher"; and the subject, as in "Aristotle."[10]

Knowledge can be taken as abstract or concrete in two ways, depending whether the subject is in the mind or outside the mind, whether it is rational or real. If the subject of knowing is outside the mind, then the concrete knowledge is the knowledge found in relation to that thing, sense knowledge. The abstract knowledge is that knowledge apart from that subject, as it exists in the mind. If the subject of knowing is in the mind, the concrete is the knowledge as a habit in the soul. It is knowing as it is in a subject. This knowledge in abstract is the mere intellectual content of the soul, or as it is spoken or most properly written. It is knowing apart from the subject. Calov expands on these three things to be distinguished in paronymous relations of terms in relation to theology. Theology is in the abstract voice and refers to doctrine. Theologian is in the concrete voice and refers to the act of knowing. The subject which is either abstracted from or predicated of is the soul of man.[11]

Gerhard calls this abstract knowledge of a subject in the mind systematic. It seems that the reason that this knowledge not as it is known but as it is in itself is called systematic is that it is has to be given an existence apart from the knowing subject. This existence is most properly in a written text, Quenstedt emphasizes this in his *Systema*.[12] Thus this knowledge is given a grammatical and logical existence apart from the mind. Yet, by extension this theology would also exist in the act of teaching through the spoken word. Yet to write or speak about knowledge demands that this knowledge be ordered in some way, if only because speaking and reading are temporal actions and there must be a beginning, middle, and end. Yet a further issue is that abstract knowledge exists in a mode of communication and thus must be systematized in order to be understood. With this basis, systematic theology could also indicate, in an improper and secondary way, the ordered knowledge in the mind that results in the written or spoken instruction.

1.1.3. Kinds of Systematic Theology

Yet the wisdom we have in systematic theology is limited in many ways. Gerhard describes this as he makes two sets of divisions in regards to theology.

10. Ibid., 2.2. Aristotle is a philosopher, and knows philosophy. One cannot predicate directly the abstract of the subject.
11. Calov, *Isagoge*, 200.
12. Quenstedt, *Theologia Didactico-Polemica* 1a, c. 1, th. 28.

First is the division between archetypal and ectypal theology.[13] Archetypal theology is God's perfect self-knowledge, and this is the standard of all true theology. Here there is no distinction between an abstract or concrete theology because there is no distinction between the subject knowing and the object known. Yet we have an ectypal or acquired theology. Concretely, this knowledge is not ours by our essence, but which we come to know. Abstractly, this knowledge, though true is both accidental, that is not from our very nature, and also finite and thus lacking in some way. Second, Gerhard divides ectypal theology into the theology of pilgrims and the theology of the blessed. In this world our theology is that of the way, that of pilgrims.[14] This theology lacks the clarity, permanence, and perfection of the theology of blessed, who have by the beatific vision an intuitive knowledge of God himself. Thus the theology we are speaking of is the imperfect knowledge of God.

Another important aspect of this ectypal knowledge of God that Gerhard speaks of it as being mostly practical. This God-given rational knowledge is ordered to an end that is not simply knowing, but action (*praxis*).[15] There are many ways in which Gerhard speaks of the practical side of knowing. Concretely this action is an action in the subject, a change in the person who has theological knowledge.[16] Abstractly and systematically the action would be the action of the knowledge itself, whether written or spoken. As we shall see the primary purpose of systematic theology is to instruct.

1.2. Definition

To reach a real definition of systematic theology we will have to analyze it according to its causes.

1.2.1. Efficient Cause

In order to determine the efficient cause of systematic theology, we must first divide it according to its source as either natural or supernatural. The natural knowledge of God is either inborn or acquired. Gerhard argues that

---

13. Gerhard, *Commonplaces* Preface, 15.
14. Ibid., Preface, 16.
15. Ibid., Preface, 11.
16. This action concretely results in having saving faith, love, the enjoyment of God, and true piety. See Ibid., Preface, 12.

since the fall this knowledge is uncertain and easily can result in error.[17] Supernatural theology is theology acquired by the light of grace. This light comes from the divine revelation given in the revealed word. Thus the principle efficient cause is the revealing God, while the instrumental cause is the word as the "medium of divine revelation."[18] For us today this instrumental cause exists adequately and only in the "written and prophetic books of the Old Testament and in the apostolic books in the New Testament."[19] Thus the efficient cause of systematic supernatural theology is God revealing himself through Holy Scripture.

1.2.2. Material Cause

The material causes of the knowledge of systematic theology are simply "the theological principles and conclusions deduced from the revealed word as from a proper principle."[20] Thus the principle in the mode of being, *modus essendi*, of systematic theology also becomes the principle of the mode of knowing, *modus cognoscendi*. From Holy Scripture dogmatic definitions can be drawn that act as the very material of theology. Yet they exist on their own apart from a knowing subject. Since principles and conclusions have a grammatical and logical basis of existence they are properly called systematic.

1.2.3. Formal Cause

The material truths of the principles drawn from Scripture must be arranged if they are to exist as abstract, systematic knowledge. Thus the form of theology is "the actual arrangement and disposition of those truths."[21] Gerhard is speaking of how these truths are ordered. He proposes many different dispositions, and thus the form of systematic theology can vary, yet this is not to say that there is not a better or worse disposition of these truths.

---

17. Ibid., Preface, 17.
18. Ibid., Preface, 18.
19. Ibid., Preface, 19.
20. Gerhard, *Loci Theologici* 25.
21. Ibid., 25, 7; see also *Commonplaces* 25.

1.2.4. Final Cause

As mentioned above, the final cause of systematic theology is instruction. It is the instruction of the word of God to people. This instruction can happen on many different levels. Gerhard makes clear in his discussion of the homonymy of the word "theology" that theology can refer simply to the faith that is common to all Christians.[22] He then quotes John Chrysostom who says that we are in a sense the teacher of ourselves.[23] Yet theology can also refer to the ecclesiastical ministers, who catechetically instruct their congregations.[24] Lastly, theology can be used only for those who have "a more accurate knowledge of the divine mysteries."[25] These last are those who have an acroamatic knowledge of theology, and could be connected to those who instruct pastors in seminaries or universities. Yet regardless of which level we see that systematic theology refers to instruction. This instruction is the internal intermediate and proximate end of systematic theology, "Information for man for his eternal salvation."[26]

1.2.5. The Real Definition

Drawing from this whole discussion, especially his analysis of the four causes of theology, Gerhard defines systematic theology in the following way, "From all the above such a definition is able to be collected: Theology (considered systematically and abstractly) is the doctrine built up from the word of God that instructs man in true faith and pious living unto eternal life."[27] Systematic theology is that knowledge which is built up by human reason from the word of God to teach other men about salvation.

2. Preaching

We will be examining two sources of Gerhard on preaching. We will begin in his *Loci*, which we were using above. Yet in this text he says that he will not speak at length about preaching, but directs the reader to turn to his discussion of preaching in his *Methodus Studii Theologici*.[28] Thus we turn

22. Ibid.
23. Ibid.
24. Ibid.
25. Ibid.
26. Ibid., 26. *Loci*, 26.
27. *Commonplaces* 31.12; *Loci* 31.
28. *Commonplaces* 26.268. In this passage Gerhard gives a summary of what he

to chapter two of the fourth section of that work, entitled "On the Practice Necessary for Sermons."[29]

2.1. Division

For the division we will examine the genus and difference of preaching. Both have to do with the duties of the ecclesiastical minister.

2.1.1. GENUS

In his *Loci*, Gerhard speaks of preaching in his discussion of the duties of the ecclesiastical minister. Preaching is an action that the ecclesiastical minister must perform. Looking at the intermediate end of the ecclesiastical minister, the conversion and salvation of men, Gerhard states that "the first duty of ministers is the preaching of the word."[30] This is because men are born in ignorance and darkness and it is through the preaching of the word of God that they are illuminated by the Holy Spirit and converted.

2.1.2. DIFFERENCE

Preaching is an action of the ecclesiastical ministry. In this action Gerhard states that the preacher has two duties (*officii*) that he must fulfill. These duties within the act of preaching distinguishes preaching from the other duties of ecclesiastical minister. Gerhard writes, "There are two other duties of ecclesiastical preachers. *Namely, the interpretation of Scripture, and an accommodation of the same to a saving use.*"[31] These two duties locate the preacher as a means or instrument between the material cause, the that

---

says in the *Methodus*. Quoting from the *Methodus*, he states that the two duties of the preacher. He also enumerates the five uses of application, stating at the end, "All that must be observed in these matters has been explained with certain rules in the aforementioned treatise." The main purpose of the rest of this passage is to argue that it is necessary that the preacher not only instruct in the true faith but also refute false doctrine, that he both teaches and reproves.

29. Gerhard, *Methodus Studii Theologici* 201. The study of preaching comes in the fourth year as one continues to examine Holy Scripture and the Loci and a study on the controversies that exist with the Calvinists and the Photians.

30. *Commonplaces* 26.265–66.

31. Ibid., 206. The two first duties of the preacher are to pray that God's word is spoken and also piously prepare and babble whatever comes to mind.

from which, the text of Holy Scripture, and the object of preaching, which is the hearers.

Gerhard divides the first duty, the interpretation of Scripture, into two parts. The first part is "the investigation of the true and genuine sense." Here we simply have the private study of Scripture; the first part is preparatory to the second part. The motion is from Holy Scripture to the habitual knowledge of the preacher. The second part is the "plain and clear exposition of the same."[32] Gerhard states that this exposition is nothing other than an explanation of the text preached on.[33] Gerhard emphasizes that it is necessary that the preacher not only know what the text says, but that he explain what he discovered to the people. This second part is completed by the public office properly, by the act of preaching, by the act of explaining what the text of Scripture literally says.[34]

The second duty, the accommodation of discovered and explained sense of the text, is also divided into two parts. The first part is the summary of the doctrines or teachings found in the text and explained in the sermon. This is a systematic act of moving from the habitual knowledge of what the text means to ordering that knowledge in a systematic way. As in the explanation of the text, in the summary of doctrine the knowledge becomes abstract. Again this first part is preparatory to the second. The second part is the application of these doctrines to the salvation of the hearers. Here the motion is from the abstract and systematic knowledge of the summary of doctrines to the habitual knowledge of the hearer.

If we analyze the first duty according to the three parts of paronymous terms we would have Holy Scripture as the subject outside of the mind from which knowledge is abstracted by the private study of investigation and made concrete again in explanation in the preaching of the sermon. Note that the abstract knowledge of the first duty is not systematic since it exists has habitual knowledge in the preacher and does not take on an existence of its own until it is actually explained to the hearers. As one can see it is very important when speaking of the abstract and the concrete to determine what the subject is. If we analyze the second duty in the same way, the subject would be the mind of the preachers from which is abstracted knowledge through the summarizing of the doctrines, which is then made habitual in the minds of the hearers by applying that knowledge to them in the act of preaching.

---

32. Ibid..
33. Ibid., 207. The text preached on is the *"Paraphrastica textus."*
34. Ibid., 206.

Thus one part of the act of preaching is simply explaining the text to the hearers. The other part is the application of what is taught in the text to the hearers. Both duties must be joined together in preaching. To take one away is to make the other imperfect and unfruitful.[35] The sermon is not simply an interpretation of the text nor simply an application to our lives. Rather, it is both. It is both expounding Holy Scripture and an application to the listeners. The connection between these two duties is the systematic of summarizing the doctrines found in the text.

2.2. Definition

Since both duties use rational means to complete its action, and this action generically consists of speaking, Gerhard freely uses the divisions found in classical rhetoric to instruct how to preach. He thus divides the rest his discussion of preaching into the five classical parts of rhetorical education: invention, disposition, elocution, memory, and pronunciation.[36] In our study we will look at the first part of this division since it deals primarily with the content of the sermon. Likewise, as we have already looked at the first duty of preaching, the exposition of the meaning of the text, we will look primarily at the second duty, that of applying the text to the hearer. As we do this we will be able to analyze this aspect of the sermon according to its causes, as we did with systematic theology.

2.2.1. Efficient Cause

We learn of the efficient cause of the sermon when Gerhard gives a general canon for all invention, whether it is of the explanation or application. The general canon simply is, "The content put forward in preaching is from the Sacred Letters."[37] He adds, "This is the only and proper source concerning divine things as a principle of difference, this is the only God given medium of salvation and of the remedy of every certain error and evil."[38] Thus the very content of the sermon must be scriptural. He elaborates on this canon through two consequences. The first is that the preacher will not indulge in long quotations from the church fathers. The reason for this is not that the

---

35. Ibid., 207.

36. Ibid. For a classical explanation of these parts see Psuedo-Cicero, *Rhetorica ad Herennium* I.ii.3ff. This text was considered authentic at that time and was widely used as a source for rhetoric.

37. Ibid., 207.

38. Ibid., 207–8.

content of these passages are not the word of God, but that these passages are not authoritative as the writings of the apostles and prophets found in Scripture. Thus the chief place must be given to quoting those passages that give a "solid foundation of faith" and which are the basis by which the church fathers are judged.[39] The second consequence of this canon is that quoting passages of pagan authors should be done very sparingly. The reason for this is that they are not the word of God at all, and God does not promise to use these passages as means of salvation. The only means he wishes to be efficacious through is his word. Thus we see that this general canon upholds sacred Scripture as the norm, exemplar cause, and efficient cause of preaching.[40]

2.2.2. Material Cause

The material cause of preaching can be divided according to its two duties. The material of the first duty is simply the passage of Scripture given, read in light of the whole of Scripture. The material cause of the second duty is the summary of doctrines drawn from Scripture. Since these doctrines have their source in Holy Scripture and have been abstracted from the mind of the knower, in this case the preacher, they can properly be called systematic knowledge.

2.2.3. Formal Cause

The formal cause of preaching is simply that it is the spoken word. The preacher uses his reason to arrange his content so that it makes sense as a spoken word. Rhetoric helps the preacher arrange his content in a way that is both clear and concise.

---

39. Ibid., 208. Two reasons Gerhard gives to quote the church fathers are first in order to give evidence to a source of consensus in the early church and second on account of how vigorous and emphatic that passage is.

40. Here we see the distinction between the normative and causative authority of Scripture at work. Yet we also see that Gerhard is clear that there can be the word of God in preaching that has the causative authority, yet not the normative authority. Scripture is the exemplar cause as it is provides models for our preaching.

2.2.4. Final Cause

Preaching is an art in which something is made, and as such it is fulfilled by an ends that is for the sake of another person.[41] Therefore, preaching does not occur for the benefit of the subject, the preacher, that he comes to understand a passage of Scripture better and is able to collect teaching from this. The main purpose, or final cause, of preaching is the application of these teachings to the hearer. Thus the object of the hearers determines the final causes of preaching.

2.2.4.1. Modes of Applying Doctrine

Gerhard states that preaching is only one mode of applying the doctrine to the hearers, and that the application of the summary of doctrines can take place in many ways. As this helps us understand the place of preaching in the church, we will look at Gerhard's divisions in detail.

First, Gerhard divides the accommodation according to the object, namely the kind of hearers to whom the preacher is accommodating the text. The first group of hearers is the infidels, who through natural theology are prepared to take up the Christian religion. The second group are the immature Christians, who need catechetical theology, which is "the fundamental parts of Christian doctrine handed on through catechetical questions."[42] The third group are the "impenitent and secure" who are to be given the condemnation of the law to lead them to sorrow for their sins. The fourth group are those who are "fascinated by erroneous opinions."[43] They need to be more properly informed and false doubts removed. The fifth group are those who are humble and contrite, that are sorrowing for their sins. To them it is necessary to give the consolation of the gospel. Lastly, the sixth group are those who are disturbed by various struggles, and they need the office of the word of God in the sense the cure of souls. Yet there are two more ways that one can accommodate the exposition of Scripture to hearers. That is when it is not addressed to a specific group of hearers but when it is either focused on an individual or when it is addressed to the whole church. The individual is most properly addressed during the rite of private confession and absolution. The whole church is most properly addressed by preaching.

---

41. Aristotle, *Nichomachean Ethics* vi.4.1140a20–21, b.8–9.

42. Gerhard, *Methodus* 215–16. It seems that Gerhard is referring the chief parts of the *Small Catechism*.

43. Ibid., 216.

Through this division Gerhard shows that there is no universal application of Scripture, but that each is specific to its object. Furthermore, since the whole church, which is addressed by preaching, is made up of many kinds of people, the uses of preaching also must vary. To explain these different uses Gerhard looks to the fivefold use of Holy Scripture.

2.2.4.2. Fivefold Use of Scripture in Preaching

Gerhard states that this variety in the uses of preaching is what St. Paul intended when he wrote in Rom 15:4, "For whatever was written in former days was written for our instruction, that through endurance and through the encouragement of the Scriptures we might have hope," and 2 Tim 3:16, "All Scripture is breathed out by God and profitable for teaching, for reproof, for correction, and for training in righteousness, that the man of God may be complete, equipped for every good work." From these verses Gerhard draws the fivefold use of Scripture: the *usus didascalius*, the *usus elenchticus*, the *usus epanorthoticus*, the *usus paedeuticus*, and the *usus paracleticus*, that is instructing, refuting, correcting, encouraging, and comforting.[44]

Gerhard explains the fivefold use of Scripture that is taken from St. Paul by looking towards the end of Scripture, which is to instruct men from evil unto salvation.[45] By these uses the remedy to the evil that changed man through the fall is introduced so that "men might be restored to pious and Christian perfection." Gerhard does this by dividing these five uses in three different ways. First, by looking at the evil that man must face. Second, by looking at the good works that the Christian does. Finally, by a useful philosophical distinction.

2.2.4.2.1. First Division of the Fivefold Use

The first division is explained in terms of the different kinds of evils that exist on account of original sin. The first evil is that in true cognition we are immature. The second evil is that in good actions we are remiss and sluggish. The third evil is that in the toleration of evil we are weak and impatient. As remedies to these three evils then are to the first the didascalic, the second the paedeutic, and the third the paraclytic uses of Scripture. Gerhard then discusses the other two uses as addition to the first two evils. First, we do

---

44. This fivefold division is first found in Hyperius, *De Formandis Concionibus Sacris* II.1. He uses the same verse, 2 Tim 3:16, as the basis of the fivefold division. See Fritz, *The Preacher's Manual*, 87.

45. *Methodus* 217.

not only lack knowledge, we believe falsely. Against this evil is the elenchitic use, which could also be called the polemical use. Second, we do not only not do what is good but we also promote and are inclined to evil. Thus there is also the epanorthotic use.

2.2.4.2.2. Second Division of the Fivefold Use

As opposites of the three evils are the three good works of the Christian: understanding the truth, doing good, bearing evil. These then are related to the three cardinal or principle Christian virtues, namely faith, love, and hope. To faith pertains understanding the truth, to love good actions, and to hope, the bearing of evil. Yet again to these three good works and virtues must be added to the opposites. There is no understanding of the good without refutation of the false, nor is there any having place for good actions without the receding of evil or sin. Again we need the fivefold use of Scripture. Gerhard summarizes, "All together, there are five members required so that so that the perfection of Christian piety may be obtain inasmuch as it can in this fallen life."[46] To these five elements of Christian perfection correspond the five uses of Scripture which instructs the hearer to them.

2.2.4.2.3. Third Division of the Fivefold Use

The last division is between the theoretical and the practical. Gerhard states, "All accommodation of Scripture is either theoretical or practical." The theoretical is concerned with the understanding of the truth and the refutation of the false, hence the didascalic and the elenchitic uses. The practical is concerned with doing good, hence the paedeutic use, avoiding the guilt of evil, hence the epanorthotic use, and bearing the punishment of evil, hence the paraclytic use.

2.2.5. Real Definition of Preaching

Preaching is a duty of the ecclesiastical ministry, a verbal act, where the minister draws teachings from Scripture and accommodates them to the whole Church. Preaching is done for the sake of instructing unto salvation, yet it does so according to the various ways in which Scripture can be accommodated to the hearer, namely teaching, refuting, correcting, encouraging, and comforting. The accommodation is taking the topics from

46. Ibid., 219.

the text and accommodating them to the people, time, and place where the sermon is being preached.[47]

SYNTHESIS

Having now analyzed both Gerhard's writings on systematic theology and preaching we can examine how the two relate. First we will look at the similarities and differences between the two. We will do this by comparing each of their causes. Second, we will look at any causal relation between them.

1. Similarities and Differences

We will examine the similarities and differences between systematic theology and preaching by comparing their causes. We will examine first the external causes, namely the efficient and final, and then the internal causes, namely the formal and material.

1.1. Efficient Cause

The principle efficient causes of both systematics and preaching are the same. They are both caused by God revealing himself through Holy Scripture. The source of the both the abstract and the concrete is the same. Their instrumental causes are also the same, insofar as it is through men set aside as teachers in the church.

1.2. Final Cause

In regards to their final causes, there are two ways in which systematics and preaching differ. First, their objects differ. Preaching is meant for the whole church, while systematic theology is usually written for a specific group, whether it is catechetical for the immature or acroamatic for those who have been called as teachers in the church.[48] Second, their end differs. Both are an accommodation of Scripture to the people in the form of instruction. That is both of them instruct concerning the word of God. The final cause of systematic theology is to instruct for the sake of true knowledge and holy liv-

---

47. Ibid.
48. Gerhard speaks of three different objects of theology in *Commonplaces* Preface, 4.2.

ing. Preaching also is ordered to instruction, but not that alone. Preaching is for the sake of correction, encouraging, and comforting. Thus in regards to the didascalic use of Scripture there is no difference between systematic theology and preaching. Yet preaching accommodates Scripture to a fuller array of ends than systematic theology.

1.3. Formal Cause

The principle difference between systematic theology and preaching is in their formal causes. Most properly systematic theology is written down while preaching is spoken. Said in another way systematic theology is a thing, an artifact, while preaching is an action. Furthermore, systematics, which is ordered to knowledge alone, is divided according to logical principles. Preaching on the other hand, which is ordered to more than just knowing but also doing, is divided according to rhetorical principles. Yet if we speak analogously they do have formal similarities. They are both rational explanations of Scripture, that is human reason gives them their order and existence. This unifying form could be called the grammatical principles that they both share. Thus in a generic and analogous sense they have the same grammatical form of theology.[49]

1.4. Material Cause

The material cause is where the most important connection between systematics and preaching is found. The material of systematics is principles and conclusions drawn from Scripture for the sake of instructing others. For preaching there is a two material causes based on the two duties of the preacher. The first duty, that of interpretation has a passage of Scripture as its sole material. Yet this act of interpretation would be the same for systematics and preaching, though for systematics draws from the whole of Scripture while preaching focuses on this or that passages. Interpretation of Holy Scripture then is the source both for systematics and preaching and provides the explanation of what the Scripture means. The next act that follows for both systematics and preaching is the summary (*collectio*) of the scriptural doctrines. This summarizing abstracts the doctrines from the subject, which is the habitual knowledge of Scripture, thus making these doctrines abstract and systematic. The summary of doctrines becomes the

---

49. It could be said that since rhetorical principles are drawn from logical, and that since to be rhetorical is to presuppose a logical grounding, that both systematics and preaching share in logical principles.

material for both systematics and the second and principle duty of preaching, that of application to the hearer. Systematics collects and summarizes these doctrines to its systematic end of instruction for the sake of instruction. The second duty of preaching also collects and summarizes these doctrines, yet for a wider application to the hearers. At the heart of preaching, the result of the first duty and the material for the second, is the summary of doctrines, which is the same material as systematics as a whole. Therefore it can be concluded that systematics and preaching are based on the same materials, the summary of the doctrines of Scripture existing in the abstract and systematically.

2. Causal Relations

We can now examine how systematics and preaching relate causally. First, we shall look at how preaching is a cause of systematics, then we will look at how systematics is a cause for preaching.

2.1 Preaching as a Cause of Systematics

Preaching is a cause of systematics insofar as the end of systematics is more completely fulfilled in the act of preaching. The end of systematics is not simply to know for the sake of knowing, it is practical since it is ordered to doing. Thus it is ordered to the fullness of the Christian life. As systematic theology, though, it only reaches this end through instruction. Yet preaching can take this instruction and apply in a richer way to the whole person and the whole church through correction, encouragement, and comfort. Thus the end that systematics is ordered to is better reached through preaching. In this way preaching can be called the actualization of systematics. Preaching is systematics in act. This conclusion could be stated in terms of the abstract and the concrete. Preaching perfects systematics in that it takes the abstract systematic knowledge drawn from the source of Holy Scripture and makes it more concrete by actually applying the systematic knowledge to the hearer, not just by instruction, but also by correcting, encouraging, and comforting. Preaching is the art of the practical science of systematics.

2.2 Systematics is a Cause of Preaching

Yet preaching cannot exist without systematic theology. Systematics is the cause of preaching insofar as preaching is based upon systematic knowledge.

Systematics is the very material grounding of all preaching. It is the source from which preaching flows. Thus Gerhard states that no one should preach who has not yet finished their study of the systematic loci. When we say that preaching is based on systematic knowledge, this is not to reject the ultimate ground being Scripture. Yet it does recognize that the divine content of Scripture can be drawn out of Scripture as the source and summarized without it losing its authority or efficacy. This abstracting of the divine content, giving it a rational basis of existence, allows it to be learned by systematic instruction and fully applied to the hearers in preaching. Preaching needs this systematic content because it is the medium by which Scripture is applied to the hearer. Without systematic knowledge, preaching has nothing to instruct or refute, and no certain basis from which to encourage, correct, or comfort.

As a corollary to this discussion it is helpful to note that there is a kind of preaching that is most properly systematic according all the causes except the formal, and in regard to the formal cause there is an analogous relation. It is didascalic preaching which shares with systematic theology the end of instruction. It seems that in Scripture this use is given priority, and thus in preaching the didascalic use must be the most important. Carl Ferdinand Wilhelm Walther, a student of Gerhard and the Lutheran Dogmaticians and also a gifted preacher, states:

> The didascalic use, for doctrine, is the one the holy apostle places before all others. It is the most important of all. It is the foundation of the other four uses. Even if a sermon is so rich in admonitions, rebukes, and comforts, if it is without doctrine, it is still a thin, empty sermon, with admonitions, rebukes, and comforts suspended as in mid-air. It is inexpressible how much many preachers sin in this respect. The preacher has hardly touched his text and doctrinal topic and already starts to admonish, rebuke, or comfort. His sermon consists of almost nothing but questions and exclamations, blessings and woes, so that the listener can hardly consider anything calmly. Far removed from going to the heart and producing true life, such preaching is much more suited to preach people to death, to kill any hunger for the bread of life, methodically to produce boredom with God's Word. It must be repugnant to every listener to be tastelessly admonished, rebuked, or comforted without first having the doctrinal foundation laid.[50]

---

50. Walther, *Practical Theology*, 64.

In the didascalic use as a foundation to the other uses we see the fullest actualization of systematics in preaching. The ultimate end of preaching is the same as systematics. This conclusion, though not stated explicitly by Gerhard himself, follows from his discussion of both systematics and preaching.

CONCLUSION

For Johann Gerhard there was no opposition between systematics and preaching. They have the same source, the interpretation of Holy Scripture, and have the same goal, the salvation of man. Systematics gives the material ground to preaching and preaching perfects and actualizes the goals of systematics. Gerhard wrote that in preaching any accommodation without both duties of explanation of the text and accommodation a use is imperfect and infertile.[51] We can say that the systematic explanation of the text without the application to the hearers is imperfect, it lacks the complete means to accomplish its ends. Likewise, any application without being grounded in a systematic explanation of the text is infertile, it lacks any ground or authority to be efficacious. If this is the case, preaching would then need systematics and systematics would then need preaching. They are distinct yet unified acts of God through his ecclesiastical ministry.

BIBLIOGRAPHY

Aristotle. *Nichomachean Ethics*. Translated by Joe Sachs. Newburyport, MA: Focus, 2002.
Calov, Abraham. *Isagoge*. Wittenberg: Hartmann, 1666.
Chemnitz. Martin. *Loci Theologici*. Edited by Polycarp Leyser. Wittenberg: Menius and Schumacher, 1653.
Psuedo-Cicero. *Rhetorica ad Herennium*. Translated by Harry Caplan. LCL. Cambridge, MA: Harvard University Press, 1954.
Fritz, John C. *The Preacher's Manual*. St. Louis: Concordia, 1942.
Gerhard, Johann. *Loci Theologici*. Edited by Eduard Preuss. Berlin: Schlawitz, 1863.
———. *Methodus Studii Theologici*. Jena: Steinmann, 1620.
———. *Theological Commonplaces: On the Nature of Theology and Scripture*. Translated by Richard J. Dinda. St. Louis: Concordia, 2006.
Hyperius, Andreas. *De Formandis Concionibus Sacris*. Basel, Oporiniana, 1573.
Martini, Jacob. *Institutiones Logicae*. Wittenberg: Fincillius, 1661.
———. *Logicae Peripateticae*. Wittenberg: Cratoniana, 1603.
Preus, Robert. *The Theology of Post-Reformation Lutheranism*. Vol. 1. St. Louis: Concordia, 1970.

51. *Methodus* 207.

Quenstedt, Johann Andreas. *Theologia Didactico-Polemica, sive Systema Theologicum.* Leipzig: Fritsch, 1702.
Rhegius, Urbanus. *Formula quaedam caute.* 1535. Wittenberg: Lufft, 1536.
———. *The Homiletical Handbook of Urbanus Rhegius.* Translated by Scott Hendrix. Milwaukee: Marquette University Press, 2003.
Walther, C. F. W. *Practical Theology.* Translated by John Drickamer. New Haven, MO: Lutheran News, 1995.

6

Assuring the Faithful
On Faith and Doubt in Lutheran Preaching

—Jacob Corzine

INTRODUCTION

... So I asked your disciples to cast it out, and they were not able." And he answered them, "O faithless generation, how long am I to be with you? How long am I to bear with you? Bring him to me."

And the father said, "... But if you can do anything, have compassion on us and help us." And Jesus said to him, "'If you can'! All things are possible for one who believes." Immediately the father of the child cried out and said, "I believe; help my unbelief!" And when Jesus saw that a crowd came running together, he rebuked the unclean spirit, saying to it, "You mute and deaf spirit, I command you, come out of him and never enter him again." ... And when he had entered the house, his disciples asked him privately, "Why could we not cast it out?" And he said to them, "This kind cannot be driven out by anything but prayer."[1]

---

1. Mark 9:17–29.

Past experience would have led the disciples to confidence that they ought, indeed, to have been able to expel the unclean spirit, but here they fail. In lamenting the faithless generation, Jesus places his finger squarely on the source of the problem: the disciples themselves were faithless in their action.[2] They did not lack faith in their ability to cast out the spirit; but that faith was no longer in God.

Jesus calls them faithless, because the disciples' faith had become turned around. They had not excluded themselves from salvation for a time, but they were having a crisis of faith, not unlike the boy's father: "I believe; help my unbelief!" Jesus' pastoral care for the disciples is twofold: first, he draws their attention to how great their unbelief is. He does this through his exchange with the father of the demon-possessed boy, particularly in v. 23. Later, when they still do not understand, he directs them to prayer. If faith is the work of the Holy Spirit in the Christian, then prayer is the external action that most naturally follows from it.[3] In it, the essence of relying on God who is entirely *extra nos* shows itself in activity that seeks all things in this God.[4] Jesus' words, designed to kindle faith in his disciples, are a reminder not to rely on themselves, but to pray.

This passage from the Gospel of Mark, with its memorable phrases, "Lord I believe, help my unbelief!" and "All things are possible for one who believes," speaks to the still relevant question of how to preach with the purpose of creating faith in the hearts of hearers, while at the same time recognizing that, for the most part, the addressees of sermons are the very baptized believers who have received faith already. The challenge is even greater in the postmodern era, in which the skill of self-referential humor is so intensely cultivated. Not just the pastor, but also the faithful know that they have faith, and they are further confident in their alleged ability to

---

2. Commentators are not in agreement about whom Jesus is referring to when he laments the "faithless generation" in v. 19. Pesch argues on the basis of the use of γενεά that the scribes are Jesus' referent (*Das Markusevangelium* 2:90). Luhrmann contends rather for faithless disciples—this seems to fit the whole of the pericope better (*Das Markusevangelium* 161). The readings hardly need to exclude each other, as is demonstrated in Lenski's interpretation, according to which the disciples are likened with the faithless scribes (*Interpretation* 377–78).

3. Luther expresses this sentiment in a sermon on Luke 17:11–19, "Das gute Herz und Glaube lehrt ihn von sich selbst, wie [der Christ] beten soll. Ja, was ist ein solcher Glaube denn eitel Gebet?" ("The good heart and faith naturally teach the Christian how he ought to pray. For what else is such faith than pure prayer?"), "Kirchen-Postille," W2 XI; *WA* VIII:360, 28–29.

4. This is the "use that very name in every time of need" of Luther's Small Catechism; (KW 352 = *BSLK* 508); cf. LC III: 8 (KW 441 = *BSLK* 663–64).

evaluate its strength or weakness.⁵ This suggests the existence of a skepticism toward any preaching of the law and sin, as the faithful already know themselves in possession of the faith that rescues from condemnation.

The question of preaching to the faithful is, in particular, a question of how and with what intention the pastor preaches the law, or—put differently—what service it performs for the preaching of the gospel to which it is attached. This will be treated later in this article. First, however, an adequate apparatus for speaking of faith must be available, and to this end a few more words must be said on the matter of faith and—in particular—doubt.

A challenge that is perhaps particularly evident in Lutheran preaching in the face of doubt is the tension that can present itself between the two foundational phrases *sola fide* (by faith alone) and *extra nos* (outside of us).

On the one hand, *sola fide* can be improperly proclaimed at the cost of the *extra nos*. The Christian may believe the pastor's proclamation that faith is the only thing necessary for salvation, and thereby entirely adequate, but in times of uncertainty, his doubt about whether he has this faith is not thereby assuaged. He is left believing that he is responsible for evoking his own faith, rather than that it is a gift of the Holy Spirit from outside of himself.

On the other hand, the *extra nos* may improperly come at the expense of the *sola fide*. Faith's source "outside of us" is proclaimed in order to be sure that the Christian not place his trust in himself. The faith, described as a gift of God over which the Christian has no influence, is thereby described as a perfect faith. When the modern Christian, in his inevitable self-evaluation, finds not a perfect faith but a faith overrun with doubt, he may conclude that he, not having the fullness of the gifts of God, must indeed have none of them.

Both extremes leave the complex reality of the Christian's experience of his own faith unaddressed. They demonstrate that, where faith itself as an article of faith comes into the crosshairs of the Christian, the dogmatic description of the matter falls short as comforting proclamation of the gospel. But the failure lies not in the inadequacy of the description, but in the inability of the Christian to see his own faith clearly. The description does not match his experience, because his sight is warped.

That the Christian does not see clearly in the act of the Christian's self-reflection is not a new observation. In the first part of this essay, it will be shown how Johannes Brenz was already attempting to parse the matter

---

5. This article will implicitly argue that discussions about "stronger" and "weaker" faith are not incompatible with Lutheran theology. The common use of these evaluations to measure and even compare the quality of Christianity of different Christians is, however, to be rejected.

dogmatically with the terms *fides visibilis* and *fides invisibilis*. Once Brenz's work has been traced, a brief review of the reception of this teaching in the history of Lutheran dogmatics will be presented. Finally, the implications of the matter for preaching, especially the preaching of the law, will be considered. By the end of the essay, it should be evident that Jesus' activity in Mark 9 is not only helpful for delineating the problem at hand, but also descriptive of the solution—not speaking about faith, but rather directing its attention outwardly, toward the work of God.

BRENZ'S CATECHISMUS PIA ET UTILI EXPLICATIONE ILLUSTRATES

Introduction to Brenz's catechism

Johannes Brenz (1499–1570) was responsible for some of the earliest Lutheran catechisms. Before the appearance of Martin Luther's Small Catechism, Brenz had already published a catechism in question-and-answer format for teaching children, and one for teaching adults. These were probably published in 1527 and 1528, and were widely received and often reprinted.[6]

The wide reception of Brenz's catechetical writings led to publications of commentaries on the same, for example by Tobias Wagner and Lucas Osiander. These works paved the way for Brenz to provide a Latin commentary of his own. This work is addressed below. Though only intended for private use, Brenz's colleagues pushed for publication. Caspar Greter was responsible for the first publication in 1551. Reprints followed in Wittenberg, Tübingen, Magdeburg, and Frankfurt am Main, with a German translation appearing already in 1551.[7] The Latin printing followed here is that of Wittenberg, 1553.

The place of faith in Brenz's definition of a Christian

Brenz's section on the Christian Religion begins by asking: "Tell the causes, on account of which you have been called and you are a Christian?"[8] The catechumen responds: "Because I believe in JESUS Christ and have been baptized into the name of Jesus Christ."[9] Brenz's commentary begins by

---

6. *Katechismus Erläutert*, XI–XII.
7. Vgl. Ibid., XII–XIII.
8. Brenz, *Catechismus Pia Et Utili*, 20. All translations are those of the author.
9. Ibid., 21.

identifying possible incorrect answers: that one was born of Christian parents, that one lives among Christians, or that one, while living among Christians, hears the sermon and receives the Lord's Supper. Rather "... it is rightly and truly answered when we say that we are therefore Christians, because WE BELIEVE in Jesus Christ."[10]

Having raised faith as the decisive and even constitutive characteristic of the Christian, Brenz proceeds to provide a three-part definition of what it means to believe in Jesus Christ:[11]

> First, to believe in Jesus Christ is to hold with a certain and firm faith that after man sinned, Christ the Son of God was immediately promised from the beginning of the world, who would expiate sin, reconcile us with God the Father, and save us in death unto eternal life, and that this Christ would be proclaimed by the prophets and time and again more and more explained.[12]

Brenz continues:

> Then, to believe in Jesus Christ is to hold with a certain and firm faith that Jesus, the son of Mary the virgin, who suffered under Pontius Pilate, is truly this Christ, who was promised from the beginning of the world and afterward was proclaimed by the prophets.[13]

And finally:

> Finally, to believe in Jesus Christ is to hold with a certain and firm faith that this Jesus Christ is the expiator of our sins and our savior, on whose account alone we stand favorably before God and are reckoned before him as just, and attain to eternal blessedness, if we truly believe in him and locate all trust (*fiducia*) for our salvation in him alone. [14]

To believe in Jesus Christ means to believe

---

10. Ibid., 22. The difference in era and in polemical orientation is evident. Brenz is still in his time exalting faith over against a magical, *ex opere operato* understanding of the sacrament. Today's emphasis on subjectivity has probably over-adjusted and could bear to be pulled in a more sacramental direction. This essay deals, with reference to preaching, with one particular area where that balance needs to be sought.

11. He admits that the definition is brief, noting that a fuller definition will follow. He means by this the exposition of the Apostles' Creed that follows at the proper place in the catechism explanation.

12. Brenz, *Catechismus Pia Et Utili*, 22.

13. Ibid.

14. Ibid., 22–23.

1. that after man sinned, God promised to send his son as savior from sin,

2. that the object of this promise is Jesus Christ, identified as the son of Mary, and

3. that this Jesus Christ truly did remove our sin and make us able to stand before God, and that he alone is worthy of our trust and confidence in this matter.

In an addendum to this three-part definition, Brenz clarifies the Lutheran *pro me*. His definition is misunderstood, or—if it is regarded as set of criteria for identifying belief, then—it is not met, if the one doing the believing does not believe "that the benefits of Christ pertain singularly to him himself, that he himself truly is one of those whose sins Christ has expiated. . . ."[15]

Here Brenz defines believing (for he is defining the verbal construction *credere in Iesum Christum* and not the nominal *fides*) chiefly according to its object. This is why he can be brief, referring the reader to the explanation of the creed that follows later. That said, he does not entirely neglect the verb *credere*: in the first two cases, it means "to hold with a certain and firm faith ("certa et firma fide tenere") and in the third case the very similar "to hold with a true and firm faith ("vera et firma fide tenere.") The verb "to believe" is circumscribed through a noun, "faith," and that faith has attributes: it is "certain," "firm," and even "true."[16] With this definition, Brenz recalls the rejection of a bare *fides historica* confessed in the Augsburg Confession.[17] Belief includes thus not only the maintenance of the historical truths of salvation in Christ, but also the maintenance of their decisive relevance for one's own standing before God.

In the section's concluding paragraph, Brenz delineates the source of faith, with an eye apparently toward the misunderstanding that one might think that "to hold with a certain and firm faith" were a work of man leading to salvation. Rather, faith in Jesus Christ "is a gift of God given . . . by the power of the Holy Spirit through the word of God."[18] The Christian is to hear God's word and to pray "that God would give us the Holy Spirit, by whose power we receive true faith and are confirmed therein."[19]

---

15. Ibid., 23.

16. One could attempt here to parse these adjectives further, likewise to consider whether their explicit attribution implies that there can be uncertain, infirm, false faith. I prefer not to do that here, but instead to follow Brenz's line of thought with minimal interruption for a few more pages.

17. Cf. AC XX:23 (KW 56–57 = *BSLK* 79).

18. Brenz, *Catechismus Pia Et Utili*, 24.

19. Ibid.

This definition of the Christian centered around the faith of the Christian forms the background for the analysis of Brenz's terms *"fides visibilia"* and *"fides invisibilia"* which follows below. There is a tension in this definition that leads Brenz to an excursus on the faith of infants: on the one hand, the Christian is characterized by an action, namely holding with a certain and firm faith to the teachings of the salvific work of Jesus Christ. On the other hand, among these teachings is the very exclusion of any action on the part of the Christian to attain his salvation: "on [Christ's] account alone we are before God in grace and are reckoned before him as just, and attain to eternal blessedness, if we truly believe in him and locate all trust (*fiducia*) for our salvation in him alone." Even as faith in Brenz's description of a Christian is focused entirely on Jesus Christ, to the exclusion of Christian activity, he seems unable to avoid speaking about the very activity of faith. This tension is inherent in the original question, "How do I know that I am a Christian?" "Because I believe in Jesus Christ." Although it would seem that Brenz is not placing the question in the mouth of a doubting Christian, the parallel to the inquiry of such a person is obvious. That would be, "How do I know that I hold to Jesus Christ with a 'certain and firm faith'?" The following depiction of his distinction between the *fides invisibilis* and the *fides visibilis* is intended to help find an answer.

The two modes of faith (fides duplex)

After providing his foundational definition of the Christian as clearly centered around the Lutheran *sola fide*, Brenz immediately takes up the question of children, who are, by all appearances, not capable of faith in such historical truths. Brenz formulates the question himself, placing it rhetorically in the mouth of the catechumen, "But what do we say, you ask, of infants? We have shown, namely, that men are Christians through faith. But infants are not seen to be capable of having faith. Can it then be that infants cannot be Christians?"[20] His answer, which spans just a few pages, is composed of a few distinct steps:

First, Brenz makes his argument by means of contraposition: In so far as it is entirely clear that the children of Christian parents are children of God and heirs of the kingdom of God, it must follow that they can also have faith. This statement is logically equivalent to that of the imaginary naysayer positing that, if children cannot have faith, it follows that they cannot be Christians. It allows Brenz to begin with Scripture passages such as Gen 17:7, Isa 49:22, and Joel 2:28, which leave beyond all doubt that children are

20. Ibid., 28.

also recipients of God's salvation, as well as Mark 9:36–37, where Jesus takes a little child into his arms. To this, Brenz adds one final fact, to which he expects the imaginary dissenter to agree: children are conceived and born in sin and therefore in need of the forgiveness of sins, which can only be attained by faith. Therefore, if children not only enter the kingdom of heaven, but also as sinners, they can do so only by the means of the forgiveness of sins, and if the forgiveness of sins can only be received by faith, it must follow that it is possible for infants to have faith.

This does not settle the discussion for Brenz. The argument by contraposition shows the dramatic consequences of denying faith to infants, but does not deal with the basis of the dissent, which is the observation that infants seem incapable of faith of the sort that Brenz describes.

He continues then by analogy: children have a true bodily life without understanding it; likewise, they are their parents' heirs before they understand this. So it ought in the same way be possible that they possess faith, even though they do not understand it. This analogy is permissible because it retains the key element of the objection: that the infant cannot understand and possesses nevertheless. An analogy between the faith of children and the faith of adults, however, Brenz finds more tenuous, "And it should thus not be thought that infants that have been accepted by God into grace would have revealed faith in the same way as adults have it."[21]

As we are here nearing the crux of the issue, a short aside is warranted. Brenz's caveat addresses not the difficulty in knowing Christ, therefore not the inability to exhibit the cognition that seems to belong to the understanding of faith he describes, but rather the difficulty in knowing one's own faith. To return for a moment to the analogy of being a worldly heir, it is not an inability to inherit that would cause a problem, but rather an ignorance that one is the inheritor at all. It would seem that Brenz has turned the discussion, silently reformulating the objection from "children seem unable to know about Christ" to "children seem unable to know that they have faith [in Christ]." The turn is plausible. Although the objection is clearly based on the child's inability to comprehend, Brenz's formulation of it focuses on the recognizable manifestation of the faith. He refers in the above quote to *fides revelata*. This use of *revelatus* is not a reference to divine revelation. The German translator of Brenz's catechism, Friedrich August Schütz, is right to translate *fides revelata* with "clear faith," "For one should not think that the children who have been received by God into grace, have such a clear faith, as do the adults."[22] That something is not revealed does not mean that it is

21. Ibid., 31.
22. "Denn man soll nicht denken, daß die Kindlein, welche von Gott zu Gnaden

not present, only that it is not plainly visible. For Brenz, as we will see, this visibility, or rather this lack of visibility, is the issue. The child's inability to comprehend consequently does double duty: it is both the instrument lacking, by which the child would be able to recognize its own faith, "even if they do not yet understand [their faith],"²³ and the element of faith lacking to the external Christian observer, "how can they have faith, when they do not yet understand?"²⁴ The rest of Brenz's argument will need to be traced in order to determine if he resolves both aspects of this objection to infant faith.

Having established by an analogy that children could possess a faith that might not be visible, Brenz shores up the same argument with Scripture. Here, the argument is *a minore ad maius*. He cites Hos 2:21-22, in which the heavens, the earth, the wheat and the wine and the oil all are engaged in "answering." To that he adds Rom 8:22, "For we know that the whole creation has been groaning together in the pains of childbirth until now." If creation can answer and groan—something we cannot see but nevertheless is attested in Scripture—how much more can a child whom God promises salvation through his Son do the same? From the next verse in Rom 8, according to which we, "who have the first fruits of the spirit" also "groan inwardly," Brenz finds then his division into two kinds of groaning: an invisible one, seen only by God, and a revealed one, seen by and known also by those who have it.

The groaning of Rom 8 is Brenz's model for a *fides duplicia*, but it is not only a model. It is clear that he regards this groaning as persuasive attestation from the Scriptures. After citing the Romans passage, he writes, "From these places of Scripture, we deduce that the groaning of creatures is double."²⁵ Then, after elaborating what he means by that, he applies it to faith, "Thus this very matter also shows that faith is double."²⁶ The groaning in Rom 8 is the groaning of those who hope but have not yet received, be it creation, waiting to "obtain the freedom of the glory of the children of God" (Rom 8:21) or we ourselves, as "we wait eagerly for adoption as sons, the redemption of our bodies." (Rom 8:23) This groaning is the expression of faith in the promise of redemption.²⁷ So Brenz presents his double understanding of faith:

---

angenommen sind, einen solchen klaren Glauben haben, wie die Erwachsenen." Brenz, *Katechismus Erläutert*, 33.

23. Brenz, *Catechismus Pia Et Utili*, 31.
24. Ibid., 30–31.
25. Ibid., 31.
26. Ibid., 32.
27. Admittedly, St. Paul speaks here of hope (ἐλπίς) but the similarity of his description of it here and the "definition" of faith in Heb 11:1 cannot be overlooked. In Rom

> Thus this very matter also shows that faith is double. But if namely faith in Christ is not divided in itself: There is, then, one faith—says Paul—but it has itself in diverse modes, in the infant and in the adult.[28]

Respective definitions of the two modes of faith and a few words about the importance of this teaching round up the section. Brenz's last three paragraphs are of particular significance here.

The faith of infants, which Brenz calls here *fides abscondita*, is not qualified in a manner that goes much beyond what has already been noted. He argues from the lesser to the greater, that if the young ravens (Ps 147:9) can cry out to God, how much more the children who are created in his likeness and received into his grace. More intriguing, however, is the reference Brenz makes to Jonah's fish. In Jonah 2:10, the Lord spoke to the fish, and it vomited Jonah out. Brenz reasons, if a fish can hear the command of God, how much more then can an infant hear his word.

For Brenz, the infant is rhetorically greater than the fish because it is a human being "created in the likeness of God"[29] and "elected to receive the kingdom of heaven."[30] It must therefore be at least as capable of hearing the word of God, which is the means by which it receives forgiveness. This is the first significant point in this paragraph: Brenz does not doubt that children can hear the word of God in a manner that is salvific for them. The second is this: the distinction between the faith of the little children and the faith of the adults to be described in a moment is not a distinction in the essence of the faith, but in its condition and mode. Brenz concludes his description of infant faith with these words: "by what means then would an infant ... not be able to hear the word of God, by which it has been forgiven through faith according to its own condition and mode?"[31] Faith is possessed in a fashion suitable to the person who receives it. Brenz does not begin here to speculate about how exactly an infant can possess faith or understand the word of God unto faith, neither about qualities of the word that would allow it to work without its words being rationally apprehended. He does not depart from his *a minore ad maius* argument.

This faith of infants, hidden except to God, is contrasted with the faith of adults, which is of a sort that also the one who has it knows of it:

8, hope is "waiting with patience" "for what we do not see." In Heb 11, faith is "the assurance of things hoped for, the conviction of things not seen."

28. Brenz, *Catechismus Pia Et Utili*, 32.
29. Ibid.
30. Ibid.
31. Ibid.

> Another is revealed faith, which not only God sees in man, but also the man himself, who by it has been forgiven, knows himself to have it and understands of what sort it is in adults. And this faith is given through the external hearing of the word of God. Just as Paul says: faith from hearing, but hearing through the word of God.[32]

The key distinction between the two modes of faith Brenz describes is that in this second mode faith is known by its possessor. Whereas, for the purpose of understanding Brenz, the *infans* may be understood as the child who is too small to even know that he has faith and nevertheless has it, the person being described as having "revealed faith" knows and to some extent is also capable of analyzing his own faith, at least so far that he can recognize the same thing in others. This mode of faith is, like the other, tied to the hearing of the word of God.

Brenz concludes the section by explaining why the distinction is important and what practically follows from it. It is important, because it affirms the salvation of little children over against the appearance that they don't have faith. Its practical consequences are an admonishment to parents to be diligent in instructing their children in true doctrine and good morals as soon as they are able to grasp such. Brenz has the dangerous consequences of sin—that one would lose the gifts of God apprehended by faith—in mind, and depicts such instruction as the means of avoiding this danger.[33]

The initial observation that there is an objection to the faith of children on the basis of their inability to reason and understand at a sufficient level does not frame Brenz's entire discussion. It serves rather only as a starting point for a series of observations about faith which, taken together, affirm the faith of the *infans*. Concluding, Brenz demonstrates his own understanding of the relationship between faith and the benefits of faith: the baptized infant, having faith, has the entire catalog of benefits. These are driven away by sin (impiety and evil deeds) so that the faith must be taught. However one does not thereby elevate an child's faith to an adult level, as though adult faith were somehow greater than infant faith, but rather one seeks to preserve the full faith given in baptism against that which would increasingly do it harm in the course of life.

---

32. Ibid., 32–33.
33. Ibid, 33.

The value of the distinction of two kinds of faith

With his distinction of two modes of faith, Brenz is addressing a disjunction between what is taught and what is seen. We cannot see that infants have faith, yet Lutherans affirm their need for it and teach that they in fact receive it in baptism. Since we believe that we can—at least in a human, limited fashion—see faith in adults, we would suppose that we ought to be able to see faith in children. This challenge is probably particular to Lutheran theology, with its distinctive emphases on original sin, the necessity of baptism, and the reception of its benefits of baptism *sola fide*.

In his treatment, Brenz does not attempt to resolve the tension created by the challenge; he only seeks to oppose its becoming normative for doctrine. Therefore he posits a different mode of the same faith particular to the infant, indicating that it is given in the Scriptures to teach this, but he does not attempt to delineate how it is essentially distinguished from the mode of faith found in an adult. The tension between the experiential observation and the teaching remains, but the teaching is affirmed over against the experience.

A note on the similarity to other distinctions

There is precedent for generalizing Brenz's distinction to apply also to those with severe developmental disabilities, those who have suffered at the hands of mentally debilitating diseases, those in comas, and—interestingly enough—those who are asleep.[34]

With Hollaz, and in the following 20th century examples, Brenz's language of *fides visibilia* and *fides invisibilia* has been exchanged for that of *fides reflexa* and *fides directa*. Here the perspective is no longer that of the person observing (or failing to observe) faith, but rather that of the person in whom the action of faith occurs. Brenz's terms and those of Hollaz, Pieper, and Bonhoeffer below cannot be directly equated with each other, but they address the same matter: the Christian is at times unable to ascertain the presence of the faith he has been promised.

In the twentieth century, the American Lutheran dogmatician, Francis Pieper, taught the distinction of the *fides directa* and the *fides reflexa*: a person can have faith without being aware of it. The faith, which believes

---

34. This comparison between those who are asleep, those who are mentally ill, and small children, can be found, for example, in David Hollaz's *Examen,* in the chapter *de gratia regenerante*. Hollaz's work is significant in its being regarded as the last dogmatics work of the age of Lutheran Orthodoxy. Cf. also Gummelt, "Hollaz, David."

the Gospel unto salvation, is *fides directa*, clinging directly to Christ as its object. *Fides reflexa* is the faith that extends from the same point, namely the believer, but returns, having the believer himself, in particular his faith, as its object. The *fides directa* looks toward Christ. The *fides reflexa* looks for the *fides directa*. For Pieper, the initial and natural application of this distinction is in describing the waking versus the sleeping, the adult versus the child. The existence of the *fides reflexa*, however, and the proper esteem for it, lead Pieper into a discussion of those times where it ought be present and is not. Of particular importance to his treatment is the fact that the absence of the *fides reflexa* is by no means to be equated with the absence of saving faith (*fides directa*). He rather maintains that the sinner's desire for grace is to be understood as faith itself.[35]

The value of Pieper's treatment is in extending the discussion rooted by Brenz in the defense of the faith of infants to the pastoral care of those among the baptized troubled by an inability to see their own faith. He calls this *Anfechtung* and the *status tentationis*. His treatment, however, lacks consideration of why the *fides reflexa* is desirable. He regards it as a good thing because it is presumed also in the Scriptures, but he does not acknowledge any relationship between the *fides directa* and the *fides reflexa* that would make the failure of the latter cause for pastoral concern.

Dietrich Bonhoeffer also draws on the distinction between *fides reflexa* and *fides directa*, in his *Act and Being*. For him, the act of reflection is perpetually inadequate to capture the *fides directa*. Also here, the child (the infant in baptism) plays a significant role, as he is not subject to the inevitable inadequacy of self-reflection, but lives rather in the objectivity of Christ, that is: faith is "fix[ed] upon baptism" as an act of God, rather than on the "I" as one—sinful—side of a relationship. For Bonhoeffer, the return to baptism is also the return to this childlike faith, which distinguishes itself by being wholly oriented toward God and free of condemning self-reflection.[36]

The broad acceptance of the distinction between two modes of faith and its uniqueness to Lutheran theology are not the only reasons that it is worth renewed attention today. The distinction provides a dogmatic foundation for engaging the pastoral-care challenge presented when self-referential, self-critical thinking is applied to faith and church life. This foundation, not an innovation, but rather a traditionally held part of the doctrine of justification by faith, describes the Christian life as a life observably oscillating between faith and doubt, while at the same time affirming

---

35. Pieper, *Christian Dogmatics*, 443–45.

36. Bonhoeffer, *Act and Being*, 157–61. As a source for his understanding of the *fides directa* and *fides reflexa*, Bonhoeffer draws on Franz Delitzsch's 1861 *System of Biblical Psychology*, 407–14.

that one's status as a child of God and heir of eternal salvation does not precariously depend on proximity to one pole of this oscillating subjectivity, but rather only on the objectivity of the divine means of grace. Both Bonhoeffer[37] and Pieper[38] note the context in which this Lutheran understanding of faith is more commonly known: in discussion of what Martin Luther called *Anfechtung* or *tentatio*.

THE WORKING OF THE WORD ON THE TWO MODES OF FAITH

In the following, working within the context of article 5 of the Formula of Concord, it shall be shown how the distinction of two modes of faith in the pastoral treatment of cases of doubt, trial, and temptation confirms the necessity of preaching law and gospel. The implications of the distinction for preaching in a manner that confirms and strengthens faith today will likewise be considered.

The preaching of the law reproves unbelief

Acknowledging two modes of faith and the intermittent ability of the Christian to see his own faith provides a helpful perspective for understanding a particular passage in FC V, "Thus, the law reproves unbelief by reproving those who do not believe God's Word."[39] At this point, in the article on law and gospel, the intention of the Formula is to delineate the proper functions respectively of the law and of the gospel. Whereas the gospel "teaches and commands only faith in Christ" and expressly does not "reprove ... unbelief," the proper function of the law is "to reprove sin and to lead to the knowledge of sin;" further, "since unbelief is a root and fount of all sins worthy of condemnation, the law also condemns unbelief." Finally, "both teachings [*sc.* law and gospel] must be alongside each other and must be taught together, but in a proper order and with the appropriate distinction."[40]

That the law continues to reveal and reprove sin means that also the Christian exhibits unbelief. This does not nullify his faith, for then he would cease to be a Christian. Rather the unbelief must be regarded as coexisting with his faith. The Formula warns about the law "lead[ing] to knowledge

---

37. Bonhoeffer, *Act and Being*, 148.
38. Pieper, *Christian Dogmatics*, 444.
39. FC SD V:19, (KW 584 = BSLK 958).
40. FC SD V:15, (KW 584 = BSLK 956–57).

of sin": it leads to presumption or despair (*Verzweiflung, desperatio*).[41] This despair is not "mere" doubt, but the utter hopelessness that follows from unresolved doubt. It is the loss of the confidence to claim Christ's salvific work for oneself (loss of the *pro me*) or the inability to recognize in oneself the work of the Holy Spirit. Using Brenz's language: to the Christian in this kind of law-produced despair, his faith has become *invisible*; and as his faith is synonymous with all the benefits of the work of Christ appropriated to him by the Holy Spirit, he is cast back onto his *fides abscondita*, by which he still desires to be saved and in fact is, but by which alone he is not able to confess that which was made true in his baptism.

The Formula of Concord's warning is a reminder that the experience of the Christian in his conscience is of no little relevance. The Christian's certainty of salvation (*Heilsgewissheit*) is rather given great importance. It is the danger of losing this certainty that necessitates that the law never be preached apart from the gospel. The loss of Christian certainty will not resolve itself; it is resolved by the preaching of the gospel.

The Preaching of the Law does not primarily cause Anfechtung, it draws Unbelief into the open

The preaching of the law within a sermon that passes the muster of FC V is always followed by a faithful preaching of the gospel. This can be seen as the work of the law occurring in a "controlled situation." This banal language is nevertheless helpful to distinguish the Christian preaching of God's law in the context of a sermon from the slew of accusations and legalisms—with and without Scriptural backing—which the Christian, and indeed, every person, is faced with all the time. In these, the law or a law is present and active but disconnected from the gospel, i.e. "uncontrolled." In the endless forms it may take, this situation of law disconnected from the gospel presents a great challenge to Christian certainty, i.e. to the strength of reflexive faith. A Christian subjected to such uncontrolled legal accusation is forced to reckon with two voices of God: the condemning voice of the law speaking in the moment and the pardoning voice of the gospel he or she has heard in the past. The situation that develops, whereby the *fides reflexa* presents more in the way of doubt than in the way of certainty, belongs to the category of *Anfechtung*; for Luther, the Christian is in a situation like that of Abraham at Mt. Moriah, forced to reckon with God telling him on the one hand that his offspring would be a great nation, and on the other to sacrifice his son. Even

---

41. Cf. FC SD V:10, (KW 583 = *BSLK* 954–55).

as a Christian has faith in Christ's salvific work, the law tells him not to, that redemption is not for sinners such as him.

In the uncontrolled situation, whether the legal accusation is divine law or purely human law is of little concern. What matters is only that it is effective in its condemnation, that also the Christian individual is stricken by it with a guilty conscience, i.e. driven toward despair. Therein, even a law that has no authority of its own is given authority. With that authority, it sows unbelief and *Anfechtung* by challenging Christians' certainty about their standing before God and leaving Christians to answer that question on their own.

It is because this sort of law-proclamation challenges the faith of the Christian on a daily basis that the law must be continuously preached from the pulpit. In the "controlled situation," the law's accusation is placed in service of the larger preaching goal of creating and sustaining faith—an activity that references the inconstant *fides reflexa*, not the *fides directa*. In the controlled situation of the law/gospel sermon, it does not create a situation in the category of *Anfechtung*, but rather "reproves unbelief," that is: in the sermon, the Law uncovers the weakness in the *fides reflexa* which serves in uncontrolled conditions as a receiving point for the accusation that leads to doubt and *Anfechtung*. The preaching of the gospel that accompanies the law then assures the Christian that divine forgiveness applies also precisely here and thus strengthens faith to withstand also accusations in this particular vein.

In preaching, not any law but only the law which has divine authority is to be employed. If it were simply the task to create doubt and banish it, any law might do. But in as far as it is actually the responsibility of the preacher not to create new doubt, but to uncover existing, well-founded doubt and then strengthen faith against it, he must preach with the authority he has, which is the authority of Scripture. This preaching has an eschatological focus: to instill a faith that will respond on the Last Day by looking to Christ. As such, the preaching task must deal with such accusations as will also fall on that day. Faith that withstands the accusation of having violated God's law will also withstand the accusation of violating human laws; the reverse cannot be so easily assumed.

It would be mistaken to understand the suggestion here as being that the goal of the preacher in preaching the law is to elucidate a situation of *Anfechtung*.[42] Rather, it remains always in the service of the preaching of the gospel. In view of the above observations on Brenz's catechism and of

---

42. Bonhoeffer warns about understanding *Anfechtung* as a "dialectical point of transition toward faith." Rather, it is the "real end of sinners, their death" (*Act and Being*, 149).

the statement in FC V, that the law "reproves unbelief," it is rather the case that proper preaching of the law and the gospel prepares the *fides reflexa* to withstand the improper preaching of the law. For if the law, in revealing sin, also draws unbelief into the open, it then effectively forces the Christian to reckon with his own lack of faith. This is, however, in the sort of preaching espoused in FC V, followed by the gospel, which creates faith in the place of that unbelief. In Brenz's language, one would say that the Christian, forced to look at himself under the condemnation of the law, becomes unable to see his own faith, where "faith" is, among other things, the sign for himself that he is a Christian. The preaching of the gospel mends the wound, leaving the faith stronger than it was before by bringing to light again that which sin and the law had obscured. Where faith has been strengthened to stand against the condemnation of God's word, both in the conscience and in the final judgment, it is certainly then also strengthened to stand against false human laws, which can condemn in the conscience although they have no voice in the final judgment.

Not quantifiable

A few notes should still be made of this conception of faith, which is by no means an exhaustive treatment. The distinctions between visible and invisible or direct and reflexive faith recognize the objectivity of the gift of faith, but are particularly valuable for their attention to the subjective aspect of being a Christian oscillating between doubt and certainty.

Brenz recognizes that children, left taught, risk losing the benefits of baptism. Properly understood, he warns against the failure of the parents to teach the child whereupon its confidence rests. Regardless of the parents' actions, the daily legalistic accusations of life will reach the child. The question is: will it, in the face of this, place its trust in the gift received, or in something else?

This makes the danger—and the reason that the *fides reflexa* must be constantly strengthened—not that the Christian slips into doubt, but that the Christian slips into such a despair that he places his faith somewhere else entirely. A change of religion or an explicit denial of salvation through Jesus Christ might be the form this takes, but it might, of course, be more subtle. At any rate, the uncertainty about the gift of faith given in baptism and the explicit rejection of it are to be sharply distinguished, although the first, left unchecked, threatens to lead to the second.

Finally, the implication that every Christian inhabits a position somewhere on a scale of sorts between extreme confidence and extreme doubt could seem to lend credence to the evaluation in American Evangelicalism that some Christians are particularly "strong." While the language of strong or weak faith certainly has its place, there is no warrant here for the rise of a kind of faith-phariasism. The very point of speaking about reflexive faith is that such reflection inevitably leads to doubt, and the treatment of such doubt always directs the Christian to stop reflecting and to look outside himself.

ASSURING THE FAITHFUL

Reflective faith is a consequence of the Christian evaluating himself and his standing before God. The uncertain result of this self-evaluation means that one could as easily speak of reflective doubt as of reflective faith. Whatever it is called, it provides strong grounds for the never-ending proclamation of the gospel *extra nos*.

FC SD V:21 distinguishes the comfort of the gospel in the strict sense from the law as follows:

> [T]he gospel . . . teaches what people should believe, namely, that they receive from God the forgiveness of sins; that is, that the Son of God, our Lord Christ, has taken upon himself the curse of the law and borne it, atoned and paid for all our sins; that through him alone we are restored to God's grace, obtain the forgiveness of sins through faith, and are delivered from death and all the punishments of our sins and are saved eternally.[43]

The gospel does not make faith visible to the Christian again by showing him where to look or what to look for in himself, but by directing his attention away from that search entirely. The gospel directs the Christian—and thereby also his faith—toward that which truly is *extra nos*, namely the forgiveness of sins won on the cross.

When the man with the possessed son was brought by Jesus to question the presence of his own faith and cry out for help, Jesus responded by giving him something to believe in: he cast out the possessing spirit and healed his son. The man in doubt about his faith was led to look away from himself entirely, and in this way his faith was strengthened. The same occurs with the disciples, who in the face of having been unable to heal the boy on the strength of their own faith are directed to prayer.

This is instructive for the homiletical task. Where unbelief is uncovered through the preaching of the law—a preaching which inevitably leads

---

43. KW 585 = *BSLK* 958–59.

a person to look inward at himself, the gospel must follow as that which draws him back out of himself to look to his salvation. In this way, assurance is provided. Those who already have received the gift of faith in its entirety are assured. Their faith is not trust in the absence of doubt, but rather trust tainted by doubt. The strengthening of faith, the assurance of the faithful, consists in uncovering this doubt and replacing it with faith. In this sense, it is certainly proper to speak, even among those who already have faith, of "creating faith" in the sermon.

BIBLIOGRAPHY

Bonhoeffer, Dietrich. *Act and Being: Transcendental Philosophy and Ontology in Systematic Theology*, edited by Wayne W. Floyd Jr. Translated by H. Martin Rumscheidt. Minneapolis: Fortress, 1996.
Brenz, Johannes. *Catechismus Pia Et Utili Explicatione Illustratus*. Wittenberg, 1553.
———. *Katechismus Erläutert*. Translated by Friedrich August Schütz. Leipzig: Friedrich Fleischer, 1852.
Delitzsch, Franz. *A System of Biblical Psychology*. Translated by Robert Ernest Wallis. Edinburgh: T. & T. Clark, 1867.
Gummelt, Volker. "Hollaz, David." In RPP 6:210.
Hollaz, David. *Examen theologicum acromaticum*, 1763. Reprint, Darmstadt: Wissenschaftliche Buchgesellschaft, 1971.
Lenski, R. C. H. *The Interpretation of St. Mark's Gospel*: Minneapolis: Augsburg, 1964.
Lührmann, Dieter. *Das Markusevangelium* Handbuch Zum Neuen Testament. Tübingen: Mohr/Siebeck, 1987.
Pesch, Rudolf. *Das Markusevangelium. Teil 2: Kommentar Zu Kap. 8,27—16,20*. Herders Theologischer Kommentar Zum Neuen Testament. Freiburg: Herder, 1977.
Pieper, Francis. *Christian Dogmatics*. Translated by Theodor Engelder and John Theodore Mueller. Vol. 2. St. Louis: Concordia, 1951.
Walch, Johann Georg. "Kirchen-Postille Evangelien-Teil." In *Dr. Martin Luthers Sämtliche Schriften*, edited by Martin Luther, 11. Groß Oesingen: Lutherischen Buchhandlung Heinrich Harms, 1987.

7

The Difference of Differentiating Address

The "We," "I," and "You," of Preaching, and the Gospel as the Gospel

—Jonathan Mumme

FLATTENED "WE" AND CONTRIVED "YOU": OBSERVATIONS FROM LUTHERAN PEWS

Words make all the difference in the world. Differences of content[1] and of tone[2] are obviously decisive. Does person, i.e. the differentiation between first, second, and third person in their singular and plural forms,[3] make a difference? It would be hard to imagine certain content conveyed as it is, if the address were changed. Could intuitive technology for the shaping of individuals' lives be marketed under itPad, ourPod, or theirPhone? Could

---

1. "If you can't say something nice, don't say anything at all."

2. "A soft answer turns away wrath, but a harsh word stirs up anger" (Prov 15:1). "Speak softly and carry a big stick" (Theodore Roosevelt).

3. In English, first person: "I" and "we"; second: "you" (singular) and "you" (plural); third: "he/she/it" and "they."

Burger King's® sell saying "Have it *our* way!"?[4] Could U.S. Senator Barack Obama have shown himself an optimistic man of the people under the motto, "Yes, *I* can!" or "Yes, *you* can!"?[5] Could you respond to your sweetheart with "We love each other," the next time that person says, "I love you."? Deprivation of differentiation of person also deprives content and restricts the delivery of what content is mustered.

This essay means to contemplate the difference—the implications—of differentiated address for the task of preaching and for the office and identity of preacher. Its point of departure is empirical: the author, a cognizant hearer of Lutheran sermons for some three decades, has experienced decidedly little in the way of differentiated address from Lutheran pulpits. The Lutheran preaching and preachers experienced do not really address the hearers as hearers by speaking to them in the second person.[6] Some Lutheran preachers will make an effort to state that certain things are done or said by God "for you." But simply tacking these two words on the end of a few third person statements hardly makes for robust second person address; as something rather contrived or even forced, this phenomenon actually shows second person address to be all too elusive.

This deprivation of the second person address is accompanied by a reticence of most Lutheran preachers to refer to themselves (and their fellow clergy[7]) in preaching. A pastor may talk about himself, often anecdotally, but beyond the anecdotal "I," the *Gegenüber* of a ministerial We is missing.[8] Ministers preaching to the pews I have occupied lack a We of ministers distinct from the You of the hearers. This deprivation of differentiated address indicates how such pastors understand of themselves, affects what they communicate to their congregations, and finally impacts the preaching of the gospel as the gospel.

---

4. "Have it your way," is a recognized advertising slogan of the company.

5. Obama's 2008 presidential campaign was conducted under the motto, "Yes, we can!"

6. Colloquialisms, such as the general American, "You know, . . ." and the rather Midwestern, "You bet," hardly amount to differentiated address.

7. As the fourteenth article of the Augsburg Confession as clarified by the Apology states that no one would preach who is not ordained, for the purposes of this article, it will be assumed that all Lutheran preachers are ordained clergy or are at least studying to be. KW 46–47 = *BSLK* 69,2–4.

8. The German *Gegenüber* stands for non-antagonistic opposition; it describes the placement of *two* things in relation to one another, a placement that maintains two distinct points. Because the English "opposition" often carries antagonist association the German term will be used. A pastor saying "we" of the colleagues of a given congregation's pastoral team does not obviate the point.

Despite the current tendency against differentiated address, such flattened speech has not been characteristic of all preachers and indeed not of some whom Christian and especially Lutheran preachers claim as teachers. "*Our* mouth has been open to *you*, O Corinthians. *Our* heart has been enlarged. *You* are not confined by *us*; rather *you* are confined by *your* affections."[9] The differentiated mode of address exhibited by Paul was not lost on Martin Luther, who in his latter sermons readily and fluidly differentiated between himself and his fellow ministers on one hand and his (other) hearers on the other by means of his mode of address. Before taking up the implications of differentiated address for the task of preaching and the office of preacher today, we turn first to observations about such address with St. Paul and with Martin Luther.

DIFFERENTIATED ADDRESS IN PAUL ON THE BASIS OF 1 AND 2 CORINTHIANS

Some preliminary observations about differentiated address, as used by St. Paul, delimit the scope of this undertaking. First, letters are not exactly sermons, and the two may not simply be equated. Paul's letters are, however, a form of address, and some directly testify to being written with the intent that they be read aloud in the church's liturgical assembly.[10] In this regard, most of Paul's epistles bear similarity to a sermon manuscript, which itself is not yet a sermon, but a document written to be delivered orally in a liturgical assembly of the church. Secondly, Paul does not everywhere differentiate between himself and his fellow ministers on the one hand and other Christians on the other. Thirdly, in letters where Paul does employ a differentiated mode of address, one cannot in every instance say with certainty whether the first person plural ("we") refers to Paul and his fellow ministers or includes all of his recipients/hearers.[11] Within these parameters it can be

---

9. 2 Cor 6:11–12; translation and emphasis mine.

10. Col 4:16 and 1 Thess 5:27. See Winger, "Orality," 200–241, 55–68; see also his "The Spoken Word," 133–51, esp. 143–48; such epistles (i.e., those not composed for a single recipient, as, for example, Philemon) are essentially preaching with appended prescripts and postscripts, whose formulation assumes oral delivery in the liturgical assembly prior to the celebration of the Holy Supper. See also Liebert, "The 'Apostolic Form of Writing,'" 433–40; the apostolic form of writing, as evident in 1 Cor, assumes oral delivery in the presence of the recipients.

11. The ambiguity of the reference of certain first person plural pronouns is sometimes highlighted by the manuscripts, where second person plural pronouns appear as variants: ὑμεῖς vs. ἡμεῖς, ὑμῶν vs. ἡμῶν, ὑμῖν vs. ἡμῖν, and ὑμᾶς vs. ἡμᾶς. See, for example, ὑμᾶς as a variant for ἡμᾶς at 1 Cor 8:8. Regarding such variants see C. E. B. Cranfield, "Changes in Person and Number" especially 280, 88–89n1: all other things

demonstrated that Paul can and sometimes does use a differentiated mode of address, wherein the first person at points refers the apostolic minister(s) and that this differentiated mode of address is not bare happenstance or just antiquated custom, but theologically significant.[12]

Paul makes ready use of the second person in his address, also referring to himself with the first person singular ("I," "me," "my"). Identifying antecedents of the first person singular and the second person plural is relatively uncomplicated.[13] Paul's uses the first person plural ("we," "us," "our") proves more difficult.[14] A number of different uses of the first person plural can and must be distinguished.[15] With a *pluralis sociativus* or "associating plural," the speaker/writer associates himself with his addressees and them with him.[16] A *ministerial plural* points to a larger group of ministers of which Paul is in some way a part.[17] With a *literary plural* Paul is simply

---

being equal, given the tendency to assimilate, a reading evidencing change in person is to be preferred.

12. A differentiated mode of first person address can also be employed in other ways; differentiation of Jewish from Gentile Christians with the latter's inclusion into a unified "we," is, for example, a powerful device in Eph 2.

13. Llewelyn, "§25 Ammonios to Apollonios," 169-77, offers some observations about differentiation in the second person. The observations are worthy but not of consequence for this inquiry and will not be pursued further here. See also Cranfield, "Changes in Person and Number," 280.

14. For a listing of the frequency of the first person (singular and) plural in the letters of the Pauline corpus see Llewelyn, "§25 Ammonios to Apollonios," 171, Table 25.1 (which takes into account both verbs and pronouns); the "phenomenon for the 1st person . . . is more complicated" (171).

15. For the content of this paragraph we follow primarily Byrskog, "Co-Senders," 232-33.

16. This is also referred to as "the inclusive 'we'" (Wallace, *Greek Grammar*, 393-99) or "the literary plural" (sic; cf. n18 below) (Llewelyn, "§25 Ammonios to Apollonios," 170). Carrez, "Le 'Nous,'" 74-86, refers to this as "Le Nous-Vous ou Nous-communauté."

17. Also referred to as the "exclusive 'we'" (Wallace, *Greek Grammar* 393-99). "Le Nous-Ministres" and "Le Nous-Apôtres" in Carrez's analysis of 2 Cor can be ordered to this category. See Verhoff for "das missionarische Wir" and "das apostolische Wir" in "The Senders," 422n17, citing Klauck, *2. Korintherbrief,* 12-13. See also Schmeller, "Exkurs," 61, "das missionarische Wir." Clear distinction cannot always be drawn between first person plural references to particular co-workers or co-senders (cf. Byrskog, n15 above) and more general references to a larger group of fellow ministers. For example, Sosthenes is mentioned in 1 Cor 1:1, but in 1:23 the "we" of the preachers indicates a wider group (cf. 1 Cor 1:12) with which further specific persons come to be associated: Apollos (1 Cor 3:4-6, 22; 4:6) and Timothy (1 Cor 4:17). At points, Paul does reference specific co-workers and co-senders, and more general reference to fellow ministers also clearly belongs to his idiom. In this article specific co-workers and co-senders are understood as belonging to this larger group and will be referred to under the category of the *ministerial plural.*

referring to himself, though making use of a plural instead of a singular.[18] In distinguishing between these uses of the first person plural, first the context and then the content of the passage are of import. However, even when careful attention is given to these "[i]t is sometimes . . . impossible to be entirely certain to what extent 'we' includes the addressees or only Paul and his co-workers."[19] In such instances the *pluralis sociativus* is to be preferred over the ministerial plural, "because what is true of all Christians is true for Paul and his co-workers, while what is true for Paul and his co-workers is not necessarily true for every Christian."[20] Both the *pluralis sociativus* and the ministerial plural are real plurals and as such are to be preferred to the literary plural.

Paul's letters to the Corinthians offer poignant example of a theologically significant differentiation between Paul and his fellow ministers on the one hand and other Christians on the other. This differentiation is evidenced and enacted by address in the second person plural, the antecedents of which are set opposite, that is *gegenüber*, antecedents of certain uses of the first person plural. Paul addresses the addressees as a "you" distinct from a particular "we" of the apostolic ministers. Two conjoining lines of observation are thus important. First, the simple fact that Paul addresses his addressees in the second person is significant; instances of this mode of address will be observed. This is, however, not to say that Paul addresses his addressees *only* in the second person; he does not. He also fluidly employs the first person, but its plural is employed in a differentiating manner, at points referencing the apostolic ministers specifically and at points including all the addressees in this "we." Therefore, secondly, instances of a differentiated "we" will be noted.

In addition to the second person plural of 1 Cor 1:3, which speaks "grace" "to the church of God that is in Corinth, to those sanctified in Christ Jesus, called holy"[21] as part of the letter's greeting, the first letter to the Corinthians is replete with second-person address. For instance, second person

---

18. See Cranfield, "Changes in Person and Number," 285. Also referred to as the "epistolary plural" (Verhoff, "The Senders," 421) or "editorial 'we'" (Wallace, *Greek Grammar*, 393–99). "Le Nous-Je" in Carrez's analysis of 2 Cor can be ordered to this category.

19. Byrskog, "Co-Senders," 232–33.

20. Ibid., 233.

21. Translation mine.

verbs and pronouns amass at 1 Cor 1:4–15,[22] 3:1–5,[23] 4:6–8,[24] 11:17–22,[25] and 15:1–3a[26]; in general chapters 4–6, 10–11, 14, and 16 exhibit high concentrations of second person address.[27]

Not only does Paul address the Corinthian addressees as "you," he also enlists a "we" that refers to himself and his fellow ministers that is distinct from a "we" shared with the addressees in general. Although "most occurrences of the first person plural reflect Paul's identification with the Christians in Corinth"[28] and are instances of a *pluralis sociativus*, other theologically significant uses of the ministerial We are also at hand in the letter. In 1 Cor 1:23; 2:6–16; 3:9; 4:1, 6–13; 9:4–5, 10–12; 15:11, 14–15, 30[29] Paul is referencing himself and fellow ministers with his use of "we." The differentiation of chapter 4 is abundantly clear. The "us" who are to be regarded as "servants of Christ and stewards of the mysteries of God" (4:1) is not a reference to Paul along with all Corinthian addressees, but rather refers to "us apostles" (4:9) with special mention in this instance of himself

---

22. E.g., 1 Cor 1:10, "I appeal to you, brothers, by the name of our Lord Jesus Christ, that all of you agree and that there be no divisions among you, but that you be united in the same mind and the same judgment."

23. E.g., 1 Cor 3:2, "I fed you with milk, not solid food, for you were not ready for it. And even now you are not yet ready."

24. E.g., 1 Cor 4:7, "For who sees anything different in you? What do you have that you did not receive? If then you received it, why do you boast as if you did not receive it?"

25. E.g., 1 Cor 11:22, "What! Do you not have houses to eat and drink in? Or do you despise the church of God and humiliate those who have nothing? What shall I say to you? Shall I commend you in this? No, I will not."

26. "Now I would remind you, brothers, of the gospel I preached to you, which you received, in which you stand, and by which you are being saved, if you hold fast to the word I preached to you, unless you believed in vain. For I delivered to you as of first importance what I also received: . . ."

27. Among these portions chap. 16 is somewhat unique, dealing with a number of organizational matters, the planning of visits, and greetings.

28. Byrskog,"Co-Senders," 241n51 lists 1Cor 1:2–3, 7–9, 10b, 18, 30; 5:4(?) 7–8; 6:3, 11, 14; 8:1, 4, 6, 8; 9:10 [sic; cf. n29 below where classified differently], 25; 10:1, 6, 8–9, 11, 16–17, 22; 11:16, 31–32; 12:13; 13:9, 12a; 15:3b, 19, 32, 49, 51–52, 57; 16:22. Cf. Verhoff, "The Senders," 418–21, for analysis and commentary on (only) the pronouns among these instances of the first person plural.

29. Byrskog, "Co-Senders," 241–44. One might consider whether 11:16 (see, for example, Verhoff, "The Senders," 418, 20) or even 15:19 might be grouped with this category. In the main Byrskog's classifications of the first persons plural in 1 Cor are very cogent, but not every instance can be decided absolutely. A definitive list of associative versus ministerial uses is neither possible (cf. n18 and n19 above)—indeed Paul can switch references of the first person plural in a single sentence (cf. Rom 3:9)—nor necessary to our purposes. *That* a differentiated "we" referring to the ministers in readily employed in 1 Cor is clear.

(4:3–4) and Apollos (4:6). The use of second person address in the context surrounding 2:2–16, namely 2:1–4, and 3:1–9, make the antecedent of "we," "us," and "our" all the more clear, but such differentiation can also take place within a single verse, as it does in 9:11: "If we have sown spiritual things among you, is it too much if we reap material things from you?"

Since even a cursory look at the theological role that differentiated address may play in the whole of 1 Cor would exceed the limitations of this essay, we will restrict ourselves to a few comments about such differentiation in the first main section of the letter, 1:10–4:21, where Paul turns his first attention to the profound divisions evident in the Corinthian church. On the one hand, a differentiation of address could be viewed as somewhat inescapable given the divisions among the Corinthian Christians.[30] However, there is not only a differentiation of division evident in statements such as "[E]ach of you says, 'I'm *Paul's*,' or 'I'm *Apollos's*,'" or 'I'm *Cephas's*,' or 'I'm *Christ's*,'" which is deemed harmful and not of Christ.[31] There is also a differentiation of office, evident simply in addressing a "you" (1:12) out of which is said, "*I* follow *Paul*"; this differentiation is not rebuked but assumed as true and divine, so long as Paul, Apollos, and Cephas are not differentiated from and pitted against one another, but rather, along with their work, seen and understood as one, being servants of Christ and stewards of God's mysteries.[32] The proper, differentiated but not divided relationship is expressed when Paul and Apollos (and by implication Cephas) stand as a unified "we" of "*Servants* through whom *you* believed, even as to each *the Lord* gave. . . . For *God's* co-workers are *we*; *God's* field, *God's* building are *you*."[33] Taking up factionalizing divisions in order to break them down, Paul does not hesitate to employ a differentiated mode of address that itself affirms a differentiation of ministers and hearers.

Paul's answer to divisions in the Christian congregation of Corinth is not perhaps the first that many Christians today might expect, namely a rejection of division by affirming undifferentiated unity and homogeneity in the church: "We're all one in Jesus; there are no differences here. So let's all get along." Rather, harmful schisms are addressed within a divine differentiation, a *Gegenüber*, of the apostolic ministers and those whom they serve. It is, in fact, precisely from the vantage point of an office differentiated and operative as such in the very address of 1 Cor that Paul can and does take up the divisions of the Corinthian congregation as he does. At the root of the

---

30. See 1 Cor 1:10: σχίσματα, schisms.
31. 1 Cor 1:12–13, translation mine; cf. 1:17 and 3:4.
32. 1 Cor 3:6–8 and 4:1.
33. 1 Cor 3:5, 9, translation mine.

divisions of the Corinthian congregation are a tendency toward and efforts at self-distinction, which is sought and achieved as wisdom and knowledge are understood and used in the way of power.[34] In this destructive[35] mix, Paul does not shift the issue from wisdom and knowledge to some other standard according to which distinction could also be achieved and out of which then division would also arise, but rather from a divinely differentiated position of apostolic minister, he rebukes the division, replacing the destructive assumption of personal and group identity by way of possessed or exercised power with the salutary Christian reality of divinely given station in which all is in fact possessed, and nothing lacks.[36] As Paul does not need to distinguish himself from Apollos, nor Paul and Apollos themselves from Cephas—and as Paul, Apollos, and Cephas are the servants and stewards they are as God has given them to be,[37] Paul may even present his and Apollos' relationship to one another as apostolic ministers as a picture of what is spiritual and mature as defined by Christ the crucified.[38] The opposite of self-distinguishing differentiation, which is achieved by the exercise of strength and power and gives rise to destructive division and schism, is the givenness of received identity and received station, which works in the way of gifts given and received, implying a *Gegenüber* alive and at work in 1 Cor, even in the very mode of address. This givenness may be understood under "grace," which itself is differentiated in relation to the addressees and to Paul.[39]

From a divinely distinct position Paul, along with his fellow ministers, addresses divisions rupturing the life of the Corinthian congregation. Already differentiated, as the mode of address attests, Paul and his fellow

34. Wisdom: 1 Cor 1:17, 19–22, 24, 30; 2:1, 4–7, 13; 3:19. Knowledge: 8:1–3, 7, 10–11 (informing especially 1 Cor 8–12). Both are related to how a word or words are spoken—to speech: see 1 Cor 1:5, 2:1–4.

35. Cf. 1 Cor 3:17.

36. The thanksgiving of 1 Cor 1:4–9 affirms the fullness of what is given and possessed in grace as a Christian theological reality that stands against the divisions that are taken up in 1:10–17. Related is the conclusion at 3:21–23 and the succinct summary of the notion in 4:7, "What do you have that you did not receive? And if you received, why boast as if not receiving?" For the relationship of "calling" (see 1 Cor 1:26) to station cf. 7:18–24.

37. 1 Cor 3:5.

38. Reading 1 Cor 2:1–3:8 in view of 1 Cor 4:5 and 9. Cf. 1 Cor 1:23. Here usage of the ministerial "we" overlaps with an intent of the *pluralis sociativus* in that there is an invitation here for the Corinthians to exhibit like-mindedness and according behavior. Efforts, however, to read a "'we' of the congregation" in 2:6–16 must undertake a good deal of theologizing prior to basic grammatical exegesis; as an example see Schottroff, "Das 'Wir' der Gemeinde," 50.

39. See 1 Cor 1:4 and 3:10.

ministers need not set themselves apart, and so are keenly poised to take up take up divisions within the life of the congregation.

2 Cor also evidences a differentiated mode of address. Address in the second person plural is readily observable throughout 2 Cor with 227 instances.[40] Additionally, a first person plural distinct from the addressees of the letter and referring to Paul and his fellow ministers is at play. Of the numerous instances of "we" in the letter,[41] many refer to Paul and his fellow ministers as such.[42] Thus, also in 2 Cor, a *Gegenüber* is clear: "The 'we' moves opposite a 'you,' that is, opposite the addressees."[43] This means, for example, that statements such as:

> But thanks be to God, who in Christ always leads us in triumphal procession, and through us spreads the fragrance of the knowledge of him everywhere. For we are the aroma of Christ to God among those who are being saved and among those who are perishing, to one a fragrance from death to death, to the other a fragrance from life to life.

are statements that Paul is making about himself and his fellow ministers.[44] This is not to say that in a second, theological sense, some such things

---

40. Carrez, "Le 'Nous,'" 475.

41. For a complete enumeration of the first person plural see ibid.

42. Carrez points to a ministerial "we" at 2 Cor 1:18–24; 2:14–16 (perhaps); 8:1–5, 18, 22, 24; 9:4; 12:11–21 (especially 12:18–19) and an apostolic "we" at 2 Cor 3:6 (to 3:6 cf. 3:1, 3); 10:4–8, 12–16; 13:8 (for 13:8 cf. 13:4–7; cf. in general 11:13, 15; 12:12). The relationship between apostles and ministers, as raised by Carrez, lies beyond the scope of this essay; both categories as pertinent to the differentiated "we," which we examine here. In addition to the passages that Carrez lists, Bryskog rightly argues the plurals of 2 Cor 1:4–8; 5:11–15; 6:1–11; and 7:2–13 refer to Paul and his co-workers ("Co-Senders," 245); see also Verhoff, "The Senders," 421: "[I[t seems to be wise to explain a plural as relating to more than one person, unless it is clear that a plural must be interpreted as an epistolary plural." The material provided by Carrez and Byrskog is not exhaustive; cf., for example, 2 Cor 1:9–14; 4:1–5:10 (especially given the use of the second person at 4:5, 12, 14–15, it seems rather obvious that a differentiation exists at least in 2 Cor 4); 10:3. Some instances are perhaps more debatable. Heavily debated are the first person plurals of 2 Cor 5:18–21; cf., for example, Wright, "On Becoming the Righteousness of God," 200–208. The fact that there is a *Gegenüber* here is abundantly clear from the first person being set opposite the second person in both 5:20 and 6:1, but argument can be made for a *pluralis sociativus* in 5:21, understanding this verse as central kerygmatic content of the preaching indicated by *parakaleo* in 5:20 and 6:1. For *parakaleo* as a verb indicating preaching see Winger, "Orality as Key," 264–66.

43. "Das Wir tritt einem Ihr, also den Addressaten, gegenüber" (Schmeller, "Exkurs," 60).

44. 2 Cor 2:14–16a; a differentiated "we" is clear on the basis of 3:1–6; note the sufficiency theme tying 2:16b to 3:6 with clear differentiation of address in 3:1–3. The motif of fragrance unto both life and death parallels the import of authority for building

cannot be understood as being true of all Christians. On a basic exegetical level they must stand as the differentiated statements they are, with this differentiation informing theological conclusions drawn from them.

Having recognized a differentiated mode of address, wherein Paul speaks as a member of a ministerial group distinct from the addressees of 2 Cor, one may then note the pointedness of the address. These "ministers of a new covenant,"[45] in addressing the addressees in Corinth, do not speak simply within that congregation, but rather "in Christ,"[46] and thus, in some sense, from without, being in themselves a "fragrance" of life (to those being saved) or of death (to those perishing) that comes and is applied to the addressees.[47] Especially where things with the Corinthian addressees pull in the direction of death and peril, the external position of the *Gegenüber* makes keen rebuke possible:

> Our mouth has been open to you, O Corinthians; our heart has been enlarged [to you]. You are not being restricted in us, but you are being restricted in your own affections. Now, [in] like exchange (I speak as to children) you also be enlarged! Do not be yoked with others, [namely] unbelievers.[48]

The goal of such pointed rebuke, delivered from a distinct position in a differentiated mode of address, is godly grief unto repentance and reconciliation to God.[49]

The possibility of what the ministers might be, not just among the addressees but also to or for them, is echoed in Paul's talk of what he and his fellow ministers have been given in this direction:

> See what is before your eyes. If anyone is confident with regard to himself that he is Christ's, let him reckon again with himself that just as he is Christ's, so also are we. For even if I boast somewhat more abundantly of our authority, which the Lord gave for building you up and not for tearing [you] down, I will not be ashamed.[50]

---

up, but also, if need be, for tearing down (cf. nn51–53 below). Similar is 2 Cor 10:3–6.

45. 2 Cor 3:6.

46. 2 Cor 2:17.

47. 2 Cor 2:16.

48. 2 Cor 6:11–14a, translation mine. The exhortation of 6:13b is repeated at 7:2, "Make room for us." Cf. n9 above.

49. See 2 Cor 7:9 and 5:18–20.

50. 2 Cor 10:7–8, translation mine; for boasting see also 10:13–15. Cf. n82 below.

Have you been thinking all along that we have been defending ourselves to you? It is in the sight of God that we have been speaking in Christ, and all for your upbuilding, beloved.[51]

The ministers' God-given authority to build up the addressees is evinced by the differentiated address. Toward this end Paul and his fellow ministers have been among the addressees (not least by way of such [epistolary] preaching). That there exist "strongholds" and "arguments" that will instead be torn down, that this authority given for building up can be flipped into something severe, is not a marker of God's gracious will, but rather of closed ears and the sad circumstance of some sorting themselves out and so being sorted out of those who are "in the faith" and "in/among" whom "is Jesus Christ."[52] Practically, this differentiated address communicates and enacts the very theological reality that underlies it; the divine authority given to the ministers for building up, or contrariwise their authority for tearing down, is affirmed and enacted by address from the differentiated position, the *Gegenüber*, of the ministerial "we."

In calling attention to disparities between Paul's (and Luther's) mode of address and that of modern preachers, a disparity among preachers evident *within* 2 Cor itself is worthy of note. As Paul distinguishes between his and others' ministry and identity over against those of the so-called super-apostles,[53] it becomes clear that these super-apostles have what status they have by way of *ability* to expound on the written word in the worship assembly.[54] Paul, along with his ministerial cohort, is who he is and has what authority he has by way of divine gift.[55] A divinely bestowed status and authority form the foundation and define the point of departure for conduct, actions, and words (including mode of address). Speaking and acting to achieve status marks and opposite course. Where a different gospel, a different spirit, and another Christ are being peddled,[56] the difference between divine monergism and synergism in the operations of the new covenant's ministry proves clarifying. Are the ministers who they are by a gifting action

---

51. 2 Cor 12:19. Here, as with 2 Cor 6:11–14a (see n48 above) there follows a reproof of sin: 2 Cor 12:20–21. Also for divinely given authority to upbuilding, see 2 Cor 13:9–11.

52. See 2 Cor 10:4–6, 8; 13:5, 10.

53. 2 Cor 11:5 and 12:11.

54. Oliveira, *Die Diakonie*, 160–61.

55. Ibid., 148. Paul received the firm conviction of being an apostle as a *gift* from God.

56. 2 Cor 11:4–5.

of God,[57] or does "ministerial" standing come by setting oneself above others by means of ability?[58] The latter understanding cannot honestly account for and appropriate the poverty and death of Christ;[59] the former can with confidence expect and bear with the dying of the ministers toward the life of those they are given to serve.[60]

DIFFERENTIATED ADDRESS IN THE LATTER SERMONS OF MARTIN LUTHER

The theological import and practical application of differentiated address, such as employed by Paul, was not lost on the sixteenth-century German friar, professor, preacher, and reformer, Martin Luther. In his mature preaching, Luther readily and fluidly appropriated both a mode and a material of address that distinguished him and his fellow ministers from other Christians. In how he addressed his hearers and in what he said to them about ministers and other Christians as such, Luther's address evidences differentiation.

Preaching, for example, on baptism in 1538 and praising with it absolution and the supper, Luther differentiates between the preachers/ministers on the catechizing side of this instruction and others who are on its receiving end. "Thus *you* amply hear of that which godly [people] should learn and know. *We* ourselves can boast with a good conscience, for *we* have taught *you* everything that God has revealed. . . . Thus I hope that *we* have fulfilled *our* office."[61] When a "we" moved opposite (*gegenüber*) a "you" in Luther's preaching, his hearers identified this "we" with the ministers: "*We*—I and *your* parsons—know, that *we* have an office of preaching that has been entrusted to *us* by God, and *we* know that *we* must answer for *our* preaching."[62] At the root of such differentiation and underpinning this

---

57. See 2Cor 3:4–6.

58. The superior position of the "super-apostles" is found in the ὑπέρ ("over and above," "beyond," "more than") of ὑπερλίαν; 2 Cor 11:5 and 12:11, cf. n55 above. Note the comparative mathematics; see 2 Cor 10:12.

59. Cf. 2 Cor 8:9. Honesty: cf. 2 Cor 11:13 ("super-apostles" as "false apostles").

60. See 2 Cor 4, especially 4:12. For this reason Paul's boast comes as the so-called "Fool's Speech" (2 Cor 11:16–33), which subverts the notion of an attained, competitive standing by making suffering and weakness the content of the inane enterprise.

61. Pr. 1698 in *WA* 46:176.16–25. Numeration of sermons ("Pr." for *Predigt*) here cited according to Aland, *Hilfsbuch*. All translations and emphases mine. "Office" reflects Luther's use of *Amt* as preferred translation for *diakonia* and cognates in such texts at 2 Cor 3:6–9; 4:1; 5:18; and 2 Tim 4:5.

62. Pr. 1849, *WA* 47:564.24–26.

practiced *Gegenüber* was not the proclivity of this preacher, but the mandate and institution of the ministry by Christ, who himself is present and active in the preaching of the ministry or preaching office:[63]

> "... To me is given [all authority in heaven and on earth. Therefore go and teach all peoples and baptize them in the name of the Father and of the Son and of the Holy Spirit, and teach them to keep all that I have entrusted you. And behold, I am with you all the days until the end of the world"]. If this were not the case, [*you*] would not be looking at me [right now], and *I* [wouldn't be looking at] *you*. If Christ had died but did not live, not another word would be spoken of him, but because his word and the scriptures are here, that is an absolutely certain sign, that he is present."[64]

Luther found ground for such differentiated address in the New Testament. Preaching on 1 Pet 5:6–7, for example, he expounded differentiated humility, namely humility in relation to the ministers/preachers and to "all others, [you] who [are] not preachers nor in the spiritual [regiment], but are who you are."[65] He interpreted 1 Pet 5:8–9 accordingly, expounding a watchfulness against the devil along the lines of the two regiments, with the ministers/preachers/clergy responsible for resisting the devil's lies according to their office, whereas the secular authorities were to resist his murderous ambitions according to theirs.[66] But his foremost teacher in differentiated address was Paul, not least in his correspondence with the Corinthians.

A stark example of what Luther could theologically and homiletically appropriate of Paul's differentiated address can be seen in a 1540 sermon on 2 Cor 3:4ff.[67] While affirming Christological, apostolic, and historic continuity of the ministry as well as the divine instrumentality of the ministers,

---

63. "The (ecclesiastical) ministry" and "the preaching office" have, on the basis of the Augsburg Confession, become Lutheran ways of speaking about the office of ministers/preachers. AC V, title; KW 40–41 = *BSLK* 58,1.

64. Pr. 1724, *WA* 46:392.19–22, reading *vides* for *video*. See Matt 28:18–20. That Luther is speaking of the sermon that is taking place is made clear by Stoltz's record of the sermon (version "S" at *WA* 46:392.31–32) "If Christ were not seated at the right hand [of the Father], this sermon would not be taking place among us." Note that "the word" and "the Scriptures" are not simply the same thing; here "the word" is referring to the preaching that is taking place. To the relationship between preaching and the Scriptures in Luther's thought cf. Mumme, "Von dem Buchstaben," 13–22, esp. 17–20.

65. Pr. 1885, *WA* 47:795.20–21. Cf. the address to elders in 1 Pet 5:1–4 and to the young in 5:5.

66. Pr. 1891, *WA* 47:839–46. For the devil as liar and murderer see John 8:44.

67. For a detailed analysis of this sermon (Pr. 1926, *WA* 49:167–70), see Mumme, *Die Präsenz Christi*, 53–92.

Luther—not only in his material but also with his mode of address—asserts a differentiation of these ministers into the active and serving side of a *Gegenüber* that belongs to the very essence of the Christian church. Speaking of the ministry or the preaching office as something entrusted to the ministers for the benefit of the Christian hearers he says:

> God entrusts to *us* his most valuable treasure, and in it are all the gifts of the Holy Spirit. . . . As John 14[:23 says,] 'We will come to him [and make a dwelling with him].' How does [he] dwell? [He dwells] there[, where] *you* have his word and preaching office (which he has given) and the tongue of the preacher [– where] *you* have baptism, [the] sacrament[, and the] keys."[68]

The dwelling and presence of God in the present among these people entails an instance that makes this presence a gift for them, unmistakably given through its delivery in a *Gegenüber* that God himself has instituted for this purpose.[69] "*You* receive grace and mercy . . . through the preaching office[. . . . Therefore] *I* am to preach and administer [the sacraments]."[70] "Now, on the other hand[, *you* are a new person], and this through *my* finger and *my* tongue."[71] In line with Paul, who addressed the Corinthians from within a ministerial We, Luther understood himself and his fellow ministers as stewards of God's mysteries,[72] a group differentiated but not separated from the people of God, existing to deliver his gifts and his presence to them as pure gift.

Decisive also for the mode of Luther's preaching was the conviction that the current ministers are the successors of the apostles, who exist as such for the salvation of those whom they serve. Paraphrasing Jesus' words in John 20:21, Luther expounds:

> "Just as the Father [has sent me, so I am sending you.]" That is, ["I am sending *you*,] so that *you apostles and [your] successors* do the same work, that I [have done], for which I also have come[. This work is] then, that *people* who are willing to be helped, be helped [and rescued] from death, [but] not those, [who] on the

---

68. Pr. 1926, WA 49:169.1–5. As substantiation for the treasure being identified as the ministry or the preaching office, see WA 49:168.34–35 and 49:169.17–18.

69. For the mandate and institution of the office of the ministry and the *Gegenüber* see n64 above and n88 below.

70. Pr. 1926, WA 49:169.30–32.

71. Pr. 1926, WA 49:169.35. Cf. 2 Cor 5:17.

72. Luther understood and expounded 1 Cor 4:1 as having to do with "the apostles, preachers, the pope [and] the cardinals" and not with "the people" (Pr. 2018, WA 51:96.9–10).

other hand [are unwilling to be helped]. This *you* also do. That is *your* regiment."[73]

Luther appropriates Paul's self- or apostolic-understanding on both theological and homiletical levels, and he communicates this as a piece of his own self- and ministerial-understanding to his hearers. Both explicitly in speaking about the office of the ministry and implicitly in his differentiating mode of address, Luther's preaching evidences another hallmark of Paul's work, namely his *confidence* as a servant or minister of Christ.

> ... [N]o Christian preacher since Paul has dared really to conceive of this notion. And if anywhere, this is the place where the ring connecting the reformation and the apostle's age closes. The boldness with which Paul speaks of his preaching office in 2 Cor 3 and 4, comes alive again in Luther.[74]

Therewith is already stated, that Luther thoroughly aligns the preaching of contemporary preachers with the preaching of the apostles.

This daring confidence can go so far as to find expression in a certain kind of boasting and what Luther refers to as a "salutary pride"[75]—salutary because this confidence and boasting do not seek status for the ministers, but rather the confidence and certainty among those whom they serve.

In a sermon preached for the first regular ordination in Wittenberg,[76] Luther exclaims and then repeats, "This confidence we must have!"[77] This confidence is that Christ himself speaks and deals with people through those whom Christ himself puts into the ministry/preaching office. Without the confidence of being an instrument, organ, and tool of Christ, a minister would better just give up preaching.[78] For this confidence underwrites and nourishes all that a preacher does; with it, Luther says, "*I* do all things with a glad heart, and *you* receive through *me* as through a mask of Christ."[79]

Would a preacher or minister speaking—preaching—of such personal confidence of his office not strike the wrong note, perhaps coming across

---

73. Pr. 1923, WA 49:138.26–29.

74. Hirsch, "Luthers Predigtweise," 16. For an exposition on confidence, boasting, sufficiency, boldness, and justification in 2 Cor, see Oliveira, *Die Diakonie*, 146–258.

75. Pr. 1372, WA 36:520.19.

76. See Pr. 1574, WA 41:457.32—458.8. For a detailed analysis of the sermon see Mumme, *Präsenz Christi*, 189–99 and 212–67. Cf. Krarup, *Die Ordination*, 183–88; and Lieberg, *Amt und Ordination*, 181–91.

77. Pr. 1574, WA 41:456.28 and 32.

78. Pr. 1574, WA 41:456.32–33.

79. Pr. 1574, WA 41:456.36–37. Further to confidence see Pr. 1926, WA 49:169.38–170.1 and (also boasting) 49:167.7–16.

as having a sort of boastful pride? Perhaps, but boasting, as confidence, is a category and so a tendency that Luther appropriated from Paul.[80] And this boastful confidence regarding the ministry is an insight that is of a piece with a decisive reformational insight regarding confidence and certainty in general; i.e. Luther *came* to this understanding:

> Once, when I was an inexperienced theologian and doctor, it seemed to me that Paul was silly, for in all his letters he often boasts of his call. But I did not understand his insight, for I was ignorant about the ministry of the word of God being so great a matter. I did not know anything about the doctrine of faith and a true conscience. For neither in the schools nor the churches was anything certain being taught, ... Therefore no one could understand the strength and power of this holy and spiritual boasting about the call, which serves first for the glory of God, secondly for the acknowledgement of our own ministry, and also for our own benefit and for that of the people.[81]

And this boasting itself finds expression in the differentiation of a *Gegenüber*:

> Poor drip that *I* am—shall *I* boast that my tongue is the pen [and] feather of the Holy Spirit?[!] And [yet] in precisely this tongue [and these] words—therein—are given and administered the gifts of the living Spirit: faith in Christ, love toward God and one's neighbor, patience and gentleness, and that *you* know, who God [is], who Christ [is], and what death [is], written in [*your*] hearts.[82]

Confidence, boasting, and even pride are salutary when they are at play for the service and well-being of others, rather than as ends in themselves for a static status of the preacher/minister.[83] Working with categories and a

---

80. For confidence see 2 Cor 3:4. For boasting see 2 Cor 10–12, especially 10:8–17 (where boasting is related to the authority and, in some sense, the jurisdiction of the apostolic ministers) and Rom 15:15–18.

81. WA 40/I:63.19–26.

82. Pr. 1926, WA 49:170.14–19. See also "bragging" (*bochen*) at WA 49.170.3–4.

83. Another side of affirming the *Gegenüber* of the office of the ministry to the congregation, as in significant ecumenical documents such as Evangelisch-lutherische / Römisch-katholische Studienkommission, "Das Evangelium," 261 (§50); Gemeinsame Römisch-Katholische/ Evangelisch-Lutherische Kommission, "Das geistliche Amt," 337 (§23); Kommission für Glauben und Kirchenverfassung des Ökumenischen Rates der Kirchen, "Taufe, Eucharistie und Amt," 570 (Amt §11); Ökumenischer Arbeitskreis evangelischer und katholischer Theologen, "Abschließender Bericht," 236 (§75); Lutherisch / Römisch-katholische Kommission für die Einheit, *Die Apostolizität der*

ministerial bearing expressed also in mode of address appropriated not least from Paul, Luther sees the certainty of the ministers as ministers and so the preachers as preachers as pertaining to and in service of the certainty of the parishioners and hearers. Shortly put, the certainty of the incumbents of the ministry/preaching office, affirmed directly (content) and indirectly (mode of address) in preaching, pertains to the certainty of salvation in the hearers and parishioners; ministerial certainty serves salvation certainty.

> And the pastor says, ["]Here I baptize[!] Thus let all people, angels, and devils know: God will accept this baptism too, and the angels will confirm [it!] Here I preach, and the words of the Gospel that I speak are Christ's [words]! Thus the devil shall let it stand and the whole world and the angels [shall] say, 'Yes!' to it." This confidence we must have. If I myself [were the one who] preaches and baptizes, I couldn't have [this] confidence that it pleases God and the angels. But since I myself do not baptize and preach, but rather he does it, who is in heaven above, I have good confidence. [I may say, "]It's your preaching, your absolution; see to it [yourself], that it is right[!]" I am an instrument: This confidence we must have![84]

The confidence or certainty of the ministers/preachers is set in a cosmic landscape where all people, their hearers included, are affected by the divine reality that gives rise to this certainty. Ministers/preachers who know that God has made them his spokesmen, stewards in the household that is his church, entrusting to them the preaching of his word, the administration of the sacraments, and the exercise of the keys, speak and act in such a way that the persons charged to their care come to know and become certain that hearing and being served by a preacher/minister is hearing and being served by God himself.[85]

The two-sided certainty alive in this *Gegenüber* of human communications reflects two *coram Deo* relationships, namely that of the preachers/ministers before God, and that of the hearers/parishioners before God. On whose behalf does the preacher speak, on whose behalf does the minister act? Any answer short of God himself does not hold for the minister, but especially not for those to whom he speaks, and those whom he is given to serve. Preaching in 1539 with an ordinand in view, Luther stresses, "If you

---

Kirche, 127 (§255) 135 (§275); and Kasper, *Harvesting the Fruits*,111 (§56) (also 79 [§41] and 151 [§76]) is simultaneously to affirm that the ministry/preaching office is also located *in* the congregation.

84. Pr. 1574, WA 41:456.25–32.
85. See Pr. 1577, WA 41:468.12–18.

are not certain, that the capacity [comes] from God, quit[!] . . . If *you* would be forgiving sins, [could you] set [the one confessing] at ease before God?"[86] Indeed, the differentiated address found in Luther's mature preaching is homiletical communication of a reality whose most pointed expression is to be found in absolution, in the loosing—or, under other circumstance, the binding—of sins.[87] Preaching on John 20:19ff, Luther declares, "From this mandate we too have the authority, that when we forgive and bind sins, we know that not we, but in fact God himself does [this], [for] we are sent by God. Thus you should listen to [the] parson not as a man, but as God."[88] As an emissary of God, the preacher does not speak as other people—even other Christians—speak, but rather as God himself.[89] A preacher is not in the same tub as a butcher or a baker;[90] his word of rebuke is a divinely ordained address, pointed at the sinner definitively from without, even outside of the interpersonal, and so is a word for the addressee *coram Deo*. When not heeded with repentance, the preacher's word closes heaven to the impenitent. "You are on the path to death! Forgive him who has angered you!"[91] This deadly reality is true, and as such, its life-giving counterpart may also be what it is, "When you hear from me: [']Your sins are forgiven you,['] then you hear that God wishes to be gracious [to you], [that] he [wishes] to justify and save [you] and deliver [you] from sin and death, so that you are just and live."[92] That there neither is nor may there be doubt on either side of this *Gegenüber*, is a phenomenon indicative of the gospel. "For if we ourselves want to waver and doubt whether we are true preachers, then the whole herd wavers in turn and the matter becomes uncertain."[93] The opposite of doubt is certainty, and the certainty of hearers, parishioners, and forgiven sinners, as such, before God, is served by the certainty of their

---

86. Pr. 1882, *WA* 47:783.34–38.

87. See Matt 16:19 and John 20:23.

88. Pr. 1923, *WA* 49:140.36–38. In relation to the laying on of hands as part of the rite of confession and absolution from the same sermon, see *WA* 49:140,7–11, "Thus you are just as bound to believe me . . . as were Christ to lay his hand on you and heal you . . . . If the servant lays [his] hands on you, even Christ himself [lays his hands on you]."

89. *WA* 40 / I:56.28—57.15.

90. See Pr. 1732, *WA* 46:447.8–10 in the context of 46:447.2–19.

91. Pr. 1651, *WA* 45:113.22–23. In the section *WA* 45:113.18–31 the distinction between the address of God and the address of the preacher disappears; cf. *WA* 45:113.24–26 and 29–31.

92. Pr. 1923, *WA* 49:139.8–10.

93. Pr. 1372, *WA* 36:521.15–17.

preachers/ministers, as such, before God. With and according to Luther, this certainty is a homiletically communicated and actuated reality.

PRELIMINARY CONCLUSIONS

On the basis of 1 and 2 Cor and the latter sermons of Martin Luther, we have observed that a differentiated mode of address has been a part of communication from Christian ministers to those charged to their care, and that this address can find expression in preaching. We have further observed that this differentiation of address—in which not only an I moves opposite a "you," but indeed a "we" can hold this position—is neither neutral nor incidental to the material of the address, but rather that the differentiated form of the address certainly affects, and in some sense even effects the material of the address.

Thus, as a preliminary set of conclusions and deductions, we may say firstly, that a divinely mandated *Gegenüber* of the ministers/preachers on the one side and the congregation on the other exists in the Holy Scriptures and in the Christian tradition, certainly within the Lutheran branch thereof; secondly, that the divinely mandated *Gegenüber* evidences itself in a differentiated mode of address that can, at times, distinguish the preacher and indeed preachers/ministers from the hearers/parishioners; thirdly, that this divine reality is perpetuated and actuated also by the differentiated address itself as it shapes hearers to acknowledge and appreciate a divinely ordered economy inherent in the Christian church.

DIFFERENTIATED ADDRESS MAKING A DIFFERENCE

If a Lutheran experience from the pews is any indication, a differentiated mode of address might be something very different for many parishioners. Does it make a difference? We would argue that it does.

On a systematic-theological level, a differentiated mode of address, or lack thereof, is indicative of an understanding of the ministry/preaching office—i.e. what it is to be a preacher/minister—in other words, indicative of an *Amtslehre* (doctrine of the ministry). Simply put, whose man is the minister/preacher? On whose behalf does he speak and act? St. Paul, Martin Luther, and the confessions of the Evangelical Lutheran Church leave no doubt about the matter: the preacher/minister speaks and acts on behalf of Jesus Christ.[94] How a preacher speaks, or does not speak, is inherently

---

94. For the Lutheran confessions see, for example, AP VII:28, "in the stead and

instructive of an understanding of the ministry/preaching office. Whether the preacher/minister speaks with a differentiated mode of address or his "we" only ever refers to the whole of the Christian congregation, an inherent ecclesiology is at play. The church is a single and unified but differentiated entity. Is there in the being that is the church a sort of differentiation wherein Christ remains a distinct head, or foundation, or key-/cornerstone, fulfilling his role and caring for the rest the entity, or is the implied ecclesiology one not just of unity but, indeed, of homogeneity?[95] Without a divine differentiation of ministers/preachers and hearers/parishioners, traditional understandings (at least Lutheran understandings) of the nature of the gospel (evangeliology) and salvation (soteriology) break down. According to the Augsburg Confession, the "bodily," eardrum-rattling word of the gospel, through which saving faith is worked and given, is an *"external* word,"[96] external not just to him or her who hears it in this or that instance, but external to *"those* who hear it." The gospel as a justifying, saving, faith-creating word is external to hearers as hearers and believers as believers. The divine *Gegenüber* of the ministry/preaching office, which is never apart from but always located in immediate ministerial proximity to the congregation, accounts for the externality of the gospel as the gospel and so for an understanding of salvation as fully good news, coming entirely from without and not in any way being required from within those who are being saved.[97] Without the ministry and therewith the preachers/ministers as an external instance for the delivering of the external word of the gospel, not only are the ministry/preaching office and the church very different creatures, but salvation is a different game, and the gospel is another gospel.

How a preacher speaks does not only communicate (an understanding of) salvation, the gospel, the church, and the ministry, but, on a practical-theological level, the mode of speech will also inform and shape how the preacher's hearers think of him; the mode of speech communicates the preacher's understanding of himself as a minister/preacher. If his speech does not evidence a differentiated mode of address which points to himself in his office as a divinely placed instance for the giving of God's saving gifts—the gospel and the sacraments—his hearers/parishioners will be less likely to view him as such or even hampered therein. If the preacher

---

place of Christ." (*BSLK* 240, 47 = KW 178)

95. Cf. Eph 2:20, Christ's position ἀκρογωνιαῖος aligns him with "the foundation of the apostles and prophets" as that which defines (or architecturally, that which squares and levels) this foundation.

96. AC V:4: German: *leiblich* (*BSLK* 58,12–13) and Latin: *verbo externo* (*BSLK* 58,16) (KW 40–41).

97. AC IV:1: Latin: *gratis iustificentur* (*BSLK* 56,4–5; KW 39).

understands himself as one of a select group of stewards of these mysteries of God and speaks as such, this will shape hearers/parishioners expectations of him and the roles they look for him to have with them. The opposite is also true. If a divinely given status as a differentiated instance in the modus of God's workings of salvation is not affirmed, also by mode of address, a different status will have to be claimed, earned, and maintained.[98]

This observation brings us to homiletics and the specific task of preaching. Firstly, we would suggest that the divine differentiation that underlies such differentiated address as is here observed and considered actually makes the task of preaching easier, for the preacher need not be concerned with making a preacher of himself by his preaching. He is a preacher and of the preachers before his preaching. Thus the task of preaching is emptied of any need or indeed temptation to serve the preacher's self or his status by preaching, and preaching can then move toward its proper end, which is the salvation and well-being of the hearers. Secondly, as one already speaking with a differentiated mode of address, preaching the whole counsel of God—including the sometimes tacitly forbidden locus on the ministry—becomes a much simpler matter, for when a preacher then does speak *about* the ministry, his material is nothing new, being already of a piece with his preaching form. Finally, the divine differentiation evidenced in a differentiated mode of address unburdens the task of preaching from what may be a, or even *the* challenge chief in the mind of many preachers: the need to relate the text to the hearers and/or to make it relevant. This observation may not serve as license for paltry study of the biblical text or insufficient sermon preparation; that would be a misappropriation of the reality here pondered. Nonetheless, if the preacher himself is the connection to God's word as speaker of God's word, then he does not need to somehow actualize the biblical text for the hearers, so that God may have a word for them. Rather, as a preacher, he finds himself caught up in the larger whole of the Triune God's mediate speaking and dealing with fallen human beings, of which the Holy Scriptures are an incontrovertible and temporally permanent part, themselves no more dead or removed from the present than the living Christ is absent from the preaching and actions of his preachers/ministers in their office.

BIBLIOGRAPHY

Aland, Kurt. *Hilfsbuch zum Lutherstudium*. 4th ed. Bielefeld: Luther, 1996.

---

98. Cf. nn55–58 above.

Byrskog, Samuel. "Co-Senders, Co-Authors and Paul's Use of the First Person Plural." *ZNW* 87 (1996) 230–50.

Carrez, M. "Le 'Nous' en 2 Corinthiens: Paul parle-t-il au nom de toute la communauté, du groupe apostolique, de l'équipe ministérielle ou en son nom personnel? Contribution à l'étude de l'apostolicité dans 2 Corinthiens." *NTS* 26 (1979/1980) 474–86.

Cranfield, C. E. B. "Changes in Person and Number in Paul's Epistles." In *Paul and Paulinism: Essays in Honour of C. K. Barrett*, edited by. M. D. Hooker and S. G. Wilson, 280–89. London: SPCK, 1982.

Evangelisch-lutherische/Römisch-katholische Studienkommission. "Das Evangelium und die Kirche ('Malta Bericht' 1972)." In *Dokumente wachsender Übereinstimmung: Sämtliche Berichte und Konsenstexte interkonfessioneller Gespräche auf Weltebene, 1931–1982*, edited by Harding Meyer et al., Paderborn: Bonifatius, 1983.

Gemeinsame Römisch-Katholische/Evangelisch-Lutherische Kommission. "Das geistliche Amt in der Kirche ('GAK' 1981)." In *Dokumente wachsender Übereinstimmung: Sämtliche Berichte und Konsenstexte interkonfessioneller Gespräche auf Weltebene, 1931–1982*, edited by Harding Meyer et al., Paderborn: Bonifatius, 1983.

Hirsch, Emanuel. "Luthers Predigtweise." *Luther: Mitteilungen der Luthergesellschaft* 25 (1954) 1–23.

Kasper, Walter. *Harvesting the Fruits: Basic Aspects of Christian Faith in Ecumenical Dialogue*. London: Continuum, 2009.

Klauck, Hans-Josef. *2. Korintherbrief*. Würzburg: Echter, 1986.

Kommission für Glauben und Kirchenverfassung des Ökumenischen Rates der Kirchen. "Taufe, Eucharistie und Amt: Konvergenzerklärungen der Kommission für Glauben und Kirchenverfassung des Ökumenischen Rates der Kirchen ('Lima-Dokument' 1982)." In *Dokumente wachsender Übereinstimmung: Sämtliche Berichte und Konsenstexte interkonfessioneller Gespräche auf Weltebene, 1931–1982*, edited by Harding Meyer et al., 545–85. Paderborn: Bonifatius, 1983.

Krarup, Martin. *Die Ordination in Wittenberg*. Tübingen, Mohr/Siebeck, 2007.

Lieberg, Helmut. *Amt und Ordination bei Luther und Melanchthon*. Berlin: Evangelisches, 1962.

Liebert, Donald Hans. "The 'Apostolic Form of Writing' Group Letters before and after 1 Corinthians." In *The Corinthian Correspondence*, edited by R. Bieringer, 433–40. Leuven: Leuven University Press, 1996.

Llewelyn, S. R. "§25 Ammonios to Apollonios (*P. Oxy*. XLII 3057) The Earliest Christian Letter on Papyrus?" In *New Documents Illustrating Early Christianity: A Review of the Greek Inscriptions and Papyri published in 1980-81*, 169–77. Sydney: Ancient History Documentary Research Centre of Macquarie University, 1992.

Lutherisch/Römisch-katholische Kommission für die Einheit. *Die Apostolizität der Kirche: Studiendokument der Lutherisch/Römisch-katholischen Kommission für die Einheit*. Paderborn: Bonifatius, 2009.

Mumme, Jonathan. *Die Präsenz Christi im Amt: Am Beispiel ausgewählter Predigten Martin Luthers, 1535-46*. Göttingen: Vandenhoeck & Ruprecht, 2015.

———. "Von dem Buchstaben, dem Geist und den Geistern: Was Martin Luther vom Heiligen Geist und von der Heiligen Schrift lehrt." *Lutherische Beiträge* 17 (2012) 13–22.

Ökumenischer Arbeitskreis evangelischer und katholischer Theologen. "Abschließender Bericht." In *Das kirchliche Amt in apostolischer Nachfolge III: Verständigungen und Differenzen*, edited by Dorothea Sattler und Gunther Wenz, 167–268. Freiburg: Herder, 2008.

Oliveira, Anacleto de. *Die Diakonie der Gerechtigkeit und der Versöhnung in der Apologie des 2. Korintherbriefes: Analyse und Auslegung von 2 Kor 2,14–4,16; 5,11–6,10*. Münster: Aschendorff, 1990.

Schmeller, Thomas. "Exkurs: Das 'Wir' im 2Kor." In *Der zweite Brief an die Korinther, Teilband 1: 2Kor 1,1—7,4*. Neukirchen-Vluyn: Neukirchener Theologie. Ostfildern: Patmos, 2010.

Schottroff, Luise. "Das 'Wir' der Gemeinde." In *Der erste Brief an die Gemeinde in Korinth*. Stuttgart: Kohlhammer, 2013.

Verhoff, Eduard. "The Senders of the Letters to the Corinthians and the Use of 'I' and 'We.'" In *The Corinthian Correspondence*, edited by R. Bieringer, 417–25. Leuven: Leuven University Press, 1996.

Wallace, Daniel B. *Greek Grammar beyond the Basics: An Exegetical Syntax of the New Testament*. Grand Rapids: Zondervan, 1996.

Winger, Thomas M. "Orality as the Key to Understanding Apostolic Proclamation in the Epistles." ThD diss., Concordia Seminary, 1997.

———. "The Spoken Word: What's Up with Orality?" *CJ* 29 (2003) 133–51.

Wright, N. T. "On Becoming the Righteousness of God." In *Pauline Theology*, edited by D. M. Hay, 3:200–208. Minneapolis: Fortress, 1993.

8

Preaching as Foolishness
—Steven Paulson

Before we get to the real question of this essay, "What is Preaching?" let us begin with a more basic question, "What is Theology?" Normally the answer is some type of "thinking." In school, for example, you are normally supposed to be "thinking," which means using your brain to figure things out according to the gift of reason.

That form of reasoning, in turn, normally means learning the special "concepts" of a discipline—learning what words "mean" by studying the history of the use of relevant words by those in the discipline. Lawyers learn the words of a courtroom, doctors learn the words that apply to the body and its health, and so theologians are likewise supposed to have a set of concepts that they should be learning so that when people hear them talk they say, that person is not a lawyer or a doctor, but a theologian. Indeed, we sometimes use the noun "theology" as an adjective modifying the word "thinking" so that a theologian is the one who is supposed to be thinking theologically.

THEOLOGY IS FOR PROCLAMATION, NOT UNDERSTANDING

The long history in the Christian church assumes something more particular about the way to "think theologically" captured in a famous phrase from Anselm of Canterbury: "faith seeking understanding" (*fides quaerens intellectum*). "Faith Seeking Understanding," was to be the title of his famous book, *Proslogion*. But though the phrase did not become his title, it has become the most famous artifact of the book when Anselm uttered his confessional prayer, "I long to understand in some degree your truth, which my heart believes and loves. For I do not seek to understand that I may believe, but I believe in order to understand (*credo ut intelligam*). For this also I believe,—that unless I believed, I should not understand."[1]

Arguing for God's existence is in itself a rather sorry affair, but what is worse is this notion that one starts with faith, like a child, and then matures in faith by adding *intellectum*. This is the way I was taught to teach religion at a Lutheran school—taking parochial country bumpkins fallen fresh from the beet truck and educating their desires in order to remove simple faith and replace it with liberal meaning, or higher desires than a beet farmer has—say the opera and Friedrich Nietzsche, or Karl Marx and social gospel.

Hegel taught along these lines, when he said that religion is a true, but lower, form of thought than philosophy—religion dealing with a "picture book" level of the world (telling stories of Adam and Eve and Moses) and philosophy dealing with a "chapter book" view of the world that gains the higher mode of pure thought. This approach to theology has a habit of dividing the world into parts: feeling, doing, and thinking. These parts are considered the three *bona*, or goods, of life, and the greatest of these (*summum bonum*) is "thinking."

In comparison to thinking, feeling (aesthetics) is considered loose, disorganized, and somewhat dangerous. "Doing" (practice/ethics) is better than feeling because it does not simply leave one with an impression (to be impressed) but allows you to impress yourself on others—to make a difference or a mark. And what school child does not want to make a difference in the world? Yet thinking is the greatest. Such a presumption goes right back to Plato and Aristotle and has never stopped since.

---

1. Migliore's textbook on theology builds on Anselm's theme, "What distinguishes theology from blind assent is just its special character as 'faith seeking understanding'" (*Faith Seeking Understanding*, 2). Anselm continued in his Preface, "In my judgment, neither this work nor the other, which I mentioned above, deserved to be called a book, or to bear the name of an author; and yet I thought they ought not to be sent forth without some title by which they might, in some sort, invite one into whose hands they fell to their perusal. I accordingly gave each a title, that the first might be known as, An Example of Meditation on the Grounds of Faith, and its sequel as, Faith Seeking Understanding. But, after both had been copied by many under these titles, many urged me, and especially Hugo, the reverend Archbishop of Lyons, who discharges the apostolic office in Gaul, who instructed me to this effect on his apostolic authority—to prefix my name to these writings. And that this might be done more fitly, I named the first, *Monologium*, that is, A Soliloquy; but the second, *Proslogium*, that is, A Discourse" (Deane, *Works of St. Anslem*, 2). Thus the great error of theology was set, and has become implacable.

The result is to make a big split between theory (thinking) and practice (applying your thoughts) in much the way that a builder of a skyscraper first has the architect picture the whole building, and the builder simply implements another's' imagination. In the end it is the architect who is remembered for the building, not the construction company. A person says, "This is a Frank Lloyd Wright building," not "This was built by Siemens and Sons."

A Lutheran, however, will not go with the crowd in this matter, but instead says something completely new. Theology is not a child-like faith seeking adult concepts by means of the irritation of doubt. Theology is not *fides quaerens intellectum*. Instead, theology (with its thinking, doing and feeling) is for something. It is a "doing," but unlike any previously imagined "doing," since it is passive. Nevertheless, theology will change the world in the most radical way possible: by preaching. So our thesis will be: theology is for proclamation instead of faith seeks understanding.

By rejecting the search for understanding we are not left with irrationalism but instead we learn how to preach. This takes a brain, and a tongue, and hutzpah, along with some other attributes that Paul lumps together and calls παρρησία (boldness) in preaching Christ.

Preachers must become bold, in particular with the gospel. As Paul says, "For I am not ashamed of the gospel, for it is the power of God for salvation to everyone who believes, to the Jew first and also to the Greek. For in it the righteousness of God is revealed from faith for faith, as it is written, 'The righteous shall live by faith.'" (Rom 1:16–17).

This means that in order to understand theology we have to tackle the more basic question: what is preaching? Proclamation and preaching are synonyms for us. Sometimes they are distinguished slightly by saying that preaching is opening your mouth and saying the gospel to sinners in order to distinguish this act from giving a sacrament. In this case we have developed a habit of using the two related words for proclamation: word and sacraments.

For this reason, "word and sacrament," have a special place in evangelical teaching as we find in the fifth article of the Augsburg Confession, "To obtain such faith God instituted the office of preaching, giving the gospel and the sacraments. Through these, as through means, he gives the Holy Spirit, who produces faith, when and where he wills in those who hear the gospel." Preaching is therefore "giving the gospel and the sacraments" as the "means" by which God gives the Holy Spirit to sinners. If we continue in this famous article, we notice immediately that the statement stands against the Anabaptists in teaching that the Holy Spirit does not come to us "without the external word of the gospel through our own preparations, thoughts, and works," but through the external word—all else excluded.[2]

In this crucial definition we learn first that the Spirit uses "means," so that the Holy Spirit is not immediate, but mediate. Further, the Spirit is not given through our own preparations whether feelings, thoughts or works. That means especially not by thinking! How then does the Spirit come? Through the external word (*externum verbum*). He comes not from inside, but from outside. And the external means is particularly and uniquely a word. Preaching is that word. So preaching is the way God gives his Holy Spirit to sinners—while they are sinners. This happens not through anything inside them, but from the outside, through the means of an external word: a little sermon.

This little sermon is not simply speaking about God, but speaking for God: Jesus said to the twelve, before sending them out for their first preaching mission, "And proclaim as you go, saying, 'The kingdom of heaven is at hand.' Heal the sick, raise the dead, cleanse lepers, cast out demons. You received without paying; give without pay. . . ." (Matt 10:7–8). "Whoever receives you receives me, and whoever receives me receives him who sent me." (Matt 10:40)

But in contradiction to this evangelical discovery, the nineteenth and twentieth centuries were often consumed with the question, "How might I speak truthfully of God, the One whom I do not see or know, who is other than me and the whole creation?" Theological thinkers of these centuries wondered, "How can my mere human words be adequate for the perfect, the total, the all-in-all of God?" Two basic attempts were made to answer this false question that reverted to the patterns of earlier theology. One is called "analogy." This assumes that creatures cannot speak directly about God, but they can do so by analogy from what they know. What do we know? We know other creatures, and so from them we can say something true about the Creator as the effect always retains some of its cause within it. This way was called the "modest way" of Thomas Aquinas. Analogy created a dualism that distinguished the realm of the divine above from the realm of the earth below with a ladder of analogical language propped up between them. What is not true in one realm may be quite true in the other. So for example, death is the case on earth, but in heaven there is only eternal life. This duality has fascinated theology and gutted preaching at the same time.

The other was a revolt against Thomas Aquinas and this modest way of teaching by analogy. It said words should not be equivocal, or shifty. They should be univocal, true in all realms—heaven and earth—if we are going

---

2. KW 40 = *BSLK* 58.

to say anything sensible about God. This emerged as nominalist teaching in the likes of Duns Scotus and William of Occam. They asserted that there are not two kinds of "being," but only one kind, and words must and do fit this one true being, or they do not. Words are thus either true or false, not shifty. Our words must be precise and unequivocal about God in order to speak properly of him. But this line of thinking also undermined preaching, since it knew nothing of a new kingdom. We cannot afford to be in this ancient (and also very recent) fight between analogy and univocity without losing preaching.[3]

Preaching is not concerned with speaking about God, but the much bolder matter of speaking for him. We cannot afford to be silenced by the difference between human and divine words, but are rather concerned with when and where those two become identical in true preaching. We call this *verbum reale*, which is the word that does not merely describe reality accurately, but creates a new reality. The word of preaching does what it says: So when you say, "The Kingdom of God has drawn near," you are not simply describing a fact or a possibility, you are bringing the kingdom itself—giving it to someone who needs it. Once you learn to deal with *verbum reale*, or *efficax*—the word that creates anew—you will no longer be giving theological opinions, points of view, or spiritual directions, but bestowing the divine word of the gospel to people who really need it. When you say the words, "I forgive you," you will not merely be stating a fact that aligns with a reality already there, nor will you be using a transcendent word that is like something we already know on earth. Instead you will be uttering the word that creates out of nothing and makes a new reality that was not there before. You will be doing what only God does, which is to create something new, out of nothing: *creatio ex nihilo*.

WHAT IS PREACHING?

When you become thus equipped, and bold, you will no longer merely be thinking theologically, but doing theology—or better yet, exercising the truth that theology is for something—it is for proclamation. So, now we will assume that theology is for proclamation—no more and no less. Then, what do we mean by preaching? As you can guess, there are many attempts at describing this, almost all of them in opposition to the key distinction between law and gospel because they are operating with a theory of analogy or univocity.

3. One can consider the struggle further in Milbank, Pickstock, and Ward, eds., *Radical Orthodoxy*.

First, we can note the obvious; preaching is some kind of public speaking. As Martin Luther often said, the qualifications for a seminarian include three things: can the fellow stand up in front of people (i.e., can he speak publicly)? Can he open his mouth and speak (i.e., does he have a big mouth)? And does he know when to shut his mouth and sit down (the gospel being a short word)?[4] Just so preaching is related not only to grammar, but to oratory or rhetoric especially as it as it was studied in the world of Greek and Roman oratory.

Consequently, the primary purpose of public speaking is always assumed to be persuasion: a sudden change in attitude.

> There is to my mind no more excellent thing than the power, by means of oratory, to get a hold on assemblies of men, win their good will, direct their inclinations wherever the speaker wishes, or divert them from whatever he wishes. In every free nation, and most of all in communities which have attained the enjoyment of peace and tranquility, this one art has always flourished above the rest and ever reigned supreme.[5]

This influenced the most important book on preaching in the Middle Ages right up to the time of Martin Luther, called *The Seventh Ring*. Its author was a Cistercian monk, Alan of Lille (1128–1202) who lived in the twelfth century renaissance of preaching that reached back to Greece and Rome to reclaim the glory of those days. Alan was interested in the secondary purpose of rhetoric, a lifelong process concerning the effect of the preaching, called "formation." Much of Christian theology and many seminaries presently are caught up in this effort to understand preaching as "formation." This inclination toward preaching as formation today claims renowned theologians like Sarah Coakley and Stanley Hauerwas. We can understand this movement best by going back to its early Christian master in *The Seventh Ring*.

Jacob's Ladder: Preaching as Formation according to Alan of Lille

To depict this effect of preaching called "formation," Alan used the story of Jacob's Ladder in which "Jacob beheld a ladder reaching from earth to heaven, on which angels were ascending and descending. The ladder represents the progress of the catholic man in his ascent from the beginning of faith to the full development of the perfect man."[6]

---

4. LW 23:227.
5. Crassus in Cicero, *De Oratore* I.viii.3.
6. Alan of Lille, *The Art of Preaching* 15.

The steps on the ladder were seven, with preaching being the highest and last:

1. Confession
2. Prayer (for grace)
3. Eucharist (for grace once it is given)
4. Careful study of the Scriptures (allows one to persevere in holding onto the gift of grace)
5. Learning to ask someone more experienced when Scripture is obscure.
6. Expounding Scripture (i.e., pounding out Scripture to others of his acquaintance)
7. Preaching (publicly giving what one has learned from Scripture).

It is indeed profound that for Alan, the top rung was not naked contemplation of God as with the mystics; there he placed earthly preaching. At first glance this appears positive. Alan concentrated his book on the highest rung and asked, what is preaching? He answered in five ways, first, by inquiring what preaching's form is (where he distinguished "surface aspects" from the treasure beneath, which predictably was "thoughts" that bear weight—since theology is really for thinking). Second by asking, who can preach? Third, who is the audience? Fourth, what are the reasons for the sermon (its context)? And finally, what is the "place" for the sermon?

His answer to the first question of preaching's form was this, "Preaching is an open and public instruction in faith and behavior, whose purpose is the forming of men; it derives from the path of reason and from the fountainhead of the authorities."[7] Instruction meant not just imparting facts, but the way to "form a life." But most importantly, this preaching was to be public ("What I say in your ear, preach upon the housetops") not secret (gnostic) knowledge imparted only to the initiated. This is an important point, because preaching is the anti-gnostic inoculation. Lying and deceiving are practiced privately in the dark. Preaching, on the contrary, is not private. So far so good for Alan; preaching is not to be given to one, but to many. Teaching can be to a single person; preaching must be for the many.

But then Alan tipped his hat regarding the content of sermons, "Public speaking is the admonishing of the people to maintain the well-being of the community."[8] How common this has become! People assume that preach-

---

7. Ibid., 15–16.
8. Ibid., 17.

ing is getting people to act communally, not individually so that preaching and the divine service as a whole are meant to make people less selfish. It is typical for Alan that the content of preaching must then include two aspects: faith and behavior. One must impart doctrine (what to believe) and behavior (what to do) exactly as the old theories of theology assumed. Therefore, theology appeals to reason's knowing of spiritual or "holy things," while ethics deals with "living the good life." Consequently, the preacher is responsible for the opening the treasure of doctrine and seeing to it that this teaching is applied throughout the week in action of the laity or religious. Alan interpreted Jacob's ladder accordingly: "preachers are the 'angels,' who 'ascend' when they preach about heavenly matters (doctrine) and 'descend' when they bend themselves to earthly things in speaking of behavior."[9]

This is a decidedly different thing than I will momentarily argue, since Alan removed the distinction of law and gospel, and in its place put the distinction between doctrine and ethics—what you know about heaven, and what you do here on earth. This is the most common of theological errors that rears its ugly head in preaching. Alan concluded that the form of preaching comes out of reason which is to direct the will in the way it should go. Reason through preaching is thus the instrument of Christian formation. Reason is serious, and cannot be diverted from its proper goal, so Alan insisted that preaching have no jokes, childish remarks, or rhythmic speaking meant to delight the ear—a theatrical display—or anything that is glittery. Too much embroidery on the cloth removes the power to reason.

Of course there are things that evangelical preachers can note to their advantage when considering Alan's understanding of the form and content of sermons, since a sermon too embroidered (too worked over) is contrived. Overworking usually means trying to get people's admiration rather than serving the benefit of the neighbor. Instead of such frivolity (Alan was a Cistercian) there must be *gravitas*—enough to "move the spirits of its hearers, stir up the mind, encourage repentance." So, he concluded that one should let the "sermon rain down doctrines, and thunder forth admonitions, soothe with praises. . . ." and so help the neighbor, not gain credit for the self. Those who gain credit for themselves are "merchants," rather than "preachers."[10]

Alan noted that neither a preacher's nor a hearer's reason is strong enough to preach with *gravitas*, no doubt because of the fall and sin. Instead, reason must be directed by authorities, just as you would have a director at a good monastery where you learn not only poverty and chastity, but obedience. Alan did hold that the chief authority was Scripture, "a theological

---

9. Ibid., 18.
10. Ibid., 20.

authority—especially a text from the Gospel, the Psalms, the Epistles of Paul or the Books of Solomon. . . " was necessary for a sermon.

But this observation broke into three fateful "kinds" of preaching that reveal the problem with his approach. One kind of sermon was the spoken word, "go and preach the gospel to every creature." The second was simply reciting the written word by reading the text aloud. Then came the problematic third: preaching "by deed." It was in this last form that Alan described the primary attribute of the preacher as "humility" that sets people "on their way and to help them make progress." For what is the ladder of Jacob other than a description of the whole Christian life as a progress up the steps of the ladder until one is perfect? Upon completion of the Christian life the preacher is imagined to disappear, and what remains is the instruction that forms the Christian for the remainder of life in heaven. No more preaching, but instruction remains forever. Then, as with any who seek to persuade, Alan said, "it is not the sharpness of the thorn that we should dwell on, but the sweetness of the rose."[11] By no means a throwaway line! Persuasion always moves to the sweet attraction rather than the thorny accusation. You catch more flies with honey than with vinegar—this always becomes the preacher's code when preaching is moral persuasion. The same soup overwhelmed the antinomian Agricola among the Lutherans.

Even though preaching was a version of persuasion for Alan, his sober approach recognized that it is acceptable to move people to tears (but "as Lucretius says, 'Nothing dries up faster than a tear'")[12] and finally, that a preacher should use examples (as this is the main way to teach). Alan held that Christian formation was progress on the ladder. Such steps were enabled by public preaching in the form of exhortation that instructs (i.e., for reason's control of the will).

The instruction was to be of two kinds: "doctrine" (spiritual things—like what heaven is like) that takes one up the ladder, and "deeds" (behavior, ethics) that return you to earth to do what is needed for others. In brief, a sermon teaches what you should know, and what you should do to be justified. Nothing could be more modern than this—perhaps without the Cistercian humility. Alan's renaissance held sway some three hundred years before someone would hear something different in Paul's letters. The medieval distinction of doctrine and ethics unseated the proper distinction between law and gospel, and the Cistercian humility unseated what Paul meant by saying that preaching was foolishness. This had to be overcome in order to unleash the power of the gospel.

11. Ibid., 21.
12. Lischer, *Company of Preachers*, 7.

PREACHING AS FOOLISHNESS: 1 CORINTHIANS 1-4

It would seem that preaching is a special type of public speaking, a genre of persuasion that uses reason as its method—until we learn what Paul did. Then the first truth of preaching is folly, "For the word of the cross is folly to those who are perishing," (there goes the whole comparison to public speaking from Aristotle to the present) "but to us who are being saved it is the power of God. For it is written [Isa 29:14] 'I will destroy the wisdom of the wise, and the cleverness of the clever I will thwart.'" (1 Cor 1:18–19) Preaching is not persuasion, it is the "word of the cross." That means, it preaches the cross: "We preach Christ and him crucified" (1 Cor 2:2).

Preaching this foolishness means giving out grace: "the grace of God that was given you in Jesus Christ" (1 Cor 1:4). And what is this grace? It is God's all-working power, which leaves nothing for you to do. This is folly to the perishing. If there is nothing for the hearers to do, then what good is persuasion? You can hear the folly, "Why bother? Why do anything, if God does all?" Well, Paul says of the Corinthian Christians, that they were "enriched (made rich) in every way," "with all speech and knowledge." (1 Cor 1:5) The proclamation of Christ is confirmed among them, so that they lack nothing (1 Cor 1:6–7). Everything is already given. Nothing more need be added. Christians do not fill the half-full cup or complete the doctrine with behavior. They do not climb any ladder. They are not lacking in any charismata (1 Cor 1:7) while they are waiting for the revealing of "our Lord Jesus Christ" (1 Cor 1:8) that will come when they see what they already have in words (hearing).

Now Paul turns to what everything in the entire world come down to, as God sees it. It is his speaking that matters. What he says must really be the case. It must hold and so weather every storm. As Paul says: "God is faithful!" (1 Cor 1:9) There is the entire doctrine of God in a nutshell. It is the whole of evangelical teaching, and what made Luther's form of preaching greater than any previous attempt (of which Alan of Lille was merely one). What is the attribute of God that matters most? Anselm said it was God's justice, along with his mercy. Others say God's attribute that matters most is goodness or love. Not so for Paul. God is faithful.

This bothered someone as wise as G. W. F. Hegel since faithfulness is what you look for in a dog. Will he come when you call? Will he stay with you when he could get meat elsewhere? But as Paul says, "Where is the wise man? Where is the scribe? Where is the debater of this age?" (1 Cor 1:20). Why is "God is faithful" so important for Paul? Faithfulness means something has been said in the form of a promise to you, and the promise-maker, or giver, is considered faithful when he sticks by the promise despite what comes. So faithfulness only means something if there is a promise to which he is faithful, and sure enough, that is what Paul means by preaching. It is not the rhetoric of persuasion; preaching is the address by God that gives you his promise. The key to it all, to grace and God's faithfulness, is that you have everything you need in that simple promise. You have every χαρίσματα you could desire. All you need in this life is to know one thing: God is faithful! If you are so lucky as to get a promise from him, he sticks by his promise when he makes it. What if the one receiving it is not faithful? Paul took that up in his letter to the Philippians: so what! God is faithful, even if his chosen Israel is not. That is all that matters. If God sticks by his promise, even if the one getting the promise does not deserve it, what must you say about the promise? It holds. It is good. It lasts. It endures.

This is why the "world did not know God through wisdom," because it thought it was climbing on Jacob's ladder up to him. Instead, what was really happening? "It pleased God through the folly of what we preach to save those who believe." (1 Cor 1:21) The world, as with Alan of Lille, assumed that reason persuades people to follow God's higher path or ladder. But to the contrary, all we do as preachers is give a promise of the cross of Jesus Christ. Not just Aristotle and the Greek speech for persuasion, this trips up everyone, as Paul says, "Jews demand signs, and Greeks seek wisdom." (1 Cor 1:22)

"Greeks seek wisdom"—which is to say, "faith seeks understanding." But Paul also found a problem with his fellow Jews, who were not looking for persuasion, but a sign. A prophet was to come and give the sign of Moses, which meant something even greater than Moses gave (Deut 18:15–18). And what is greater than Moses? How do you do better than the law of Moses? A better law, perhaps? No, Paul recognized that you give a new word, which is the gospel. But the Jews wanted a sign, not the gospel. The sign would tell them that suffering had come to an end, and the gift of their election would finally appear. But that is not what Paul means by grace. The sign seeks glory, and glory is the receipt of what is due—not the surprising gift of something that is not due. That is why glory concerns signs rather than wisdom. Wisdom understands a thing presently, signs await a future glory. Christ's cross overthrows both those who seek wisdom, as faith seeking understanding, and those who seek signs in anticipation of the glory that is soon to arrive (כְּבוֹד יהוה). But what does a dead Jesus do to persuade you of anything? The sign of the cross strikes one as pointing in the wrong direction. Where is the glory in that? For this reason, to the Jews Paul's preaching is folly.

"But to those who are called, both Jews and Greek, Christ the power of God and the wisdom of God. For the foolishness of God is wiser than men, and the weakness of God is stronger than men" (1 Cor 1:24–5). Here we have a sudden reversal, since God's weakness is stronger than anything among creatures. But Paul's reversal is not a simple, worldly reversal in which one group conquers another. It is the victory of Christ by using the foolishness of preaching to bring down and to lift up, to destroy and create new. So Paul says, "[C]onsider your call, brethren; not many of you were wise according to worldly standards, not many were powerful, not many were of noble birth; but God chose what is foolish in the world to shame the wise, God chose what is weak in the world to shame the strong, God chose what is low and despised in the world, even things that are not, to bring to nothing things that are." (1 Cor 1:26–28) This is the dialectic, or the working, of law and gospel. And so Paul aligns this in columns with wise/powerful/noble overthrown by foolish/weak/lowly.

Thus we come to the matter of the true attribute of a preacher: boasting. Paul states that the dialectic of law and gospel so works "that no human being might boast in the presence of God. He is the source of your life in Christ Jesus, whom God made our wisdom, our righteousness and sanctification, and redemption; therefore as it is written, 'Let him who boasts, boast of the Lord.' [Jer 9:24]" (1 Cor 1:29–31). Preachers do not boast in themselves, but in Christ. It is true that Christ is not only the center of Scripture but the center of any sermon, but Christ can be used badly or preached poorly. "When I came to you, brethren, I did not come proclaiming to you the testimony [mystery] of God in lofty words of wisdom. For I decided to know nothing among you except Jesus Christ and him crucified." (1 Cor 2:1–2) Christ crucified serves no purpose for reason or for those looking for a sign. There is no earthly scheme of power, glory, wisdom or strength which makes Christ crucified its announcement and declaration. Specifically, this does not work with a legal scheme, where you do something meritorious and God rewards you. Crucifying Christ is no merit.

Here Paul then gives his famous dichotomy, "And I was with you in weakness and in much fear and trembling and my word (λόγος) and my proclamation (κήρυγμα) were not [in the form of] persuasive words of wisdom, but in demonstration of the Spirit and power." (1 Cor 2:3–4) Paul's preaching was not persuasion. Instead, it was demonstration [actualizing—a token] of the Spirit and power. Persuasion tries to get you to look at the same thing differently—perhaps from a different point of view. But the thing remains the same. Persuasion seeks only a change of "perspective." What Paul did was to change reality. This is what we mean when we say that preaching is actually doing something, not just talking about it. It is *verbum reale*. Paul's words were not persuasive wisdom, but demonstrative Spirit and power—dynamite, actually giving them, not just talking about them. That is what Christ crucified does. He does not ask you to look at things from the perspective of the little guy, or the poor, but instead gives you power. But the power does not enable you to do a work of the law. It is the power of what Christ did and the impact that has on you. What is that? He took your sin and killed it. You are free! That is the great power unleashed by these words, "that your faith might not rest in the wisdom of men, but in the power (δύναμις) of God." (1 Cor 2:5) Here is the dynamite of the public speaking that preaching is. It is what God is doing that matters here, not what you are doing. The sermon does not move its hearers to accomplish something; it does not move them to tears. It addresses them with what God is doing, not just has done. The power is here and now, and it is God's. If there are any tears they come later out of joy.

Paul quickly makes clear he is not talking about irrationalism or what the Greeks would call "skepticism," a position of doubt and the critique of everything. "Yet among those who have come to their end (τέλειος) we do impart wisdom, although it is not a wisdom of this aeon, or the rulers of this aeon, who are coming to nothing." (1 Cor 2:6, translation mine) What does Paul mean here? To what "end" do the faithful come? Not the pinnacle of the law, as it was for Alan of Lille; that would make them virtuous and perfect on the top rung of Jacob's ladder. It finishes the old attempts to grasp for power in the world. Now that God has demonstrated his power, applied it, made it actual, those who received a preacher are over and done as old creatures, and the new has begun. This gives the wisdom of a new aeon, not the attempt in the old world to gain a new perspective. Those who have no preacher are not arriving to a τέλος but simply coming to nothing.

Then Paul plays a dangerous, but necessary, game with the gnostics (the religious secret knowers) who teach that they have a wisdom only the initiated can get concerning how to climb Jacob's ladder. Paul says, "But we declare the wisdom of God, a mystery that has been hidden, which God decreed before the ages to our glory." (1 Cor 2:7, translation mine). God decreed it, or said it before the ages, thus he predestined it. But this has been hidden—a mystery—until now! Until when? Until the moment you get your preacher, which means until the crucifixion of Christ is preached presently for you. Paul tells us clearly, "None of the rulers of this age understood this; for if they had, they would not have crucified the Lord of glory. But as it is written, 'What no eye has seen, nor ear heard, nor the heart of man conceived, what God has prepared for those who love him [Isa 64:4].' God has revealed to us through the Spirit. For the Spirit searches everything, even the depths of God." (1 Cor 2:8–10)

1 Corinthians 3 arrives at the problem that plagues the Corinthian church: once you have a preacher, and that one is the spiritual man (1 Cor

2:14–15) then the first thing people do is to make him a local hero. That is, a cult of personality, or a person of power. In other words they separate the words and the person, and idolize the person, rather than hear the word. The reverse also happens, to hate the person rather than hear the word.

Paul says first, "But I, brethren, could not address you as spiritual men, but as men of the flesh (σαρκίνοις), as babes in Christ. I fed you with milk, not solid food; for you were not ready for it; and even yet you are not ready, for you are still of the flesh (σαρκικοί). For while there is jealousy and strife among you, are you not of the flesh, and walking like old men." (1 Cor 3:1–3)[13] What are anthropoids after all? They are people without a preacher! Without a preacher they are running around like chickens with their heads cut off trying to persuade others of their opinion. They have no promise, no faith, nothing to run to in time of trouble—falsely comfortable in good times and without any trust in bad. They have no one to give them the word of Christ that forgives.

After addressing the joint (and not factionalizing) work of preachers, who on the single foundation of Jesus Christ (1 Cor 3:4–23) Paul comes to his great definition of preachers, "Let a man reckon us as assistants (ὑπηρέτας) of Christ and stewards (οἰκονόμους) of the mysteries of God." (1 Cor 4:1, translation mine) The key attribute of the preacher is none other than that of God himself, "As for the rest, what is to be sought in the steward is that they be found faithful." (1 Cor 4:2, translation mine) Paul is not concerned that he is currently being judged and found wanting by people in Corinth, who are comparing him to Apollos or Peter or for that matter to Christ.

> But with me it is a very small thing that I should be judged by you or by any human court. In fact, I do not even judge myself. For I am not aware of anything against myself, but I am not thereby acquitted. It is the Lord who judges me. Therefore do not pronounce judgment before the time, before the Lord comes, who will bring to light the things now hidden in darkness and will disclose the purposes of the heart. Then each one will receive his commendation from God. (1 Cor 4:3–5).

The only commendation a preacher seeks is this, "You have been faithful. Not to the law, but to Christ, that is, to his promise of forgiveness of sins which is the meaning of his grace that he alone gives." Grace is not a power in the worldly sense. This is why many Bible historians of recent

---

13. ἄνθρωπον (3:3) does not refer to "ordinary men" as the RSV has it, a form of a common mistranslation, as if Christians were extraordinary. That is not the meaning of "pneumatic man."

centuries have made the mistake of thinking Paul does not concern himself with the forgiveness of sins. That reflects a false assumption that grace is giving something other than forgiveness, which means the gift is power in the old world. But Paul is making his case throughout that this grace, this gift, is not a power; it is a weakness. It is not a possession; it is a freedom. It is not a quality of virtue; it is a new life, "I have applied all these things to myself and Apollos for your benefit, brothers, that you may learn by us not to go beyond what is written, that none of you may be puffed up in favor of one against another." (1 Cor 4:6) After all, what puffs up? The law. What does it mean to live according to Scripture then? To find the promise of Christ's crucifixion, and apply it.

> So, who judges you? What do you have that you did not receive? If you received it, why boast as if you had not received it? Already you are filled! Already you have become rich! Without us you have become kings! And would that you did reign, so that we might share the rule with you! For I think that God has exhibited us apostles as last of all, like men, sentenced to death; because we have become a spectacle to the world, to angels and to men. (1 Cor 4:7–9)[14]

In this way, Paul leads us to the next great teaching on preaching as foolishness, which compares preachers and hearers. Hearers of the word are kings! Already! There is not anything higher than to be a hearer of the proclamation. In fact, it would be nice if the hearers took the bull by the horns and ruled accordingly. Then the preachers would rule with you. But as it is, the apostles are not on the top of a church pyramid, but on the bottom—exhibited like caged animals sentenced for death. Even angels watch this sport as they get thrown to the lions! Preachers are, after all, sentenced to death. That is what the end of holding the office of preaching is. No wonder preaching is foolishness. Who would want to do it knowing this? Thus he says,

> We are fools for Christ's sake, but you are wise in Christ. We are weak, but you are strong. You are held in honor, but we in disrepute. To the present hour we hunger and thirst, we are poorly dressed and buffeted and homeless, and we labor, working with our own hands. When reviled, we bless; when persecuted, we endure; when slandered, we entreat. We have become, and are still, like the scum of the world, the refuse of all things. (1 Cor 4:10–13)

---

14. RSV slightly revised.

So, in the end, Paul contrasts the hearer and the preacher in a set of opposites: filled/empty, rich/poor, alive/dead, honor/humiliation, homeowners/homeless, blessed/reviled conciliated/slandered. So, in the end, what is the preacher? The preacher is περικαθάρματα, the "scum of the world" and περίψημα, the "refuse of all things." Preaching is foolish in the world because in the end the preacher is garbage and scum, just as the Lord planned it.

But before we conclude the matter of preaching as foolishness, and confirm that preaching is not persuasion in any common sense, Paul ends by giving us one more metaphor for a true preacher, specifically an apostle like Paul to Corinth:

> I do not write this to make you ashamed, but to counsel you as my beloved children. For though you have myriad guardians[15] in Christ, you do not have many fathers. For I became your father in Christ Jesus through the gospel. I appeal to you, then, become imitators of me. (1 Cor 4:14–16, translation mine)

Mimesis is not a way of acquiring knowledge, but is the direct imitation of Paul the preacher. "Preach like I do," he is saying. How is that? What is preaching? It is learning the distinction of law and gospel and giving these words to the ungodly. It is not climbing Jacob's ladder in doctrine and descending in ethics. It is not the rhetoric of persuasion. But it is power. The dynamite of his preaching is in the Word, who is Christ—crucified, and so in the simple word of Christ: "I forgive you." Anything else is fluff, or "puffed up," but has no dynamite in it. Unfortunately for the time being, this power is hidden under the sign of its opposite—weakness.

So Paul gave the Corinthians a final word on the foolishness of preaching, "But I will come to you soon, if the Lord wills, and I will find out not the talk of these arrogant people but their power. For the kingdom of God does not consist in talk but in power. What do you wish? Shall I come to you with a rod, or with love in a spirit of gentleness?" (1 Cor 4:19–21). Such is the question of a father who knows when children have been caught up in false preachers who confused persuasion with their proper work, which is the foolishness of letting the word do its work as *verbum reale*.

BIBLIOGRAPHY

Alan of Lille. *The Art of Preaching*. Translated by Gilian R. Evans. Cistercian Fathers 23. Kalamazoo: Cistercian, 1981.

Cicero. *De Oratore*. Translated by E. W. Sutton. Cambridge, MA: Harvard University Press, 1967.

15. The same word is used in Gal 3:24–25 for pedagogues, teachers, disciplinarians.

Deane, Sidney N., ed. *Works of St. Anselm*. Chicago: Open Court, 1903.
Lischer, Richard, ed. *The Company of Preachers: Wisdom on Preaching, Augustine to the Present*. Grand Rapids: Eerdmans, 2002
Migliore, Daniel L. *Faith Seeking Understanding: An Introduction to Christian Theology*. 2nd ed. Grand Rapids: Eerdmans, 2004.
Milbank, John, Catherine Pickstock, and Graham Ward, eds. *Radical Orthodoxy: A New Theology*. London: Routledge 1999.

9

Paraenesis in Preaching
Some Systematic-theological Considerations for a Homiletical Problem[1]

—Hans-Jörg Voigt

INTRODUCTION

In their book, *Möne Markow der neue Amerikafahrer* (*Möne Markow, The New American Pastor*) Johannes and Theo Gillhoff give a wonderful description the preaching practice of a true blue village pastor from Warkentin in Mecklenburg, Pastor Brümmerstädt.[2] The novel bears a strong connection to the history of The Lutheran Church—Missouri Synod in that the main character, Möne Markow, becomes a pastor of that church. The novel opens Möne Markow's childhood in Mecklenburg for the reader and lets him or her experience something rather interesting—something related to

---

1. These considerations were presented as a paper to the pastors' convention of the Southern District of the Independent Evangelical Lutheran Church (the *Selbstständige Evangelisch-Lutherische Kirche [SELK]*, Germany) and to the homiletics class of its Practical-theological Seminar for vicars/curates. Followed by an exercise, the whole took the form of a workshop. The oral form of the paper has, in the main, been retained for this printed version.

2. Gillhoff and Gillhoff, *Möne Markow*, 40–41.

our topic—from the preaching practice of the Lutheran Church in Mecklenburg. There one reads,

> Pastor Brümmerstädt hurled forceful admonitions into the conscience of his flock; with great gravity he emphatically smote their evil spirits straight on the head and with the staff of woe flogged them on the inside, so that the ears of the Old Adam got a thorough boxing. Especially pride and immorality did he make the objects of his castigation. . . . And he did not fail to set before their eyes the demise of the world and the final judgment with thunderous voice and powerful words. Of this day none knew when it would come, and on it each and every one would have to give an account of his stewardship, be he master or servant, maid or maiden, old or young.
>
> And many a little lady below him in the pew sunk her head to her breast and fervently pleaded, "Dear God, just not tomorrow, it's my laundry day!" And then, all of a sudden, a totally different Pastor Brümmerstädt stood in the pulpit. It was no longer the commanding, admonishing, chastising man, whose voice rang as the thunder of judgment. The ominous clouds had retreated from his brow; the storm had cleared away, and now a soft, quiet rain came falling down. A warm, touching tone lay in his voice, and great joy and gentleness radiated from the man as he now began to speak of in moving words of the praise of God.

Perhaps no genre of speech is so related and even bound to a particular time as preaching. And indeed even of the renowned sermons of the nineteenth or eighteenth centuries, hardly a one could be preached today, especially as Pastor Brümmerstädt is supposed to have stood in the pulpit for an hour and a half. It is, however, certainly clear that the village pastor, Brümmerstädt, of Lutheran Mecklenburg (at least so far as he is portrayed by authors Johannes and Theo Gillhoff) was practiced in the art of distinguishing law and gospel, and in doing so did not shy away from powerful admonition.

Paraenesis, is from the Greek παραινέω, meaning "to advise strongly, recommend, urge."[3] In New Testament scholarship paraenesis denotes ethical admonitions with specific connection to a congregation or grouping of Christians. In the gospels Matt 5–7 and Luke 6:17–49 are worthy of special note; in Paul's letters Rom 12, Gal 5–6, Phil 4, 1 Thess 4–5, Col 3–4, and Eph 4–6. Given this biblical paraenesis, it is necessary for preachers to deal with paraenesis in preaching. In these considerations I am operating under the

3. BDAG 764.

assumption, that paraenetical preaching is to be equated with the so-called third use of the law.[4]

Paranaesis entails problems for preaching practice in Protestant circles, and in contemplating this topic I cannot help but be under the impression that digging into the subject on simply a systematic-theological level would come up short. Thus these considerations, in a sort of multidisciplinary fashion, are intended for both systematic- and practical-theological deliberation and appropriation. And I think that this sort of systematic- and simultaneously practical-theological approach is a basic requirement for Lutheran preaching, for the remarks of the Lutheran confessions understand themselves as an interpretation of Scripture, and as guidance toward rightly understanding Scripture. For preaching and pastoral what I am driving at here may be brought under the heading of "comfort." "As Lutheran confessions are formed one is, not least with controversial theological questions, always asking about that which is pastorally relevant and about which solution, given it being founded in Scripture, is helpful, comforting, and proper for pastoral care."[5]

1. AN EXAMPLE OF THE PROBLEM

In order to illustrate this problem I have selected a prominent example of a sermon from the nineteenth century: a sermon preached by C. F. W. Walther on the Fifth Sunday after Trinity, which in 1845 was the feast day of John the Baptist. In selecting a sermon from Walther I am well aware of his worthy contributions in the founding and theology of The Lutheran Church—Missouri Synod, whose influence is also not to be underestimated in the very predecessor churches out of which the Independent Evangelical Lutheran Church of Germany was born.

In this particular sermon Walther was preaching on Luke 1:57–80. Toward the end of the sermon one finds this:

> Oh, well is it with you, if you would then humbly speak to God, saying, "Oh, Lord, I too am a fruitless tree, who is thus worthy to be chopped down by you and thrown into eternal fire." Then the gospel says to you, "See your salvation! For your salvation is not in your works or worthiness, but—oh, rejoice and be glad!—'in the forgiveness of your sins, through the tender mercy of our God, through which the dawn from on high has also broke upon you, that he appear to you, who sits in darkness and the shadow

---

4. Cf. SD VI (KW 587–91 = *BSLK* 962–69).
5. Klän, "Herausforderungen," 13.

of death, and guide your feet into the way of peace.'" That you must then firmly believe and, in order that you remain in this faith, daily and hourly call upon God and not let his word out of your heart. Behold, in this way do you come to the knowledge of your salvation; in this way you come to forgiveness and so will you finally be saved.

Now, blessed[6] are those who hear the word of God and keep it! I have shown you the way, so now make haste and follow it! ...[7]

To this sermon section I now directly oppose Walther's own Thesis XIV from his evening lectures on law and gospel, in which he himself writes:

Tenthly, God's word is not rightly divided, when one demands faith as a requirement for justification and salvation,[8] as if a person not solely through [faith], but also because of faith, that is on account of faith and in view of faith before God is justified and saved.[9]

In his study Barnbrock rightly calls attention to an insurmountable tension between Walther's preching practice and the statements of his evening lectures on law and gospel.[10] In the section of the sermon just quoted Walther is, in the first instance, preaching the law. On the receiving end of this sermon the sinner has already recognized that he is a "fruitless tree," who deserves to be thrown into the fire. Then Walther proclaims the gospel by addressing the pericope directly to the individual hearer, "that he appear to you . . ." Then, however, follows the paraenetical call to faith: "That you must then firmly believe and, in order that you remain in this faith, . . ."

In countless sermons today one can see that this sequence is entirely typical. In simplified form it can be presented as: 1. the preaching of the Law in its accusing function; 2. the preaching of the gospel with the promise of forgiveness and God's grace; and finally 3. ". . . so now let us!"—believe, do, act—in the sense of the third use of the law.

6. "*[S]elig*" has stronger connections to "salvation" ("*Seligkeit*") in German than in English; see n8 below.

7. Barnbrock, *Die Predigten C. F. W. Walthers*, 191.

8. "*Seligkeit*"; see n6 above.

9. Walther, *Die rechte Unterscheidung*, 3; translation mine. Cf. English translation in *Law and Gospel*, trans. Tiews, 4.

10. Barnbrock, *Die Predigten C. F. W. Walthers*, 358, "Walther's propositions about preaching, as he develops them in his evening lectures on the proper distinction between law and gospel, stand in rather distinct tension both to his understanding of preaching, as presented in his *Pastorale (Pastoral Theology)* as well as to his own preaching practice."

The identifying features of such preaching practice have been fleshed out by Manfred Josuttis in a study that remains unsurpassed to this day.[11] These are the perspicuous piling up of conditional words (since, therefore, so, because of) and verbs relating to the human will (let [us], must, may, can, should) at the end of the sermon. So, too, the piling up of question marks may be reckoned to the identifying features of such sermons.

2. SYSTEMATIC-THEOLOGICAL RAPPROCHEMENT

2.1 Is Paraenesis Law or Gospel?

In considering paraenesis in view of law and gospel, the definition of the Formula of Concord is first to be called to mind. Both law and gospel are works of the Holy Spirit, the law being an *opus alienum* and the gospel an *opus proprium*.[12] Then the Solid Declaration, by way of a Luther citation, states, "Everything that proclaims something about our sin and God's wrath is the proclamation of the law, however and wherever it may take place."[13] One would not simply assign paraenesis to this definition, if it in fact intends to guide and instruct baptized, redeemed Christians as they travel their path of faith. Of this the Solid Declaration speaks a bit later, "Nonetheless, reproving sin and teaching good works remain the proper function of the law."[14] To this description paraenetic address can be assigned when it in fact teaches of good works and Christian life.

However, the Solid Declaration's definition of the gospel, which follows its definition of the law, certainly does not fit with paraenetic address, "On the other hand, the gospel is the kind of proclamation that points to and bestows nothing else than grace and forgiveness."[15]

2.2 Concerning the Third Use of the Law

It is not Article V but rather Article VI of the Formula of Concord, which treats the third use of the law, that brings greater clarity in the question about the systematic-theological placement of paraenesis and its assignment as address in the preaching of the law and of the gospel. The point of

---

11. *Gesetzlichkeit*.
12. SD V:11 (KW 583 = *BSLK*, 955.23–31).
13. SD V:12 (KW 583= *BSLK*, 955.39–42).
14. SD V:18 (KW 584 = *BSLK*, 957.30–33).
15. SD V:12 (KW583 = *BSLK*, 955.42—956.12).

contention behind Article VI was whether those who have been born again learn good works from the law and therefore the law is still to be preached to them, or whether they without the preaching of the law, by the prompting of the Holy Spirit do what God demands of them.[16]

However, given that human beings do not attain to perfect sanctification in this life, but remain sinners, the Solid Declaration cites Rom 7, "Therefore, in this life, because of the desires of the flesh, the faithful, elect, reborn children of God need . . . the law's daily instruction and admonition."[17] The good works that flow from faith are works in accord with the will of God, that is to say the law of God, but they are not fruits of the law but rather of the Spirit.

In this light "the law" can be defined as "the revealed will of God, which aims at the work of human beings." Above all the law shows the inability of human beings to carry out such work, but it also gives direction and content for the actions of pardoned sinners. "The gospel," on the contrary, is to be defined as "the action of God, which aims at the salvation of human beings." Against this backdrop the exhortations of paraenetic address come to stand on the side of the law, for they contain the will of God and aim at the action of human beings.

Paraenesis's alignment with the workings proves itself in the practice of preaching in that with people of sensitive and alert consciences paraenesis can flip into the sin-identifying function of the law. Werner Elert underscores this with his denial of a third use of the law. The law always accuses: *lex semper accusat*.[18] Naturally, Elert also knows that the law has an instructing function. In Elert's case, though, this function coincides with the first and second functions of the law.[19]

For the practice of preaching the result is that a third use of the law, also in the form of New Testament paraenesis, cannot be separated from the preaching of the law in its *usus elenchticus*, its accusing function. Thus, if at all possible, the highly typified way of structuring a sermon as presented above (law, gospel, "so now let us . . . !") is to be avoided.

---

16. SD VI:2 (KW 587 = *BSLK*, 962.16—963.18).
17. SD VI:9 (KW 588 = *BSLK*, 965.10–14).
18. See AP IV:128 (KW 141 = *BSLK*, 185.53–54).
19. Silcock, "Freiheit und Gesetz," 13.

2.3 From What does a Preacher Expect Change in the Life of the Congregation—from the Law or from the Gospel?

In all of the frustrations that come in the daily life of a congregation comes a question that is decisive for preachers: "From what to I expect changes for good in the life of the congregation and in my own life?" Does one expect such change from the preaching of the law or from Christian exhortations, which also are aimed at the action of human beings, or is it the preaching of the gospel that works such change?

To this the Solid Declaration of the Formula of Concord gives answer:

> For the law indeed says that it is God's will and command that we walk in new life. However, it does not give the power and ability to begin or to carry out this command. Instead, the Holy Spirit, who is given and received not through the law but through the proclamation of the Gospel (Gal 3[:2, 14]) renews the heart.[20]

The preaching of the gospel, the comforting promise of salvation, alone works change in a person's life, and in the life of a congregation. This is a statement of faith, which makes allowance for the supernatural power of the word of God. The living voice of the gospel works as it were sacramentally, as a *sacramentum audibile*[21] in cooperation with the *verbum visibile* of the sacrament. However, a paraenetic instrumentalization of the gospel mixes law and gospel.

3. SUMMARIZING THESES

1. By the Holy Spirit the preaching of the gospel works renewal and change in the life of the baptized.

2. Paraenesis aims at the action of the baptized and is thus to be equated with the third use of the law.

3. Paraenetic address itself must also be overtaken by the comfort of the gospel.

4. Depending on the given life circumstances of an individual hearer, paraenetic preaching can exercise the penalizing and killing working of the law, as well as give helpful and guiding direction for the fruit-producing life of the redeemed.

---

20. SD VI:11 (KW, 589 = *BSLK*, 965.36—966.2); Gal 3:2,"Let me ask you only this: Did you receive the Spirit by works of the law or by hearing with faith?"

21. See Sasse, "Word and Sacrament, 24.

5. A paraenetic instrumentalization of the gospel mixes law and gospel. (As in, "I did that for you. What are you doing for me?")

CONCLUSION

As a closing to these contemplations about preaching, law, and gospel, Martin Luther brings a fitting word:

> Oh that it would please God to have the bishops, parsons, and rulers of this Christian people solemnly receive such teaching at this time. For who can preach, unless he is an apostle? And who is an apostle but he who brings the word of God? And who can bring the word of God but he who has heard God? Can one, however, call him an apostle, who recites nothing but his own dreams and human statutes and philosophical doctrine to the people? Indeed, he is a thief, a murderer, a spoiler and strangler of souls, who is not sent, but comes from himself. And this the afflicted and fearful consciences recognize all too well. For as often as God's word is preached, it makes happy, broad, certain consciences, for it is a word of grace and forgiveness, and what is more—a good and sweet word.
>
> But when one preaches man's word, that makes a sad, cramped, and quaking conscience in oneself, for it is a word of the law, of wrath and of sin. It shows what man has not done, and what he should in fact do.[22]

BIBLIOGRAPHY

Barnbrock, Christoph. *Die Predigten C. F. W. Walthers im Kontext deutscher Auswanderergemeinden in den USA.* Hamburg: Kovač, 2003.

Gilhoff, Johannes, and Theo Gilhoff. *Möne Markow der neue Amerikafahrer.* Berlin: Gebrüder Weiss, n.d.

Josuttis, Manfred. *Gesetzlichkeit in der Predigt der Gegenwart.* Munich: Kaiser, 1966.

Klän, Werner. "Herausforderungen für die kirchliche Verkündigung in einer nachchristlichen Welt: Eine Betrachtung über die Bedeutung der Ansage von Gesetz und Evangelium in unserer Zeit und Welt." *Oberurseler Hefte* 47 (2007) 11–28.

Sasse, Herman. "Word and Sacrament: Preaching and the Lord's Supper." Translated by Norman Nagel. In *We Confess the Sacraments*, 11–35. St. Louis: Concordia, 1985.

Silcock, Jeffrey. "Freiheit und Gesetz." *Oberurseler Hefte* 47 (2007) 13.

Walther, C. F. W. *Die rechte Unterscheidung von Gesetz und Evangelium.* St. Louis: Concordia, 1901.

---

22. WA 17/II:256.16–30.

———. *Law and Gospel: How to Read and Apply the Bible, A Reader's Edition*. Translated by Christian C. Tiews. St. Louis: Concordia, 2010.

10

Liturgical Preaching
The Pitfalls and the Promise

—John T. Pless

One of the fruits of movements for liturgical renewal in the last half of the twentieth century and first decade of the present century has been an accent on the nature and character of the sermon in the context of the liturgy, "Liturgical preaching is biblically oriented, kerygmatically controlled, eucharistically directed proclamation of the Word through the sermon as an integral and contributing part of the liturgy of the church gathered together in Christ's name to celebrate his presence, power and promise."[1]

The Austrian priest, Pius Parsch, would stand as something of a pioneer with his five volume work, *The Church's Year of* Grace, published in English in 1964.[2] Prompted by *Divino afflante Spiritu* promulgated by Pius XII in 1943, Roman Catholic exegetical scholars were free from former restraints to engage the Scriptures and the laity encouraged to read the Bible devotionally. The movement toward more direct involvement with the Holy Scriptures along with ecumenical and liturgical impulses nurtured by Vatican II would be reflected in Parsch's work which saw the liturgy as reflective of the Scriptures and the Scriptures at home in the liturgy. In *The Church's*

---

1. Bass, "An Introduction to Liturgical Preaching," 30.
2. Parsch, *The Church's Year of Grace*. For more on Parsch, see White, *Roman Catholic Worship*, 90–91; Kwatera, "Pius Parsch," 29–35. Similar in format to Parsch is the four volume set by Nocent, *The Liturgical Year*, which provides commentary on the revised Roman lectionary in light of liturgical reforms introduced by Vatican II.

Year of Grace, Parsch provides a liturgical commentary on the readings for daily office as well as each Sunday of the church year. This integrative approach to Bible and liturgy would accent the homily as being of one fabric with the liturgy, a doxological commentary connecting the lectionary to the contour and content of its ritual structures.

Something of a Lutheran parallel to Parsch's work is the four volume set by Fred H. Lindemann, *The Sermon and the Propers* published in 1958. In addition to providing commentary on the propers for each Sunday of the Christian year, Lindemann included actual sermons (both his own and others). The first volume includes an apologetic for the chief service each Sunday and festival day being the full service of both the word and the Sacrament of the Altar. Lindemann's work would serve as a widespread resource for pastors in The Lutheran Church—Missouri Synod in the decade of the 1960s until the adoption of the three-year lectionary offered by the Inter-Lutheran Commission on Worship (ILCW) largely rendered it obsolete.

A sampling of other authors indicates a growing impetus toward liturgical preaching among American Lutherans. George Bass, a professor of homiletics at Northwestern Lutheran Seminary in Minneapolis, published *The Renewal of Liturgical Preaching* in 1967, providing a theological rationale for the sermon as an integral part of the liturgy as well as critique of the standard lectionary then in use by Lutherans in North America. The well-known Swedish theologian, Gustaf Wingren's book *The Living Word in the Preaching and Mission of the Church,* first published in English translation in 1960, includes a chapter on liturgical preaching under the heading "God speaks—Man Listens." Here Wingren asserts that preaching is an "exposition of the Christian year"[3] which gives order and shape to the proclamation of living voice of Christ in the midst of the congregation. Bo Giertz, in a volume of essays growing out of a symposium on the unity of the church, contributed a chapter, "The Meaning and Task of the Sermon in the Framework of the Liturgy," in which he argues that the sermon and the liturgy have a reciprocal influence on each other as "the sermon works the life which the liturgical forms must fill out."[4] In the same volume, Conrad Bergendoff writes on "The Sermon in the Lutheran Liturgy," making the case that preaching "presupposes a community of believers," and that the communal form of this assembly is expressed in the liturgy as it receives and transmits the word.[5]

---

3. Wingren, *The Living Word,* 195.
4. Giertz, "The Meaning and Task," 137.
5. Bergendoff, "The Sermon," 131–32.

Clearly, an accent on liturgical preaching emerged in North American Lutheran churches and was accelerated by the adoption of *Lutheran Book of Worship* (1978) and *Lutheran Worship* (1982). Shaped in varying degrees by the resurgence of liturgical preaching in the Roman Church as well as a turn on the part of many Protestants toward lectionary-based preaching, Lutherans absorbed language and images from others in their own attempts to articulate an approach to preaching that was said to be liturgical and sacramental.[6] While the recognition of the liturgical character of the sermon is salutary, does the Lutheran theology of preaching itself carry within itself deeper resources while avoiding pitfalls inherent in approaches growing out of the variegated liturgical movements of the twentieth century? In other words might there be a means of critiquing the way that liturgical preaching has been described and implemented in recent decades, that at the same time provides for finding a more sure-footed way to affirm that, in and through the sermon, God is acting to forgive sins and strengthen faith for the sake of Christ crucified and raised?

Preaching must avoid a schism between the sermon and the sacrament. Luther states the case:

> So the word and the sacraments should not be divided, for Christ has comprehended the sacraments in the word. And without the word, one could not take comfort from the sacraments. Indeed, one could not know what the sacraments were! It is, therefore, not just a great blindness and error but rather a miserable abomination that the Papists preach about forgiveness of sins and yet forget the word, on which everything depends, and direct the people to monkey business—seeking the forgiveness of sins by their own devotion and works."[7]

In this house postil on John 20:19–31 from April 16, 1531, the Reformer seeks to make clear the fact that Christ has comprehended the forgiveness of sins acquired on the cross in the word which delivers and bestows the treasure. It is through this word of forgiveness, which is integral to both sermon and sacrament, that the fruits of Christ's redeeming work are handed over to sinners.

The oft-used phrase "Word and Sacrament" is more than a cliché, as it indicates a coordinate relationship that canned be pulled apart without emptying preaching of its evangelical potency and reducing the Lord's Supper to anthropocentric cultic activity. Rather, liturgical preaching is the Lord's work through the proclamation of the gospel to create and sustain

---

6. Here see West, *Scripture and Memory*, 25–64.

7. LW 69:399.

faith as it anchors hearers in the promises of Christ embodied in baptism, absolution, and the Sacrament of the Altar.

Here Hermann Sasse is particularly helpful. Sasse observes that according to Luther, "This sacrament is the gospel."[8] Preaching the Lord's Supper is nothing other than an exposition of the words of institution since they "contain the whole gospel."[9] Likewise, to preach baptism and the absolution is to preach the gospel, "Baptism is the gospel, because the whole gospel is contained in it, not only in words but also in what our Redeemer does in his mighty rescue of us from sin, death, and the devil. Absolution is the gospel, the forgiveness of sins, the anticipation of the verdict of justification that will come in the last judgment."[10] But each must be preached in its particularity.

What is given in the sacraments determines for Sasse how they are preached. They are not the "representation" of Christ's past work in the way of Odo Casel.[11] The death of Christ is not made present in the sacraments. It is a unique and unrepeatable historical event. Rather, in baptism, the baptized is joined to the death of the crucified and risen Lord so that the future of this Lord is now the future of the one who in faith clings to the promise of this Christ. In the Lord's Supper, the church is engaged not in cultic reenactment but in the receiving of the benefits of Christ's death given now by his body and blood under bread and wine. Thus the sacraments are preached as gospel.

Gerhard Forde also engages liturgical preaching, suggesting that the split between sermon and sacrament is avoided by recognizing that preaching itself is a "sacramental event"; in his words, "Preaching in a sacramental fashion is *doing* to the hearers what the text authorizes you to do to them."[12] If the text condemns, the preacher condemns; if the text consoles, the preacher consoles. This means that preaching is not merely explaining a text but letting the text itself stand as God's address to the living present. Forde asserts that if preaching is not seen as sacrament it will crumble into theological instruction or ethical exhortation, collapsing perhaps into a psychologized reading of the biblical narrative as the preacher seeks to gain a connection with his auditors with statements like, "No doubt there were times in your life when you felt abandoned like the Psalmist or perse-

---

8. Sasse, "Word and Sacrament," 23.
9. Ibid.
10. Ibid., 25.
11. Ibid., 26. For more on Sasse's critique of Odo Casel, see Pless, "Hermann Sasse," 47–51.
12. Forde, "Preaching the Sacraments," 91.

cuted like Paul." Such approaches relegate the sacraments to like more than appendages to preaching, "When this happens the sacraments too gradually degenerate into automats for dispensing a mysterious quantity called 'grace' that has lost its relation to the gospel story."[13]

Here the sermon comes to function as something of a preparation for grace which is delivered elsewhere as the preacher calls upon his hearers to "remember their Baptism" or points them forward to the Lord's Supper which is yet to come. This is illustrated by rather perfunctory and obligatory remarks about baptism or the Lord's Supper at the end of the sermon. The late James Schaaf, who taught at Trinity Lutheran Seminary in Columbus, Ohio, quipped that the former model of the sermon as three points and a poem has been replaced by the sermon as three points and a few words about the sacraments. Such preaching attempts, most often, to artificially justify itself as sacramental by forced insertion of references to baptism and the Lord's Supper into every sermon. This can be avoided where the sermon itself is understood as functioning sacramentally.

Forde himself provides an example of just this kind of sacramental preaching in a sermon on Col 2:20–3:4 under the title, "You Have Died." Clearly the immediate context of this pericope is Paul's baptismal teaching stated in Col 2:12, "you have been buried with him in baptism." Yet Forde preaches the sermon without an explicit reference to baptism. Beginning his sermon with the assertion, "You have died, and your life is hid with Christ in God! I expect you did not reckon when, for whatever reason you bestirred yourself to show up here today, that you were going to a funeral,"[14] Forde moves to announce to his hearers that they are already dead. They have shown up for their own burial. Their funerals are now. It is too late to do anything about it. It is not simply that you will die, but that you are dead and your life is now hidden with Christ in God. A striking feature of this sermon is that Forde preaches baptism without ever mentioning baptism. The action of baptism as death and resurrection is not preached descriptively or by way of analogy. He is not preaching about dying and living. Instead the preacher forthrightly proclaims the baptismal death. Hearers cannot miss what baptism gives or bestows even though the word "baptism" never crosses the preacher's lips.

A dual problem surfaces when sermon and sacrament are severed. "Without a sacramental understanding of the Word, preaching degenerates into mere information; without preaching, sacraments degenerate into

---

13. Ibid., 99.
14. Forde, "You Have Died," 215.

'magic.'"[15] Without preaching, the sacraments can become ritual enactments done to "realize" or "re-actualize" the presence and power of a God who is thought otherwise to be absent. Even as preaching anchors and makes unmistakable the "for you" of the sacraments, so the sacraments keep the audible word of preaching from evaporating into inwardness. Hence Forde,

> Most of Protestantism tried to solve the problem of magic, by simply rejecting the objectivity, the externality of the sacraments in favor of preaching understood as a word addressed to our subjectivity, our inner 'decision.' The sacraments degenerated into the symbols of what goes on within, signs of our dedication and the like. Thus the word basically disappeared into the inner reaches of the soul, rarely to be heard from again, gradually degenerating into pop psychology and greeting card sentimentality.[16]

When liturgical preaching is reduced to commentary on the drama of ritual action it forsakes its character as "a speech-act in the form of a divine *promissio*."[17] Deeply influential on American Lutherans through his students Eugene Brand and Robert W. Jenson,[18] the Heidelberg theologian Peter Brunner asserted that, in preaching, "Our task is not primarily to expound a text but to interpret an action that takes place in our midst."[19] Brunner's definition was congruent with and reinforced an approach to liturgical preaching that was more akin to commentary than proclamation. The sermon itself functions to illustrate or explain an action that is going on elsewhere, in the rites and ceremonies of the liturgy or in the act of celebrating the sacrament itself. The sermon itself then is not seen as the living word of Christ rooted and normed by a text of Holy Scripture but as an instruction in how to understand, participate in, or sensually experience the liturgy.

Oswald Bayer is suggestive of a more evangelically-faithful approach. Drawing on Luther, Bayer writes, "The evangelical understanding of the word of the sermon preserves Luther's great hermeneutical discovery, which,

15. Forde, "Preaching the Sacraments," 100.

16. Ibid., 105.

17. Bayer, "Preaching the Word," 202.

18. Eugene Brand was a leading architect of the *Lutheran Book of Worship* (1978) and the author of a popular introduction to the liturgical theology it embodied, *The Rite Thing*. Robert W. Jenson is a well-known systematic theologian celebrated for his ecumenical work. Jenson is the author of *Visible Words*.

19. Brunner, *Worship in the Name of Jesus*, 157. For a careful critique of Brunner, see Olson, "Liturgy as 'Action,'" 108–13; and Olson, "Contemporary Trends in Liturgy," 110–57.

strictly speaking, is his Reformation discovery. Namely, *that the linguistic sign itself is the thing; it does not represent a thing that is absent but it presents a thing that is present.*"[20] The sermon, then, is not discourse that points to something going on either in the heart of the hearer or in the communal action of the assembly. It is itself the speaking of the Lord's words—both law and gospel—which carry with them the Lord's own authority to kill and make alive, to convict and comfort. The preacher is authorized to assert God's word in human speech. As Bayer says, Luther does not, like modern spiritualistic thinking, "differentiate strictly between God and human being, Word of God and human speech."[21]

Preaching takes place within the context of the divine service. Hence Bayer identifies the sermon "as a particular part of the Christian divine service, a special type of speech need[ing] to be in harmony with the criterion and essence of the entire divine service."[22] The testamentary words of the Lord which give his body and blood for the forgiveness of sins form the matrix in which the sermon is found. Bayer sees the word of Christ in his supper as guarding the preacher against three homiletical missteps identified at least implicitly by Forde: theorization, moralization, and psychologization.[23] In the Lord's Supper, God is approaching the human being with the word of promise attached to his body and blood. This word of promise is not an appeal to action or a description of some other reality to be made complete by understanding, involvement, or observation. Even so, the word of preaching is promissory, to be received by faith alone.[24]

---

20. Bayer, "Preaching the Word," 202. Also, "That the verbal sign itself is the matter itself, that it presents not an absent but rather a present matter, that was Luther's great hermeneutical discovery, his reformatory discovery in the strict sense of the word. He made this discovery first of all in his investigation of the sacrament of penance (1518). That the sign itself is already the matter and event itself means in view of absolution that the sentence 'I absolve you of your sins' is not merely a declaratory judgment of what already is, thus presupposing an inner, proper absolution. The word of absolution is rather a verbal act, which creates a relationship—between God in whose name it is spoken, and the person to whom it is spoken." Bayer, "Martin Luther," 54. For Luther, the sermon itself must be an actual absolution.

21. Bayer, *Martin Luther's Theology*, 265.

22. Bayer, "Preaching the Word," 201.

23. Ibid. Also see Elert, *The Structure of Lutheranism*: "[T]he Gospel not only gives information concerning a new relationship between him who hears it and God; but it brings this relationship about—only, however, by calling attention to Christ" (65); and again: "Justification is no psychic change; it is a word of God spoken to the sinner" (87).

24. Here see Luther's words in *The Babylonian Captivity of the Church* (1520) "For anyone can easily see that these two, promise and faith necessarily go together. For without the promise there is nothing to be believed; while without faith the promise is useless since it is established and fulfilled through faith. From this everyone will readily

Preaching, like the Lord's Supper, delivers the forgiveness of sins accomplished on the cross. Both sermon and sacrament are "for you." Tapping into Luther's famous words against Karlstadt and the enthusiasts that redemption was won at Calvary but distributed in the sacrament,[25] Albrecht Peters concludes, "Preaching that is not centered on proclaiming the alien righteousness of Christ affords no deliverance; unless *Solus Christus—sola gratia—sola fide* is proclaimed publicly, even if one were to perform Christian deeds and keep on uttering the word Church with one's mouth, salvation would be absent; God's wrath and condemnation would be all that is there, since neither God nor the true Church can be truly present without proclamation. For each individual, even though one were to remain in the community of the Church and honor word and sacrament in an external way, such a person would finally be seeking to become righteous on the basis of his own efforts alone, which means that he has excommunicated himself inwardly and has rejected salvation in Christ."[26]

The catechism is the compass which navigates liturgical preaching so that God's speaking and giving are distinguished from the Christian's activities. Preaching is not evocative of an innate knowledge of God nor the

---

gather that the mass, since it is nothing but promise, can be apprehended and observed only in faith. Without this faith, whatever else is brought to it by way of prayers, preparations, works, signs, or gestures are incitements to impiety rather than exercises of piety" (LW 36:42).

25. Writing in 1525, *Against the Heavenly Prophets in the Matter of Images and Sacraments*, Luther says, "We treat forgiveness of sins in two ways. First, how it is achieved and won. Second, how it is distributed and given to us. Christ has achieved it on the cross, it is true. But he has not distributed it or given it on the cross. He has not won it in the supper or sacrament. There he has distributed and given it through the word, as also in the gospel, where it is preached. He has won it once for all on the cross. But the distribution takes place continuously before and after, from the beginning to the end of the world" (LW 40:213–14). Then a few lines later, Luther continues, "If now I seek the forgiveness of sins, I do not run to the cross, for I will not find it given there. Nor must I hold to the suffering of Christ, as Dr. Karlstadt trifles, in knowledge or remembrance, for I will not find it there either. But I will find in the sacrament or gospel a word which distributes, presents, offers, and gives to me the forgiveness which was won on the cross. Therefore Luther has rightly taught that whoever has a bad conscience from his sins should go to the sacrament and obtain comfort, not because of the bread and the wine, not because of the body and the blood of Christ, but because of the word which in the sacrament offers, presents, and gives us the body and blood of Christ, given and shed for me. Is this not clear enough?"(LW 40:214) Also note the Large Catechism: "Therefore it is absurd for them to say that Christ's body and blood are not given and poured out for us in the Lord's Supper and hence that we cannot have forgiveness of sins in the sacrament. Although the work took place on the cross and forgiveness of sins has been acquired, yet it cannot come to us in any other way than though the Word" (LC V:31, KW 469 = BSLK 713).

26. Peters, *Commentary: Creed*, 286.

cultivation of the religious imagination, but rather speaking of God's law and gospel, both of which are outside the hearer.[27] The catechism is geared for repentance and faith so that God's law creates contrition and his gospel vivifies by forgiving sins. Luther recognized that without the orientation of the liturgy by this catechetical compass, the introduction of a revised order would be inadequate.[28] When he prepared the German mass of 1526, he stated that this "German service needs a plain and simple, fair and square catechism."[29] Luther would provide just such a catechism in 1529.

Using catholic texts known from the western liturgy (Apostles' Creed, Lord's Prayer, the baptismal formula, and the words of institution in the Lord's Supper) Luther would provide preachers with an outline of the shape and content of the doctrine to be preached. Luther's catechisms, both the small and the large, were born in the pulpit. Heinrich Bornkamm describes the birth:

> *The Large Catechism* is one of Luther's greatest artistic achievements. From this initial work a second sprang forth, *The Small Catechism*. While the mastery of the larger work lies in the wealth and liveliness of its articulating the faith, the beauty of the smaller work lies in the precision with which it made matters of faith luminous and memorable. Without the preparatory condensation of the catechetical sermons into *The Large Catechism*, there would have been no crystallization of the entire substance into *The Small Catechism*.[30]

Not only were the catechisms derived from preaching, they would serve the hearers in providing a hermeneutical framework to understand the sermon, giving both preacher and hearers a common language.

An evangelical distillation of the Holy Scriptures, the catechism "moves the Scripture, the confession of the church, and our daily life into the light of the last day,"[31] arming the Christian for life and death. The theological structure of the Small Catechism is geared to the proper distinction of law and gospel. Luther departs from the traditional, medieval ordering of the chief parts as Lord's Prayer, Apostles' Creed, and Ten Commandments.

27. Here see Bayer, "If the only effective way of dealing with the past is justification of the ungodly, and if the only effective way of dealing with future is a resurrection from the dead, and if both can only be a creation out of nothing, then the word that does it all is not a 'natural' word—immanent—possibility within human beings and their world but must come from the outside" ("Preaching the Word,"197).

28. LW 53:26.

29. LW 53:64.

30. Bornkamm, *Luther*, 601.

31. Peters, *Commentary: Ten Commandments*, 20.

He explains his rationale for the sequencing of the decalogue, creed, and Our Father:

> Thus the commandments teach man to recognize his sickness, enabling him to perceive what he must do or refrain from doing, consent to or refuse, and so he will recognize himself a sinful and wicked person. The Creed will teach and show him where to find the medicine-grace which will help him to become devout and keep the commandments. The Creed points him to God and his mercy, given and made plain to him in Christ. Finally, the Lord's Prayer teaches all this namely, through the fulfillment of God's commandments everything will be given him. In these three are the essentials of the entire Bible.[32]

Liturgical preaching is catechetical preaching not so much because it is didactic (although it certainly will teach the faith) but because it is actually doing what the catechism confesses. The catechism guides the preacher in understanding that the law/gospel distinction is not a formulaic template into which the text is squeezed. Rather, the catechism confesses the God who exposes sinfulness in the endless variety of manifestations of its root cause in the failure to fear, love, and trust God above all things. Luther's explanations to the individual commandments are open-ended. They not only prohibit certain vices but positively impose a demand for positive action that is never satisfied. The creed confesses the work of the Triune God in such a way that the second article reflects the Christological festivals of the church year.[33] Luther's explanation of the work of the Holy Spirit in the third article sharpens the necessity of preaching, for "I believe that I cannot by own reason or strength believe in Jesus Christ, my Lord, or come to him; but the Holy Spirit has called me by the gospel, enlightened me with his gifts, sanctified and kept me in the true faith."[34] Here Luther is doing more than making a descriptive statement about the necessity of divine monergism in conversion; he is speaking of the reality that the believer is

---

32. LW 43:4.

33. Peters, *Commentary: Creed*. Peters writes, "The Gospel of the Second Article finds its center in the cross and resurrection of Jesus . . . But the Good News of our salvation unfolds within the circle of festivals that celebrate Christ; thus, Luther's sermons for the various festival occasions consciously expand and deepen the catechism's 'short children's sermons.' The reformer orients the individual sermons for festivals, time and again, on the basis of the appropriate sections from the Apostles' Creed . . . The garland of Christ festivals decorates and makes real the chief article of our redemption. Even in his festival sermons, Luther tirelessly reiterates the 'for us' aspect; he deepens a practice from the late Middle Ages that used the church year to impress the Creed of the minds of the listeners" (163–64).

34. *Luther's Small Catechism*, 17.

forever dependent on the gospel for faith to be sustained. His exposition of the Lord's Prayer demonstrates the cruciform nature of Christian existence lived under the cross and with the promise of the resurrection.

Then to the catechetical trilogy of the decalogue, Apostles' Creed, and Lord's Prayer, Luther adds material on Holy Baptism, the Sacrament of the Altar, and eventually confession/absolution. God preaches his word in the water of baptism, giving us his name to call upon.[35] The grammar of the absolution, "I forgive you your sins," is the grammar of preaching. In the Sacrament of the Altar, the forgiveness of sins is unmistakably "for you." The forgiveness of sins lies at the heart of the sacrament. Luther drives this home with the triple repletion of "given for you" and "shed for the forgiveness of sins" in the sixth chief part. Bayer observes:

> Luther does not concentrate on the threefold repetition of the two phrases 'given for you' and 'shed for the forgiveness of sins' just by chance. God's turning toward the sinner, the promise that creates faith, empowered by the death and resurrection of Jesus Christ, cannot be summarized any more succinctly and specifically then by these words. This must be stated clearly as a critique of the depersonalizing speech about the 'bread of life' or the diminution of the Lord's Supper to become a generic love-fest. The Lord's Supper is not some diffuse celebration of life but is defined in a precise way in its essence by means of the connection between the word of Christ that has the effective power and the faith."[36]

The catechism's confession of the Lord's Supper as Christ's gift bestowing the forgiveness of sins drives the preaching of the sacrament, avoiding imagery and language that would override the testament that the Lord has established.

Catechetical anchorage prevents the slippage of liturgical preaching into artistic attempts to probe out of any text that has do with water or

---

35. Here see Paulson, "Graspable God," 51–62. This article is in itself an example of liturgical-catechetical preaching as Paulson demonstrates that how the divine promise of baptism is done is not left to the recipient (the baptized) but the giver (God). God preaches his name into the water for faith to grasp.

36. Bayer, *Martin Luther's Theology*, 272. Also see Korby, "The Use of John 6": "The forgiveness of sin is both the beginning and the goal. We do not start with the forgiveness and then move on to something higher, greater, or better. The East saw the gift of immortal life as the gift of the Eucharist. The West saw the immaculate offering of the church to her Lord—but in the communion only an appendix with the forgiveness of sins (but not of mortal sins so as not to degenerate the sacrament of penance). The mystics saw in the Lord's Supper the mystery-laden liquification of the individual in the awe. But Luther concentrates on the center, the forgiveness of sin" (131–32).

washing a connection to baptism. Not every reference to bread or eating and drinking is grounds for a sermon on the Lord's Supper. Forced and fanciful exegesis yields impressionistic preaching which leaves the old Adam intact, providing him with space to manipulate the text for his own survival, rather than facing a Lord who kills and makes alive. The catechism answers the question, "How can water do such great things?" with "Certainly not just water, but the word of God in and with the water does these things."[37] In similar fashion "How can bodily eating and drinking do these things?" is answered with "Certainly not just eating and drinking do these things, but the word here written, 'Given and shed for you for the forgiveness of sins.'"[38] Even as these catechetical questions draw us to the word of promise, so liturgical preaching must deliver the goods of the promise and not get lost in analogies to washing and meals.

Rightly understood, the liturgy not only sets the context for the sermon but itself reinforces what preaching is accomplishing. In the sermon, as in the liturgy, the Lord carries the action of the verbs, delivering and bestowing his gifts through his words which are "spirit and life" (John 6:63). "It must be apparent that there is no competition and that the spoken and visible word complement each other perfectly, supporting and reinforcing each other so that they save us."[39] Preaching and the sacrament are not be played off against other. The diminishing of one leads to the diminishing of the other. The abuses of liturgical preaching as poetic commentary on ritual action or a mere prelude to the sacrament need not deprive us of a genuinely evangelical understanding of the sermon as the proclamation of the word of the cross whereby the Triune God sustains and strengthens terrified consciences by the absolution. Such is the task of Lutheran liturgical preaching.

BIBLIOGRAPHY

Bass, George. "An Introduction to Liturgical Preaching." *Response* (1978) 30.
Bayer, Oswald. "Martin Luther." In *The Reformation Theologians*, edited by Carter Lindberg, 51–66. Oxford: Blackwell, 2002.
———. *Martin Luther's Theology: A Contemporary Interpretation*. Translated by Thomas H. Trapp. Grand Rapids: Eerdmans, 2008.
———. "Preaching the Word." In *Justification is for Preaching*, edited by Virgil Thompson, 196–216. Eugene, OR: Pickwick, 2012.
Bergendoff, Conrad. "The Sermon in the Lutheran Liturgy." In *The Unity of the Church: A Symposium*, 125–32. Rock Island, IL: Augustana, 1957.

37. *Luther's Small Catechism*, 24 (KW 359 = BSLK 516).
38. Ibid., 31 (KW 363 = BSLK 520).
39. Forde, "Preaching the Sacraments," 101.

Bornkamm, Heinrich. *Luther in Mid-Career 1521–1530*. Translated by E. Theodore Bachmann. Philadelphia: Fortress, 1983.

Brand, Eugene. *The Rite Thing*. Minneapolis: Augsburg, 1970.

Brunner, Peter. *Worship in the Name of Jesus*. Translated by Martin Bertram. St. Louis: Concordia, 1968.

Elert, Werner. *The Structure of Lutheranism*. Translated by Walter A. Hansen. St. Louis: Concordia, 1962.

Forde, Gerhard. "The Meaning and Task of the Sermon in the Framework of the Liturgy." In *The Unity of the Church: A Symposium*, 133–41. Rock Island, IL: Augustana, 1957.

———. "Preaching the Sacraments." In *The Preached God: Proclamation in Word and Sacraments*, edited by Mark C. Mattes and Steven D. Paulson, 147–74. Grand Rapids: Eerdmans, 2007.

———. "You Have Died." In *A More Radical Gospel: Essays on Eschatology, Authority, Atonement, and Ecumenism*, edited by Mark C. Mattes and Steven D. Paulson, 215–17. Grand Rapids: Eerdmans, 2004.

Jenson, Robert W. *Visible Words: The Interpretation and Practice of the Christian Sacraments*. Philadelphia: Fortress, 1978.

Korby, Kenneth F. "The Use of John 6 in Lutheran Sacramental Piety." In *Shepherd the Church: Essays in Pastoral Theology Honoring Bishop Roger D. Pittelko*, edited by Frederic W. Baue et al., 129–44 Fort Wayne: Concordia Theological Seminary Press, 2002.

Kwatera, Michael. "Pius Parsch, Evangelist of the Liturgy." In *How Firm a Foundation*, edited by Robert L. Tuzik, 2:29–35. Chicago: Liturgy Training, 1990.

Luther, Martin. *Luther's Small Catechism with Explanation*. St. Louis: Concordia, 1986.

Nocent, Adrian. *The Liturgical Year*. Translated by Matthew O'Connell. Collegeville, MN: Liturgical, 1977.

Olson, Oliver K. "Contemporary Trends in Liturgy Viewed from the Perspective of Classical Lutheran Theology." *Lutheran Quarterly* (1974) 110–57.

———. "Liturgy as 'Action.'" *Dialog* (1975) 108–13.

Parsch, Pius. *The Church's Year of Grace*. 5 Vols. Translated by William G. Heidt. Collegeville, MN: Liturgical, 1964.

Paulson, Steven D. "Graspable God." *Word & World* 32, no. 1 (2012) 51–62.

Peters, Albrecht. *Commentary on Luther's Catechisms: Creed*. Translated by Thomas H. Trapp. St. Louis: Concordia, 2011.

———. *Commentary on Luther's Catechisms: Ten Commandments*. Translated by Holger Sonntag. Saint Louis: Concordia, 2009

Pless, John T. "Hermann Sasse and the Liturgical Movement." *Logia* 7, no. 2 (1998) 47–51.

Sasse, Hermann. "Word and Sacrament: Preaching and the Lord's Supper." Translated by Norman E. Nagel. In *We Confess the Sacraments*, edited by Norman E. Nagel, 11–35. St. Louis: Concordia, 1985.

West, Fritz. *Scripture and Memory: The Ecumenical Hermeneutic of the Three-Year Lectionaries*. Collegeville, MN: Liturgical, 1997.

White, John F. *Roman Catholic Worship: Trent to Today*. New York: Paulist, 1995.

Wingren, Gustaf. *The Living Word in the Preaching and Mission of the Church*. Translated by Victor C. Pogue. Philadelphia: Muhlenberg, 1960.

11

The Real Presence and Liturgical Preaching[1]

—John W. Kleinig

Imagine two advertisements in two different places. The first advertisement is by the side of a busy road through the countryside. It has two words on it, "Free Meal!" That is all it says. It is a good sign. Yet people do not take any notice of it because it does not tell them where to go to get that meal. The second sign is in front of a restaurant. And it has three words on it, "Free Meal Here!" Both these signs have the same message. Yet the second sign is quite different from the first because of where it is placed. Its location tells you where you can go to receive a free meal. The liturgical preaching of the gospel is like that second sign. Its location is as significant as its message. Since the preacher stands together with Jesus in God the Father's presence, he can present God's gifts to his hearers.

There is a chapel in a Protestant seminary in Australia that contradicts this most graphically. Behind the communion table in its sanctuary there are three lovely stained glass windows inspired by the words of the angel to the women in Matt 28:5–6. The first left window has the words, "Do not be afraid!" The third right window has, "He is risen." But the central window, which dominates the sanctuary, has, "He is not here." That, sadly, does not just sum up the Zwinglian theology that is taught there, but, despite

---

1. The first draft of this paper was given at The First Andrha Pradesh Lutheran Symposium at Guntur in India in January, 2007. It has been slightly edited for printed publication.

the Lutheran teaching on Holy Communion, it also could be said of the preaching of far too many Lutheran pastors. All too often they preach as if Christ were not with his disciples in the divine service; they preach as if they did not stand in the presence of the Triune God, Father, Son and Holy Spirit. And that makes their preaching unreal, ineffectual, and unpastoral. They, quite unwittingly, promote a kind of practical Christological atheism in their preaching.

When we preach the word of God in the divine service, we proclaim a great mystery, something hidden from sight and all our other senses, something invisible and yet far more real that all that seems most real to us, the mystery of Christ present among us. St Paul speaks of it in this way in Col 1:25–27:

> I became a minister according to the stewardship from God that was given to me for you, to make the word of God fully known, the mystery hidden for ages and generations but now revealed to his saints. To them God chose to make known how great among the Gentiles are the riches of the glory of this mystery, which is Christ among you [plural], the hope of glory.

Here the apostle Paul depicts himself as a mystagogue, a person who initiates others into a mystery by his preaching. That mystery is the real presence of the risen, glorified Lord Jesus with his people in the church. The mystery is located there. There Paul discloses the mystery of Christ's real presence to the saints, those who are united with Christ and so share in his holiness. There he reveals the hidden presence and activity of the risen Lord to them by preaching God's word to them, the gospel that proclaims Christ and brings 'life and immortality to light' for its hearers (2 Tim 1:10). Apart from God's word they have no access to the risen Lord Jesus; apart from it they have no knowledge or experience of him even though he is there among them. That word proclaims Christ's presence to them and introduces him to them. It initiates them into the mystery of Christ in that place, something that no eye has seen, no ear has heard, and no human heart has ever conceived (1 Cor 2:6–10). The disclosure of his hidden presence there in that assembly gives the faithful a glimpse of glory, a foretaste of heaven here on earth.

In 1 Cor 4:1 Paul describes himself and his colleagues as "stewards of the mysteries of God." That does not just apply to him; it applies to every pastor. We pastors are all stewards of God's mysteries. By our preaching we proclaim the mystery of Christ. We do speak for an absent Christ; we speak for Christ who stands amongst us in the divine service and is there invisibly present with us.

The service of word and sacrament depends upon the presence of the risen Lord Jesus. It is located where he is located with the Father in the heavenly sanctuary.[2] It only works as it is meant to work because it is done there. Apart from him, it does not work properly, nor can it work properly anywhere else. He works in it and makes it work. We therefore make things difficult for ourselves as pastors by focusing on what we do when we preach. We concentrate on ourselves and on our message, rather than on Christ and his gifts to us. We speak and act as if we did everything. So something strange occurs. The same Lutheran pastors that believe in justification by grace and the real presence of Christ in Holy Communion all too often preach as if this was not true. They preach as if Christ were not present and active in the divine service. They preach as if they did not stand with the risen Lord Jesus in the presence of God the Father. And so the mystery of Christ is obscured; the gate of heaven is shut; present access to God's grace is lost. They get in the way of Jesus and shut him out. They dislocate themselves and their hearers from him.

When we gather for worship Christ serves us and gives his gifts to us there and then, in that place. He involves us in his service of God the Father. Worship is divine service, God's service of us in Christ and our service of God through Christ. And that makes all the difference for us in our preaching. We do not proclaim an absent Christ who lords it over us from afar, but we proclaim the risen Lord Jesus who is present with us to serve us. Everything is done in his presence. We pastors hand on what we receive from him, just as he gives us everything that he receives from his heavenly Father. He is the preacher and the liturgist in every service that we conduct. We work together with him. He uses our mouths to speak to the people of God, just as he uses our hands to hand out his body and blood to them. He is the speaker; he is the giver. We are his agents and instruments.

THE LOCATION OF THE RISEN LORD JESUS IN THE DIVINE SERVICE

The ministry of Jesus that began with his baptism did not end with his ascension. When he ascended he made it quite clear to his apostles that he would be present in the church with his disciples to the close of the age (Matt 28:20). After his ascension he became invisibly present with them in

---

2. For the importance of location for Luther Yeago, "The Catholic Luther," 37–41; and Kleinig, "Where is your God?," 168–84, which is a revised version of the essay in *All Theology Is Christology*, 117–31. This and my other articles may be accessed in John W. Kleinig Resources Publications at www.johnkleinig.com.

such a way that he was no longer bound by the normal limitations of time and space and matter. In the introduction to the book of Acts Luke goes one step further. He says, "In the first book, O Theophilus, I have dealt with all that Jesus began to do and teach, until the day when he was taken up, after he had given commands through the Holy Spirit to the apostles whom he had chosen." The key word here is "began." Luke claims that Jesus continues his work in word and deed through the ministry of word and sacrament in the church. That is why we read from the gospels in the divine service. That is why we preach from the gospels in our sermons. The readings from the gospels are so important for us in our worship because Jesus continues his work in the church. They therefore do not just tell us what Jesus said and did long ago; they tell us what Jesus says and does each Sunday when we gather together in his presence. They make sense there because they tell us what is happening there.

The story of the appearance of Jesus to the two disciples on the road to Emmaus in Luke 24:13–35 shows us how Jesus continues his ministry in the present age.[3] It happened, as you all know, on the evening of Easter Sunday. The two unnamed disciples had heard about the resurrection of Jesus, but did not understand the significance of what they had heard. When Jesus joined them on their journey, they did not at first recognize him. As far as they knew he was dead and gone from them. So Jesus made himself known to them in two stages in two locations. First, he preached himself to them from the Old Testament as he walked with them on their path. Yet, even though their hearts burned with joy as he spoke, they still did not recognize him. Then, when they had invited him to stay overnight with them as their guest, he acted as if he was their host when they sat down for the evening meal. He took the bread, gave thanks, broke it, and gave it to them, just as he had done when he instituted his holy supper three nights earlier. They recognized him there in the breaking of the bread, Luke's term for Holy Communion (Luke 24:35; cf. Acts 2:42, 46; 20:7). As soon as they recognized him he vanished from their sight.

That story gives us the basic theology of worship in the early church. Each Sunday the risen Lord Jesus, who travels with us through life as our unseen guide, makes himself known to us in the divine service. This happens in two stages. First, Jesus uses the word of God from the Old Testament to preach himself as the crucified and risen Lord. Then he hosts a meal in which he feeds us with his own body and blood.

---

3. For a comprehensive examination of this theme, see Just, *Luke 9:51—24:53*, 972-1020.

We discover two things about preaching from this dramatic account. First, Jesus himself is the preacher in our congregations. He is also the message; he preaches himself to us in the divine service. By his word he speaks to us there in that place. We human preachers are merely his mouthpieces, his spokesmen. He says, "He who listens to you listens to me" (Luke 10:16). Second, the preaching of the gospel is closely connected with the Lord's Supper. What Jesus tells us about himself he gives to us in Holy Communion. The same Jesus who preaches himself to us in the gospels and in the sermon that proclaims the gospel gives himself and all his gifts to us in the Lord's Supper. There he presents the body and blood that he offered up for us by his death on the cross. So preaching goes hand in hand with the administration of the sacrament. By preaching of the gospel we tell our people what Jesus gives to them in Holy Communion; by offering Christ's body and blood to them we give them what we have preached, Jesus and his gifts. In his Large Catechism Luther says, "For here in the sacrament you receive from Christ's lips the forgiveness of sins, which contains and conveys God's grace and Spirit with all his gifts . . ."[4]

DOING HEAVENLY WORK ON EARTH

Jesus himself taught the twelve apostles about his hidden presence and work with them in the divine service in Matt 18:18–20. He said:

> Truly, I say to you, whatever you bind on earth shall be bound in heaven, and whatever you loose on earth shall be loosed in heaven. Again I say to you, if two of you agree on earth about anything they ask, it will be done for them by my Father in heaven. For where two or three are gathered in my name, there am I among them.

Since the early church, this passage has quite rightly been used to teach what happens in the divine service. It tells us three things about our location and task as preachers.

First, we pastors do not gather the members of our congregations; God the Father gathers them together. The congregation then is God's assembly, his church, the people gathered by him in his presence. We minister there in his assembly, the church of God.

Secondly, we pastors do not lead our congregations in worship; Jesus does that. We act in his name as his agents and representatives. He is present where two or three gather in his name. In the service of word and sacrament

---

4. LC V:70; Tappert, 70 = *BSLK* 721–22.

Jesus bridges the gap between heaven and earth and joins these two spheres for us. Thus, since Jesus is present and active in the assembled congregation, we pray together with Jesus and work together with him. We speak in his name and pray in his name. Together with Jesus and in his name we do heavenly work here on earth; we do the work of God the Father by praying to him and by speaking his word.

Thirdly, like the apostles we pastors work together with God the Father and the risen Lord Jesus in their mission of binding and loosing here on earth. We bind the conscience of people by teaching God's law and announcing God's judgment on sin; we loose people from guilt and condemnation by teaching the gospel and pardoning sinners (John 20:21-23). We bind the powers of darkness by praying for their deliverance from them; we loose people from the grip of Satan by proclaiming God's word and enacting the sacraments. Thus Jesus involves us in his administration of his Father's grace here on earth. In the divine service we pastors work with Jesus in judging sin and pardoning sinners. Together with Christ and in his presence we use his keys, the keys that open the door into the Father's house, the keys that pardon sinners and give them access to his grace (Matt 16:19) for only through the forgiveness of sins can sinners approach God the Father unafraid with a good conscience in the full assurance of faith. We admit forgiven sinners to the Father's presence by admitting them to the Lord's Supper. Because they have been pardoned and justified, they have unrestricted access to his grace in the divine service. Thus the forgiveness that we proclaim in Christ's name is the key that opens the door to the Father's gracious presence; it gives people access to heaven there on earth.

When we preach we do so under an open heaven. It is significant that Jesus only began to preach after his baptism. There, as had been prophesied in Isa 61:1-3 God the Father anointed him with the Holy Spirit as the Messiah and commissioned him to preach the gospel. There, too, heaven was opened up for him and the people who were united with him in baptism (Matt 3:16; Mark 1:10; Luke 3:21). He therefore preached under an open heaven. And so too do we! In John 1:51 Jesus promises that those who hear us will, like Nathanael, "see" heaven open before them in the divine service. In a sermon on this text Luther explains how this is so:

> Before the advent of Christ heaven was closed, but in and through Christ heaven stands ajar again. Now Christians see heaven opened, ... The Heavenly Father still addresses these words to us: "This is my beloved Son!" ... When you are baptised, partake of Holy Communion, receive the absolution, or listen to a sermon, heaven is open, and we hear the voice of

the Heavenly Father; all these works descend on us from the open heaven above us. . . . Still we hear God speaking to us from heaven; we call and cry to Him, and He answers us.[5]

Jesus continues his ministry of word and deed in the church today. It is true that he completed his work of redemption at his resurrection and ascension. That work is finished. But that is not the end of the story. Through the preaching of the gospel and the enactment of the sacrament he now delivers the benefits that he gained for us by his death. Just listen to how Luther helpfully distinguishes the ongoing work of Jesus in the church from the work of redemption:

> We treat of the forgiveness of sins in two ways. First, how it is achieved and won. Second, how it is distributed or given to us. Christ has achieved it on the cross, it is true. But he has not distributed or given it on the cross. He has not won it in the supper or the sacrament. There he has distributed it through the Word, as also in the gospel, where it is preached. He has won it once and for all on the cross. But the distribution takes place continuously, before and after, from the beginning to the end of the world.[6]

THE LOCATION OF PREACHING IN CHRIST'S PRESENCE

In 2 Cor 2:17 Paul explains the connection between preaching and the presence of Christ in the divine service:

> For we are not, like so many, peddlers of God's word, but as men of sincerity, as commissioned by God, in the sight of God we speak in Christ.[7]

Paul mentions two things about the context of his preaching as well as the preaching of Timothy and us.[8] As preachers we, like Paul and Timothy,

---

5. LW 22:201–2 = WA 46:712.7–22.

6. LW 40:213–14. He adds on p. 214, "If now I seek forgiveness of sins, I do not run to the cross, for I will not find it given there, . . . But I will find in the sacrament or gospel the word which distributes, presents, offers, and gives to me the forgiveness which was won on the cross." = WA, 18:203.28—204.

7. The last part of this sentence is repeated in 2 Cor 12:19.

8. Note Paul's use of the ministerial "we" for himself and for Timothy as co-authors of this letter (2 Cor 1:1).

speak God's word in Christ; we speak as God's word in the presence of God the Father.

When we pastors preach in the divine service we stand in the presence of God the Father. He has called and commissioned us to preach his word. So we pass on what we receive from him. We preach in his presence. This is symbolized by the architecture of our churches. They are usually divided into two parts, the nave that represents this world and the sanctuary that represents the heavenly world. The pulpit stands between God and the congregation. When we preach we bring the Father's word and his blessings to his people here on earth. We take what comes from him and we offer it to our hearers. The impact and effect of our preaching comes from speaking his word there in his very presence.

God's word differs from human words because it is filled with his Holy Spirit. Because it conveys his Holy Spirit it is life-giving and effective; it does what it says.[9] It does not just speak about forgiveness, it forgives our sins; it does not just speak about reconciliation, it actually reconciles us with God the Father; it does not just speak about eternal life, it gives us eternal life; it does not just speak about cleansing and holiness, it makes us clean and holy before God. So when we speak God's holy word, we speak the Holy Spirit to our hearers. In our preaching we enact God's word as law and gospel; we use the keys to bind and loose, to pronounce God's judgment on sin and to forgive sinners who repent. Our preaching opens the door to the Father's house and ushers people into his heavenly presence; it gives people access to the grace of God the Father here on earth.

We preachers can do all this because we were joined with Christ and united with him. His location determines our location. When we preach we do not stand in our own shoes and act by ourselves in the presence of God the Father. Since we are in Jesus we stand in his shoes; we represent him; we speak and act on his behalf.[10] Our vestments remind us that we preachers, as it were, dress up in him and represent him. He speaks to the people through us. He uses our mouths to speak the Father's word and our hands to pass on the Father's gifts to his people. His presence makes us God's agents and

---

9. For more on this see Kleinig, "The Work of the Holy Spirit," 15–22.

10. The words of the condemnation in the German version of the fifth article of the Augsburg Confession refer to the ministry of the word in this way, "Condemned are the Anabaptists and others who teach that we obtain the Holy Spirit without the embodied word of the gospel through our own preparations, thoughts, and works." *BSLK* 58.11–15. The term "the embodied word," "*das leiblich Wort*," comes from Luther. By this vivid expression Luther connects the incarnate Son with the word that is heard in the readings from the Scriptures, spoken in the absolution, proclaimed in the sermon, sung in the liturgy, and enacted in baptism and the Lord's Supper.

ambassadors. Since he is present with us, we can, if we are faithful to our calling, administer the grace of God in our preaching.

All three persons of the Holy Trinity are equally involved with us pastors in our preaching. Through baptism and faith all God's people stand in the presence of the Triune God; all members of the church have access to the Father through the Son by the Holy Spirit. We pastors have an additional privilege. We have been appointed by the Triune God to speak for him in the divine service. More correctly, he has appointed us so that he can speak his life-giving word to others through us there in that location. This means that Jesus uses us to preach the Father's word to our people and to give his Holy Spirit to them through his word. So when we preach we join with Jesus in delivering the grace of God the Father and his Holy Spirit from heaven to earth.

Note how Luther emphasizes God's location in his vivid description of the involvement of Jesus in our preaching:

> ... pastors are nothing but channels through which Christ leads and transmits His Gospel from the Father to us. Therefore wherever you hear the Gospel properly taught or see a person baptized, wherever you see someone administer or receive the Sacrament, or wherever you witness someone absolving another, there you may say without hesitation, "Today I beheld God's Word and work. Yes, I saw and heard God himself preaching and baptizing." To be sure, the tongue, the voice, the hands, etc., are those of a human being; but the Word and the ministry are really those of the Divine Majesty Himself.[11]

LITURGICAL PREACHING

Since we pastors stand together with Jesus in the presence of God the Father, this has far-reaching consequences for our preaching. I would like to mention only one such consequence. Since we preach together with Jesus, we can be sure that, whatever he promises us in his word, he delivers to us in Holy Communion.[12] This means that the most obvious application for any text from the gospels is to be found in the celebration of the Lord's Supper. By our preaching we tell our hearers to go there to receive him and his gifts for themselves from him. There they can pray confidently for those things

---

11. LW 24:67 = WA 45:521.7—522.1.

12. In his Small Catechism (VI:6) Luther summarizes this by speaking of "forgiveness of sins, life, and salvation," Tappert, 352 = BSLK, 520.

that he has promised.[13] Let me illustrate this briefly by considering the festive half of the church year in that light.[14]

In Advent we proclaim the two comings of Christ, his coming in his incarnation and his coming at the end of the world. The same Lord who has come and who will come comes to us as our judge and savior in Holy Communion. So we sing, "Blessed is he who comes in the name of the Lord," and pray that our Lord Jesus will come to each of us personally in the sacrament by saying, "Amen. Come Lord Jesus!" (1 Cor 16:22; Rev 22:20).[15]

At Christmas we proclaim the wonderful mystery of the incarnation, the embodiment of God's Son. We preach the good news that the eternal Son of God took on a human body to save us bodily from death. The same Lord who became flesh for us (John 1:14) gives us his flesh (John 6:52–56). In the sacrament he gives us his glorified human body and blood to heal us in body and soul[16] and make us clean and holy for life with God the Father (Heb 9:14; 10:29; 13:12). There we, in turn, offer our bodies as living sacrifices, holy and acceptable to him (Rom 12:1).

During the season of Epiphany we proclaim the theophany of God the Father, his visible appearance to the world in the humanity of Jesus. We therefore see God the Father in Jesus as he says, "Anyone who has seen me has seen the Father" (John 14:9). The same Lord who disclosed the glory of God to his disciples long ago still discloses the glory of the Father to us in Holy Communion. Like Simeon, we receive our Savior and see our salvation with our own eyes when we take the body of Jesus in our hands (Luke 2:25–32). We see the glory of our God right there for us to contemplate as we receive Christ's body and blood.

During Lent we proclaim the sacrifice of Jesus for our sins and the forgiveness of sins through faith in him. Jesus, the Lamb of God who suffered for us and died for our sins, gives us his blood to drink for our release from sin. In Holy Communion he takes away our sins and gives us his own righteousness. His blood, which he sprinkles on our hearts (Heb 12:24) cleanses us from sin (Heb 9:14) and makes us holy (Heb 10:29); it protects us from

---

13. Note the prayer for the "Divine Service, Setting Four," in LSB 209, "Grant us Your Holy Spirit that we may faithfully eat and drink of the fruits of the cross and receive the blessings of forgiveness, life, and salvation that come to us in His body and blood."

14. This is inspired, in part, by von Schenk, *The Presence*.

15. This prayer comes after the Words of Our Lord in "The Divine Service, Setting Two" of LSB 179. See also Lockwood, *1 Corinthians*, 632–33; and Brighton, *Revelation*, 657–58.

16. See the wording of the formula for the dismissal of communicants in LSB 164, 181, 199, 210, 218, as well as Luther's description in the *Large Catechism* (V, 68) of the sacrament as "a pure, wholesome, soothing medicine which aids and quickens us in both soul and body." Tappert, 454 = BSLK, 721.

JOHN W. KLEINIG   The Real Presence and Liturgical Preaching   189

the devil and gives us the victory over him (Rev 12:11).[17] As we celebrate it we proclaim his death until he comes at the close of the age (1 Cor 11:26).[18] Before we receive his body and blood we ask him as God's Lamb to have mercy on the whole world and to grant us and all people peace.

During the Easter season we proclaim the victory of Jesus over death and his gift of eternal life to us here and now in this life. The same Lord Jesus, who appeared to his disciples on Easter Sunday by standing among them (John 20:19–23) and ate with them (Luke 24:36–43; Acts 10:41) makes himself known to us in the breaking of bread (Luke 24:13–35). There we meet with him. There he gives us his own eternal life through his life-giving body and blood as he promised, "Whoever feeds on my flesh and drinks my blood has eternal life" (John 6:54a).[19] By that he not only dwells in us, making our bodies living shrines for him (John 6:57; cf. 1 Cor 6:19) but he also ensures that he will raise us bodily from the dead on the last day (John 6:54b).

On Ascension Day we proclaim the exaltation of Jesus as the King of heaven and earth and his invisible presence with us, free from all the restrictions of time and space. Raised bodily from the dead, he entered his Father's presence with his blood (Heb 9:12). In Holy Communion the same Jesus who has been exalted as our Lord and our great High Priest in the heavenly sanctuary, so that he could give his body and blood to all people all over the world, ushers us through a new and living way, the way of his flesh, into the Father's presence in the heavenly sanctuary; there we now can approach the Father's presence, the throne of grace, through his flesh and with his blood (Heb 10:19–22).

At the Feast of Pentecost we proclaim the gift of the Holy Spirit to the church fifty days after Easter. On that Sunday Jesus poured out his Spirit on all his disciples who had gathered together in one place. And he continues to do that every Sunday in the divine service. There Jesus offers us his Holy Spirit as we hear his word and as we receive Holy Communion. There he stands among us, as he did on Easter Sunday, and says, "Receive the Holy Spirit" (John 20:22). There he gives the same Spirit for "all" of us to "drink" that he gave at Pentecost (1 Cor 12:13).[20] His body and blood are our

---

17. See Kleinig, "The Blood for Sprinkling," 124–35.

18. These words are given after the Words of Our Lord in the "Divine Service, Setting Two" of LSB 179.

19. Note Melanchthon's assertion in AP XXII:10, "The sacrament was instituted to console and strengthen terrified hearts when they believe that Christ's flesh, given for the life of the world, is their food and that they come to life by being joined to Christ." Tappert, 237–38 = BSLK, 331.

20. While most commentators restrict this to the gift of the Spirit in baptism, it

"spiritual"[21] food and drink (1 Cor 10:3–4); as we eat his body and drink his blood we receive the Holy Spirit again and again.[22]

CONCLUSION

Pastors preach liturgically when they connect the sermon with the location of Christ in the divine service. That emphasis on the liturgical location of preaching is something that I learned from my teacher Dr. Sasse.[23] It is true that the gospel can be preached apart from the liturgy as a word of witness to anybody anywhere and as missionary preaching to the world. But the proclamation of the gospel in evangelism reaches its goal in the baptism of its hearers and their incorporation into the liturgical assembly. The preaching of the gospel does not just initiate people into the church; it takes its proper place there in the service of the church. Sasse drove this point home dramatically on one occasion by referring to the location of the pulpit between the font and the altar in the church. In liturgical preaching, he said, pastors first lead people from their place in the world to the font and their union with Christ in baptism. Then they lead their people from the font to the altar and the presence of the Father in the heavenly sanctuary. After that they send them back with Christ and his Holy Spirit to serve as holy priests where God has located them in the world, in their God-given station and vocation.

Liturgical preaching presupposes the real presence of the risen Lord Jesus in the congregation of the faithful people of God and his delivery of salvation to them from heaven to earth. Preaching is done under an open heaven. Pastors stand there with the angels and the whole communion of saints in the presence of God the Father, Son, and Holy Spirit. They speak God's word to their hearers and deliver God's gifts to them there. They proclaim the free gift of God's grace in the place where it is given. They announce, "Come and get it! Free salvation here and now!"

---

makes better sense to regard this as an allusion to the Lord's Supper, which, in the ancient church, baptized adults received for the first time in the same service as their baptism. Paul's use of the perfect passive may indicate that this is an ongoing gift from God.

21. "Spiritual" here means that it is has to do with the Spirit; it is Spirit-filled, Spirit-giving. See Lockwood, *1 Corinthians*, 322 and 325–36.

22. For a discussion on the ongoing reception of the Holy Spirit, see Kleinig, *Grace Upon Grace*, 46–49; and "The Work of the Holy Spirit," 15–22.

23. Kleinig, "Sasse on Worship," 106–22.

BIBLIOGRAPHY

Brighton, Louis A. *Revelation*. St. Louis: Concordia, 1999.

Just, Arthur A., Jr. *Luke 9:51—24:53*. St. Louis: Concordia, 1997.

Kleinig, John W. "The Blood for Sprinkling: Atoning Blood in Leviticus and Hebrews." *LTJ* 33 (1999) 124–35.

———. *Grace upon Grace: Spirituality for Today*. St. Louis: Concordia, 2008.

———. "Sasse on Worship." In *Hermann Sasse: A Man for our Times?*, edited by John R. Stephenson, 106–22. St. Louis: Concordia, 1995.

———. "Where is your God? Luther on God's Self-Localisation." *AJL* 11, no. 4 (2009) 168–84.

———. "Where is your God? Luther on God's Self-Localisation." In *All Theology Is Christology: Essays in Honor of David P. Scaer*, edited by Dean O. Wenthe et al., 117–31. Fort Wayne: Concordia Theological Seminary Press, 2000.

———. "The Work of the Holy Spirit in Worship." *LTJ* 44 (2010) 15–22.

Lockwood, Gregory J. *1 Corinthians*. St Louis: Concordia, 2000.

Schenk, Berthold von. *The Presence: An Approach to Holy Communion*. New York: Kaufmann, 1945.

Yeago, David S. "The Catholic Luther." *First Things* 61 (1996) 37–41.

12

The Preacher's Tongue and the Hearer's Ear

Compelled by the Spirit[1]

—David Petersen

QUESTIONS FROM EUCHARISTIC PIETY AND CENTRALITY

Increased Eucharistic piety has brought difficulties for American Lutherans. The most burning issue is infant communion. That particular topic requires serious theological inquiry and contemplation. Even as we continue to grow in our realization that a worthy reception for the Holy Communion is not based upon an intellectual understanding of the Sacrament, obtained, like a Jewish Bar Mitzvah, post-pubescent, but upon faith, we have to wrestle with the limits of when the Holy Communion is appropriate for a baptized believer. Yet if that is the most burning or difficult issue, there are others. Can the Holy Communion be rightly administered outside of a congregation, such as on a college or seminary campus? Should the Holy Communion be celebrated at funerals and weddings, which are largely ceremonies for the

---

1. This paper was originally delivered at the St. Michael's Liturgical Conference at Zion Evangelical Lutheran Church in Detroit, Michigan on September 28, 2013. Slight modifications from the oral delivery have been made for printed publication.

public outside of the Church?[2] These things were not burning issues for most American Lutherans at the founding of The Lutheran Church—Missouri Synod. Pastors and parishioners of the LCMS have been forced to deal with them at a practical level, but I am not sure that they have actually been handled theologically in the LCMS.[3] Other than my discomfort with infant communion, but inability to fully speak strongly against it, the struggle for me has been trying to articulate a theology of the word and preaching which acknowledges the Eucharist as the central and defining sacrament of the Christian and the church while still maintaining its own centrality and importance.

Some might propose that there is no tension between preaching and the Sacrament. Yet if that were the case, if there were no tension, then why have we so often heard, if not said, things like, "the Eucharist delivers when my preaching fails?"[4] This assumes that the Eucharist never fails the faithful. It assumes that the Eucharist delivers grace and strengthens faith to all those who receive it worthily. There are other assumptions in this statement, though. If the Eucharist delivers to the faithful when preaching fails, then preaching must, at least from time to time, fail. It must have the ability to not always deliver the gospel to the faithful. Why is it, or how is it, that preaching can fail and the Sacrament of the Altar cannot fail apart from unbelief or hypocrisy on the part of the communicant? Is it accurate to say

---

2. See, for example, the questions and answers section of the tract, "Theology and Practice of The Lord's Supper." In section 2, under the title "Extracongregational Services," the report gives a long list of requirements, "If under special conditions it is desired that an occasional transparochial service be held, the following steps would preserve the observance of the above Scriptural guidelines and also provide for good order. a. Requests for extracongregational Communion services on a Circuit, District, Synodical level should be discussed first of all with the pastoral adviser of the group. Consideration should be given to these questions: 1. Is the reason for a Communion service consonant with the Scriptural and Confessional meaning and intent of the sacrament? (cf. Ap XXIV:68; FC SD VII:59). 2. Will the sacrament be offered only to members affiliated or in fellowship with The Lutheran Church—Missouri Synod in an atmosphere where confessional integrity can be preserved? b. The counsel of the District President should be sought. c. A host congregation should be secured, and the pastoral adviser should work closely with this congregation in making the necessary preparations. d. The celebrant at the service of Holy Communion should ordinarily be the pastor of the host congregation."

3. I am unaware of the aforementioned document from the LCMS's Commission on Theology and Church Relations (CTCR, see n2) ever being addressed even though it is now common for the Holy Communion to be offered on its seminary campuses without a host congregation or pastor.

4. I was unable to find this exact sentiment in print and must simply rely on personal, anecdotal evidence.

that the preacher can ruin the sermon but that the celebrant cannot ruin the Sacrament?

The question is not that difficult, but it does need to be articulated and not just assumed. Our preaching can fail due to the preacher's sin. The Holy Communion cannot fail due to the celebrant's sin in the same way; that is, it cannot fail to deliver the gospel to the faithful as long as the words and elements are used.[5] This is a vocational hazard. In a way similar to a negligent father harming his children, a negligent preacher harms his flock. The vocation of preacher differs from the vocation of celebrant. A celebrant is only a voice in the Office of the Holy Ministry established by the Lord. A negligent and even abusive father who gives his child a glass of orange juice can be one who harms the child in many ways, and yet at the same time the juice provides vitamin C for the child despite the father's other failures. So too a negligent preacher, while harming his flock, might still serve them as the Lord's servant with the administration of the sacraments despite himself. In preaching, however, the preacher is called upon to do more than recite and hand over something that the Lord effects by his word. In preaching, the preacher is to interpret and apply. His knowledge, personality, and skill are involved, and negligence has consequences for the flock.[6]

At the same time, there is a promise. God established the Office of the Holy Ministry, and he provides through imperfect fathers and imperfect pastors. Love covers a multitude of sins. The Lord uses earthen vessels to carry his Spirit to his people. He is faithful to his word. He has established the authority of the Office of the Holy Ministry in which his preachers have been sent. It is because all authority in heaven and on earth has been given to him that preachers are sent to preach and to baptize. Therefore, the authority of preaching is Christ's own authority. His authority must be definitive and therefore must be discernible.

It is surprising at first, but Luther may have valued preaching above both the reading of the Scriptures and the Sacrament. I suspect that we modern, confessional Lutherans in America tend to value the Sacrament over preaching, and that we are in danger of, if not actually, undervaluing

---

5. I am intrigued by a comment from a colleague in this regard, but I have not had a chance to parse it out or explore it yet, "The Sacrament requires preparation by the communicant. The sermon requires preparation by the preacher."

6. My original intent with this paper was to explore this statement by Brooks: "Preaching is the communication of truth by man to men. It has in it two essential elements, truth and personality" (*Lectures on Preaching*, 5). This definition is well known in Protestant circles and is commented on in nearly every serious book on homiletics. I suspect that while it grates on Lutheran ears, Brooks is on to something. The Office of the Holy Ministry does not exist apart from the persons (and their personalities) that the Lord calls.

preaching. While I do not think that we overvalue the Sacrament, I do think statements such as "the Eucharist delivers when my preaching fails" hint at this and also show that we might be a bit insecure about the authority in which we have been sent. A careful reading of the Lutheran confessions and consideration of the topic can help to bring balance to preaching and Sacrament and to place the Bible into its role as source. Lutherans can be unashamed of the authority of the preacher and the centrality of the sermon without falling into the error of sacerdotalism.

Fortunately, if there has been an error, if we have undervalued preaching and overvalued the Bible or have misunderstood the relationship of sermon to Eucharist and gospel,[7] it has been mitigated by tradition. The liturgy has reined us in where our understanding might have failed. Our actual practice, like traditional architecture, is not out of balance. If anything requires some adjustment, it is only our attitude, that is, how we think about these things. That is not insignificant. Ideas have consequences. How we think about the sermon shapes how we prepare and how we behave in the pulpit. Yet the change is easier and less immediately obvious than a change in practice. Nonetheless, while I think we need to modify our thinking about these things in order to bring them into line with the Scriptures and the Lutheran confessions, I am not proposing a dramatic shift or new Reformation, but simply that we restore the sermon to its rightful place as the authoritative word of God, the gospel itself, in the service.

PART 1: THE QUESTION "WHY PREACH?"

Context of the Question

The question that has driven my study for this paper is "Why preach at all?" Redeemer Lutheran Church, which I serve in Fort Wayne, IN, has enjoyed daily communion during Advent, Christmastide, Lent, and the first week of Easter for the last thirteen years. We have always had a sermon at every service. We rarely use, devotionally, material from the fathers or Luther at the mass; rather, we normally hear a sermon from the pastor that he himself has written, even if it is a recycled sermon or one that he has rewritten from someone else. It has been my personal practice, almost without exception,

---

7. Consider this statement from Reed: "The Gospel is the liturgical summit of the first half of the Service, the 'Office of the Word'" (*The Lutheran Liturgy*, 281). That same language and idea is also echoed in Kinnaman, *Worshiping with Angels and Archangels*, 21. This paper will demonstrate that Luther, at the least, and probably also the Augsburg Confession, holds that the sermon is the high point of the service of the word. The typical physical majesty of pulpits also confesses this idea in architecture.

to preach also at all pastoral calls wherein the Eucharist is celebrated, such as shut-in and hospital visits. From time to time, I have wondered what is behind this compulsion. Is a sermon necessary at every mass? Is not the reading of the Gospel, the *verba*, and the reception of our Lord's body and blood sufficient for what ails us?

Outside of the penitential seasons and the feasts that follow, we enjoy daily Matins at Redeemer. While there is always a sermon at the mass, I feel no such compulsion for a sermon at an early morning, weekday Matins. We usually use a devotional reading from one of the fathers or some great light, but the pastor or liturgist simply reads it as it is written. He does not preach or comment on the reading nor does he modify it. Why does such a devotion not serve equally well at the mass? Why not use great sermons from the past? How could those sermons not be better, both in content and rhetoric, than anything that the modern preacher might say? Even if I were capable of preaching with the eloquence of St. Chrysostom, could I pull that off every day for sixty days straight? Why not gather up the best of Christian preaching and simply read it? And if that would be edifying and good, as it seems it would, why preach at all? Not even Chrysostom or Leo preaches with the authority of Paul. Why not just read the Bible out loud for thirty minutes instead of preaching a sermon? To sum it up, how could reading a sermon from the fathers not be superior to our preaching, and how could reading the Bible not be superior to any human work?

I find it fascinating that neither I nor my people are tempted by those ideas. My people do not hold me in the same regard as they hold St. Paul or St. Chrysostom, yet they would be sorely disappointed if I simply read sermons from Chrysostom or the Bible. I was called to preach, and they want me to preach. They might be bored to tears or even dread the sermon, desperate that they would end sooner, but there is something in them that wants the preacher to preach. Why is that? The idea of using patristic sermons or reading the Bible seems to me to be perfectly logical and consistent with the principle of *Sola Scriptura* and what we say about the Bible. Yet even as an idea not put into practice, just my suggestion of it fails to satisfy. Something in the hearer wants the pastor to say something. In a similar way, something in the pastor wants to speak. That something, simply put, is the Holy Spirit. He imbibes the preacher's tongue with holy, interpretive speech necessary for salvation, and he tickles the hearer's ears to be itchy for his truth and for evidence that the preacher is speaking authoritatively.

Augustana IV and V: The Bible Alone?

It is a bit surprising, in a sense, but neither Article IV nor V of the Augsburg Confession extol the Scriptures. Article V states:

> To obtain such faith God instituted the office of preaching, giving the gospel and the sacraments. Through these, as through means, he gives the Holy Spirit who produces faith, where and when he wills, in those who hear the gospel. It teaches that we have a gracious God, not through our merit but through Christ's merit, when we so believe.[8]

The idea of simply handing out Bibles for the sake of evangelism does not find support in the Augsburg Confession. What the Confession confesses is that God has established the office of preaching in order that men would obtain justifying faith, that is, that which delivers forgiveness of sin and righteousness before God out of grace for Christ's sake. The Confession does not say that God inspired the Bible for this purpose nor that he called all Christians to witness for this purpose. While it might be argued that those ideas simply are not addressed and therefore are not contrary to the Confession, what the Confession is emphatic about is that God has instituted the office of preaching in order to deliver justifying faith to humanity. The mass demands preaching because preaching has been instituted by God. As confessed in Article V, preaching—not the reading of the Bible—is the central activity of the Church for the salvation of the world.

I had mistakenly thought that I could find a foil to this in the Gideons International. I was surprised to learn that they also understand that the Bible must be accompanied by a personal witness. They call that witness "conversational evangelism." To be sure, they do not locate this in the Office of the Holy Ministry; nonetheless, they do not advocate letting the Bible speak on its own. They recognize the necessity of interpretation and application. Their current website states, "For our members, presenting the gospel usually begins with presenting someone with a Personal Workers Testament. However, conversational evangelism goes beyond the simple giving of a gift."[9]

Before we go further, we need to note that there are no passages in the Confessions which limit Holy Scripture. The idea, however, that a man might be converted by the Scriptures, apart from the church and the office of preaching, is foreign to the Confessors. It seems that even the Gideons sense this. For us, however, it needs to be stated that preaching is no more

---

8. KW 40 = *BSLK* 58.
9. "News: USA."

a piece of adiaphoron than Holy Baptism or the Holy Communion. The office of preaching, and not just personal witness, is the means of the means in Article V. The means for Article V, through which God "gives the Holy Spirit who produces faith, where and when he wills, in those who hear the gospel," are the preaching of the gospel and the administration of the sacraments. For those means to be delivered, he instituted the office of preaching. Thus, the office is the means of the means. While the article does not make exclusive claims for the office, neither in contrast to the personal witnessing of the laity nor to the bare Scriptures, those things are never stated to be divine, and therefore necessary, institutions.

Predigtamt

The German title "preaching office" (*Predigtamt*) in Article V is not accidental.[10] Even if the most defining and central sign of the church is the Holy Communion, the most defining and central character of the Office of the Holy Ministry is preaching. The office was instituted for preaching and the Sacraments, but the chief and defining duty is preaching. Thus, the office itself demands that the preacher preach and not simply read someone else's sermon. That is not to say it can never be done or that it is wrong to rewrite other people's sermons, but at some point, with some regularity, the preacher is to preach as the one sent for that purpose.[11]

10. Philipp Melanchthon, the author of the Augsburg Confession, seems to prefer the term *Prediger* in the Apology to the Augsburg Confession as well, using it thirty times while only using *Pfarrer* three times, though his favorite term seems to be *Priester*, which occurs seventy-nine times. The Latin title is *De Ministerio Ecclessiastico*. So also the terminology in the article itself is slightly different, "*docendi evangelii*."

11. LSB *Agenda*, 165–66, 70. The LSB Rite of Ordination never asks the candidate to promise to preach, only that all his preaching and teaching and administration of the sacraments be faithful to the Scriptures, creeds, and confessions. The Rite of Installation, however, in the final admonition to the pastor, is explicit, "Go, therefore, and be a shepherd of the Good Shepherd's flock. Preach the Word of God; administer the holy Sacraments; offer prayer for all the faithful; instruct, watch over, and guide the flock among which the Holy Spirit placed you." See also Martin Luther,

> From this it follows that whoever does not preach the Word, though he was called by the church to do this very thing, is no priest at all, and that the sacrament of ordination can be nothing else than a certain rite by which the church chooses its preachers. For this is the way a priest is defined in Mal. 2[:7]: "The lips of a priest should guard knowledge, and men should seek instruction from his mouth, for he is the messenger of the Lord of hosts." You may be certain, then, that whoever is not a messenger of the Lord of hosts, or whoever is called to do anything else than such messenger service—if

The Spirit-filled Office and Romans 10

In Article V of the Augsburg Confession, Philipp Melanchthon connects the Holy Spirit to the office there specified. The Holy Spirit is given to the people through the means of giving the gospel and the sacraments which are given through the office of preaching. Melanchthon's argument follows the argument in Rom 10 even though it does not cite it:

> For the Scripture says, "Everyone who believes in him will not be put to shame." For there is no distinction between Jew and Greek; for the same Lord is Lord of all, bestowing his riches on all who call on him. For "everyone who calls on the name of the Lord will be saved." How then will they call on him in whom they have not believed? And how are they to believe in him of whom they have never heard? And how are they to hear without someone preaching? And how are they to preach unless they are sent? As it is written, "How beautiful are the feet of those who preach the good news!" But they have not all obeyed the gospel. For Isaiah says, "Lord, who has believed what he has heard from us?" So faith comes from hearing, and hearing through the word of Christ. (Rom 10:11–17)

The King James Version renders the present participle in verse 14 as "preacher." The English Standard Version, quoted above, translates it as "someone preaching." Though it is subtle, the single noun "preacher" is more concrete than "someone preaching." The preacher is not someone who occasionally preaches, in the way that some people occasionally bake cakes or turn a wrench. The preacher is not a hobbyist. He is one who is sent for this purpose and who is utterly defined by it. It might seem an exaggeration for us, but the point for Melanchthon in Article V is that there is no "hearing

---

I may so term it—is in no sense a priest; as Hos. 4[:6] says: "Because you have rejected knowledge, I reject you from being a priest to me." They are also called pastors because they are to pasture, that is, to teach. Therefore, those who are ordained only to read the canonical hours and to offer masses are indeed papal priests, but not Christian priests, because they not only do not preach, but they are not even called to preach. Indeed, it comes to this, that a priesthood of that sort is a different estate altogether from the office of preaching. Thus they are hour-reading and mass-saying priests—sort of living idols called priests—really such priests as Jeroboam ordained, in Beth-aven, taken from the lowest dregs of the people, and not of Levi's tribe [1 Kgs 12:31]." LW 36: 113.

of the Gospel" apart from preachers sent by the Holy Spirit. For how will they hear without a preacher?[12]

The critical text, followed by the ESV, has "word of Christ" rather than the KJV and majority text's "word of God." The critical text seems to be working under the assumption that the scribes were accustomed to the phrase "word of God," especially in the context of Rom 10 where the Scriptures have both been invoked and quoted. Thus, it would seem that they were prone to modify Paul's original "word of Christ" to the more familiar "word of God." I suspect the critical text is correct. Paul is contrasting the word of Christ with the Scriptures. Faith comes not from hearing the Bible (that is, the Scriptures) but by hearing the word of Christ.

Whichever phrase is used, "word of God" or "word of Christ," the phrase stands directly parallel to the word "Gospel" (εὐαγγελίῳ) in verse 16. The gospel, Paul says, was not obeyed, or more literally, not "underheard" (ὑπήκουσαν). In reference to the beautiful feet, verse 15 uses the verb form of gospel, evangelize, for preach, and a substantive form of the adjective "good" (εὐαγγελιζομένων τὰ ἀγαθά). Thus the word of Christ is the good news-ing of the good. Both in the immediate context and in the larger framework of Romans, what must be heard is the gospel in the narrow sense, not simply the word of God in the broad sense. The distinction then in "word of Christ," as opposed to simply "word of God," is fitting, even if not necessary.

What is meant by the genitive, "of Christ" or "of God," in this case is also worth some consideration. The Lutheran exegete R. C. H. Lenski takes it as a simple possessive. Faith comes from hearing what Jesus spoke, that is, his actual words and utterances. Lenski, however, does understand that this is not only the "utterances that fell from Christ's lips" but is also the "utterance of faith" that is heard far and wide. It seems unlikely, however we take the genitive, that anyone would think that hearing an actual repetition of the utterances of Christ is what is meant here. Despite Lenski's claim that the word of Christ means the utterances of Christ, he demonstrates that he

---

12. It is noteworthy that Luther's definition of the gospel in the Smalcald Articles begins with the preached word, then moves to the sacraments, and then to the mutual conversation of the brothers. Again, we see the primacy of preaching. "We now want to return to the gospel, which gives guidance and help against sin in more than one way, because God is extravagantly rich in his grace: first, through the spoken word, in which the forgiveness of sins is preached to the whole world (which is the proper function of the gospel); second, through baptism; third, through the holy Sacrament of the Altar; fourth, through the power of the keys and also through the mutual conversation and consolation of brothers and sisters. Matthew 18[:20]: 'Where two or three are gathered ...'" (KW 319 = *BSLK* 449)

also understands that this word of Christ is also Jesus speaking through the preachers and inviting sinners to follow him.[13]

Like any Koine grammarian, Daniel Wallace gives a long list of how the genitive is used in the New Testament.[14] Besides the idea of a simple possessive, the two that are the most interesting in this context are the material and content genitives. Consider the difference between a bucket constructed of iron, which we might call a "bucket of iron," and that same bucket filled with tennis balls, which we might call a "bucket of balls." A bucket of balls is not made of balls but filled with balls, while a bucket of iron is not filled with iron but is made of iron. "Bucket of iron" then would be a genitive of material. "Bucket of balls" would be a genitive of content. Is the "word of Christ" which bestows faith upon those who hear it made of Christ, as a bucket of iron is made of iron, or is the "word of Christ" filled with Christ in the way that a bucket of balls is filled with balls?[15]

The question is significant: What is the relationship of Christ to the saving gospel? Is he its source, its content, or its material? Is he its possessor, its benefactor, or its end? In some ways, all of Wallace's categories can bring light to the gospel, and we probably fail in the most shallow of ways if we try to pigeonhole the significance of the "word of Christ" too closely to one aspect of the genitive. The question, however, has bearing on Article V of the Augsburg Confession. St. Paul says that faith comes from hearing through the word of Christ, but only to those who hear because a preacher has been sent. Melanchthon says that the Holy Spirit produces faith, where and when he pleases, in those who hear the gospel as it has been given through the office of preaching. Preaching then must be the word of Christ. Whatever that means, whatever sort of a genitive it is, it must mean, at the very least, that preaching carries Christ's authority and not simply the preacher's.

Have We Said Too Much?

I suspect that some would understand this treatment of these passages from Romans and the Augsburg Confession as sacerdotalism, but this is the contention of the Augustana. The *Lutheran Cyclopedia* defines sacerdotalism as the "view according to which the laity can establish relation with God only

---

13. *Romans*, 668.
14. *Greek Grammar*, 77–137.
15. The distinction here between ῥῆμα and λόγος is not significant. But lest we hear echoes of John's prologue, we should note that Paul uses ῥήματος, "utterances, sayings, or words" in Rom 10:17 and not λόγος.

through priests."[16] The Augsburg Confession does not indicate that the laity can *only* establish a relationship with God through the office of the preaching, nor am I aware of the Lutheran confessions talking about justification in any place as the Christian establishing a relationship with God. Neither do the confessions imply that ordination has placed an indelible character upon pastors. Yet, the Lord did institute the office of preaching in order to create saving faith in the hearers. I suppose then we might well say that the Lord has instituted the office in that he might establish a relationship with the laity, whether or not they might establish a relationship with him in some other way or not. This is then not the error of sacerdotalism, no matter how uncomfortable or inconvenient it might be. It is necessary that we confess that the Office the Lord has instituted bears Christ's own authority and promise and that its purpose is to create and deliver saving faith to God's children.

The Catechisms: Where is the Sacrament of the Altar?

Martin Luther's explanations to the Third Commandment in the catechisms are interesting not only in their emphasis upon preaching, but also in their lack of concern for the Holy Communion. Should the Small Catechism's explanation not read, "We should fear and love God so that we do not despise preaching and His Word, nor neglect the Holy Communion, but hold God's Word and preaching sacred, gladly hearing and learning it, even as we faithfully receive the Lord's body and blood according to His promise?"[17] According to the "Rite for First Communion Prior to Confirmation" in the LSB *Agenda*, the children are asked, "Do you intend to continue to hear and receive the instruction of your Lord, confess your sins, and receive the Lord's Supper faithfully through your life?" In both LSB's "Rite for Confirmation" and "Rite for the Reception of Members by Transfer or Profession of Faith" the candidates are asked, "Do you intend to hear the Word of God and receive the Lord's Supper faithfully?"[18] In every way that people become adult members of our congregations, we ask them to pledge not only to hear the Word of God and preaching faithfully but also to receive the Holy

---

16. Lueker, *Lutheran Cyclopedia*, 690. See also the fuller definition: Jacobs and Haas, *The Lutheran Cyclopedia*, s. v. "Sacerdotalism, Relation of the Lutheran Church to."

17. *Luther's Small Catechism*, 12. The actual reading in the Small Catechism that is most widely used in the LCMS is, "We should fear and love God so that we do not despise preaching and His Word, but hold it sacred and gladly hear and learn it."

18. LSB *Agenda*, 26, 30, 33.

Communion faithfully. How is that missing from Luther's explanation of the Third Commandment in the Small Catechism?[19]

The Sacrament is likewise missing from the Large Catechism's treatment of the Third Commandment. Luther writes:

> It used to be thought that Sunday had been properly observed if one went to mass or listened to the Gospel being read; however, no one asked about God's Word, and no one taught it either. Now that we have God's Word, we still fail to eliminate this abuse, for we permit ourselves to be preached to and admonished, but we listen without serious concern. Remember, then, that you must be concerned not only about hearing the Word, but also about learning it and retaining it.[20]

It might be argued that Luther assumes the hearing of Bible readings and the reception of the Sacrament in worship, yet he explicitly states that those things are not enough. What he is against, of course, is a mechanical view of the Sacraments or the idea that the Sacraments are our work meant to appease God's wrath. Luther has to be read in his own context. Some of what is behind his concern and emphasis is certainly seen in his comments in 1532 on Ps 51. There he writes:

> This is the doctrine for which we bear not only the name "heresy" but punishment, namely, that we attribute everything to hearing or to the Word or to faith in the Word—these are all the same—and not to our works. Yes, in the use of the Sacraments and in confession we teach men to look mainly at the Word, so that we call everything back from our works to the Word. The hearing of gladness is in Baptism, when it is said: "I baptize you in the name of the Father and of the Son and of the Holy Spirit" (Matt 28:19); "He who believes and is baptized will be saved" (Mark 16:16). The hearing of gladness is in the Lord's Supper, when it is said, "This is My body, which is given for you" (Luke 22:19). The hearing of gladness is in confession, or, to call it by its more proper name, in absolution and the use of the keys: "Have faith. Your sins are forgiven you through the death of Christ." Though we urge the people to the Sacraments and to absolution, still we do not teach anything about the worthiness of our work or that it avails by the mere performance of

---

19. One answer, at least, might be that Luther was writing a systematic treatment of the faith that was meant to be taken as a whole. Faithful reception of the Sacrament of the Altar is taken up in the Questions and Answers. That may be the case, but it seems a strange thing to not include in the discussion on worship.

20. KW 399–400 = *BSLK* 585.

the work, as the papists usually teach about the Lord's Supper, or rather about their sacrifice. We call men back to the Word so that the chief part of the whole action might be the voice of God itself and the hearing itself.[21]

Nonetheless, even in that context, I find the quote from the Large Catechism disturbing. There is real merit in hearing the gospel read and in receiving the Holy Communion. Too much emphasis on our learning and retaining what is taught in the sermon can also easily be abused and mis-shaped into works righteousness, in a way just as deadly as the false view of the sacraments as effecting what they do *ex opere operato*.

Preaching versus the Bible

More directly related to our topic is Luther's contrast of what he calls "God's word" with the reading of the gospel. This stands parallel, though the mirror image, to his equivocation in the Small Catechism of preaching and the word of God. His argument here in the Large Catechism is that a person does not, or at least may not, hear God's word in the reading of the gospel at the service unless there is preaching and admonition, which the person must then strive to retain and learn. Not only is Luther lacking an emphasis on the Sacrament in his explanation of the Third Commandment, but so also he seems to elevate the explanation of the text, preaching, above the text itself.

Vilmos Vajta explains some of this. He states that Luther "demanded more than lessons from the Bible. To him 'using Scripture' was not tantamount to 'reading Scripture.' It implied the preaching of the word by which the redemptive facts of the Bible could be applied to the congregation." Because the Bible could be either misinterpreted or misunderstood, simply hearing the gospel read was not enough. Even as the Sacrament was of no value apart from faith, so also the Bible was of no value without faith. Vajta continues, "The divine nature of the Word is as hidden in the Bible as it was in the manger of Bethlehem or on the cross of Calvary. Faith is needed to find the Word of God in the Bible."[22] Thus, Luther locates the birth of

---

21. LW 12:369–70.

22. Vajta, *Luther on Worship*, 75–76. In its deliberations about the word of God this paper is concerned mainly with the relation of preaching and the Scriptures, but it has been impossible to not also consider the relationship of preaching to the Sacrament of the Altar The concerns about Luther's explanation of the Third Commandment were not sought. They came about as his equivocation of the Word of God and preaching were considered. For a fuller examination and defense of Luther's view of worship, I reference Vajta's work. Vajta underscores what we have already stated about the necessity

faith and the key to hearing God's word not in the Bible reading, but in the sermon.

Luther's 1523 Treatise on Worship

This idea and the abuses he is responding to comes out in Luther's treatise "Concerning the Order of Public Worship, 1523." There he writes:

> Now in order to correct these abuses, know first of all that a Christian congregation should never gather together without the preaching of God's Word and prayer, no matter how briefly, as Psalm 102 says, "When the kings and the people assemble to serve the Lord, they shall declare the name and the praise of God." And Paul in 1 Corinthians 14 [:26–31] says that when they come together, there should be prophesying, teaching, and admonition. Therefore, when God's Word is not preached, one had better neither sing nor read, or even come together.[23]

This document, written six years earlier than the catechisms, helps to put Luther's emphasis and possible oversights in the catechisms into context.[24] He was specifically concerned with medieval abuses tied to the idea of a functioning of the sacraments *ex opere operato*, which resulted in either no preaching or foolish, meaningless preaching.[25] Luther's corrective was to emphasize faith and preaching. His correction might have been a slight overreaction. As already indicated, wrongly taken, Luther's emphasis could be as misleading and abusive as the medieval abuses. Nonetheless, Luther maintained that every gathering of the congregation for worship, with or

---

of preaching and preachers, but he also brings Luther's sacramental theology of worship into play. On p. 109 he writes:

> Worship, as we have concluded, is God's work of love by which he imparts to us the fruits of the redemption in Jesus Christ. This work is done through the Word and the sacraments. But we also found that the Word must be preached and the sacraments administered. It is not enough for the Word to rest between the covers of the Bible, nor for the Sacrament to be de dis-played in the tabernacle on the altar. The Word is a message. It must be heard. It needs messengers. The Sacrament is a gift. It must be received. It requires administrators.

23. LW 53:11.

24. I have striven to be careful to not claim that this treatment has considered every aspect of Luther's theology of worship or surveyed all of his writings.

25. Luther states that God's Word had been silenced by "un-Christian fables and lies, in legends, hymns, and sermons." LW 53:11

without the Holy Communion, must include "prophesying, teaching, and admonition" on the word of God.

Later in the same document, he explains the relationship of the Bible and the sermon in a surprising way. He writes:

> The preacher, or whoever has been appointed, shall come forward and interpret a part of the same lesson, so that all others may understand and learn it, and be admonished. The former is called by Paul in I Corinthians 14 [:27] "speaking in tongues." The other he calls "interpreting" or "prophesying," or "speaking with sense or understanding." If this is not done, the congregation is not benefited by the lesson, as has been the case in cloisters and in convents, where they only bawled against the walls.[26]

Luther considers the reading of the Bible to be "speaking in tongues." Without interpretation, the Bible will lead to confusion and chaos. He considers the sermon to be the "interpreting" or "prophesying," or "speaking with sense or understanding." In the next verse, St. Paul writes, "If there is no one to interpret, let each of them keep silent in church and speak to himself and to God" (1 Cor. 14:28). If Luther's reading is correct, then St. Paul is saying to never read the Bible in church unless there is a sermon. Luther's remarks here may be taken as polemical hyperbole but he is not exaggerating in his opinion that the preacher speaks by the Spirit and that his explanations are necessary for faith. The Bible does not stand alone.[27]

The Preacher's Authority

Carl Fickenscher attempts to answer a question similar to ours in his essay "The Divine Preaching of Jesus: As One with the Authority of Scripture." His question is "What authority do Christian preachers have and how is it different from that of Christ?" He argues that Christian preachers do not enjoy the personal authority that Jesus had due to his divinity, but that they share in part of the authority that he had because both Christ and Christian preachers stand upon the authority of the Scriptures. He is arguing against the idea that the preacher's authority is based in Christian experience or in some democratic ideal. His survey of our Lord's use of the Scriptures is helpful, but his argument for the authority of Christian preaching being based

---

26. Ibid., 12.

27. The slogan *Sola Scriptura* has never meant the Bible stands alone but that the Bible alone is authoritative to determine doctrine in contrast to the idea that the Bible and tradition determine doctrine.

upon the authority of the Scriptures is thin. For the most part, his argument hinges on the distinction between the rabbis and Jesus. Fickenscher writes:

> The difference between Jesus and the scribes was not chiefly a personal one (great as that may have been) but was a matter of the way each conveyed the message of the Scriptures they supposedly shared. Jesus rightly declared the living and life-giving Word of the Old Testament while the scribes missed its spirit completely. Why was Jesus recognized as one having authority? Because Jesus stood firmly on the authority of Scripture.[28]

The analysis requires some clarification. The authority of Jesus was not recognized because he claimed to stand firmly on the authority of Scripture and the rabbis were claiming some other authority. They both claimed to stand on Scripture. Yet the Lord's authority was recognized and the rabbis' was not. The Lord's authority was recognized because his interpretation rang true while that of the rabbis did not. That must be what Fickenscher means by "the way each conveyed the message." The way of Jesus was the correct interpretation. The way of the rabbis was false. What distinguished them then was not claims of authority, but content. Jesus surprised the audience with his authority because, as Fickenscher points out through Edersheim, the preaching of Jesus was an "unfolding of the Old Testament's inmost, yet hidden meaning."[29] What made his authority manifest was his correct interpretation and application of the Scriptures.

Still, that is not enough to move to the authority of modern preachers. The distinction needs to be made between what makes the authority manifest and the authority itself. The authority of Jesus is not, in the first place, in either his divinity nor is it in the Scriptures. His authority to preach was in his anointing. The Spirit of the Lord had been poured upon him that he would preach the good news to the poor. In that anointing, in the river that divided heaven and hell and the wilderness from the Promised Land, he was declared to be the beloved Son that people were to hear. His anointing was an anointing for preaching. In a similar way, Christian preachers have been anointed to preach. Fickenscher rightly points out that their source is the Scriptures even as it was the Lord's source, but their authority is not the Scriptures, it is the sending. Thus, the Rom 10 text above, "How will they preach unless they are sent?" That authority, the authority to preach in Christ's stead, is recognized in their right interpretation and application of Scripture.

---

28. "The Divine Preaching of Jesus," 30.
29. Ibid.

Application Today and Conclusion

The preacher desires to preach because he has been sent to preach and because the Bible requires interpretation, that faith might be implanted and strengthened. The hearers desire the preacher to preach his own sermon and not simply to read a patristic sermon or read the Bible, that they might hear the word of Christ for the strengthening of their faith and that they would discern whether the preaching has the authority of Christ.

I suspect that in our calmer context, and without the immediate medieval abuses of an *ex opere operato* understanding of the sacraments' operations or of a lack of sermons afflicting us, we might faithfully gather midweek for Matins or Vespers without a sermon, despite Luther's insistence that we not do so. Yet at the same time, in order to be safe from the errors of the past, and to maintain a proper understanding of the necessity of faith for benefit in the Sacrament in particular, it seems a wise practice to insist upon preaching at every mass and that the majority of those sermons be mostly the preacher's own words. In this our practice need not be modified, but our attitudes could be adjusted. Preachers and hearers alike should reverence faithful preaching as Spirit-given holy speech that creates and sustains faith in God's children, not simply as brief lectures or periods of instruction.

The Augsburg Confession, the catechisms of Martin Luther, and Luther in his treatise "Concerning Public Worship" exalt preaching not the Bible. The word of God is of no use apart from faith. The idea that the Bible could be used on its own in worship, apart from preaching, is a faulty, *ex opere operato* view of the Scriptures' function that is contrary to the Lutheran confessions. Hearers need preachers sent by the Holy Spirit to explain and to apply God's Word to them, that they might hear the gospel and by the Spirit's grace, believe. Preaching is essential to the mass because faith is essential to the mass. This understanding explains Luther's use of 1 Cor 11 to call the Bible speaking in tongues and the sermon the necessary interpretation. That exegesis may not be as far-fetched as it sounds at first. The Holy Spirit invoked and called down at ordination compels the preachers to preach because the people need faith, and faith comes by hearing the word of Christ, that is, the redemptive facts of the Bible applied to the congregation. That same Spirit compels the people to hear, not only that they would obtain faith (which is the main purpose of preaching) and that they would learn and retain the redemptive facts of the Bible applied to them, but also that they would discern the preacher's authority and recognize his words as the very word of Christ. Is this not what our Lord means when he says to the apostles, "The one who hears you hears me, and the one who rejects you rejects me, and the one who rejects me rejects him who sent me." (Luke 10:16)?

BIBLIOGRAPHY

Brooks, Philip. *Lectures on Preaching*. New York: Dutton, 1907. http://openlibrary.org/books/OL23310403M/Lectures_on_preaching (accessed October 7, 2013).
The Commission on Worship of The Lutheran Church—Missouri Synod. *Lutheran Service Book Agenda*. St. Louis: Concordia, 2006.
Fickenscher, Carl C., II. "The Divine Preaching of Jesus: As One with the Authority of Scripture." In *The Pieper Lectures: Preaching through the Ages*, edited by John A. Maxfield, 16–34. St. Louis: Concordia Historical Institute and The Luther Academy, 2004.
Gideons International. "News: USA." http://www.gideons.org/News/LocalNews.aspx (accessed September 26, 2013).
Jacobs, Henry Eyster, and John A. W. Hass, eds. *The Lutheran Cyclopedia*. New York: Scribner's Sons, 1899.
Kinnaman, Scot A. *Worshiping with Angels and Archangels: An Introduction to the Divine Service*. St. Louis: Concordia, 2006.
Lenski, R. C. H. *The Interpretation of St. Paul's Epistle to the Romans*. Columbus, OH: Wartburg, 1945.
Lueker, Erwin L., ed. *Lutheran Cyclopedia: A Concise In-Home Reference for the Christian Family*. St. Louis: Concordia, 1975.
Luther, Martin. *Luther's Small Catechism with Explanation*. St. Louis: Concordia, 1991.
Reed, Luther D. *The Lutheran Liturgy*. Philadelphia: Muhlenberg, 1947.
Theology and Practice of the Lord's Supper: A Report of the Commission on Theology and Church Relations of The Lutheran Church—Missouri Synod as prepared by its Social Concerns Committee. May 1983. http://www.iclnet.org/pub/resources/text/wittenberg/wittenberg-msynod.html (accessed October 1, 2013).
Vajta, Vilmos. *Luther on Worship: An Interpretation*. Translated by U. S. Leupold. Philadelphia: Muhlenberg, 1958.
Wallace, Daniel B. *Greek Grammar: beyond the Basics*. Grand Rapids: Zondervan, 1996.

13

Gloomy Revelations or Comforting Doctrines?

—Esko Murto

THE ISSUES OF GOD'S ELECTION, THE BONDAGE OF THE WILL, AND ORIGINAL SIN IN PREACHING AND PASTORAL CARE

Concerning the topics of God's election, the bondage of the will, and original sin, Lutherans face criticism from both mainline "liberal" Christianity and "conservative" evangelicals. To some, the views held by the Lutheran confessions appear depressing and gloomy, utterly at odds with the affirming and empowering message of humanist preaching. To others, these doctrines seem to serve as excuses for lukewarm Christianity and as ways to provide theological justification for spiritual sloth.

While it may often hold that Lutheran theologians are adequately equipped to defend their confessional stance in theological debate, the questions of homiletical and pastoral application of these doctrines may turn out to be trickier. The road from the pastor's study into his pulpit or confessional booth may be hard to navigate, sometimes so much so that these doctrines are deemed true, but "unpreachable," i.e. without use in actual homiletic work.

This essay seeks to explore the aforementioned doctrinal topics whilst asking the question of their practical use in pastoral work. It is assumed that the reader is familiar with at least the rudimentary ideas of the Lutheran confessional writings concerning these topics so that they will not be extensively explained. Some points will be made concerning theological content and possible misunderstandings often attributed to these doctrines, but the ultimate goal nonetheless lies in their use and application in congregational life.

Due to the author's personal history as well as the spiritual history of many of his parishioners, this essay will approach its topic largely from the viewpoint of Nordic Pietism (a term really too broad to be used as anything more than a vague description of one's theological background). As such, questions or objections raised by more liberal, mainline Protestantism are not given much consideration. Motivation for this work stems from practical experience in preaching, teaching, as well as discussing and applying pastoral care in congregations where many members have a history in spiritual traditions that have legalistic tendencies while often downplaying the severity of original sin, promoting ideas of free will in matters of conversion and staying silent about God's election. Through pastoral ministry, it has become clear to the author that these doctrines are not simply theological points to be subscribed to for the sake of properly bearing the title 'confessional,' but more than that, that they should be treasured and put to use in preaching and spiritual care.

PREACHING AS GOD'S MEANS OF ELECTION

The doctrines of bound will and original sin can hardly be handled without dealing with questions of God's omnipotence concerning evil things and his election of believers and unbelievers. Maintaining God's omnipotence as well as the goodness of his will is nigh impossible in the absence of certain distinctions. One of the most crucial is the distinction between the *hidden* God and the *revealed* God.

"Hidden God" (*Deus absconditus*) is used (at least by Martin Luther) to describe God as he is in his lofty majesty, as all-powerful, mysterious ruler of the universe. This God is known by no one, and humans cannot directly deal with him. This is the God who affects everything, but is affected by none. The hidden God directs all things according to his will, and gives both good and evil, happiness and suffering. The hidden will of the hidden God draws up a plan that no one knows except him, a plan that is inevitably carried out, down to the finest detail. Luther states, "Hidden in his majesty,

God does not mourn death nor remove it, but instead causes death, life and everything in everything. In this realm, he has not bound himself to his word, but has reserved freedom and power over all."[1]

The hidden God in his incomprehensible power can seem fascinating, but in times of trial he causes fear and terror more than anything else. This God is the "consuming fire" (Heb 12:29) and to fall into his hands is truly a fearful thing (Heb 10:31). Philosophers speculate about the hidden God and Calvinists try to systematize him, but Luther's approach was different: fear him and flee for your life!

Safety from the horror of God's hiddenness is found in his self-revelation. Through the word of God, people are able to find a revealed God (*Deus revelatus*). This God is not mysterious and unapproachable. On the contrary: he brings forth his will in both law and gospel, reveals them to people, and commits—even binds himself—to these words. This is the way Christians are meant to seek God and deal with him.

Another distinction, quite similar to this, is used in describing the ways people attempt to find God. The "uncloaked God" (*Deus nudus*) means God apart from his word, outside the revealed promises. He is naked, incomprehensible and impossible to find. Any attempts at finding this God will lead into spiritual confusion and even despair. The God mankind is able to find is God "clothed" in the means of grace (*Deus vestitus*). Through the means of grace, people come into contact with the God who reveals himself, and, in Christ, becomes known to them and even forms a relationship with them.

The difference between revealed, clothed God and hidden, naked God is also the difference between preached and confessed God and the God not preached, not confessed. Therefore, when approaching the question of God's eternal election, the Lutheran confessions clearly and purposefully refuse to speak of it as though it was something enacted by the hidden God. Christians are not called to confess the hiddenness of God; the Scriptures never reveal this side of the matter and believers should refuse to ponder it. Philosophically, one might come to the conclusion that God elects some to be saved and purposefully condemns others. Faith, however, stems not from philosophy but from theology, and theology is based on God's revelation, not human speculations.

On this account, the Lutheran confessions reject the notion that God's election makes preaching unnecessary. "God does not call apart from means. He calls through the Word, which he has commanded us to preach, the word of repentance and the forgiveness of sins."[2] Similarly is rejected

---

1. LW 33:140.
2. FC SD XI:27 (KW 645 = *BSLK* 1071).

the notion that preaching would be a mere formality, a play even, while the actual election happens according to God's hidden will. Accepting this would mean that "God, who is eternal truth, would contradict himself. God condemns such vice in people when they say one thing but think and intend something else in their heart."[3]

The impact this understanding has on preaching and pastoral ministry becomes apparent when the full meaning of the means of grace for God's election is confessed. In and through these means God makes his election, because in and through them his will is made known. Therefore the Lutheran church also confesses:

> We retain private absolution and teach that it is God's command that we "believe this kind of absolution and regard it as certain, that we are truly reconciled with God when we believe the word of absolution, as if we had heard a voice from heaven," as the Apology also explains in this article. This comfort would be taken away from us completely if we could not conclude from his call, which takes place through Word and sacraments, what God's will towards us is. Such a view would also destroy and deprive us of the foundation, namely, that the Holy Spirit most certainly wills to be present, effective, and active through the Word as it is preached, heard and considered.[4]

Confessing that people are entirely passive (*pure passive*) in regard to their own salvation, is not saying that salvation and God's election would take place without using the means of grace. What must be understood is that the efficient cause (*causa efficiens*) in these means is neither the one receiving them nor the one administering, but God alone. The pastor, when preaching or administering the sacraments, is not acting on his own nor should the members of his congregation view him so; instead, he is there to represent Christ and to speak on his behalf.

> They represent the person of Christ on account of the call of the church and do not represent their own persons, as Christ himself testifies: "Whoever listens to you listens to me." When they offer the Word of Christ or the sacraments, they offer them in the stead and place of Christ.[5]

It turns out that, when questions concerning God's hidden will and the potentially terrifying notions of predestination arise, the Lutheran answer is

---

3. FC SD XI:35 (KW 646 = *BSLK*, 1074).
4. FC SD XI:38–39 (KW 647 = 1074–75).
5. AP VII/VIII, 28 (KW 178 = *BSLK* 240).

not a philosophical one, but neither is it a theological one, not at least in so far as theology is understood in its academic sense. The answer is homiletical. As Gerhard Forde puts it, "The God whom we can discover ourselves is always a hidden God, literally a God not preached. . . . The only way to overcome the problem of the hiddenness of God not preached is by God preached."[6]

BONDAGE OF THE WILL SERVING THE FREEDOM OF THE GOSPEL

The Lutheran understanding of the effects had by original sin on one's spiritual capabilities has sometimes been criticized for destroying the idea of human will, and thus rendering man into a mere animal or, even worse, a machine. A person without freedom of will and thought is likened to a mere marionette, forcibly following the whims of the puppeteer. This, however, is not what Lutherans mean when they speak of the human will being bound. It is crucial to note the difference between the will being bound and the will being nonexistent. The Lutheran church confesses that people, even after the fall, have a will, and that this will is very active. They are capable of thinking, planning, wanting, and willing, and then of acting according to their will.

The problem mankind encounters in spiritual matters is not lack of will, but rather the lack of freedom from which this will suffers. Man's will is active and capable of desiring things, yet unable to freely choose the object of desire. In this way, man is bound in his decisions. Sin causes people to exercise their will in ways that ultimately and unavoidably lead them farther away from God, rather than bringing them closer to their Creator. In his Heidelberg disputation of 1518, Luther claimed, "Free will, after the fall, exists in name only, and as long as it does what it is able to do, it commits a mortal sin." (Thesis XIII)[7]

Original sin causes a person to be *incurvatus in se ipsum*, "turned into himself." People are able to exercise their will when choosing among the options presented, but being *incurvatus* means being so tightly curved inward on oneself that options in spiritual matters are consequently severely limited. The will is, so to speak, free to pick any item from the menu, but it is not free to choose what options are presented, just as a hallucinating person might be able to make choices within his hallucination, but is not free to decide to step out of it. As a result, God is not there for the will to

---

6. Forde, *Captivation*, 78–79.
7. Forde, *Theologian*, 52.

choose. Quite on the contrary, the will actively opposes God. The Formula of Concord confesses:

> In such a case it can be really said that the human being is not a stone or a block of wood. For a stone or a block of wood does not resist the person who moves it; neither does it understand or feel what is being done to it. In contrast, people resist God the Lord with their will until they are converted.... Such people can do absolutely nothing toward their own conversion and are in this case much worse than a stone or a block of wood. For they resist the Word and the will of God until God awakens them from the death of sin and enlightens and renews them."[8]

Experience supports this. A person not believing in Christ would not describe his thoughts or notions as being similar to those of a rock or log. Such a person truly considers, thinks, and forms their own opinions concerning religious matters. Their thoughts are genuinely their own, their attitudes truly arising from their heart. They are free—free to not believe in God. As long as the borders of this freedom remain uncontested, they truly believe themselves to be free, and in some sense they really are. Only when Christ is being preached will the captivated nature of their will begin to emerge.

An unbelieving person is therefore not in a state of "decreased responsibility," and no one can accuse God of forcing that person into anything. Rejecting Christ is something people do out of their free will, and similarly the sins they might commit are done out of their hearts, and not something violently forced upon them by an outward power.

The gospel, the good news, is that God, despite their will, comes to save humankind. C. S. Lewis described the wonder of his own conversion thus:

> The Prodigal Son at least walked home on his own feet. But who can duly adore that Love which will open the high gates to a prodigal who is brought in kicking, struggling, resentful, and darting his eyes in every direction for a chance of escape? The words *compelle intrare*, compel them to come in, have been so abused by wicked men that we shudder at them; but, properly understood, they plumb the depth of the Divine Mercy. The hardness of God is kinder than the softness of men, and His compulsion is our liberation."[9]

---

8. FC SD II:59 (KW 555 = *BSLK* 894–96).

9. Lewis, *Joy*, 229.

Following Luther, the Lutheran confessions unconditionally reject all attempts of reserving man some, even ever so slight role in his salvation. The Formula of Concord (FC EP. II:2-4) meticulously rejects a means of expression that might be used to support the notion that a person has free, or even partially free will in the matter of his own salvation.

It must be nonetheless noted, that these confessional statements deal specifically with the unbelieving person's capabilities for creating saving faith in himself. The sharp rejection of free will in this question does not mean that in actual conversion or in the Christian life following conversion, a person's will would remain in its original state, always only resisting God. Among the rejected expressions is also the saying, "Human will resists the Holy Spirit before, during and after conversion."[10] Rather, it is confessed that, in conversion itself, the Holy Spirit causes reluctant unbelievers to become eager, so that the persons can and will, because of the Holy Spirit, accept the grace offered. So even in this regard, the Lutheran confessions do not describe men as mere rocks or logs, but calls them active and willful.

The same can be seen taking place also in the life following conversion. "After this conversion of the human being the reborn will is not idle in the daily practice of repentance but cooperates in all the works of the Holy Spirit that he accomplishes through us." (FC II:88) A regenerate soul is not in the same position as before, and the Formula even goes as far as to call a believer's will "freed," *arbitrium liberatum*. Christians are not enslaved to sin, and no longer utterly bound in unbelief and ungodliness. Rather, it is confessed that believers "not only hear the Word but are able to assent to it and accept it—although in great weakness."[11]

Central to Lutheran anthropology is the struggle between the "Old Adam" and the "new creation." The believer is fully and completely righteous, and at the same time utterly, incurably sinful (*simul iustus et peccator*). This is true in the face of God, but also in the person's own, inner life. The believers are free when it comes to their regenerate selves, yet at the same time, due to their sinful flesh, the desire for evil and numerous sins remain in them. This creates a permanent state of conflict within the believer. Faith and unbelief are fighting one another; there is a struggle between carnal sins and good works. All this creates anguish and woe within one's soul, resulting in hardships mostly unknown to unrepentant people who are content in their unbelief.

> Because in this life we receive only the first fruits of the Spirit and our rebirth is not complete but rather only begun in us, the

---

10. FC SD II:82 (KW 560 = *BSLK* 905-6).
11. FC SD II:67 (KW 557 = *BSLK* 898-99).

struggle and battle of the flesh against the Spirit continues even in the elect and truly reborn. For one can detect not only a great difference among Christians—one is weak, another strong in the Spirit—but within each Christian, who is at one moment resolute in the Spirit and at another fearful and afraid, at one moment ardent in love, strong in faith and hope, and at another cold and weak."[12]

Preachers would be wise to remind their parishioners that this kind of spiritual anguish should not be seen as a cause for despair, as it is rather oftentimes a sign of true Christian faith. Faith grows through struggle and leads into struggle, as the conflict between old Adam and new man heightens. As Martin Luther put it, "just as we cannot get along without eating and drinking, so we cannot get along without affliction and suffering. Therefore we must necessarily be afflicted of the Devil by persecution or else by a secret thorn which thrusts into the heart, as also St. Paul laments."[13]

With the help of the Holy Spirit, Christians overcome these temptations and remain in true faith, unless they purposefully and with clear understanding reject God's commandments and despise the call to repentance. Such is called "grieving the Holy Spirit," and leads to a hardened heart and spiritual death. Both Melanchthon in the Apology of the Augsburg Confession, and Luther in the Smalcald Articles confess that saving faith cannot remain alongside mortal sins, i.e. grave sins that are freely committed with willful consent, "Therefore the faith that receives the forgiveness of sins for the heart that is terrified and fleeing sin does not remain in those who succumb to their lusts, nor does it coexist with mortal sin."[14] The distinction is between sin that rules men (*peccatum regans*) and sin that is ruled by Christ and the Holy Spirit (*peccatum regnatum*).[15]

When preaching about the bondage of the will, one must skillfully reveal and reject the many ways with which people might reserve at least some role for themselves in their salvation. The preacher must boldly confess that their salvation is not in any regard dependent on their decisions or deeds. A

12. FC SD II:68 (KW 557 = *BSLK* 899).
13. "Sermon at Coburg on Cross and Suffering" (1530) LW 51:207.
14. AP IV:144 (KW 142–43 = *BSLK* 188).
15. "Luther emphasizes that saints, too, may fall and much more easily than might be expected. In fact, they even fall frequently. According to the Reformer, however, what makes a difference here is whether these falls occur 'deliberately' or 'out of weakness.' Even if a saint falls often 'because of weakness,' he or she will not be denied forgiveness. However, if Christians fulfill the desires of the flesh 'deliberately' and in a 'carefree' manner, they are being deceitful and do not regard sin as sin anymore. The outcome of this, in turn, is that they no longer cry to Christ for mercy, and so they lose the Spirit of Christ and 'die.'" Mannermaa, *Christ Present*, 71.

chain is only as strong as its weakest ring, and if the sinner is left *any* role in his salvation, it will logically become the central role in no time.

At the same time, however, one must realize that Lutheran doctrine does not dictate the experience and emotions one must have, can have, or cannot have concerning conversion. "I decided to follow Jesus" can be an accurate description of the experience many Christians have. Such an experience need not automatically be labeled as problematic; instead it can be, if understood correctly, a valid description of what took place in one's heart when the Holy Spirit made a reluctant unbeliever into an eager one. Together with the Formula, it is right to confess that God is able to renew and regenerate man's will, and this can cause some people to experience "choosing Jesus." The Confessions are not written with the purpose of regulating human emotions concerning their conversion, but rather, focusing on accurately determining the efficient cause (*causa efficiens*). Is the Holy Spirit confessed to be the sole agent in one's conversion, or does there still remain some attempt to save oneself through deeds or decisions?

How will this monergism affect the way Lutherans preach? If God is the one doing all the work in our salvation, can the preacher still appeal to his hearers, admonishing them to believe in Christ and live godly lives? C. F. W. Walther explains this in the following manner:

> In this thesis, we are not claiming that it is wrong for a pastor to demand—even passionately—that his listeners have faith. That was what all the prophets demanded, all the apostles, and, yes, even the Lord Jesus Christ Himself. When we demand faith, we do not lay down a demand on the Law. Rather, we extend the sweetest invitation, saying to our listeners, "Come, for everything is now ready." If I invite a half-starved person to sit down to a well-set table and to help himself to anything he likes, I do not expect him to tell me that he will take no orders from me. In the same way, the demand to believe is to be understood not as an order of the Law, but as an invitation of the Gospel. No, the error we are addressing is that man can produce faith in himself.[16]

It should be remembered that preaching God's word is a real means of grace which creates and conveys the reality it speaks about. God's word is an efficacious word (*verbum efficax*) and therefore the declaration: "believe the good news!" brings along the Holy Spirit who, according to God's plan, creates true faith in those who hear such preaching.[17] This is even more certain

---

16. Walther, *Law and Gospel*, 287.
17. "His Word—his self-revelation—is *verbum efficax*; it is 'promise' in the

when one is preaching to believers, saying: "bear good fruit!" Then the Spirit is present, using these words as his tool, kindling love and producing good works in those who hear the word. Their hearts can, even if weakly, accept this preaching, growing stronger and more eager through it.

While Lutherans reject synergism in all of its forms, it is still worthwhile to retain and further develop preaching that boldly challenges the hearers to accept God's word and do good works. Such preaching is not the kind of "pietism" confessionally bound Lutherans ought to reject, nor should it be considered "law" in the sense that it terrifies the conscience and drives the hearer to despair. While it is true that people in themselves have no power to believe in God or to do good works, this simple declaration is not yet gospel. The gospel, the good news, is not based on what we are unable to do, but on what God is able to do. True enough, if a person is in despair and spiritually exhausted by a false theology of free will, simply telling him how utterly and completely impossible it is for him to save himself may be merciful—in the same manner that it is merciful to put down a lame horse. The gospel, however, is much more than just that.

ORIGINAL SIN AS A RELEASE FROM THE TASK OF PRODUCING PERFECT CONTRITION

Concerning original sin and ways of preaching about it, an interesting detail can be found in Luther's statement in the Smalcald Articles, "The inherited sin has caused such a deep, evil corruption of nature that reason does not comprehend it; rather, it must be believed on the basis of the revelation in the Scriptures."[18] Luther's notion is helpful to anyone perplexed by the gravity of Lutheran doctrine concerning the original sin. Further developing this claim, trusting that such an addition would be approved by the reformer, one could go on to say that besides intellect, the reality of our sin surpasses also our emotional capabilities. Hence, original sin is "such a deep ... corruption of nature that reason *and heart* do not comprehend it, rather, it must be believed."

Original sin surpasses the believer's ability to rationally understand or emotionally experience it. Sin corrupts not only our deeds and thoughts,

---

categorical sense, *promissio*. It does not make a promise in the sense that it sets something forth as an expectation and thereby puts you off until later. *This promise is much more; it is its own fulfillment; it fulfills itself, and this actually does not take place at a later time, but at the very moment it is uttered; it is* promissio *as a valid promise that takes effect immediately."* Bayer, *Luther's Theology*, 114.

18. SA III:1, 3 (KW 311 = *BSLK* 434).

but also the very senses we use for judging our actions and moral position. After the fall, man's mind as well as his heart are damaged so that he is unable to fully realize his own state. This leads to a state where so-called "perfect contrition" becomes impossible, in other words, where sinners are unable to become fully aware of all their sins and make complete confession.

The criteria for "perfect contrition" are numerous, but one historical requirement was to enumerate all sins because only those explicitly mentioned could be absolved. Late medieval piety even knew guides written with the purpose of helping penitents to become aware of all of their sins so that they might be listed when making a confession. Still, consciences could not find solace, as Luther's biographical writings attest. He continues in the Smalcald Articles by making a bold shift away from such practice when describing his understanding of true contrition:

> This repentance is not fragmentary or paltry—like the kind that does penance for actual sins—nor is it uncertain like that kind. It does not debate over what is a sin or what is not a sin. Instead, it simply lumps everything together and says, "Everything is pure sin with us. What would we want to spend so much time investigating, dissecting, or distinguishing?" Therefore, here as well, contrition is not uncertain, because there remains nothing that we might consider a 'good' with which to pay for sin. Rather, there is plain, certain despair concerning all that we are, think, say, or do, etc.
>
> Similarly, such confession also cannot be false, uncertain, or fragmentary. All who confess that everything is pure sin with them embrace all sins, allow no exceptions, and do not forget a single one. Thus, satisfaction can never be uncertain either. For it consists not in our uncertain, sinful works but rather in the suffering and blood of the innocent Lamb of God, who takes away the sin of the world' [John 1:29]."[19]

Roman Catholic spirituality still carries along the notion of perfect contrition. "When it arises from a love by which God is loved above all else, contrition is called 'perfect.'"[20] The main difference between perfect and imperfect penitence is found in the person's motivation: if contrition is awakened by true love for God, it is perfect; if motivated by fear of punishment, it is imperfect. From a Lutheran viewpoint such a distinction is a clear example of diluting the gospel with the demands of the law. The law demands love, but can never create it in a sinful human being; true love for

---

19. SA III:3, 36–37 (KW 318 = *BSLK* 446–47).
20. *Catechism of the Catholic Church*, §1452.

God can only exist where sins have been forgiven. The law fulfils its very purpose when it terrifies the conscience and drives the penitent sinner to seek forgiveness from God. Therefore, demanding true love for God as a prerequisite for perfect contrition is to expect the fruits of forgiveness to exist prior to forgiveness itself, hence putting the proverbial cart before the horse.

Contrition, whether perfect or imperfect, should never be considered a condition for forgiveness or an efficient cause of it. Remorse, sorrow over one's sins, penitence—whatever word one might use, is not yet the repentance Lutherans seek. True repentance has two parts: to "have contrition and sorrow . . . about sin, and yet at the same time to believe in the gospel . . . that sin is forgiven and grace obtained through Christ."[21] Both Judas and Peter felt grave remorse for their sins (Matt 27:3 and Luke 22:62), but only Peter was forgiven—because he returned to Christ. Mere contrition is not yet true repentance, if faith is still lacking.

Even when crude forms of works-righteousness are rejected, a more subtle form of legalism can prevail and continue troubling consciences, tempting Christians to offer their troubled consciences as an atoning sacrifice to God. The idea, rarely expressed but sometimes felt, is that God has mercy only on those who have sufficient grief over their sins. Hymns as well as conversion stories and testimonies often describe how utterly wicked, miserable, guilty, and hopeless the repentant sinner felt in front of God's terrifying judgment seat. When such deep emotional experiences are missing, the penitent may be tempted to think there is something thoroughly wrong in his spiritual life, that in some way his conversion is not adequately genuine. In some way, such a notion hits home perfectly. The shocking realization of the Laodicean nature of one's heart may be perfectly accurate, even if the consequences inferred from it are often false.

When temptations take this form, Luther's claim concerning the original sin surpassing our understanding proves its worth in pastoral care. The sinfulness of the human heart is so deep that reason cannot understand it, and it is similarly impossible for our emotional life to fully realize and experience the gravity of our crimes. The lukewarm numbness of the heart is a sign of nothing more than original sin affecting the Christian's emotional life. The depth of our sin is something we must believe according to God's word, because we cannot sufficiently see or feel it. The hardness of our hearts should definitely be included among the things we confess as sins. However, it would be a grave mistake to think that there is no true repentance or forgiveness unless our mind succeeds in enumerating all

---

21. AC XII (German) (KW 44 = *BSLK* 66–67).

our offenses or our heart manages to feel sufficiently agonizing pangs of conscience. Even the etymology of the word might help to understand this; conscience is based on knowledge (*scientia*) of your sins, not necessarily any concrete experience of them.

To put it more sharply: perfect repentance—be it measured cognitively (ability to enumerate sins) in regard to motives (love of God rather than fear of punishment) or emotionally (sufficient feelings of guilt)—is attainable only by a person without any sin. Anyone with sin is incapable of perfect repentance, so long as repentance is evaluated by examining the repentant person themselves. This is good news: the blood that was poured on the cross does not need to be supplied with our tears of remorse, as if only then our sins would be washed away.

Nonetheless, it might be worth noting that a sense of guilt is often coupled with or even superseded by a sense of shame and worthlessness. In pastoral care, it is usually necessary to address both sides of the matter. The doctrine of original sin can be a harsh, but still true reminder, not only of our wicked state but also, indirectly, of our inherent worth and dignity.

Sin, by its very nature, is not something that primarily describes the quality of a person, but rather his relation. To have sin or to commit sin is always something that is expressed in relation to something else. People may not need the knowledge of God's law to realize they are lazy, short-tempered, or dishonest. Seeing these things as sinful, however, requires them to realize that there is someone they are responsible to concerning their misconduct and shortcomings. One can be truly sinful only *coram Deo*, in the eyes of God (which, incidentally, means that frustration from just breaking your own ideals or failing in your own ambitions does not count as true Christian penance).

Calling all people sinful, then, means treating all people are responsible. And while that notion should justly terrify us, it also brings along a certain affirmation of worth and dignity. Rocks, plants, or animals are not considered responsible for their actions, but people are. The demands and accusations of God's law reveal that humans, even in their fallen and depraved state, are still held responsible, they are still considered and judged as beings with the high and noble calling of being God's likeness and image. The harsh love of God says, "I expect more from you and I won't leave you alone as long as you keep going wrong," instead of, "I don't consider you worth my time anymore."

A final note concerning original sin in preaching and pastoral care deals with the notion of guilt, or lack of guilt, associated with concupiscence, "the evil desire." At least in the more liberal mainline churches, it is now largely considered self-evident that nothing can be considered sinful that is not freely chosen. The fact that such claims are made among Lutherans proves how weak and shallow the understanding concerning the original sin has become. Involuntary sin is at the heart of the whole concept of original sin. As the Augsburg Confession states, "all human beings . . . are conceived and born in sin . . . and full of evil lust and inclination."[22]

Conservative Christians sometimes bring forth the distinction between inclination to evil and evil deeds themselves, and then claim that the former is not yet sinful, but becomes so if the person gives in to temptation and commits evil deeds. Presently, this distinction is often used to soften the scandalous claim that homosexuality is sinful. The claim, therefore, is that while practicing homosexuality is a sin, homosexual orientation in itself is not sinful.

While the distinction is reasonable when considering human relations (there is a real difference between wanting to kill someone and actually pulling the trigger) and the way our sins harm our neighbor, the distinction is too shallow to explain away our sinful desires in front of God. The Augsburg Confession clearly states that desire for evil, concupiscence, is in itself a real sin. (AC II:2)

The need to explain away the sinful nature of evil desires may stem from a weak understanding of the Lutheran *simul iustus et peccator*. The harsh bedrock of original sin, if nothing else, proves that it is utterly impossible for a Christian to stop sinning in this life. If this verdict is too much to bear, then a need arises to explain concupiscence away. Lutherans, however, are free to confess sin in all its forms, at the same time putting their trust on the forgiveness freely and abundantly given in their baptism. The condemnation and punishment applies only to those who are "not born anew through baptism and the Holy Spirit."[23]

Failure to confess original sin in all its severity blunts the law, and allowing the error of free will into preaching dilutes the gospel. What results, is a crisis in preaching and pastoral care, indeed, a crisis of the whole pastoral office itself. What remains of the pastoral office is merely a pompous version of a bible salesman or a spiritual consultant service—a weak alternative to the full meaning of the preaching office that is supposed to be the office of the stewards of the secrets of God's household, ministers who serve their Lord by allowing him to make his election here and now through the preached word and the administered sacraments. Hence, a clear understanding of original sin, the bondage of the will, and God's election, is a treasure to be cherished and used in service of the Gospel.

22. AC II (German) KW 36, 38 = *BSLK* 53.
23. AC II (German); KW 38 = *BSLK* 53.

BIBLIOGRAPHY

Catechism of the Catholic Church. Vatican City: Libreria Editrice Vaticana, 1994.

Bayer, Oswald. *Martin Luther's Theology. A Contemporary Interpretation.* Grand Rapids: Eerdmans, 2008.

Forde, Gerhard O. *On Being a Theologian of the Cross.* Grand Rapids: Eerdmans, 1997.

———. *The Captivation of the Will. Luther vs. Erasmus on Freedom and Bondage.* Edited by Steven Paulson. Grand Rapids: Eerdmans, 2005.

Lewis, C. S. *Surprised by Joy.* Orlando: Harcourt, 1955.

Mannermaa, Tuomo. *Christ Present in Faith. Luther's view of Justification.* Translated by Kirsi Stjerna. Minneapolis: Fortress, 2005.

Walther, C. F. W. *Law & Gospel: How to Read and Apply the Bible.* Edited by Charles P. Schaum. Translated by Christian C. Tiews. St. Louis: Concordia, 2010.

14

Learning to Lament
Preaching to Suffering in the Lament Psalms

—Jeremiah Johnson

THE PROBLEM OF SUFFERING

When I arrived at my first parish, Julie and Dan (not their real names) were already engaged, and I had the privilege of being their pastor as they entered this new season in their lives. Dan and Julie faced multiple job changes, family issues, and several relocations and did so with a firm confidence in their Lord. But as time went on and they desired the gift of a family, they faced the complex and heart-wrenching realities of infertility. What was at first an eager desire soon became a longing emptiness that cast a long shadow over their lives. Finally, the Lord granted them a child, although Julie's pregnancy was a tenuous one. It seemed that every few weeks raised new complications. Julie found herself on bed rest twice, and during the second session, at about the end of the second trimester, she gave birth prematurely.

Life in the neonatal intensive care unit is difficult and anxious. The prognosis for Dan and Julie's child looked good at first, but he suddenly took a turn for the worst, and after two unsuccessful surgeries, his life slowly slipped away. Dan baptized him, and he spent the final moments of his life in his mother's sobbing arms.

Julie's response was far worse than I imagined. With surprising vitriol, she raged against her Lord and any who presumed to speak for him. I have rarely seen such desperate anger, like a wounded animal who lashes out for dear life. My pastoral care for her was fraught with failures, but this much was also clear: Julie lacked the means for mourning. She had no language for her grief. When Julie's anger and despair welled up, instead of being channeled, it overflowed the riverbanks and flooded her life with a destructive bitterness. This is certainly not to say that Julie's grief or anger or bitterness were illegitimate, but without any proper vehicle with which to express it, it wreaked havoc on her life. I will not presume to know what it is like to lose a child so young. That burden has not been given to me, but this experience left a deep and enduring impression on me and convinced me of this truth: we are in desperate need of learning to lament.

Anyone who has been to a funeral can testify to the fact that we struggle with how to mourn. In the face of death, many well-intentioned friends and family members attempt to "fix" the problem of mourning by somehow justifying the circumstances of a death with words like, "She's not in pain anymore," or "God needed him more than we did," or more egregiously, "I'm *sure* he is in heaven now," implying that a Christian's name being written in the book of life somehow extinguishes all sorrow in this age. Putting the best construction on it, the responses of family and friends stem from a deep-seated longing to relieve the suffering of loved ones. In our eyes, sorrow is the problem, and so we fumble about in search of some remedy to "fix" the problem of mourning.

Our attempts to solve the "problem" of mourning have not gone unnoticed by the funeral industry. One funeral home in a town neighboring that of my first parish handed out the *Transitions* newsletters, a publication filled with articles about grief and tips on how to speak to those who mourn. In one particular issue, the primary article has a list of fourteen things to say (or not to say) to someone who is grieving. It includes salutary advice like "Don't try to lessen the loss with easy answers," "Share your memories," and "Don't rush the survivor." Analysis of this advice aside, the very fact that these sorts of publications are common in the funeral industry indicates that, as a culture, we struggle not only with our own mourning but also with how to speak with others who are mourning.

Our problem with mourning is certainly not limited to funerals. All kinds of suffering: cancer, job loss, divorce, family strife, and mental illness, are often met with our American, problem-solving approach. Chronic pain is met with incessant optimism. Divorce is met with a litany of justifications. Family strife is met with an endless barrage of advice. This is not to dismiss optimism or outrage or sound advice. But what is so often lacking from suffering of every kind is the willingness and ability to genuinely express our pain and loss.

When all you have is a hammer, everything begins to look like a nail, and in the eyes of American pragmatism, sorrow and pain are simply more nails to be pounded. This is even reflected in how we talk about mourning. We talk about "getting over" a loss, "working through" grief, "moving on," or the "road" to healing. Our language portrays mourning as an obstacle that we must suffer but ultimately overcome. In reflecting upon his own son's death, Nicholas Wolterstorff articulates this struggle as "coping" versus "overcoming."

We live in a time and place where, over and over, when confronted with something unpleasant we pursue not coping, but overcoming. Often we succeed. Most of humanity has not enjoyed and does not enjoy such luxury. Death shatters our illusion that we can make do without coping. When we have overcome absence with phone calls, winglessness with airplanes, summer heat with air-conditioning—when we have overcome all these and much more besides, then there will abide two things with which we must cope: the evil in our hearts and death.[1]

To use Wolterstorff's terminology, we find it hard to face suffering, foremost in death, because we cannot overcome suffering but only cope with it. And our solution-oriented focus towards suffering displaces both our capacity and willingness to express our grief.

In contrast to our pragmatic approach to mourning, the Scriptures speak in the language of lamentation, which gives authentic voice to our suffering and does not lay the burden of overcoming upon our own backs. It is, therefore, the thesis of this essay that American Christianity needs to rediscover the biblical practice of lamentation, not as a gimmick or a principle, but because lamentation is an appropriate and faithful response to the sorrow that fills our fallen world. Moreover, this is the case because, in his priestly office, Christ himself laments for us, on our behalf, unto the age to come, where the need for lamentation will pass away.

Sadly, however, American Christianity has neglected lamentation and has often been complicit in the pragmatic response to suffering. In a context that often sells itself on "positive" messages and upbeat worship services, the Biblical practice of lamentation is practically foreign to American Christians today. I believe that our modern aversion to lamentation fits hand-in-glove with how poorly we usually deal with suffering in the church. This poverty of properly addressing suffering is further evidenced by many funeral sermons, which attempt to alleviate grief with encouragements like, "We

---

1. Wolterstorff, *Lament*, 72–73.

should be *happy*; she's in heaven now." The homiletical lacuna of lamentation is likely related to the fact that the church shies away from lamentation in both scripture and song. Anecdotally, I can count the number of sermons I have heard on the lament psalms on one hand. Others, including Howard Wallace[2] and Glenn Pemberton have noticed this same trend of neglecting lament. Our modern aversion to lamentation is also demonstrated in our hymnody. Austin Holt conducted a study of several modern hymnals of various American denominations, comparing the breakdown of their genres with the genres of the psalms. He found that our modern hymnals are disproportionately weighted towards hymns of praise and thanksgiving and lacking in hymns of lamentation.[3]

I am convinced that we American Christians need to learn to lament once more, and lay our distresses before the Father who not only hears our pleas, but gives us the very words with which to express them, and I believe that key to the restoration of lamentation is the *preaching* of these psalms.

---

2. Wallace, *Words to God*, 135–37.

3. Holt surveyed three hymnals: *Songs of Faith and Praise* (Churches of Christ) *The Presbyterian Hymnal*, and *The Baptist Hymnal*, categorizing their hymns as: praise, thanksgiving and trust, lament, teaching and encouragement, or other. In contrast to the psalms, these hymnals contained vastly more hymns in the praise and thanksgiving categories and far, far fewer in the lament category. Laments comprise 40% of the psalter, whereas laments comprise only 12–18% of these hymnals. Looking at the data further only revealed a deeper disparity. Many of hymns in these hymnals that are categorized as laments are barely comparable to their counterparts in the Psalter. Pemberton summarizes the findings:

> This comparison of our hymnals to the Psalms reveals two significant and alarming results. First, we have almost completely lost the biblical language of lament. . . . Few of our lament songs correspond to the kind of lament in the Psalms: what constitutes 40 percent of the book of Psalms (60 laments out of 150 psalms) comprises only 3 percent of SOFP (*Songs of Faith and Praise*) . . . , 2 percent of BH (*The Baptist Hymnal*) . . . , and 7 percent of PH (*The Presbyterian Hymnal*). . . . In other words, absent from our laments are the themes most prevalent in the laments of the Psalter: the problem of enemies, unmerited suffering, and God's failures to act or respond. (Pemberton, *Hurting*, 39)

I noticed this same dearth of laments in a popular children's songbook from Concordia Publishing House, *Little Ones Sing Praise*. Preparing some children's devotional materials, I was searching for a song that might complement well the mourning Israelites in the Babylonian captivity, but there is not even one song in *Little Ones Sing Praise* that has some element of lament in it. This prompts me to ask, do we ever expose our children to lament? If not, does this contribute to why we seem to have such an aversion to it as adults?

Why the lament psalms? The church has relied on the psalms as its prayer book, and for good reason. The lament psalms in particular are almost entirely primary discourse, the psalmist's words to God.[4] In light of our own deficient dialogue with the Lord, these words are both welcome and necessary for us. They give us a voice with which to speak back to God, and in God's own words.

Why *preaching* the lament psalms? This dialogue should not be limited to prayer. If we are fundamentally ignorant about how to speak with God about our own suffering, then should not the pulpit be the place where we are tutored in this divinely given discourse? Not only is the sermon an opportunity to teach lament, but it is especially appropriate because the sermon is, by nature, a *corporate* activity. Even as deeply personal as the lament psalms are, the Scriptures are never individual property. Thus the primary discourse of the lament psalms is not simply the words of one Christian, but the words of the whole church. As Bonhoeffer argues, they can only be the words and experience of the church if they are first the words and experience of Christ.

No individual can repeat the lamentation psalms out of his own experience; it is the distress of the entire Christian community at all times, as only Jesus Christ has experienced it entirely alone, which is here unfolded. Because it happens with God's will, indeed because God knows it completely and knows it better than we ourselves, only God himself can help.[5]

THE LAMENT PSALMS

Before we engage in any kind of homiletical reflection on the lament psalms, we would do well to consider two more fundamental questions. First, what is a lament? What are its identifiable characteristics? Second, what does a lament do? What effect does it have on a reader? How does it enable us to speak to God?

What is a lament? Since the work of Herman Gunkel, scholarship on the psalms has utilized his classification system for the psalms or some variation thereof. Both Gunkel's and most other classification systems include

---

4. Although this list is by no means exhaustive, a few good examples would be Pss 6; 10; 13; 17; 36; 42; 52; and 77.

5. Bonhoeffer, *Psalms*, 47.

the category of lament,[6] which comprises forty percent of the Psalter.[7] Of course, the psalms themselves do not have the categories explicitly attached to them, so any system of classification is, by nature, an imposed construct. Nevertheless, these classification systems allow us to group psalms with similar characteristics and discuss them as a larger set.

So what characterizes these psalms? The psalms of lament are prayers specifically seeking deliverance from some kind of crisis. The crises in the psalms are varied: crop failures, sickness, moral degeneration, gossip, national security, and more. The lament psalms often have five common elements: an address to God, complaint, request, motivation, and confidence in God and his action.[8] Not all of these five elements are present in every lament psalm, but many of these psalms share three or more of these elements.

For example, Ps 43 begins with the address and a request from God for vindication.

> Vindicate me, O God, and defend my cause against an ungodly people, from the deceitful and unjust man deliver me! (Ps 43:1)

This request is immediately followed by the psalmist's complaint.

> For you are the God in whom I take refuge; why have you rejected me? Why do I go about mourning because of the oppression of the enemy? (Ps 43:2)

In contrast, the final verse expresses a confidence in God's salvific action.

> Why are you cast down, O my soul, and why are you in turmoil within me? Hope in God; for I shall again praise him, my salvation and my God. (Ps 43:5)

Another key feature of the lament psalms is their widespread use of first to second person discourse: "I" to "you." This is not a unique characteristic of the laments, but a widespread feature of all the psalms. For example, Ps 13 is mostly a first to second person discourse between the psalmist and the Lord.

> How long, O LORD? Will you forget me forever? How long will you hide your face from me? How long must I wrestle with my thoughts and every day have sorrow in my heart? How long

---

6. Bellinger, *Psalms*, 21. Gunkel distinguished between community laments and individual laments. This is a perfectly legitimate distinction but quite unnecessary for the sake of this essay.

7. Pemberton, *Hurting*, 32.

8. Ibid., 65.

will my enemy triumph over me? Look on me and answer, O
LORD my God. Give light to my eyes, or I will sleep in death;
(Ps 13:1–3)

Other examples of first- to second-person discourse include Pss 16, 17, 22, 28, 30, 38, 44, 54, 55, 61, 63, 64, 77, and 101, to name only a few. This feature has long led the church to identify (although not exclusively) the psalms as prayers.

Having discussed what a lament is, let us consider what a lament does. Put succinctly, the lament psalms give us a divine grammar with which to speak to God in the midst of our suffering, and we need a divine grammar because we do not know how to speak to him.

Before his turn towards orthodoxy, Augustine reviled the rhetorical simplicity and mundaneness in the Scriptures. It was, for all practical purposes, a book estranged from him. He was a foreigner to the Scriptures. But he "eventually realized that his estrangement from Scripture lay within *him* and his refusal to allow it to question him."[9] How much of our exegesis attempts to make the Scripture (and especially the psalms) palatable to our sensibilities and comfortable for our lifestyles? How frequently do we object to a doctrine because we cannot bear the implications of it? Augustine's recognition that the Scriptures are a foreign word to us because we are estranged from them is crucial to our openness to being changed by the word of God. Brian Brock rightly says of Scripture, "It is as strange and eternally different from our common sense as is Christ himself."[10]

Augustine's recognition of the psalms' foreignness to us indicates a universal problem for all Christians. We do not know intrinsically how to speak about God, much less how speak to him about our suffering. When the disciples asked Jesus to teach them to pray like John had taught his disciples, the implication was that they did not know *how* to pray.[11] The lament psalms presume a similar deficiency on behalf of the reader, who learns how to pray from them and with them. Consider, for example, Ps 38.

> Those who seek my life lay their snares; those who seek my hurt speak of ruin and meditate treachery all day long.
>
> But I am like a deaf man; I do not hear, like a mute man who does not open his mouth.
>
> I have become like a man who does not hear, and in whose mouth are no rebukes.

---

9. Brock, *Singing*, x.
10. Ibid., xi.
11. Luke 11:1.

But for you, O LORD, do I wait; it is you, O Lord my God, who will answer. (Ps 38:12-15)

In light of the treachery of his enemies, the psalmist is at his end; he no longer responds to them. He is defenseless. His only hope is to wait for the Lord's answer and vindication.

So it is *our* words that fail us. We do not know how to speak to God about our suffering. In light of our own deficient dialogue with the Lord, the words of the lament psalms are both welcome and necessary for us. Instead of looking inward for God's response, the Lord speaks *extra nos* through the psalms. Not only does he provide *his* end of the conversation, he also provides *ours*. He gives us words to speak to him, and he responds to us. Although these words provided to us articulate the frustration, pain, longing, and grief within us, these words are not from within us. In this sense, they are confession, "to say with" the Lord.[12]

By praying the psalms we learn a discipline of prayer so that no longer do our hearts pray by themselves, with the consequent confusion between our feelings, sighs and wishes, etc. and prayer. Rather we find ourselves able to speak with God "whether the heart is full or empty." If we follow the prayer discipline of the psalms, we find ourselves molded in character as pray-ers.[13]

In summary, the lament psalms are prayers seeking deliverance from some sort of crisis. They are identified as prayers because they are dominated by first to second person discourse between the psalmist and God. One of the functions of a lament is to provide a divine grammar for bringing our lamentations before the Lord, without which we would be unable to adequately address him. Not only do the laments provide our end of the conversation, but also God's end of the conversation.

PREACHING THE LAMENT PSALMS

The Herald and the Pastor

What does a "lament sermon" look like? How does one preach a lament sermon? The lament psalms present unique homiletical challenges and opportunities not often encountered in other texts. In presenting the distinctiveness of preaching on the laments, it is helpful to recall Thomas Long's

---

12. In writing to Marcellinus, Augustine makes a similar observation. Gregg, *Athanasius*, 108–10.
13. Wallace. *Words to God*, 70.

images of the preacher as "herald" and the preacher as "pastor."[14] These two images are useful not only because they are common and theologically sound images of a preacher, but for the purposes of these reflections particularly because the lament psalms bring a homiletical dimension that does not fit cleanly into either of these categories. Holding both images in view we can more clearly see the challenges and opportunities both images provide in regard to the preaching of lament.

The image of the herald is exemplified by the Old Testament prophetic declaration, "Thus says the Lord." The herald's primary role is to be the mouthpiece of God. He does not meddle with the message, but the herald delivers it to its recipients as God's words rather than his own. Karl Barth used this image, albeit for more than just preachers, to emphasize the divine origin of the herald's message.

> Proclamation is human language in and through which God Himself speaks, *like a king through the mouth of his herald,* which moreover is meant to be heard and apprehended . . . in faith as the divine decision upon life and death, as the divine judgment and the divine acquittal, the eternal law and the eternal gospel both together.[15]

The herald is objective. He is not "floating an idea" or proposing a theory. He is proclaiming an objective message from God. This message is *extra nos*, not an invention of the herald.

The image of the pastor leans more towards the subjective. The pastor is more concerned about how the divine message will be received by his hearers. "Thus says the Lord" may be true, but a sermon cannot be limited to raw proclamation.

For the preacher as pastor, the needs of the hearers (not necessarily their wants) take on much more prominence than they do for the herald. The preacher discerns these needs, we may even say diagnoses these needs, and then strives to be of help by intervening with the gospel, by speaking a word that clarifies and restores.[16]

The pastor certainly must know the divine proclamation, but he also must know how those who listen will hear it. He must know about their lives and their hearts in order to deliver this message adequately.

---

14. Long, *Witness*, 24.
15. Barth, *Doctrine*, 57 (emphasis mine).
16. Long, *Witness*, 31.

Intercessory Preaching

Both the image of the preacher as herald and the preacher as pastor neglect one powerful dimension of the lament psalms: intercession. Both the pastor and the herald speak words from God, the former with an objective edge and the latter with a subjective edge. But in both cases, it is primarily a one way conversation from God to man. But the laments introduce something infrequent in other Biblical texts, words to God. As we noted earlier, many of the psalms are prayers, first person addresses to God. Consider this appeal for God's help in Ps 28:

> To you, O LORD, I call; my rock, be not deaf to me, lest, if you be silent to me, I become like those who go down to the pit. (Ps 28:1)

Or this statement of confidence in Ps 102:

> But you, O LORD, are enthroned forever; you are remembered throughout all generations.
>
> You will arise and have pity on Zion; it is the time to favor her; the appointed time has come. (Ps 102:12–13)

The herald may be well equipped to deliver messages from God, but he does not speak to God on behalf of the people. Even the pastor, who is concerned with the needs and the life context of his hearers is still primarily concerned with what he will say to them, not what message he will bear to the Lord from them. But the lament psalms open up the door to a different image of a preacher: the preacher as an intercessor.

The pastoral office is grounded in the authority given him to do certain things in the stead of Christ. In the baptismal rite, the pastor baptizes in the first person, "*I* baptize you," but he does so in the name of the Father, Son, and Holy Spirit.[17] In absolution, the pastor forgives in the stead of Christ. In the Small Catechism, Luther explains concerning the question "What is confession?" ". . . that we receive absolution, that is forgiveness, from the pastor as from God Himself, not doubting, but firmly believing that by it our sins are forgiven before God in heaven."[18] Again, the pastor speaks in behalf of Christ when proclaiming the absolution in the LSB, ". . . in the stead and by the command of my Lord Jesus Christ, I forgive you all your sins in the name of the Father, Son, and Holy Spirit."[19] The office of the pas-

---

17. LSB 270.
18. Luther, *Luther's Small Catechism*, 26.
19. LSB 185.

tor is entirely reliant upon the office of Christ. He would have no office apart from Christ's office, and this includes the office of preaching.

The image of the herald and pastor both correspond most closely to Christ's prophetic office. This office is primarily a proclamatory office—it is a declaration *from* God, not an appeal *to* Him. The Lutheran dogmatician Francis Pieper argues that Christ's prophetic office is extended on earth today by teaching and preaching in the church.[20] So it is reasonable to conclude that the preaching office relies upon the prophetic office of Christ. But is preaching limited to the prophetic office of Christ?

Hebrews describes the priestly office of Christ in some detail.[21] As priest, Christ intercedes for his people in both prayer and sacrifice (Heb 5:1–3, 7; 7:25–28; 9:11–14). Christ's intercessory role is perhaps best illustrated in the High Priestly Prayer of John 17. "I pray for them. I am not praying for the world, but for those you have given me, for they are yours." (John 17:9) In this prayer, Jesus asks the Father for the disciples' protection (17:11, 15) joy (17:13) sanctification (17:17) unity (17:21) and glory (17:22). Even on the cross, Jesus intercedes for those who mock him, saying, "Father, forgive them, for they do not know what they are doing."

Because the lament psalms also frequently address God as a pray-er, the preaching of these psalms could reflect Christ's priestly office in addition to his prophetic office. Preaching according to Christ's priestly office would offer words *to* God in behalf of our hearers in addition to words *from* God. But this kind of intercessory preaching is no mere homiletical novelty. Intercessory preaching reflects what Christ already does when he takes the words of the psalms on his own lips.

It was the point of the New Testament writers in having Jesus speak as if the words of the psalms were his own words. But Jesus continues to pray the psalms, Bonhoeffer asserts, and so becomes an intercessor for his people. Believers who pray the psalms do so as part of the body of Christ. Verses in the psalms may not, on occasion, be the immediate prayer of one part of the body. Even so they can be the prayer of other parts. In this way, the words of God become our words to God and God hears God's people when the pray the psalms, praying in the words of Jesus, the Word of God.[22]

So what does intercessory preaching look like? One possibility is infusing prayer into the sermon. In a sermon on Ps 31, the preacher might actually cry out to God for the congregation simply using the words of the text, "Incline your ear to me; rescue me speedily! Be a rock of refuge for

---

20. Pieper, *Christian Dogmatics*, 339.
21. See Heb 2:17; 3:1; 4:14; 5:6; 8:1; 10:11.
22. Wallace, *Words to God*, 77.

me, a strong fortress to save me!" (Ps 31:2) The preacher might also expand on this plea, telling the Lord some of the specific crises that he knows his hearers are experiencing. The sermon would, at least in part, sound like a prayer from the entire congregation to God. But the sermon would also proclaim the psalmist's confidence as if it belonged to the congregation. "But you heard the voice of my pleas for mercy when I cried to you for help. . . . Be strong, and let your heart take courage, all you who wait for the Lord!" (Ps 31:22, 24) Intercession would be met with proclamation. The preacher would declare both words *to* God and words *from* God.

Standing Astride the Eschatological Gap

When the preacher steps into the pulpit, he stands astride two ages. On the one hand, he echoes the words of John and Jesus, proclaiming in this age that the reign of heaven is at hand.[23] On the other hand, he proclaims how Christ will return and restore all things in the age to come.[24] Long, using his images of pastor and herald frames this tension like this:

> The pastor's question, "How are we to live through the day?" must always be held in tension with another question, "How can we live toward the tomorrow of God's promised future?" Here the herald image corrects the pastoral one.[25]

But for any preacher who is sufficiently attuned to his hearer's lives, this is an exceedingly difficult tension to manage. When Jesus proclaimed the immanent reign of God, it was accompanied by signs and wonders of that inbreaking reign. He healed the sick, cast out demons, cleansed the lepers, and even raised the dead. When the crowds heard the proclamation about His reign, they received its eschatological firstfruits. The modern preacher, however, rarely has such reinforcement. When he preaches the present reign of God, it does not immediately cure Aunt Ethel of cancer or give Mr. Robinson his job back or even raise Jim and Karen's daughter from the dead. The full restoration of God's reign awaits the parousia. But that makes it difficult to preach to those who are suffering in the present.

This tension between the ages, this eschatological gap should not and cannot be solved by the preacher. Jesus' words at the end of John 16 should tell us this much. "I have told you these things, so that in me you may have peace. In this world you will have trouble. But take heart! I have overcome

---

23. Matt 3:2; 4:17.
24. Acts 3:21.
25. Long, *Witness*, 34.

the world." (John 16:33) On the one hand, we cannot turn a blind eye to our present hardships, opting instead to focus only on the age to come. On the other hand, we cannot shunt our eschatological hope in favor of addressing our present needs. The tension between the present and the future age must remain a tension, and the lament psalms help us to articulate this tension faithfully.

Psalm 130 demonstrates a remarkable eschatological hope in the face of present despair. In the first two verses, the psalmist describes himself as crying out from the depths of the deep. "Out of the depths I cry to you . . . let your ears be attentive to the voice of my pleas for mercy!" (Ps 130:1–2) In the face of his present despair, the psalmist waits with hope. This is hardly wishful thinking, but a living hope. The Lord's future arrival is just as certain (if not more so) than the rising of the sun (130:6). The theological keywords "steadfast love" and "redemption" (130:7) ground this future hope in the Lord's promises and actions.

In Ps 61 the psalmist pleads for safety and refuge, and he looks both to the past and to the future for hope and confidence in the Lord's gracious action. Verses three and four provide a powerful contrast. First, the psalmist recalls the Lord's past protection, "for you have been my refuge, a strong tower against the enemy." (Ps 61:3) This past action is coupled with a request for future deliverance. "Let me dwell in your tent forever! Let me take refuge under the shelter of your wings!" (Ps 61:4) This pattern of past action and future confidence is repeated in verses five through eight. God has heard past vows and made the psalmist the recipient of a God-fearing legacy (61:5). Based on this, he asks that the king's life and reign would be extended to eternity (61:6–7) The psalmist's response of praise, then, extends back into the daily present (61:8).

Psalm 42 also couples the psalmist's present despair with confidence in the Lord's future deliverance. He laments his apparent present abandonment by God. "My tears have been my food day and night, while they say to me continually, 'Where is your God?'" (Ps 42:3) But then the psalmist chastises himself and confidently asserts the Lord's future deliverance, "Why are you cast down, O my soul, and why are you in turmoil within me? Hope in God; for I shall again praise him, my salvation and my God." (Ps 42:5–6) Again, at the end of the psalm, the psalmist expands his lament,

> "I say to God, my rock: 'Why have you forgotten me? Why do I go mourning because of the oppression of the enemy?' As with a deadly wound in my bones, my adversaries taunt me, while they say to me continually, 'Where is your God?'" (Ps 42:9–10)

But he then chastises himself, confirming his trust in the Lord, "Why are you cast down, O my soul, and why are you in turmoil within me? Hope in God; for I shall again praise him, my salvation and my God." (Ps 42:11) Note how the questions, "Why have you forgotten me?," "Why do I go mourning . . . ?," and "Where is your God?" are not answered, save only by the counter question "Why are you [soul] in turmoil?" and the exhortation, "Hope in God." These unanswered complaints express but do not resolve the eschatological gap.

I have heard people complain that the lament psalms do not provide answers for their present troubles. In one sense, this is precisely why the lament psalms should be preached, because they do not peddle easy answers or seek to resolve the eschatological tension between the present age and the age to come. These psalms, on the one hand, are bluntly honest about our own present suffering, our deep despair, our raging enemies, and our sense of abandonment in the midst of our darkest hours. On the other hand, the laments are also brazenly confident not only in the Lord's past faithfulness, but especially in his future action.

The lament psalms do not provide us an answer to our suffering, but how to speak in the midst of it. They provide no answer to our suffering, because there is no answer, save only the answer that we find in the death and resurrection of Christ.

To be sure, the psalms request fellowship with God in earthly life, but they know that this fellowship is not completed in earthly life but continues beyond it, even stands in opposition to it (Ps 17:14–15). So life in fellowship with God is always already on the other side of death. Death is, to be sure, the irrevocable bitter end for body and soul. It is the wages of sin, and the remembrance of it is necessary (Pss 39 and 90). On the other side of death, however, is the eternal God (Pss 90 and 102). Therefore not death but life will triumph in the power of God. We find this life in the resurrection of Jesus Christ and we ask for it in that life to come.[26]

CONCLUSION

One does not need to be Christian to know that suffering is an unavoidable part of life in this age. Our lives and the lives of our neighbors all testify to this truth. The American culture has been plagued with an overly pragmatic approach to dealing with suffering that views it simply as something that needs to be fixed and rushes to repair it, and unfortunately the church has often become complicit in this error, attempting to "solve" the problem of

---

26. Bonhoeffer, *Psalms*, 61–62.

our mourning with optimism and denial. These failed attempts to short-circuit our suffering belie a more fundamental problem: we do not know how to speak to God in the midst of our suffering.

But where our own words fail, God provides a divine grammar for us to speak in the lament psalms. These psalms are not only words *from* God but also words *to* God. And if the practice of lament is to be restored, the whole Church needs to be tutored in this foreign grammar, and this tutoring begins in the pulpit.

Preaching the lament psalms relies not only on the prophetic office of Christ, but also on his priestly office. The lament psalms provide the preacher with the opportunity to speak to God in behalf of his hearers, and thereby also shape their own pleas to the Father. Furthermore, the lament psalms instruct the preacher how to stand in the eschatological gap between the suffering of the present age and the restoration of the age to come without neglecting either one.

Ultimately, the lament psalms are not merely a different and novel way to speak about suffering. The lament psalms link our suffering to the one who suffered on our behalf, and God's future action in which the laments express such profound confidence is fully realized in the person and action of Christ. So when the preacher preaches lament, it is never mere mourning. Lamentation is fully expressed only in the light of Christ's death, resurrection, and return. And finally, in the parousia, he will turn our mourning into dancing.

BIBLIOGRAPHY

Barth, Karl. *The Doctrine of the Word of God, Church Dogmatics*, volume 1. Translated by G. T. Thomson. Edinburgh: T. & T. Clark, 1936.
Bellinger, W. H. *Psalms: Reading and Studying the Book of Praises*. Peabody, MA: Hendrickson, 1990.
Bonhoeffer, Dietrich, and Eberhard Bethge. *Psalms: The Prayer Book of the Bible*. Minneapolis: Augsburg, 1970.
Brock, Brian. *Singing the Ethos of God: On the Place of Scripture in Christian Ethics*. Grand Rapids: Eerdmans, 2007.
Gregg, Robert C. *Athanasius: The Life of Antony and the Letter to Marcellinus*. London: SPCK, 1980.
Long, Thomas G. *The Witness of Preaching*. Louisville: Westminster John Knox, 1989.
Luther, Martin, and Sara Tyson. *Luther's Small Catechism, with Explanation*. St. Louis: Concordia, 2005.
Pemberton, Glenn. *Hurting with God: Learning to Lament with the Psalms*. Abilene, TX: Abilene Christian University Press, 2012.
Pieper, Franz. *Christian Dogmatics*. Vol. 1. Saint Louis: Concordia, 1951.

Wallace, Howard N. *Words to God, Word from God: The Psalms in the Prayer and Preaching of the Church*. Aldershot, UK: Ashgate, 2005.

Wolterstorff, Nicholas. *Lament for a Son*. Grand Rapids, Eerdmans, 1987.

15

The Preacher as Physician for the Sick in Spirit

—Jakob Appell

I will prescribe regimens for the good of my patients according to my ability and my judgment and never do harm to anyone.[1]

INTRODUCTION

Johann Gerhard's monumental *Loci Theologici* lists metaphors in the Holy Scriptures for the pastoral office, among them "physician." His brevity suggests that the metaphor appears rarely. He notes only one passage (Jer 30:13) and concludes from it that "ministers of the Word are like physicians of states, inasmuch as they point out how to forestall or even heal and remove the greatest illnesses: sin, the wrath of God, and punishments."[2] This essay seeks to highlight this underdeveloped metaphor by considering several important aspects of what it means to be a pastor and preacher to the sick in spirit. Exploring the task of preaching under the metaphor of pastor as physician for the sick in spirit may renew interest in the physician-metaphor for the pastoral office as well as understanding of what a pastor is called to be and do. A word will be spoken in the conclusion about the limits of the

---

1. From the *Hippocratic Oath* (500 BC) an oath historically taken by physicians.
2. *Theological Commonplaces*, 46.

analogy, but these limits do not detract from its legitimate use. The main part of the essay will focus on preaching in its similarity to the physician's diagnosis, prognosis, and prescription of medicine.

THE PASTOR AS PHYSICIAN

The Licensed Physician

The physician's office bears considerable responsibility. This demands that only qualified people are licensed and that those who license physicians (*Socialstyrelsen* in Sweden) interrogate the life and health of the patients. The right qualifications include not only knowledge but also the ability to transform knowledge into successful diagnostics and medication. When unsuitable persons are licensed, the reputation of all medical care falls into disrepute. Ultimately, the physician answers to those who license.

The same holds for the pastoral office. It can only be received from the Lord of the church, the same who had compassion on people without a shepherd (Matt 9:36) encouraged prayer for laborers into the harvest, and answered the same prayer by carefully appointing the twelve apostles (Matt 10:1–4). The Lord of the physicians cared for the people's eternal health. The trustworthiness of the church demanded the faithfulness of the apostles. The Lord himself saw to their training and capacity to transform knowledge into the diagnostics of the law and the medication of the gospel. The apostles likewise ensured, like physicians, that new men were suitable before receiving the office through prayer and the laying on of hands. When congregations began asking men among them to become their pastors, it was by churchly activity that they were licensed. Still, it is ultimately Christ to whom the pastor must give account.

The physician, given the office, acts on behalf of licensing authorities and the hospital and need not prove his worth to his patients. Wearing official clothes, the physician represents the hospital much more than himself. Associated with medical care and the hospital, he cannot act in his own name. He is there for the patients, not the patients for him. Neither is he in charge of the medicine; the hospital is, whereas he only prescribes medicine. Where the skills of physicians vary, the medicine itself has reliable healing power.

A pastor receives the office from the Lord through the church. He acts on behalf of Christ, the Physician, and represents the Church, to which he is called. He need not prove his worth, rather he is sent by the Lord to people whom the Lord sees as "harassed and helpless." This is the physician's strength in both good and bad times. His clerical clothes are meant to free him from his own person. Neither is it his job to invent the medicine. He stewards only what he has received (1 Cor 4:1). The medicine is the washing of regeneration (Holy Baptism) the life-giving word of God in preaching and counseling, "the medicine of immortality" (the Lord's Supper) and the good news of recovery in Holy Absolution. The medicines have in common the promise of Jesus to be present with his life and healing, with the forgiveness of sins. The power is in the medicine, neither in the office-bearer nor in his skills.

Physicians need broad knowledge. They must know the content, aim, effects, and proper (and improper) application of the medicine. Another important area of knowledge is anatomy and pathology. The physician needs to know about the normal and the sick condition of patients, have general knowledge of the human nature, see the relationship between physical and psychological health, understand how diseases arise and change, and recognize how the body responds to treatment. This is necessary in order for the physician to make a proper diagnosis and thus prescribe proper medication. Careless diagnostics leads to diminished effectiveness in treatment, even though the power of the medicine in itself is unchanged. What makes a physician really skillful is therefore the capacity to diagnose—knowing and understanding the patient and her problem—and to prescribe proper medication.

Pastors likewise need broad knowledge as spiritual physicians. They learn the content of the medicine from the Scriptures, its aim from the dogma, its effects from church history, and its application from pastoral theology. What the medicine is not and how it cannot be used is recognized from the history and experience of the church. The pastor's medicine is very potent: Christ himself in word and sacraments. Justification by faith alone is the article on which the whole hospital stands. But the pastor knows not only his potent medicine; his skill as a physician grows with experience, by which he develops insight into the often complex sicknesses of the patients. Pastors need training in the crucial art of diagnostics. Even pure gospel preaching will suffer from poor diagnosis, i.e. from not being rightly handled (2 Tim 2:15). Luther speaks of the one rightly understanding law and gospel as the true physician, "a Doctor of Holy Scripture."[3]

The office of physician as a metaphor for the pastoral office helps pastors understand their office, identity, and responsibility. What the pastor is lays the foundation for what he does. A true doctor handles medicine and patients rightly, which ultimately leads us to what pastor-physicians do.

3. WA 36,25,29 (from Plass, *What Luther Says*, 732).

Before moving into the task of preaching, which in the way of our analogy is the physician's diagnosis, prognosis, and prescription of medicine, we must first discuss the pastor-physician's identity as pastor.

Physician and Pastor

The patient's willingness to receive the instructions of a physician depends much on the physician's attitude. Although he relies on the physician, the patient also feels the difference between empathy and professional distance. The patient looks for the former, not only for the right answer. Compassion shown can be half the medication. To this end, the pastor as physician must be tempered by the pastor as shepherd.

The Danish homiletician Leif Andersen, in his *Texten og tiden*, describes the postmodern man as allergic to authorities.[4] A pastor, though sent with authority, needs to proclaim like a shepherd. Those hearing the sermon are vulnerable and may leave at any time. The trust they place in the pastor must be managed with deep respect. Empty talk, predictable answers, or poorly prepared sermons will only contribute to the tiredness of words common in our day. Even doctrinally correct sermons can lack something essential. The pastor as shepherd sees what Jesus, the Shepherd, saw: "He had compassion for them, because they were harassed and helpless, like sheep without a shepherd" (Matt 9:36). The Physician and Shepherd saw what the people could not see and did not just say doctrinally correct things or give simplistic solutions. And the Shepherd saw—what they also could not see—himself dying for them and leading them to the knowledge of the truth (1 Tim 2:4). The Samaritan woman at the well moved, during her meeting with the Overseer-Shepherd, from being hostile, afraid, and ashamed of the truth, to the liberation and restoration of the truth (John 4). The medication of the truth is the end, shepherding is the means. "The shepherd leads to waters where I find peace" reads Ps 23 translated from Swedish (*Svenska folkbibeln*).

An important duality for pastors is therefore to speak, on the one hand, for God to men, and, on the other hand, for men to God. This duality is found also in the physician's office. He is the expert, but the patient's description of the sickness, the vulnerability and the fear he shows, are also important. The physician listens carefully, empathizing with the patient, giving a voice to the feelings he/she has, and so helps the patient to be honest. The duality is biblical. In the psalms, God's own word gives voice to man's

---

4. Andersen, *Teksten og tiden*, 33ff. In the following, some of his thoughts are collected.

feelings, complaints, and inability to understand God. God's word itself gives honesty to man. The pastor, therefore, upholds a duality in his role as pastor. In line with the liturgical symbolism, he faces the congregation and speaks on behalf of Christ, but he is also, like a shepherd, one with the flock, facing God.[5] A physician with a shepherd's mind sees himself in the place of the patient, but he remains the physician! "To the weak I became weak, that I might win the weak" (1 Cor 9:22). Applying this duality to preaching, it becomes important that the reality of sin, unbelief, fear, and suffering is not described as though it were distant from the preacher's own reality. Still, he speaks the word of God that heals. The description is not a fictive world in which the pastor in reality has never been. He himself needs the life of daily repentance and the poverty of spirit in order to lead the flock to the same life. He needs to be himself the vulnerable patient at the Physician's feet.

The Good Shepherd laid down his life for the sheep. The pastor-physician sees his task in light of the Chief Physician's task. The task is not to be served, but to serve the many for whom Jesus died. For some pastors, it means holding back a desire to explain everything and aspiring toward a higher degree of empathy, listening and giving word to the sheep's description of reality. For others, it means holding back the habit of giving correct answers (which might have become clichés and simplifications) and problematizing what the sheep actually experience when hearing correct answers. For some, it means holding back the tendency to bind people to themselves, making them dependent and reliant on the pastor in an unhealthy manner, when in fact they need to grow in independence and responsibility. And some may have to hold back the desire to be right about everything, and instead express at times insecurity and vulnerability, in order to help the sheep themselves to express vulnerability and honesty in the face of things not so simple and self-evident. A pastor who in this way lays down something that is habitual to him, lays it down for the sheep, like the Good Shepherd.

THE PASTOR-PHYSICIAN AND PREACHING

In order to proceed to preaching, which belongs to the doing of the pastor, the significance of that pastor's being as physician for the sick in spirit has first been explored. Preaching can never be mere technique. Preaching is pastoring. It is what pastors do to the sick in spirit. The main elements of

---

5. Moses, for example, as God's appointed leader, accuses the people of disobeying the Lord and yet stands before the Lord on behalf of his people asking for mercy. Cf. Exod 32:32.

this to be explored are the diagnosis, prognosis, and prescription of medicine. Physicians usually see patients one at a time, while pastors in the task of preaching see a body of people, although composed of individuals who are sick in spirit. This tension is also part of the picture to be painted in the section.

Preaching as Diagnosis

Even before the physician's examination of a patient takes place, he is aware of the need to draw a potentially complex picture of the patient's problem. The more a physician can add to this picture, the better the conditions for examination. Such foreknowledge becomes for the pastor in the preaching situation the *only* source of information for diagnosis. He never comes to the conversation which for the physician leads to diagnosis; he simply diagnoses the whole congregation, which may even be full of strangers. It follows that broader and deeper foreknowledge of the sick in spirit leads to better diagnosis. But before preaching as diagnosis is addressed, the idea of diagnosis must be introduced.

Stomach pain can occur for various reasons: food poisoning, stress, cancer, appendicitis, psychosomatic reasons, etc. Painkillers may not be wrong, but they are not a medication taking the disease seriously. At times, the physician is unable to identify the problem and can do nothing but give such a prescription. But a physician properly looks for the cause of the symptoms in order to identify what needs to be cured. A key to success is understanding the patient. Through listening to the patient, the picture of the disease appears. The physician may try to help the patient remember things that may have caused, or worsened, the disease. He needs to know what to look for in order to ask the right questions. Comparisons to other patients and pictures of diseases help. Insights into how men react to sicknesses are significant. People describe things as better or worse than they are; they may distort or withhold information that would have facilitated the physician's diagnosis. The physician listens critically, as the patient may hold conscious or subconscious resistances. The resistance may be caused by many things. Some are hesitant to see a physician. All manner of fears may contribute to this hesitancy. Faith is needed, the belief that the physician can actually help and the medicine actually cure.

Also the pastor must draw a complex picture, but in the preaching situation, he is not even able to talk to the patient in order to fully address his or her situation. On the one hand, the people he sees from the pulpit have one thing in common: the sickness of sin. On the other hand, sin is a complex reality which relates similarly to the soul as the disease to the body. The pastor's preaching will depend on his understanding of man and the complexity of sin. Just like the physician who has listened carefully to his patients, the pastor has gained insight into the soul of man—not only in the confessional or through counseling, but also in his many daily interactions with people. He learns to understand how people prettify, worsen, or distort the truth about themselves, even though honesty would have facilitated, to their benefit, the pastor-physician's preaching. The conscious or subconscious resistance may be mistrust towards the church, the pastor, or the medicine—perhaps caused by bad experiences of the same. Some hope to recover on their own or make their own medicine of good feelings, which makes the injury worse. It is often the naked, and feared, truth that causes the resistance. People are rather happily ignorant of how bad things are, of how deeply wounded or afraid they actually are, than cognizant of the disease within. This is true despite the fact that medicine exists and can help. People need a certain degree of trust in the pastor-physician, which in itself is a work of the Spirit through the gospel, and they need hope that the medicine will work before they can even think about exposing themselves and dealing with the mess within. Understanding the fear of vulnerability and weakness, the consequences, the declaration of sickness, the shame associated with sensitive sins: all this belongs to the insights the pastor needs in preaching to the sick in spirit.[6]

Preaching as Prognosis

When diagnosis is given, the disease explored and described, and the physician ready to prescribe medicine, he gives a prognosis for the recovery. The medicine might have side effects or expose other diseases. Its effect may be slow. The medicine may initially be considered inadequate but must be taken regularly to have its full effect. The patient might react negatively to the medicine, especially if the recovery is slow, but he is not to take other medicines or doubt the effect. He may not give up prescribed medication and reach instead for painkillers. What the physician says in the prognosis is meant to give confidence during treatment and encourage patience with the medication.

    Likewise in preaching, the prognosis of God's word is given to encourage persistence in the use of the means of grace. The gospel is powerful medication. The pastor-physician must be heard and the medicine must

---

6. It may not be forgotten, that the pastor's insight into his own spiritual sickness is also an important source for drawing a picture of the state of his hearers.

be taken. The prognosis warns against replacing the medication with the search for emotional satisfaction or the temptation to escape. In the parable of the sower, Jesus gives a prognosis of the work of God's word in a person's life. The medicine's power is unchanging (the seed) but outward or inward circumstances might change or destroy the soil of the soul. Birds, thistles, and stony ground identify the three classical enemies of the soul: the devil, the world and the flesh. These are real enemies that will affect the treatment and recovery.

To biblically exemplify the idea of prognosis, the apostle Peter will be used here as an example patient. Peter was a spiritually sick person who met the chief Physician himself. In this case, the physician knew about sick Peter long before Peter knew him. "You did not choose me, but I choose you" (John 15:16). If Jesus would have given a prognosis based on the effects of himself in Peter's life (which is what the means of grace effect in the life of the Church) it may have looked something like this:[7]

The Call

Peter was called by Jesus while fishing.[8] He experienced a miraculous catch of fish, an extraordinary gift from God. He reacted with fear, "Depart from me, for I am a sinful man, O Lord" (Luke 5:8). At the same time, Peter did not want Jesus to leave, so when Jesus had assured Peter that he did not have to fear, he became willing to listen. The prognosis shows that the medication is initially perceived as strong, often causing the patient to consider refraining from medicating, or leading him to believe that the treatment has concluded. But the medication must continue. The purpose of the prognosis is to foresee the effects of the initial experience of divine intervention and help people persist with the medication.[9]

---

7. The pattern of the following prognosis is not randomly chosen but follows the pattern of *ordo salutis*. The point is not to highlight this particular homiletical tool, but to show a custom in the history of the church that follows the idea of prognosis. In this essay, *ordo salutis* follows the version of Giertz in *Life by Drowning*.

8. The catch of fish in Luke 4 is often considered the call of Peter, while it remains uncertain whether the occasion in John 1:35–51 is another and chronologically earlier calling event.

9. In *ordo salutis* this is the *call*. Events and experiences catching the spiritual attention of a man belong to the call, making him want to become a Christian. The work of the Spirit has begun in him. It has been warned that many want to stay in this phase of feelings, by looking for further spiritual experiences, and not look for the deepening gained by the use of God's word and prayer.

Enlightenment through the Law

The medicine continued to affect Peter and he grew in discipleship. After another miraculous experience, the feeding of the five thousand, the crowds followed Jesus, but when he intended to continue medication, most of the crowd left. As noted, the prognosis knows of the risk of giving in. The medication was not what the crowds had hoped for. But in Peter's case, loyalty to the medicine grew with use. When Jesus asks "Do you want to go away as well?" Simon Peter answered him, "Lord, to whom shall we go? You have the words of eternal life" (John 6:67–68). He had grown to understand that the medicine is too valuable to be abstained from. Perhaps he struggled with doubts and longed for "happiness pills." When most people withdrew and were critically scornful, it is likely that both rational and emotional questions arose. The significant hold in Peter's heart was, thanks to the medication, Jesus' "words of eternal life," not his miracles, his popularity, or the emotional experiences, but a steadfast word answering his thirst for eternal life. There was a conviction that the medicine works.[10] It also had its effect when Peter gave his great confession (Matt 16:13–20). But the malignant disease in his heart hit back just after the confession when Peter became the spokesman for Satan, as he expressed the simple "things of men." It is noteworthy that Peter does not at this point understand the necessity of the cross, wherefore the medicine needs to dig deeper.

The prognosis declares that complex side effects can appear. After three years of medication, Peter had grown into a proper Pharisee. When Jesus foresaw his denial, Peter replied, convinced that his loyalty and commitment had grown stronger than that of the other disciples, "Though they all fall away because of you, I will never fall away" (Matt 26:33). He deemed himself faithful not only in theory, but in practice, "I will lay down my life for you" (John 13:37). Peter's fear of rejection showed itself here, and not dissimilarly later, when he denied Jesus in the courtyard of the high priest.

The prognosis describes how, through this complex process, the medicine reaches the deeper layers. It is no longer searching individual sins or a general sinfulness, but the deepest fears and misguided longings. The pride that had grown over the previous three years was in reality a lack of self-awareness. There was nothing wrong with the medicine. "I have prayed

---

10. *The enlightenment through the law* follows the call. The disciple who now pays attention to the word of God and is serious about his faith tends to search the things a Christian ought to do and to be. It goes well, initially, since he had never before cared about Christian living. Loyalty toward the Lord is visible and measureable. In his own eyes, he is a decent disciple. Here, it is common that the deepest fear develops pious mechanisms of defense and that misguided longing searches for satisfaction in the Christian fellowship.

for you that your faith may not fail. And when you have turned again, strengthen your brothers" (Luke 22:32). The medicine struck Peter's poor self-awareness. This is a painful process, one which the pastor himself also undergoes. The pastor also fears conflict and is dependent on appreciation. Peter calls himself loyal because he fears rejection. The prognosis shows that self-awareness both exposes self-deception (pride) and causes despair. When Peter faced his actual identity, he wept bitterly. Self-insight is painful, but a necessary phase in the medication. Peter realized that his desire to lay down his life for Jesus was not matched by his power to do so. Fidelity of the heart was ultimately lacking. Fear and self-defense reigned in his heart. Ironically, the seed was thereby sown for Peter to realize a hard-gained insight: He must not lay down his life for Jesus, rather it is Jesus who had come to lay down his life for Peter, to be loyal where Peter failed, and to confess where Peter swore. Even if it seems like the medication (Jesus' presence in Peter's life) had suffered a setback, it was quite the opposite occurring as Peter found himself in the deep darkness of self-awareness.[11]

Enlightenment through the Gospel

Many would naturally quit medication at this point of apparent failure, not realizing that true self-insight is born through such pain. Following the prognosis, a patient can be aware that the medicine reaches deeper into that deep darkness. The risen Lord, through the angel, told the women, "Go, tell his disciples and Peter" (Mark 16:7). The betrayal of Peter was hidden in an empty tomb and he wanted Peter to hear what he now could say in all its fullness, on Easter evening: "Peace be with you" (John 20:21). Then Jesus showed them his wounds. "Upon him was the chastisement that brought us peace, and with his stripes we are healed" (Isa 53:5b).[12] Here is the ground

---

11. *Enlightenment through the law* continues in a second phase, when pride is replaced by despair. Both pride and despair are the work of the law. The disciple recognizes the things missing. He feels that he cannot be Christian even if he wants to. Fear exposed in pious circles of Christians makes this difficult, and misguided longing is perceived as self-centeredness.

12. The law prepares the way for *the enlightening by the gospel*. One's own, broken cisterns hold no water, and in facing the living waters of the gospel, the "yes" of faith is awakened. The fear that had reigned in the disciple is facing competition in the things given in Christ. Justification means that the disciple, who sought "everything" in himself and others without satisfaction, finds satisfaction. Christ had everything he longed for and searched for in others and in himself. The ground was already laid and another ground cannot be laid—the ground to the inner well flowing with eternal and living waters (John 7:37–39). The cornerstone is laid in Jesus' death, delivered in the well of baptism. The one satisfying his thirst in Christ knows to satisfy the thirst in him. "From

for justification, and Jesus' own word has the power to create faith. The medicine has such power, on which the prognosis encourages the doubting patient to ponder.

The medication of Peter had to continue. Also this is part of what the prognosis describes. There are potential setbacks and obstacles despite the progress of faith. A while later Jesus met Peter again at the Sea of Tiberias. Three times Jesus asked Peter if he loved him (John 21). In this dynamic dialogue, Jesus touches the remains of Peter's brokenness. Two times Jesus asked Peter if he loved him with perfect love (ἀγαπάω) but the humbled Peter replied quietly that he loved him with brotherly love (φιλέω). The third time, Jesus descended to the level claimed by Peter. Since it was the third time, Peter was reminded of the threefold denial and that his betrayal was not even worthy a brotherly love. Peter replied with grief, appealing to Jesus to see beyond who he is and what he does, to see that he actually loved Jesus. "You know everything." And Jesus, knowing everything, knew that Peter loved him—because Jesus, despite Peter's denial, did not reject him. He had accepted him through the forgiveness of sins. Acceptance and appreciation is founded in Christ, not oneself. Peter's greatest fear, Jesus' rejection, was unfounded. In Christ, he had no need to fear at all, not even death.[13] In this way, he was set free to actually love Jesus.

Preaching as prognosis does not come to an end with Peter's faith in Christ and his love towards the Lord. Both Peter's life and the experience of the Church teach that the medication reaches its goal when faith is given and yet that faith has to be nourished by persistent medication as the realities of unbelief, fear, and misguided longing remain present.

Sanctification

The prognosis alerts the patient of "the two natures," as exemplified by Peter. Ironically, Peter would eventually be right in his promise, "I will lay down

---

faith for faith, as it is written, 'The righteous shall live by faith'" (Rom 1:17).

13. Enlightening by the gospel means both justification and regeneration. In the tradition of *ordo salutis*, the use of the term is rather complex. Baptism is the washing of regeneration (John 3:5; Titus 3:5) but if we, according to the pattern of Peter, see the post-resurrection meeting between Jesus and Peter as an event in which the grace and life of Christ changes Peter and his inner fountain, then we need, following the pattern of *ordo salutis*, to consider that event as "regenerative." But perhaps it is wiser to use terms such as "awakening" or "recovery" for the one born again in Holy Baptism, which can be found also in the NT. "Awake, O sleeper, and arise from the dead, and Christ will shine on you" (Eph 5:14). An apparent weakness in the many variants of *ordo salutis* is that the place and effect of the sacraments (especially baptism) in a Christian's life are rather absent.

my life for you," when he had found satisfying acceptance in Christ, when perfect love had cast out enough fear and ultimately the fear of rejection through death. Peter ended his life as martyr (John 21:19). But even though the prognosis described such a medical breakthrough in Peter's life, it continued to emphasize the power of sin and its ability to have success. Such became true in Peter's life as well. The same fear of rejection that once drove Peter to promise "I will never leave you" and to swear on the courtyard "I do not know the man," drove him long after to withdraw from communion with gentile Christians, "fearing the circumcision party" (Gal 2:11). The prognosis describes realistically how Peter is both sick, well, and recovering. On the complex road of sanctification, on which justification by faith is the only realistic reality, Peter has put his trust in Jesus by allowing him to be his Physician, on Jesus' own initiative. And where Jesus is, "he who began a good work" will bring it to completion (Phil 1:6). He became "to us wisdom from God, righteousness and sanctification and redemption" (1 Cor 1:30).[14]

No matter how the journey will look for the individual, there is in Peter's story an example of a prognosis which can encourage the pastor-physician to consider preaching as prognosis. Preaching as prognosis proclaims the power of the medicine and the need for persistence in medication, especially in challenging phases of life, but also man's own responsibility and that the deceitful heart will take every opportunity to escape and give in to unbelief, fear, and misguided longing. The medication can be interrupted by the desire of the patient, which is constantly troubled by the enemies described by Jesus in the parable of the sower and the soil. The prognosis is realistic in the sense that it never guarantees success, but simply encourages persistence on the medicine, "He who has ears, let him hear" (Matt 13:9).

The pattern of prognosis described, often called *ordo salutis*, has the benefit of describing the reactions of the soul in the encounter with the medication of God's Spirit. In its best forms, *ordo salutis* prescribed proper medicine for people in different situations and soul conditions, and encouraged trust in the Physician, with the purpose of inspiring patience in

---

14. *Sanctification* follows justification and regeneration. The disciple knows his weakness, the fear and his misguided longing, and therefore searches for and finds his strength in the Lord. The fear and the misguided longing are now perceived as lies in his life, still holding a firm grip on heart and mind, but yet defeated by the truth. "Do not be conformed to this world, but be transformed by the renewal of your mind, that by testing you may discern what is the will of God, what is good and acceptable and perfect" (Rom 12:2). As the disciple continually replaces the lies of his fears and misguided longings with the truth of God's word (about what he is and has in Christ) like a plug in the hole, he begins lifting his eyes away from himself, laying down his mechanisms of defense, and trying to discern what God's will is (instead of the "spiritually motivated" protections from fear and the "piously defended" satisfactions of misguided longing).

the medication. A preacher thinking in terms of prognosis is aware of the fact that every Peter needs different directives in different stages, and takes the many stages into consideration in the preaching situation. The whole spectrum can be present in the church. Among both baptized and unbaptized, there are those who are indifferent, skeptical, hostile, impenitent, disappointed, longing for various things, and also those wanting to believe. Rightly understood and applied is *ordo salutis* not a static stair, but an investigation of man's spiritual condition which the preacher may find useful in his diagnosis and medication.

Preaching as Prescription of Medicine

In the analogy of this essay, the aim of all preaching is to medicate. Jesus made himself to be the medicine of the church, but he gives himself in different "packages" with specific purposes tailored to the diagnosis and the prognosis. Since the preacher-physician speaks on behalf of Christ, his presence in preaching is part of the medication. As a servant of the word, the physician leads the sick by the help of God's Spirit into the truth. Indeed, the sick person is to see that the diagnosis comes from God in his word, that the prognosis is meant to encourage persistence in hearing and studying this word, and that the truth found in the Holy Scriptures reveals the medicine. The word of Christ gives Christ (John 6:63; Luke 10:16) who is both Physician and medicine.

The sacraments as medicine will be highlighted in what follows. The point is not to include every aspect of the sacramental theology, but to give a few glimpses of how preaching can speak of the sacraments as medicine prescribed in response to the diagnosis of the sick.

The Medicine of Holy Baptism

The medicine of Holy Baptism is not a medication which loses its effect after the baptismal ritual itself. Peter's calling can be likened to baptism. It changed Peter's life and defined what followed. Jesus chose Peter, without Peter's request, leading Peter to ask Jesus to leave him. The story continues showing how Peter grows, not in this new identity but in his old one, until he reaches the top of the mountain of pride and falls. What seemed to be a failure for Jesus illustrates beautifully that the grace of his calling rests upon Peter (in a parallel sense, the grace of baptism). After years of "discipleship," Jesus must still tell Peter "when you have turned again. . ." (Luke 22:32). Peter's faithlessness does not undo Jesus' faithfulness.

Preaching baptism means to cast light on a medicine already given or with which one begins. The disease is not the true identity, but Christ, who has given himself to the baptized, clothed him with "the garment of salvation," and covered him "with the robe of righteousness" (Isa 61:10). He is promised full healing, justification on account of Christ's sacrificial death. The baptized is under the care of the Physician who covers his life with baptismal grace. Tirelessly, Jesus works with and prays for the baptized to strengthen his new identity.

The Medicine of Holy Absolution

The medicine of Holy Absolution follows after baptism. "The one who has bathed does not need to wash, except for his feet" (John 13:10). Forgiveness is continuously needed, not only because of actual sins, but also for the purpose of renewing the identity given in the washing of regeneration.

Preaching confession and absolution reminds the hearer of the reality taking place in the beginning of the divine service but also encourages personal visits to the physician, who has been given a special mandate by Christ to hear confessions. "If you forgive the sins of any, they are forgiven" (John 20:23a). Confession and absolution is also meant to be spiritual prophylaxis, regularly used, where the sick continuously describes the condition of the disease (which is hard, yet liberating) and hears the recovering statement of the physician. It also gives the physician the opportunity to specify the diagnosis which in the preaching can only be general, and to adjust the medication. Some may need encouragement to overcome inner resistance, others may need guidance on specific issues. An essential part of preaching as prescription of medicine is to "leave the office door open" for individual confession and absolution and counseling, so that uncertainty and spiritual pain are not left untreated.[15]

The Medicine of the Lord's Supper

One way to speak about preaching the Lord's Supper as medicine is to highlight Jesus' speaking of man as hungering and thirsting. Jesus spoke of man's deepest desire to which He himself was the answer. Jesus expresses man's deepest longing in terms of hunger and thirst and describes his body as true food and his blood as true drink. The deepest hunger is met by the

---

15. During the awakening, many sought out pastoral counseling after services, sermons, and private devotions in order to ask for precision in the diagnosis and the medication.

bread of Christ's body and the deepest thirst by the drink of Christ's blood. After receiving the body and blood, the most powerful healing dwells in the depths of the spiritually sick person. The apostle boldly states, "It is no longer I who live, but Christ who lives in me." (Gal 2:20). The tradition of calling this sacrament "the medicine of immortality" perhaps follows the words of the Physician, "Whoever feeds on my flesh and drinks my blood has eternal life . . ." (John 6:54).

Preaching the Lord's Supper emphasizes the spiritual reality of Christ in us. There is no greater medicine. Christ satisfies the deepest thirst, a thirst revealed through the preaching of diagnosis. Christ is the living waters and preaching directs the thirsty to the true fountain in the Lord's Supper. Faith knows that the Physician knows how powerful the medicine is, and needs no further explanation than the promise given by the Physician to be himself the medicine.[16]

The medicines have much in common, but speak differently to the sick in spirit. Where the diagnosis is accurate, the right medication follows naturally. The pastor-physician knows what needs to be given in order to ensure recovery, strengthen recovery, and picture recovery also as a final (heavenly) reality.

CONCLUSION

"Physician" has not often been used as an analogy for the pastoral office. As explored in this essay, it clarifies certain elements in the pastoral identity and brings light to the task of pastors, especially the task of preaching. Physicians, like pastors, are entrusted an office, answer to those giving the license, and represent the hospital in times of healing and of death. A pastor speaks on behalf of Christ, the Chief Physician, who entrusted the office and the medicine. The pastor meets the sick in spirit as a physician, searching carefully for the truth in order to give a proper diagnosis and right medication, but also leading the sick like a shepherd to that truth, no matter how painful it is. Preaching is like the physician's diagnosis, prognosis, and prescription of medicine. The hardest part is often the diagnosis, and having a broad and deep understanding of people becomes key. Prognosis follows. Here, preaching proclaims the power of the medicine and the need for persistence in medication. The sick need different directives in different stages. Finally, preaching as prescription serves to offer not only salvation and healing, but also the faith needed to "take" the medicine. "Faith comes

---

16. Because this medicine is so powerful, the apostle warns for the abuse of it (1 Cor 11:17–34), which highlights the need for the physician to give proper diagnosis.

from hearing, and hearing through the word of Christ" (Rom 10:17). The Chief Physician is Christ himself, speaking through the voice of the pastor-physician, and Christ gives himself in the medicines of Holy Baptism, Holy Absolution, and Holy Communion, administered by the pastor-physician. These medicines speak differently to the sick and match the different concerns picked up in the diagnosis.

The strength of an analogy is its ability to picture a reality which can otherwise be difficult to describe holistically. However, that strength is inevitably limited by the object of comparison. A physician, looking for the health of the body, can ultimately only try to slow the irresistible forces of death. The pastor, primarily looking for the health of the soul, which can be eternally secured, does actually mean the eternal health of the body as well, since Christ's atonement for sin led to victory over death and hell. Likewise, sin differs from the reality of sickness, since sin remains in the mortal body until the death. Justification becomes the source of recovery already now, and yet a reality not fully visible until the resurrection of the dead. In the meantime, the medicine works, sanctifying man. To the Physician, who for us became "wisdom from God, righteousness and sanctification and redemption" (1 Cor 1:30b) be all glory now and forever.

BIBLIOGRAPHY

Andersen, Leif. *Teksten og tiden: En midlertidig bog om forkyndelsen.* Vol. 1. Fredricia: Lohse, 2006.
Gerhard, Johann. *Theological Commonplaces: On the Ecclesiastical Ministry.* Part 1. Edited by Benjamin T. G. Mayes. Translated by Richard J. Dinda. St Louis: Concordia, 2011.
Giertz, Bo. *Life by Drowning: Enlightenment through Law and Gospel.* Translated by Eric R. Andrae. Cottenham, UK: Target, 2013.
Plass, Ewald M., ed. *What Luther Says. A Practical In-Home Anthology for the Active Christian.* St Louis: Concordia, 1959.

16

Present Preaching

—Daniel J. Schmidt

WHAT MAKES A GOOD SERMON?

I like good sermons; I like to listen to them, and I want my congregation to hear them from me. But it has always been difficult to say what makes a sermon good, and there are a number of reasons for this. First, hearers falling asleep during the sermon is something not precluded even by apostolic preaching.[1] Second, people have experienced good preaching throughout the history of the church. Thirdly, the great effect some sermons have does not always seem to be what the divine author intended.[2]

So what makes a good sermon? The vast amount of homiletical literature available makes answering this question a daunting challenge. Should we learn from the church father Chrysostom again?[3] From the predicant

---

1. Acts 20:9.
2. This also includes sermons by successful preachers who define the gospel in economic or political terms. Cf. O. C. Edwards's analysis of Martin Luther King Jr.'s influential preaching with the lack of distinction between the two kingdoms (*History*, 707).
3. Cf. Edwards's analysis of this church father's biblical interpretation, content and style, and his sermon on the statues (ibid., 77–87).

friars of the high Middle Ages,[4] from Luther,[5] the great orthodox Lutheran theologians,[6] or the impressive English preachers of the nineteenth century[7]? Should we study the annual volumes of the Yale Lectures on Preaching from 1871 to the present?[8] What about the New Hermeneutic?[9] And what about the New Homiletic that rose in its wake?[10]

These questions immediately open the door the related discipline of rhetoric. In North America, the sermon has always been considered a category of public speech. An orator who catches one's attention in the beginning and keeps it until the end is appreciated. Good speakers move others to stand up for their faith, their country, and the rights of the less privileged. Basic rhetorical abilities are indispensable for any project.

Rhetorical knowledge was sometimes gained first-hand from the great classical tradition of the western world.[11] But more often it was handed down in condensed form and included in standard chapters of the homiletical textbooks.[12] This shortcut led to a mechanical use of figures of speech and sermon structures in many pulpits.[13] In some traditions, such knowledge

---

4. Both the Franciscans and the Dominicans were at first orders of wandering beggars who preached publicly. Numerous homiletical aids were created for their ministry (ibid., 211). Cf. Edwards's treatment of this movement under the aspects of "Preaching as an Art," "Thematic Preaching and Scholasticism," "Preaching Aids," and "Popular Preaching" (ibid., 211–38).

5. There is much to be learned from Luther's *Invocavit* sermons (see Leroux, *Luther's Rhetoric*).

6. For example, the sermon postils by Valerius Herberger or Johann Gerhard.

7. The so-called "Three Bs" are among the most highly regarded preachers in America in the second half of the nineteenth century: Horace Bushnell, Henry Ward Beecher, and Phillips Brooks. Theodore Graebner, professor for philosophy and New Testament at Concordia Seminary in St. Louis in the early twentieth century, cites as homiletical examples the Presbyterian Lyman Beecher (1775–1863) and the Baptist Alexander McLaren (1826–1910) (*Manual*, 24, 42ff.).

8. A study of *The Heart of the Yale Lectures* reveals that the "new homiletic" in the second half of the twentieth century benefited from the "old" much more than any of its pioneers or adherents acknowledged.

9. See Pfitzner, "Problem," 347–48, 56.

10. The term "new homiletic" was widely adopted following the 1969 publication of Randolph's book *The Renewal of Preaching: A New Homiletic Based on the New Hermeneutic*, which gave a description as well as a vision of this movement.

11. E.g., Kennedy, *Rhetoric*.

12. Two of the classics in North American homiletics are Brooks's *Lectures on Preaching* and Broadus's *On the Preparation and Delivery of Sermons*. It seems that the role rhetoric played in North American homiletics in the twentieth century was both a contributing factor and an effect of the periodic revisions and reprints of these two works over a period of a hundred years.

13. There is widespread criticism within the "new homiletic" of a standard,

was mainly acquired from listening to experienced speakers. This is true especially in the African American way of preaching with its tradition of the chanted sermon, the pattern of call and response, the skilled employment of emotions, and the art of storytelling.[14] Persuasion of the hearer is a rhetorical end essential where a social gospel is preached.[15] The place of rhetoric in homiletical textbooks is undisputed in North America.[16] It is presupposed in a cultural and denominational setting where the notion is widely held that the sermon's primary goal is to move people to action.

Cultural aspects also affect our perception of a sermon. A certain sense of humor employed intentionally by a preacher presupposes the same sense of humor in his hearers. The best parts of a sermon preached in English by a bilingual Hispanic preacher to a similar audience may be lost on a monolingual English hearer. And the fine irony of some of the divine words of scripture cannot be used to season the preaching in many African languages to which irony is unknown.

What, then, makes a good sermon? No matter how often a preacher hears the sentence "That was a good sermon!" at the exit of the sanctuary, one particular pastor's response is always appropriate, "That remains to be seen." Where the living voice of the gospel resounds from the pulpit, a spiritual battle is being fought.[17] Our sinful nature, though not averse to entertainment, habitually blocks out any notion that the spiritual disease we suffer from may be congenital and terminal, that the human heart is rotten to the core, and that there is nothing but for the old nature to die with Christ and a new nature to rise with him. It loathes the idea that we need to be treated continuously with the word of God.[18]

We can therefore rely neither on market research nor on audience response testing. We rather strive for sermons which speak God's word to his people according to its divine purpose. The responsibility is spiritual and the question theological. This does not imply an easy answer, nor does

---

three-point sermon structure, which, according to Baxter, was prominent over several generations (*Lectures*, 226).

14. See Edwards, *History*, 431, 539, 542, 723, etc.

15. Ibid., 648-49.

16. Cf. Wardlaw, "Homiletics," 245-46.

17. Chrysostom's sermon on the statues and Luther's *Invocavit* sermons are vivid examples of this general character of the sermon. This is however just as important in baptism and funeral sermons, and not insignificant in other cases (see above, n3 and n5).

18. The imagery of Christ the physician is an important aspect of the theology of Wilhelm Loehe (see Raschzok, "Das geistliche Amt," 85, 89). It is found also in Walther's "Pastoraltheologie" (105), and in the hymns of the church (see TLH 322:3).

it relieve any preacher of the responsibility to hone his exegetical and rhetorical skills, continue learning from his fellow preachers,[19] and study the particular culture of his hearers. But it will hopefully uncover some aspects of preaching which will be helpful to both preacher and hearer.

Dealing with this question will therefore be based on what the Scriptures and the Lutheran confessions teach about the word of God.[20] It will be drawn from the experience of the Lutheran church with the living proclamation of the gospel throughout many centuries, cultures, and languages. It will show that Lutheran preaching is "present preaching." And it will reveal that this statement has two sides, referring both to the "presence" in preaching and to preaching in the "present tense."

PRESENCE IN THE SERMON

Presence in preaching means that God is present in his word. The Holy Scriptures are to be regarded as God's own speaking, recorded in writing: Through the written word he continues to speak to all subsequent generations including our own.[21] The preacher's responsibility is to present to his hearers what the author of those words intends, be it the prophet or apostle, or ultimately the Triune God who used their voices long ago to speak to us today. This calls for considerable care on the part of the preacher lest he put into the mouths of the sacred authors his own ideas or those of his day. It is also an argument for a clear distinction between scriptural facts and details filled in in an effort to present the text in a lively, three-dimensional context. Finally, it is a reminder to the preacher that it is not his job to parade his own spiritual insights before an audience. The Lutheran church is right in insisting on thorough exegetical training of her pastors. And it places on all Christians the responsibility of judging what they hear on the basis of God's word.

Both preacher and hearer stand in the sermon in God's holy, eternal presence. This should motivate the pastor toward good preparation. The notion that the Holy Spirit will give an unprepared preacher the right words as he steps into the pulpit emanates from a very different spirit. The notion of beginning sermon preparation early in the week and ruminating on the

---

19. Cf Lischer, *Preachers*.

20. See AC V, VII; SA III,iv; FC V, VI, etc. This includes the doctrine of law and gospel.

21. See e.g., Pss 22–31.

nascent sermon over several days may be attributed to a certain work ethic,[22] but it is also the practical-theological consequence of this spiritual truth.

A preacher who conveys the conviction of God's presence in the sermon will also incite the hearers' prayer that they remain attentive. Humanly speaking, this is a greater challenge today than in earlier ages. The hearer needs to understand the spiritual nature of the word of God and its proclamation. Such spiritual insight has to come from the sermon itself and be supported by all parts of Christian education in the congregation.

This leads to the second important aspect of presence in the sermon. The gospel is ever contemporary in the sense that its hearers are present in it throughout the ages.[23] When they hear the living voice of the Lord uncovering sin and portraying Christ as the Savior, when grace is announced to those who repent, it includes all human beings of all times.[24] We can give nothing to atone for our sin, and the offering of sacrificial lambs in the temple has been impossible since the destruction of Jerusalem in 70 AD. How important then for us to be told by the apostle of the Lord that "Christ our Passover lamb" was "sacrificed for us."[25] This application of the first person plural to the present hearers is no anachronism but the theological application of God's historic act of salvation "once and for all," and it goes hand in hand with the proper application of law and gospel: It makes it impossible for the hearer at any time to deflect the blows of God's law with the argument that it was really meant for someone else far away and long ago. Moreover, it is a great comfort to a sinner with a broken heart not to be told to feel good about himself but to have a pastor who pronounces such a person just and righteous here and now.

This means that any sermon is preached for those who are present when it is preached.[26] It knows that there are faith goals as well as love (or life) goals. A sermon downloaded from the internet, composed by somebody who has never been in the same room with the hearers, is like food off the supermarket shelf: The hearers do not starve, but they rarely get their proper diet. A preacher may gain an occasional insight from it, but he must not forget that he is dealing with patients coming to Christ as their physician. They need to get "what the doctor ordered." They need be able to grasp what they hear, to benefit from such teaching, to apply it for their own

22. See, e.g., Craddock, *Preaching*, 101.
23. See Acts 2:39, etc.
24. Thus the warning Rev 22:18–19.
25. 1 Cor 5:7.
26. In his contribution to *The Preacher's Workshop Series*, Deffner (*Real Word*, 6ff.) cites five basic categories of human needs according to Abraham H. Maslow.

reproof and correction, and for training in righteousness, that as people of God they may be complete, equipped for every good work.[27]

A good preacher knows his people in their homes. Putting this to spiritual use gives him a considerable advantage over any guest preacher—though a sound grounding in biblical anthropology as well as rhetorical experience sensing the reactions of the audience do narrow the gap when a pastor is preaching from a different pulpit.[28] In addition, this prevents him from dividing believers into "real Christians" and others, and bars any notion on the part of the hearers that the law is meant only for those who "need" it.

Experience tells us that "a house going preacher has a church going congregation." A preacher who lives with his congregation, who listens to his members and prays for them during the week, will not be afraid to engage their sins and needs in the pulpit. He will not shoot shotgun-style at all possible sins, nor will he rage about the "evil world." He talks about sins his hearers are committing or are likely to commit.[29] He is concerned not so much with what they want to hear but with what they need to hear from God in a particular place and time. This is what C. F. W. Walther called "contemporary" preaching in the true sense.[30]

One of the most influential homiletics teachers of the Missouri Synod in the twentieth century, Gerhard Aho, taught his students to start with a thorough exegesis of a particular word of Scripture. Then, remembering that being human means to suffer from a most serious disease called original sin, they should look for its concrete manifestation in the passage which is symptomatic of the underlying spiritual problem or malady.[31] An example may be the exodus of the Israelites from Egypt. They began to murmur against God as they saw the predicament they were in, but not God. This is our problem, too, time and again. We do not murmur against Moses, and we may not complain loudly against God, but we may grumble with our hands

27. 2 Tim 3:16–17.

28. In his analysis of Luther's *Invocavit* sermons, Leroux demonstrates how the hearers with their expectations, objections, and actions are included in Luther's sermon by the use of particular rhetorical means (speaking in character, use of the first person plural etc., see Leroux, *Rhetoric*, 37, 61, 65).

29. This point was emphasized by Aho in his Sermon Theory classes. Cf. Baxter, *Lectures*, 72.

30. Walther, *Pastoraltheologie*, 105–6. Cf. Leroux, *Rhetoric*, "Presence is that element of proof that is created when a speaker makes a focused-upon subject more impressive, significant, and real to the audience" (30; emphasis original). See also the treatment of rhetorical tactics under the heading "Presence" (ibid., 32–37).

31. "Our task in preaching is to analyze the surface symptoms in terms of the more basic malady, sin" (Aho, *Sermon Theory I.*,12).

by praying less regularly, or with our feet by staying away from church. Hoping to feel God more directly and looking for something tangible, we may seek other kinds of worship and turn to more emotional ways of preaching.

The goal of preaching is defined by what God's word wants to accomplish. Preaching to a concrete group of people also means to preach with a clear goal. In the approach of Caemmerer and Aho, this goal is closely connected to the symptom or spiritual problem revealed in a Bible passage and manifest in the congregation.[32] It is unlikely that Moses preached a long sermon to the Israelites in Exod 14. But its goal has been recorded in Scripture, "Fear not, stand firm, and see the salvation of the Lord which he will work for you today." (14:13) Whenever this passage of Scripture is preached in the twenty-first century, it is with the same divine goal: That God's people stand firm in the faith and see what the Lord is doing for their salvation. Toward this goal, God continues to speak to us today.

However, if a hearer only had to try hard enough to accomplish such goals, to become stronger in faith and more faithful in action, then the preacher's rhetorical skills and the inspiration he provides with his words and his personal example would be paramount in preaching.[33] The incarnation of the son of God would be relegated to a distant past and original sin would no longer affect human beings as much as it used to.[34] The doctrine of law and gospel would be history, and the Bible would serve only as a source of inspiration or a textbook on how to make the most of one's life.[35]

If not for the presence of the Triune God in his word, this would be our situation as we study the sermon text for the following Sunday and as we open our Bible in the pulpit and turn to the congregation. But a preacher always starts his preparation as a listener, and the voice he hears is not the echo of his own but that of his maker and his judge, his redeemer and his comforter. Preacher and hearer have a place in Christ's work of salvation, but they do not contribute to it. There can be only one kind of work righteousness in Christian preaching: the righteousness of Christ who has done everything the law requires, and who has done it for us. Where systematic

---

32. Aho, *Sermon Theory I*, 12. On the triad of goal, malady and means cf. the division of systematic theology according to *finis* (goal) *media* (means) and *subiectum* (the sinful subject, i.e., humanity) in Lutheran Orthodoxy (Preus, *Theology*, 156).

33. Brooks defines preaching as "the bringing of truth through personality" (Wilson, *Preaching*, 78). Robinson speaks of the weight of the preacher's character (Baxter, *Lectures*, 40); Forsyth of the "sacramental quality of his personality for his message" (ibid., 24). Similarly John A. Broadus, Jesse Burton Weatherspoon, John Killinger, R. E. O. White, et al.

34. See, e.g., Farmer, *Servant*, 265.

35. Cf. Randolph, *Renewal*, 98.

theology speaks of the imputation of this righteousness to the individual believer, homiletical theory speaks of its application. The gospel means that God gives us what he demands from us.[36] With regard to the sermon, this means that the divine goal revealed to us in a passage of Scripture is accomplished by its divine author alone.

Thus a third aspect moves into focus. Following his elder colleague Caemmerer, who taught in St. Louis, Aho trained his students to look for the means in addition to the malady and the goal.[37] In Exod 14, this is the Lord acting to direct the course of nature in order to safeguard his people. The dead end opens up to reveal a passage to safety.

Understanding the nature of the word of God and of its proclamation in the sermon is an act of faith brought about by the Holy Spirit through the word. It relieves the preacher of undue pressure under the many expectations of his hearers as he starts to prepare his sermon. Looking for the goal, the problem, and the means in his passage helps him to see the presence of the congregation in God's word and the presence of God's word in the congregation.

The rise of the so called "new homiletic" in the 1960s and 1970s was due to a combination of factors. The three-point sermon had come to be regarded as a standard format that had lost its edge.[38] The development of mass media went hand in hand with a fresh interest in rhetoric and audience response.[39] New models of communication spurred an interest in new ways of preaching.[40] The new hermeneutic coined the phrase of the "word event" whose application to the sermon seemed only natural.[41] The revolutionary atmosphere of the 1960s questioned all kinds of authority and provided an argument for various experiments with "dialogue preaching" in the following decades.[42] Many of these were short lived (and rightly so)[43] but they brought back to mind a classical rhetorical truth: The hearer plays a decisive role in any kind of oral communication.[44]

36. Cf. Walther, *Law and Gospel*.
37. Aho, Sermon *Theory I*, 14–15.
38. Edwards, *History*, 800.
39. See Levering, "Development," throughout; Blackwood, *Preparation*, 30.
40. A watershed for a renewed interest in the relationship between form and content in preaching is the publication of *Design for Preaching* by Henry Grady Davis in 1958. See also Craddock, *Authority*, 43; and White, *Guide*, 87.
41. Wilson, *Practice*, 63.
42. See Lischer, *Theology*, 3–4. Cf. the programmatic title of Eggold's book "Preaching is Dialogue."
43. Cf. Lowry, *Plot*, xvii.
44. Otto, *Die Kunst*, 73, 76.

Good preachers have always been convinced of this. This is no accident. It is the consequence of the theology of the word: God is present in his word, and it addresses the contemporary hearer. Preaching does not just convey cognitive information; it works decisive changes in those who hear it. Or, as the orthodox Lutheran theologian Salomon Glassius put it: God communicates himself.[45] This conviction is therefore deeply imbedded in biblical theology. It is at the basis of every good sermon preached throughout the history of the church. It is the essence of apostolic preaching and based on an apostolate which mandates the messenger to speak in the name of Christ, with Christ binding himself to such speech and acting through him.[46] It is the mark of an understanding of the preacher's office as an integral part of the ordained ministry. It may not prevent people from falling asleep under the pulpit, but it has the power to wake up those who are dead asleep in their sins and to raise them to new life.[47]

PRESENT TENSE PREACHING

The reformers spoke of the *viva vox evangelii*: the living voice of the gospel.[48] They were willing to lay down their lives for it because they were convinced that this word saves those who trust it from sin and death. They knew they were accountable for their teaching and preaching before the living God. God is present in his word: What a responsibility and what a privilege for those to whom it has been entrusted in this world, Christians in and under the pulpit alike. God comes to us through the proclamation of the gospel. He unites himself with us through his body and blood as the elements of the sacrament are consecrated through the divine word and received in faith through the same word.[49] We find ourselves included in the word as it continues to be preached, and the word dwells in us. It reveals our sin, but more than that: it reveals to us the word incarnate, Christ our salvation.

Human condition remains the same before God throughout the ages, and the Scriptures are to be preached at all times. With C. F. W. Walther we affirm that such preaching is meant to be ever contemporary. The church is not like a person grown old who spends his time reminiscing about the past. We do not speak in an ancient language which few can understand.

---

45. Glassius. *Arbor vitae*, 136. I am indebted to Armin Wenz for this contribution.

46. See Rengstorf's exposition on the Jewish apostolate (TDNT 1:407–47, The Later Jewish Institution of the 20–414. שָׁלִיחַ).

47. Eph 5:14; Rev 2 and 3.

48 WA 12, 259. Cf. Eggold, *Dialogue*, 19–20, 26.

49. FC VII:6–9, etc.

We preach what God has done in the past because it applies to us today. He has done it for us; he is God-With-Us. In this sense, Christian preaching is, in its essence, preaching in the present tense. We preach to those who are present to hear us.

Of course, our daily life differs considerably from that of Abraham, Rachel, Simon the Tanner, or Lydia, the seller of purple goods.[50] Outwardly, the local and global culture in the beginning of the third millennium AD has little in common with theirs. We live on different sides of the Enlightenment and of the technical, scientific, and digital revolutions of the last three centuries.[51] Ours is meant to be an age of reason, not of superstition. Man has come a long way since he started to believe in himself and his abilities. And many believe that it is impossible to bridge this great divide.

Following this track, there is a notion that the hearers of the sermon should not be burdened with anything that has no plausible explanation. Preaching the miracles as historical events might throw a hearer into confusion by confronting him with a worldview other than his own. A general way to avoid such tension is to use a scripture passage as a cache of pleasant thoughts. The preacher pulls out as many as time allows, the listeners nod in appreciation, and both go home feeling better about themselves and the world.[52]

Another approach is to draw a lesson from the ancient text. With little regard for the original situation of an event or a word recorded in the Scriptures and apart from the real life characters that were part of it, a timeless truth is distilled from a Bible text. Sermons based on individual verses are especially prone to this tendency.[53]

A similar method is the symbolic interpretation of biblical events. The boat of the disciples tossed about by the storm and the waves becomes a metaphor for the contingencies of human life. The prison Paul finds himself in is said to represent our fears and worries. Leprosy comes to stand for our sinful nature. This kind of interpretation carries some degree of biblical justification. The apostles do interpret certain Old Testament events allegorically.[54] Disease and everything else that threatens our life in this world

---

50. Acts 9:43; 16:14.

51. According to Jensen, the digital revolution brought about the end of the "Gutenberg Age" and the beginning of a new age (*Thinking*, 56 and throughout). Cf. Randolph, *Preaching*, 8, 54.

52. Cf. Buttrick's critique of the so-called textual sermon in *Homiletic*, 18.

53. Cf. Jones, *Principles*, 95ff.; Craddock, *Authority*, 145ff. Reu explicitly alerts his readers to this dangerous tendency (*Homiletics*, 315ff.).

54. Rom 5:14; 1 Cor 10:4; Gal 4:24–25, etc.

is a consequence of man's fall into sin.[55] The creator who saves from physical harm and the Savior who has broken the power of sin and death are one and the same. However, unless God's concrete actions in the course of this world are preached as such, this message risks conveying the impression that he performs symbolic acts rather than personally (and in the flesh!) confronting the consequences of the disobedience of mankind.[56]

These approaches have in common that they deal with the historical gap between our situation and that reflected in the biblical passages basically by annulling it. The same applies to an understanding of the sermon as an inspirational talk based on ancient, divine words. The writers of the biblical books were inspired, and the preacher uses their words to inspire the congregation. But what good is inspiration to anyone unless he is renewed through justification and sanctified continuously by the Holy Spirit who imputes to him the saving work of Christ?[57]

By contrast, the hearers can be invited to go back in time with the preacher. He opens the hatch to a rhetorical time machine by asking them to imagine that they are spies secretly scoping out Jericho with Joshua.[58] He tells them to sit down among the children of Israel by the river of Babylon and to cry with them at the memory of the destruction of the temple in Jerusalem and the loss of the divine worship ordained by the true God.[59] This method does not restrict preaching to the cognitive realm. It engages the hearer emotionally. Listening becomes an experience.[60] This can be quite effective. But it remains essentially a trick. The hearers are no Jewish spies. Most likely, they have no training for such a job. And they would not last long in ancient Jericho with their accent and their Sunday suits and ties. Neither are they Jews in exile, far from their home and unable to worship God according to his divine ordinances. They are after all sitting in the middle of a Christian worship service in a sanctuary built around an altar and a baptismal font. This method may be employed occasionally to highlight individual points, but its usefulness for preaching biblical texts is limited.

The great divide needs to be bridged. But the historical situation on either side must be respected. In his study, the pastor conducts a thorough exegesis of the text. He sincerely meditates on the spiritual situation of his

55. Rom 7:24, 8:22; 1 Cor 15:22.

56. Central in this regard is the resurrection of Christ; see 1 Cor 15:13–14.

57. See, e.g., AP IV:132–35.

58. Num 13. Cf. Craddock's critical view of this method in his preface to Lowry, *Plot*, xvi–xvii. See also Lowry, *Authority*, 97.

59. Ps 137.

60. This is a major reason for the new homiletic's emphasis on narrative preaching and "story." Cf. Jensen's books *Telling the Story* and *Thinking in Story*.

congregation. And he brings both together in his sermon. Such an in-depth study of the text as well as of the hearers in their respective situations is a mark of responsible preaching. The past as well as the present belong to the history of God with his people, both are to be respected in their own right. If God works in history to save this world, then our approach to the written documents of these acts cannot be ahistorical.

One possible way of bringing both sides together in the sermon is to swing back and forth between the biblical setting and the setting of the present-day hearers. The preacher should take care, however, to avoid the effect of a tennis game on spectators in the front seats: trying to keep an eye on the ball as it flies back and forth over the net is tiring. Prolonged, this procedure drains the hearers' concentration.

These caveats do not bar such methods entirely from the pulpit. Preaching and teaching from the inspired words of God (whether oral or written) is something that occurs even within the holy scriptures. The later writers are faced with the same difference between Then and Now. The psalms confess the mighty deeds of the Lord in the history of his people and proclaim them anew.[61] Jesus cites the law and the prophets.[62] Paul refers to the faith of Abraham, which was counted to him as righteousness and explains, "It will be counted to us who believe in him who raised from the dead Jesus our Lord"[63] Thus a word of God from the time of the old covenant becomes significant for the Christians to whom he writes. In a similar way, the letter to the Hebrews summarizes the history of God with his people before the coming of Christ.[64]

This does not mean that the contrast between different times and situations is ignored. The opening sentence of the same letter summarizes the difference as well as the continuity of God's speaking then and now, "Long ago, at many times and in many ways, God spoke to our fathers by the prophets, but in these last days he has spoken to us by his Son."[65] And what does the Son say? "You have heard that it was said—but I say to you."[66] This contrast marks the beginning of a new situation. The law remains to be fulfilled to the last iota. But the Son of God has now come to do it.[67] The Canaanite woman is told that he is sent only to the sheep of the house of Israel.

61. Pss 66; 78 (esp. vv. 3–4).
62. Matt 5:17, etc.
63. Rom 4:24.
64. Heb 11:1—12:1.
65. Heb 1:1–2.
66. Matt 5:43.
67. Matt 5:17–18.

But the insistence of her faith receives a sign that the dividing wall is about to fall.[68] The "nations" were excluded from God's people, but Christ brings both together as one new man.[69] The ceremonial laws of the old covenant are no longer binding on those who are part of the new creation.[70]

But in spite of this development in the history of salvation, man's spiritual situation remains the same: he is born as a sinner and can do nothing to save himself from sin's consequences. Man's belief in himself was not an original idea of the Enlightenment.[71] The fast growing list of mankind's achievements does not include a remedy for the spiritual disease called original sin. Attempts to explain the world apart from the one true God were made long before. The real gap is not between the characters that make up the cast of past biblical events on the one side and modern people on the other. The gap is between the holy God and sinful man. This is why Gerhard Aho taught seminarians and ministers to look for this spiritual malady in every sermon passage. Its surface symptoms differ from time to time and from one culture to the other, but its effect on human beings remains the same. Therefore sin still needs to be diagnosed today for what it is. The law needs to be preached.

But there is something even more important that stays the same: God is faithful. His gracious intention to save man from this condition remains unchanged throughout history. With him, promise and fulfillment are one; he does what he says. Otherwise it would have been pointless to write down the spoken word or for the written word to be copied and handed down from one generation to the next over the last three millennia. Anyone who continued to believe and preach words spoken to those who lived before him would have been deceiving himself.[72] But generations of Christians trusted that God is present in his word and that it was meant for them as well.

In this sense, biblical preaching is present tense preaching. What God has done and said in the past is applied to sinners and their lives at the present time. The tradition of Christian preaching continues not as long as preacher and hearer find relevance in it for their lives, but until the end of the world, because today's hearer and preacher are as relevant to God

---

68. Matt 15:24–28.
69. Eph 2:15–16.
70. Col 1:16–19.
71. Cf. Gen 11 (Tower of Babel) and the perseverance of semi-Pelagianism in the history of the church.
72. E.g., in Ps 44.

as those of the past.[73] In the light of the word of God, the situation of the first hearers of a biblical passage becomes transparent for the lives of their present counterparts because it is the same God dealing with the same human nature.[74] This does not mean that both blend into one, indistinct image. Moses did not think of cyberbullying when he received the eighth commandment. A Christian man has no command to marry his brother's childless widow. But the spiritual problems encountered in a congregation today are a sounding board for God's diagnosis and treatment as witnessed by the Holy Scriptures. Thus the sermon will address the spiritual problem and God's goal in overcoming it at both ends of the timeline. The preacher acknowledges the distance in time while focusing on the spiritual separation of the sinner from the holy God. He declares guilty all sinners present in the worship service including himself, and announces grace to those who repent and believe. He forgives and retains sin. God's eternal judgment is pronounced here and now. That is present tense preaching.

This corresponds to the nature of the word of God. There is an existential urgency here that is unequaled by any words "produced by the will of man."[75] We do not extract a few extra ounces of relevancy from ancient texts that have had their time. In the apostolic ministry, the minister is bound without exception to the will of the one who commissioned him. He speaks not in his own authority as a pious Christian (or a gifted speaker) but in the authority of the Triune God who binds himself to this ministry. God judges sin today as he did in the past. The same measure will apply on the Day of Judgment. His word does not return to him empty. It hardens the heart of those who reject it; it moves to repentance those who receive it. No sin removed today by his word of grace will be brought up again on the last day. That is preaching God's word from the past in the present tense for the future—for a sinner to have an eternal future with God.

Present tense preaching then is closely linked to the forensic aspect of the word of God and to its objective character.[76] Different people hear the same word differently according to their experiences and their present situation. They associate different things with particular verbal and non-verbal

---

73. Cf. Pfitzner, "Can I make my analysis of human existence the final yardstick for the relevance of the Word of God?" ("Problem," 355).

74. In his third *Invocavit* sermon in 1521, Luther, in dealing with the conflict in Wittenberg, cites the example of Paul's action in Athens in Acts 17. Luther is "obviously contemporizing the Athenian context" and "has imported Paul to 16th century Wittenberg and, implicitly, himself back to first-century Athens!" (Leroux, *Rhetoric*, 82).

75. 2 Pet 1:20-21.

76. Rom 1:16; 2; 3.

signs.[77] Every preacher can tell stories of people who heard things he never said. But this does not mean that the word spoken from the pulpit has no meaning in itself. It only confirms that certain models for the process of communication are insufficient.[78] The acoustic form is not a neutral container into which the preacher packs what he wants and sends it to the hearer who in turn unpacks it. This is why a preacher needs not only to talk to the parishioners, but also to listen to them. House calls are part of the sermon preparation. The same is true of many chance conversations that started with a casual remark in the church hall or in the supermarket checkout line. The human receptor is part of the communication process. But scriptural doctrine does not distinguish between the human word spoken in the sermon and the word of God as if it were basically impossible for one to become the other.[79] That the divine word means nothing to a sinner who rejects it is also part of its effect. Taking into account human nature there are at least two reasons why listeners hear things that were never said. Adapting Paul's statement that for now we see God's reality "as in a mirror dimly" (1 Cor 13:12) we may say that we hear the proclamation of his word imperfectly because of the many noises around us and within our heart. On the other hand, hearers sometimes hear things they need to hear even though the preacher did not intend to say them: God who has given his church the ministry of preaching also gives his Holy Spirit who accomplishes in the hearer's heart what he wants despite the limitations and imperfections of the preacher.[80]

Jesus Christ continues to commission messengers by calling men into the ministry. He is the living word of God, the Word made flesh. Through this word, the whole world has been made and is sustained until the last day.[81] In a present tense sentence that goes against all grammatical rules, in

77. Attempts have been made to take this notion of postmodernism to the extreme. An "open work" of art is said to have no meaning apart from that which comes about in the subjective reaction of the receptor. But modern advertising, for instance, would not work unless there was sufficient agreement on the meaning of words and symbols among the targeted customers. In 2011, the German philosopher Markus Gabriel and his Italian colleague Maurizio Ferraris declared the end of postmodernism and the beginning of a new realism.

78. E.g., the model that mirrored the functioning of telephone and radio technologies (sender—transmitter—receiver).

79. Cf. Barth's theology of the word of God as expressed in his *Kirchliche Dogmatik*, I/1:52, 96, etc.

80. Cf. the discussion in the ancient church on the validity (and hence efficacy) of sacraments performed by apostate priests.

81. John 1:3; 2 Pet 3:7.

Greek as well as in English, he says, "Before Abraham was, I am."[82] He is the eternal "I Am," the word that will remain forever. When we receive it, we receive him and he dwells in us with everything his word promises: forgiveness, justification, and eternal life. Declared righteous in the present, we no longer live in fear of the final judgment in the future.

This is an existential truth. It turns everything around. It is much more exciting than to pretend that we are gathering manna in the desert in the early morning with the Israelites, or bringing down solid walls with the sound of our church instruments. This is about our very existence. We are headed for eternal death. But Christ is here to turn our life around.

A preacher who makes it his habit to base his sermon preparation on the original text and a careful study of the relationship of the individual words as well as the thought process will make exciting discoveries in his preaching ministry. He will find that many passages show a clearly dramatic format.[83] An example is the prisoners' transport from Palestine to Rome of which Paul is part (Acts 27:13-44). Their ship hits a storm in the Mediterranean Sea and runs aground a sandbank off the island of Malta. The sailors expect the loss of many lives. Against all odds all 276 people on board make it safely to the island. This account lends itself to be retold in much detail. It also offers vivid images for a metaphorical application by reminding the hearers how quickly a life can be shipwrecked and how God comes to the rescue. But there is a spiritual depth to it that manifests itself in a dramatic reversal of roles. While the Roman soldiers are about to kill their prisoners to prevent their escape, one of these saves everybody's life. Paul is a prisoner of the emperor of Rome, but he has been briefed by the one who is above all earthly armies, all political powers, and all forces of nature.[84] The soldiers take instructions from the prisoner. Not a single life is lost. What a demonstration of the sovereignty of the Lord for Paul and those around him. What a powerful sermon on the power of the word of God which saves his apostle so that with him it may reach the capital of the western world. Here the reader begins to sense that Paul has a freedom that is greater than that

---

82. John 8:58.

83. The dramatic "loop" consisting basically of conflict, aggravation, and resolution is central to Eugene L. Lowry's contribution to the new homiletic. It was described by the German dramatist Gustav Freytag in 1863 (*Die Technik*) and introduced into the homiletical discussion in the 1940s and 50s by Blackwood (*Preparation*, 162, cf. 268) and Davis (*Design*, 182; see also 163, 174ff.). I am indebted to David R. Schmitt, St. Louis, for pointing out the connection with Freytag.

84. Acts 27:21-44. On the reversal of the earthly hierarchy cf. Mary's words in the *Magnificat*, Luke 1:51-52.

of the body, and a life that surpasses the martyr's death he is going to suffer in Rome.

A preacher discovering this dramatic climax in his study can draw appropriate conclusions from it and take them into the pulpit, "God is greater than our fear," or "He who trusts in the Lord is never forsaken." He can talk about how God still saves people today and sees them through many storms in their lives. But he can also involve the hearers in these dramatic discoveries in the course of the sermon, just as he discovered them during the week:[85] that God acts here against all expectations, that he reverses the ranks of authority, that he saves many lives for the sake of one prisoner who is practically dead already. And the hearers begin to sense how improbable and unlikely it is that God would save them who are prisoners of the ruler of this world. They come to understand that his will to save is the reason why he still keeps this dying world turning. He still wants us and many others to hear the word of life that is stronger than the physical death we are going to suffer.

This dramatic format is not limited to narrative parts in the Scriptures. It also characterizes many of the doctrinal passages. It is of existential importance. And it calls for the undivided attention of the hearer.

Thus, "present preaching" also has to do with staying focused. Just as the preacher stays with the hearer throughout the sermon, the preacher wants the hearer to stay with him. This takes work from both of them. If the sermon text follows the pericopal readings or is announced beforehand, the reader can prepare himself by reading it at home before the service. He will ask the Holy Spirit to help him concentrate. He can practice putting all other thoughts on hold during this time under the word of the Lord. The preacher for his part can learn from good orators at all times to speak clearly, to lay out an audible line of thought, and to set clear goals.[86] He can allow for the gradual loss of concentration on the hearers' part by including summary statements and transitions, allowing them to catch up with the progress of thought before moving on, and thus to reach the conclusion together with him.[87]

---

85. The emphasis on inductive (as opposed to deductive) preaching was an important contribution by Craddock (see *Authority*).

86. See Aho, *Skeleton*. By contrast, Aho (following Luccock) speaks of the "Jericho sermon . . . in which the preacher . . . marches around the outside of a subject seven times making a loud noise. The preacher is convinced that the walls will fall down. For the hearer, they rarely do" (ibid., 8–9).

87. See Aho, *Sermon Theory I*, 27–32.

RETURNING TO THE QUESTION: WHAT MAKES A GOOD SERMON?

"Preaching in the presence of God," "preaching for those who are present," and "preaching in the present tense"—all these work together to ensure that the preacher does not deliver a lecture from the pulpit, but engages the hearers personally and directly in the spiritual battle for their lives. It is a house call and a counseling session with the congregation as a whole. Whether or not the preacher prepares a full manuscript during the week, he is not so much writing a sermon as preparing for it. His goal is not to read to his members, but to talk to them. Some preachers prefer to have the manuscript in front of them, but, with increasing experience, manage to speak from it rather than reading it. Others practice to speak freely from an outline or a number of keywords.[88] In any case, more than one preacher has experienced that God gives him words in the pulpit which he did not plan, because he has entrusted to him the very individuals seated before him. Thus a preacher learns that with all the work he continually puts into his preparation, it is not he who speaks but the living God. And he marvels at this incredible truth: that God entrusts his precious, life-saving, eternal word to a weak, sinful person like himself, and that he gives his Holy Spirit with it in order to accomplish what he sends it for. A sermon preached on this basis is a good sermon.

BIBLIOGRAPHY

Aho, Gerhard. *The Lively Skeleton. Thematic Approaches and Outlines.* The Preacher's Workshop Series. Vol. 4. St. Louis: Concordia, 1977.
———. *Sermon Theory I.* Ft. Wayne, IN: Concordia Theological Seminary Press, 2012.
Barth, Karl. *Kirchliche Dogmatik.* Vol. I/1, *Die Lehre vom Wort Gottes: Prolegomena zur Kirchlichen Dogmatik.* Münich: Kaiser, 1932.
Baxter, Batsell B. *The Heart of the Yale Lectures.* New York: Macmillan, 1947.
Blackwood, Andrew W. *The Preparation of Sermons.* London: Church Book Room, 1955.
Broadus, John A. *On the Preparation and Delivery of Sermons.* Philadelphia: Smith, English, 1871.
Brooks, Phillip. *Lectures on Preaching: Delivered Before The Divinity School of Yale College.* London: Allenson, 1877.
Buttrick, David. *Homiletic: Moves and Structures.* Philadelphia: Fortress, 1987.

---

88. Broadus positively refers to the practice of a thorough preparation of a written manuscript combined with a free delivery based on a full outline (*Preparation*, 326). Jones discusses the range of possibilities from reading or memorizing the manuscript to a delivery based on a detailed outline all the way to an improvised speech (*Principles*, 189ff.).

Craddock, Fred B. *As One without Authority. Revised and with New Sermons*. St. Louis: Chalice, 2001.
———. *Preaching*. Nashville: Abingdon, 1985.
Davis, Henry G. *Design for Preaching*. Philadelphia: Fortress, 1958.
Deffner, Donald L. *The Real Word for the Real World*. Preacher's Workshop 3. St. Louis: Concordia, 1977.
Edwards, O. C., Jr. *A History of Preaching*. Nashville: Abingdon, 2004.
Eggold, Henry J. *Preaching is Dialogue: A Concise Introduction to Homiletics*. Grand Rapids: Baker, 1980.
Farmer, Herbert H. *The Servant of the Word*. London: Nisbet, 1942.
Freytag, Gustav. *Die Technik des Dramas*. Leipzig: Hirzel; English translation: *Technique of the Drama* (Chicago: Griggs, 1896).
Glassius, Salomon. *Arbor vitae: Der Baum des Lebens*. Jena, 1629.
Graebner, Theodore. *A Manual for Classroom and Preacher's Desk. Part II: Sermons Classified according to Content*. St. Louis: Concordia, 1919.
Jensen, Richard A. *Telling the Story: Variety and Imagination in Preaching*. Minneapolis: Fortress, 1980.
———. *Thinking in Story: Preaching In A Post-Literate Age*. Lima, OH: C.S.S., 1993.
Jones, Ilion T. *Principles and Practice of Preaching*. New York: Abingdon, 1956.
Kennedy, George A. *Classical Rhetoric and Its Christian and Secular Tradition from Ancient to Modern Times*. Chapel Hill: University of North Carolina Press, 1980.
Leroux, Neil R. *Luther's Rhetoric. Strategies and Style from the Invocavit Sermons*. St. Louis: Concordia, 2002.
Levering, William Henry. "The Development of the Field of Homiletics in America from 1960–1983." PhD thesis, Temple University, 1986
Lischer, Richard, ed. *The Company of Preachers: Wisdom on Preaching, Augustine to the Present*. Grand Rapids: Eerdmans, 2002.
Lischer, Richard. *A Theology of Preaching: The Dynamics of the Gospel*. Rev. ed. Durham, NC: Labyrinth, 1991.
Lowry, Eugene L. *The Homiletical Plot: The Sermon as Narrative Art Form*. Louisville: Westminster John Knox, 2001.
Otto, Gert. *Die Kunst, verantwortlich zu reden*. Gütersloh: Kaiser, 1994.
Pfitzner, Victor C. "The Hermeneutical Problem and Preaching." *CTM* 38 (1967) 347–62.
Preus, Robert D. *The Theology of Post-Reformation Lutheranism*. Vol. 1, *A Study of Theological Prolegomena*. St. Louis: Concordia, 1970.
Randolph, David J. *The Renewal of Preaching: A New Homiletic Based on the New Hermeneutic*. Philadelphia: Fortress, 1969.
———. *The Renewal of Preaching in the Twenty-First Century: The Next Homiletics, with Commentary by Robert Stephen Reid*. Eugene, OR: Cascade, 2009.
Raschzok, Klaus. "Das geistliche Amt bei Wilhelm Löhe. Impuls in eine amtsvergessene Kirche." In *Wilhelm Löhe. Erbe und Vision*, edited by Dietrich Blaufuss, 80–109. Lutherische Kirche, Geschichte und Gestalten 26. Gütersloh: Gütersloher, 2009.
Rengstorf, K. H. "Ἀπόστολος." In TDNT 1:407–47.
Reu, M. *Homiletics: A Manual of the Theory and Practice of Preaching*. Chicago: Wartburg, 1924.

Wardlaw, Don M. "Homiletics and Preaching in North America." In *Concise Encyclopedia of Preaching*, edited by William H. Willimon and Richard Lischer, 243–52. Louisville: Westminster John Knox, 2000.
Walther, C. F. W. *Americanisch-Lutherische Pastoraltheologie*. St. Louis: Concordia, 1875.
———. *The Proper Distinction Between Law and Gospel*. St. Louis: Concordia, 1929.
White, R. E. O. *A Guide to Preaching: A Practical Primer of Homiletics*. Grand Rapids: Pickering and Inglis, 1973.
Wilson, Paul S. *The Practice of Preaching*. Nashville: Abingdon, 1995.

17

The Path from the Text to the Sermon
A German Preacher Takes Stock of Methods from America[1]

—Gottfried Martens

INTRODUCTION

This essay must begin with a confession: I really know very little about practical theology. What is more, I can claim no overview about the newer academic discussions in the area of homiletics, and that is especially true for German homiletics, since I never participated in a homiletics course here in Germany. Thus I can only speak from the background I have, namely what I learned about homiletics during my studies in the USA, and above all, from my own experiences in the congregation.

The method by which sermons develop in normal congregational circumstances is very different than one might have been taught in his studies. The idea that a preacher might free up one or two days each week in the course of congregational work to apply himself wholly to sermon preparation—uninterrupted by all outside influences—in order to follow all of

1. Translator's note: The following was delivered as an address to the Practical Theological Seminar of the Independent Evangelical Lutheran Church (*Selbstständige Evangelisch-Lutherische Kirche*) of Germany. It has been modified slightly from its lecture form. Translation by Jonathan Mumme and Rachel Mumme.

the many steps he once learned toward the creation of a sermon, possibly even in written form, will always be brought quickly back to reality. Simply put, I too consider writing sermons a central task of my service in the congregation; I do not belong to the species of pastor who honestly first gets around to writing his sermon on Saturday night at 11 p.m. Quite the opposite: my sermon writing day is, *horribile dictum*, Monday, and if that does not work, then I want to be finished with the sermon by noon on Tuesday at the latest. I simply cannot work creatively under pressure. Nevertheless, the situation in which the sermon must be written often looks like this: the preacher would like to sit down and begin working on the sermon, but then the phone rings and a long conversation follows, the Kindergarten teachers ask for a meeting, and today's hospital visitation cannot be put off. In the midst of all of that, the week's sermon should emerge, and I sit there thinking, "I only have X hours left and the clock is ticking. Or, Holy Week draws threateningly near and I know that five sermons need to be written quickly. How, in the face of that do I keep myself from panicking and do the sermon work that needs to be doing in a very levelheaded way?

Here I mean to show how I go about this work, as I learned to in the USA, and how I modified such method for myself. I am very conscious that the way I write a sermon might today seem completely antiquated. Nevertheless, I stand by it, not only because I hold this path from text to sermon to be helpful and practical, but also, because I believe with regard to its contents that the method can be theologically substantiated.

A LOOK AT THE "NEW HOMILETIC" IN THE USA

To rule out any misunderstandings right from the beginning, when I here address "North American Preaching Models" I do not by that mean the "new homiletic" which has arisen in the last thirty years in the USA and has, in the meantime, also been taken up here in Germany. A simple introduction is provided by the book from Martin Nicol, *Einander ins Bild setzen: Dramaturgische Homiletik*.[2] On the contrary, this "new homiletic" criticizes and breaks with homiletics as I still learned the discipline at Concordia Theological Seminary (Fort Wayne, IN) twenty years ago and utilize today in my sermon preparations.

To indicate what this "new homiletic" about I offer a few key points from Martin Nicol's book:

---

2. The title could be translated, "Making Pictures of One Another: Dramaturgical Homiletics."

- The "new homiletic" opposes an inductive understanding to a discursive understanding of the sermon, still common today; it is not about "explaining a truth of the faith" (deductive) but instead to share experiences of the faith (inductive)."[3] Above all, however, the sermon is not about "conveying a truth to the hearers, but rather about catching them up in a movement, in which they themselves can have experiences and gain insights. The paradigm for preaching is no longer the academic lecture with thesis and arguments, but rather the movie with pictures that move people."[4]

- Related to this, the "new homiletic" emphasizes the unity of content and form against the view that the sermon is essentially only about content, while the form is something second-tier or external.

- For this reason the "new homiletic" tries to grasp the sermon as "event," and this essentially as an aesthetic category. At the same time this entails the sermon no longer being a "talk about" something. Rather it is a "talk in;" preaching means "preaching from within." "This kind of sermon tries . . . not to speak *about* comfort, but rather to comfort."[5]

- Correspondingly, the "new homiletic," as presented by Martin Nicol, attempts to understand the sermon as "art among arts" (*Kunst unter Künsten*). It is no longer about "thinking in ideas," but rather "thinking in story." Thus Nicol pleads for a "dramaturgical homiletic," which is about letting lines of suspense unfold.[6]

- In his thoughts on preaching, Nicol also places substantial focus on the integration of the sermon in the liturgy, in order that it does not remain a foreign object in the dramaturgy of the entire divine service, which only interrupts and disturbs the liturgical "journey into mystery."[7]

- As far as his hermeneutical thoughts go Nicol explicitly turns against the thought implied by the title of this work: "from text to sermon." In doing so, he is being consistent, contrasting that notion with his formulation, "from event to text," which means "that starting from inspired understanding of biblical words, pictures, and narratives, I move on to inquire about the form of the text in the Bible."[8] How-

3. Ibid, 25.
4. Ibid.
5. Ibid., 55.
6. Ibid., 36.
7. Ibid., 38.
8. Ibid., 59.

ever, in doing do, the following also applies, "In a complex preaching process there can be absolutely no more linear paths. Hermeneutical progress always happens in circular motion."[9]

Closing this synopsis of Nicol's presentation of the "new homiletic," we must note that one can certainly take numerous ideas from him. Helpful is his insistence that the sermon is not primarily about information, and that this insight also must correspond with the form of the sermon. His criticism of the mechanical use of the "three-point" sermon structure, which he outlines or rather caricatures, is also helpful. Likewise, one must nod to him as speaks against a haphazard way of writing a sermon from one idea and association to the next, and pleads for planned formulation, for the development of a sermon structure that the hearers can follow. Important, too, are his admonitions that a sermon is never just a monologue, but always a form of interaction, and that for this reason speaking freely instead of reading a sermon is not an indifferent matter, but rather belongs to the very essence of the sermon's form.[10]

Nevertheless there are some decisive questions to be put to the "new homiletic" and how it conceives of preaching, and these prompt me in principle to hold fast to the method of sermon preparation attacked so vehemently by the "new homiletic":

- In the form presented by Nicol, conceiving of preaching as the "new homiletic" does mean appropriating a reception hermeneutic (*Rezeptionshermeneutik*) which rests on the premise "that texts do not simply represent reality, but rather that they, like works of art, in the process of reception, sometimes bring forth from themselves completely different realities than those after which the texts might have been modeled in the first place. It is in interplay with contexts that texts become intelligible (intertextuality). What is true for the reception of texts can also be asserted for their production. Biblical texts are then the (provisional) result of a process of tradition that is primarily oral, thus again belonging to an interplay between texts and contexts."[11] Theologically, this hermeneutical decision is taken on board by denying that preacher and hearers are situated opposite one another in preaching. As Nicol says, "The discursive sermon presupposes an understanding of the preacher that is to be explained and communicated by the raised position of the pulpit. Ultimately this model only functions when the preacher by virtue of his office is still accorded authority in matters of

9. Ibid.
10. Cf. Ibid., 118–19.
11. Ibid., 60–61.

faith. When the hearers claim a competence for interpreting in matters of faith this model loses its foundation."[12] If one drops the pietistic misinterpretation of the discursive sermon, according to which the preacher in the pulpit is communicating his personal insights, then the way that the "new homiletic" conceives of preaching is fundamentally aimed at dissolving the notion that the word of God and faith are situated opposite one another at dissolving the *extra nos* of this word, and at an entirely new way of understanding and stipulating the authority of this word. And this has consequences:

- Under the premises mentioned the sermon can only retain an aesthetic function; it opens a field for the giving of meaning. However, the sermon is "representative rather than effective action,"[13] as Nicol openly states referencing Schleiermacher. If the sermon is only understood as representative and thus also as interpretive event and in this sense as a work of art, the hearer then approaches it with his own interpretive competence with the result that something such as truth first emerges in this encounter. Putting it cautiously, this definitively curtails an understanding of the sermon as a means of grace, in which God himself—judging and saving—goes to work on the hearers. The change of subject taking place here is unmistakable.

- Ostensibly the claim being made here is then taken up pneumatologically in conceiving preaching as "event." However, even though Nicol distances himself from an existential-theological restriction of the concept of event, this does not change the fact that also in his own thinking preaching only "becomes" event now and then, in a way not subject to human beings. In this way of thinking about things the Spirit is not at all bound to the word. The approach that Nicol takes is and remains Barthian-Reformed. Accordingly, incarnational thinking is missing in the hermeneutic that he supports; God's binding his action to very particular historical events and also to the texts that are tied to them and thus remain normative instance over against those with whom they interact is not taken seriously. To say it again in Nicol's own words, "Preaching as artwork is open. It opens up plurality of understanding, a plurality that can be construed as an echo of plurality in the workings of the Holy Spirit."[14]

12. Ibid., 24–25.
13. Ibid., 43.
14. Ibid., 63.

- Finally, after reading Nicol's book I still have a final, very practical objection. To me his way of thinking about preaching seems amply aloof and aimed at a throng of hearers from the educated classes that is familiar with works of art and knows about interpreting them. Telling in this regard is Nicol's use of the term "small change." Hartmut Hauschild, my mentor when I was a vicar, was always impressing upon me that I was not to be dolling out hundred dollar bills in my sermons, but rather "small change"—not playing around with material of which the people knew not what do or make, but with something they could handle. Nicol, on the other hand criticizes making "small change" in sermons (although he is certainly right in the example that he brings up to make his point).[15] Nicol means to give food for thought against a much more down-to-earth and simple understanding of preaching and composing sermons, namely conceiving of these as a craft. He says, "With a craft one rightly awaits that it succeed, that it produce a perfect product."[16] However, I would be willing to bet that this is not the only possible understanding of craft. Even less can I cozy up to his alternative: sermon as work of art.

In what follows I wish to present craft—a craft, however that claims no perfection, but indeed knows that the Holy Spirit binds himself to the always imperfect, finite, human word; *finitum capax infiniti*.[17]

SERMON AS BATTLE/BATTLEFIELD

As a contrast to Nicol's aesthetic understanding of preaching, I prefer to understand and portray the sermon as a battle—as a battle both first and foremost in the theological sense, but then also in the psychological sense.

When one understands preaching in this way, the hearer is not so to speak in a neutral position as one looking at a piece of art, nor does he assume an active, contributing role as interpreting subject. Rather, the sermon wades into the battle between old and new man, between flesh and spirit, which takes place in each baptized person who hears a sermon. Or the sermon runs directly into opposition from the old man in those not yet baptized. In preaching the preacher steps into this battle armed with

15. Ibid., 99.
16. Ibid., 70–71.
17. Translator note: "The finite is capable of the infinite." This christological conviction, which underpins Lutheran sacramental theology, stands as a line of demarcation to the conviction that "the finite is not capable of the infinite" and sacramental theology/-ies formulated in accord with it.

the word of God, which is "living and active, sharper than any two-edged sword, piercing to the division of soul and of spirit, of joints and of marrow, and discerning the thoughts and intentions of the heart." (Heb 4:12)

When this happens the old man, in a host of ways, puts up a fight against what he hears: he approaches the sermon with the attitude that what is said really does not do much, will take far too long, and will be boring, but not just for that reason; it is really just an interruption to worship anyway. Or, he approaches the sermon with the attitude that what is said is always the same and is old hat that everyone already knows. Or, from the outset, he expects decent entertainment from the sermon and judges the sermon afterward by how it measured up to this expectation. The human brain's response of overstimulation, which affects us all, he utilizes to switch our ears to "ventilation" mode, so that all that goes in one goes out the other. And naturally he puts up a real fight when frontally attacked in the sermon; he finds a thousand reasons why this must be a terrible sermon to attack him in such a way, since what it pointed out about him was done, said, thought, or neglected with only the best of intent.

In preaching I do not presume that the people sitting before my pulpit have left a victorious battle of the new man against the old behind them long ago and are now like newborn babes long only to savor the pure, spiritual milk of the word of God as much and as long as possible. I do not assume this, not only because I know myself as one who listens to sermons (everyone knows that pastors are especially poor hearers of sermons) but also because the word of God itself opens our eyes to see who the hearers of this word are and what takes place in them under the workings of this word of God in law and gospel.

In this respect, Martin Nicol was exactly right: the sermon is not some information about something. This would not do justice to its character as a battle and would actually require a neutral, inquisitive hearer. Rather, Nicol's characterization of the sermon as "forensic discourse"[18] is correct, even though he himself clearly opposes this understanding of the sermon in his further treatment of it. However, "battle" means even more; it means that I know that in preaching I am dealing with an opponent, who from the beginning of the sermon to its closing sentence is trying to evade me, who does not want to hear what is being said to him. On this opponent the preacher must always have his eye.

Consequently the sermon, which is a battle, always has an essential dialogical character: it addresses the hearer, not with some politely distant formality, but rather with the biblical "you" of God's speaking to man. It

---

18. Cf. Nicol, *Homiletik*, 41.

seeks to grasp man in his flight from God and face him up to the demand and promise of God's word by responding to the listener's blockades, addressing them, and consequently knocking his own weapons out of his hand. This approach applies, one may note, beyond preaching to other work in the congregation; it is decisive that we take instances of resistance seriously and take it upon ourselves as preachers and pastors to address them openly. In this way we prevent resistance, opposition, and antagonism from continually building up. This is a very effective method for timely release of pressure from the kettle, before it boils over.

At the same time, from what has already been said, it becomes clear that this battle with the old man definitely has a dimension that extends to the psychological. The old man even utilizes the very way that we are composed as creatures to evade the word of God. It is therefore helpful and important that in the writing of the sermon we always bear in mind that in many cases, we are dealing with listeners who are less and less practiced in listening and must give them very concrete, technical help to make this listening easier and enable them to follow the sermon as it goes along. From the first sentence to the last the sermon is actually a battle for the attention of the hearers. I reiterate that attention can be held much better by speaking freely than by reading a sermon in lecture fashion. One can quite quickly read from the faces of the hearers, observing whether they are really following or not, whether they are still reacting or not. Then one also much sooner sees when the hearers begin to cast stolen glances at their watches, though their concern for the time need not of itself faze a preacher. Half of them holding their watches to their ears is another matter.

Incidentally, the fact that the sermon is a battle does not mean that it is always or even essentially polemic in its tone. Ultimately, the sermon is first and foremost promising proclamation of the gospel. But even this promise and comfort of the gospel encounters a heart that wants to close itself to this promise and not let itself be comforted. Thus even promising and comforting are not spared this battle.

Finally and above all, the fact that the sermon is a battle means this: I am trying to achieve something with my sermon, and it has a clear goal. Of course I know that I cannot achieve this goal with my listeners by my own reason or strength,[19] that I am not the one who is able to kill the old man and work faith in the hearer. Nevertheless, I am working toward a goal with my sermon, because I assume that the word of God as found in Holy Scripture, which I am to proclaim—that this word itself already intends such a goal and desires to accomplish something with the hearer. So, borrowing a

---

19. Cf. SC II:6 (KW 355 = *BSLK* 511–12).

word from the apostle, I do not run aimlessly; I do not box as one beating the air (1 Cor 9:26). Rather, I always have the sermon's goal clearly in mind and do not let it go until I have finally achieved it.

THE WAY FROM THE TEXT TO THE SERMON

Having laid some groundwork about the sermon one comes to the practical question: How do I get from the text[20] to the sermon?

I will begin right in the middle of the sermon preparation. Naturally I began with prayer, asking the help of the Holy Spirit in all that I have ahead of me. By this point I have already read the text in its original language and translated it, and thereafter read it in Luther's translation, which will be used in the divine service. I have reflected upon the text personally, read commentaries and sermon-helps for this pericope, and have gathered my thoughts together about how the statements of the pericope could be ordered in a systematic-theological way. At the same time, all kinds of thoughts and reactions that this text has set off for me go swirling around in my head. What kinds of reactions might this text elicit in the hearers? What kinds of problems does it address with them? What kinds of obstacles it might encounter when it is heard? And in my head are also swirling all sorts of thoughts about everything that I could say about this text. And all this is still rather disordered and jumbled.

Now it is time to put things in order. I do not do this by trying to work out something like a scope of the text. Manfred Seitz rightly criticized this "scope method" in his seminal essay, "Zum Problem der sogennanten Predigtmeditation"[21] and instead suggested a differentiated summary of the exegetical work under the key words "intention," "kerygma," and "idion." I find this method of summary extremely helpful; I use it in preparing every sermon, in order to clarify what I have read and pondered to this point. The "intention" answers the question, "What was the text wanting to accomplish in the hearers at that time?"[22] This answer is an important aid in the subsequent formulation of the sermon's goal; it takes seriously the fact that the

---

20. The word "text" is used here in a very technical sense. I specifically avoid using the word "text" in the sermon. That which we are to preach is not just a "text," not just some literary product; rather, in this text God himself speaks. If this text is his word, we should in the sermon deliberately name the subjects behind the "text": the prophets and apostles, and, behind them, God. Thus we are spared many hermeneutical errors. For this insight I thank the former director of the SELK's Practical Theological Seminary, Rev. Horst Nickisch.

21. Seitz, "Predigtmeditation," 21–32.

22. Ibid., 27.

original text had a goal in mind. Under "kerygma" Seitz understands answer given to the following questions: "How do the theological statements of the text sound when logically joined together?"[23] In my experience as a preacher it has proven itself helpful at this point simply to ruminate the lesson until I know it by heart (that is, if the lesson is not too long); so doing the links and connections that Seitz mentions get sniffed out. Even the wording of the sermon lesson should be so familiar to me that I am at home with its thoughts and how they progress. Finally, the "idion" answers the question, "Given its form and content, wherein does the uniqueness of this text consist?"[24] The question about the formal uniqueness of the text should show itself in the shape of the sermon; herein Nicol is essentially correct. Narrative, poetic, and texts that present an argument all suggest a different ways of shaping the sermon. The question about the uniqueness of the text's content is, finally, a decisively important aid against finally preaching ourselves to death sooner or later, given that in so many sermon lessons the same message seems to be presenting itself over and over again. We do ourselves and our hearers a favor when we let this idion play an important role in shaping the content of our sermons.

After determining the intention, kerygma, and idion I move directly to the question about "goal," "malady," and "means," which is what the sermon is all about. These terms are unmistakably American English expressions, which pithily summarize the homiletical teaching of the St. Louis professor, Richard Caemmerer, as developed in his book *Preaching for the Church*.[25] "Goal" specifies what the sermon means to accomplish with the hearers. "Malady" describes the attitude, condition, or situation of the hearers, which opposes this goal; to put it another way, the "malady" describes the point of departure, from which the hearers are to be lead to the goal. The "means" points finally to that by or through which the hearers are lead from the malady to the goal. If this were advertising one would speak of the "motivation," but in this context that expression is too weak. Theologically the means is nothing less that the gospel in the specific form, in which it presents itself in the sermon lesson.

As simple as these questions are it is in fact worthwhile to invest some time in answering them. To begin with, the three questions about goal, malady, and means cannot actually be answered independent of one another or even one after another; rather all three are directly and inextricably related

---

23. Ibid.

24. Ibid.

25. See especially 87ff. Caemmerer taught at Concordia Seminary from 1940 through the mid-1970s.

to each other. Only when the answers each relate to one another and yield a coherent sense have I answered them in a meaningful and expedient way.

At the same time the answers to these three questions make a serious and salutary reduction necessary: the answers to these three questions should each be formulated in a single and not too sizeable sentence. In the formulation of the answers to the questions about the goal and malady "the hearers" are the subject of the sentences, whereas in the answer to the question of means God, Christ, or the Holy Spirit is. Only by way of reduction to such short sentences can I keep the sermon from being a form of boxing where fists swing about in the air (cf. 1 Cor 9:26) now and then trying to land a punch, but finally hitting no target and reaching no goal. For the success of a sermon it is decisively important to exercise restraint, to let that precious thought that the preacher would really like to include fall to the side. Precisely in readying such restraint the triad of goal, malady, and means is very serviceable; it helps me achieve clarity about what direction I am now thinking to go in the sermon.

For a proper understanding of goal, malady and means it is very important that these have their place in the homiletical reflection that precedes the sermon's formulation, and not in the exegetical synopsis of the sermon lesson. The Word of God does indeed first uncover our malady, and the malady is thus something necessarily different than the problems that we sense and experience in the congregation. However, I must be very precise in sniffing out what concrete expression this particular malady takes in that congregation that I will have in front of me when preaching the sermon. Take, for example, a sermon lesson on 1 Thess 4:1–8 for the twentieth Sunday after Trinity, where Paul addresses the men of the congregation in Thessalonica, warning them against the fornication they were practicing. There may be congregations in which this is in fact a very timely topic, but if I know that on Sunday I primarily have elderly women in front of me, then the malady of the congregation in Thessalonica does not correspond exactly to the malady of the congregation to which I am preaching on Sunday. Thus I need to think about where I, taking my point of departure from this text, can locate the malady in this congregation. If my sermon ends up giving these ladies a good warning about lewd living, I have missed the malady as clearly as when I would have complained about the moral decline of the world today and its youth in front of this congregation. For in preaching, the malady is always about the malady of those hearing the sermon and not about the malady of others. Shortly put: only by precisely specifying the malady can I keep myself from building straw men, whom I then noisily shoot down in my sermon, leaving myself feeling like a champion marksman, but having never even got the Old Adam in his concrete form in my sights.

Here I have begun with the malady, and indeed this suggests itself with many sermon lessons. It makes sense first to ask where I, in the sermon lesson, can find the hearers with their needs, their guilt, their lost state before God. Where are the obstacles and instances of resistance to the goal being reached that are to be overcome? But one quickly sees that in doing so the goal keeps pressing itself into view, and formulating the sermon's goal is certainly not as simply as may first appear. First of all the goal does not have to be identical to the "intention" that the exegetical study produced. That which has already been noted about the malady is also true of the goal: the formulation of the goal is the result of homiletical reflection. Further one must keep an eye on the relationship between the goal and the malady: they must relate to one another, but the formulated goal must be more than the negation of the malady; it must be positive and must, of course, at the same time be grounded in the biblical text. First and foremost the goal should be formulated as concretely as possible. Only when a goal has been precisely formulated can the preacher steer precisely in its direction. Here we find ourselves in a certain dilemma: the more concrete the formulation of the goal the greater the danger of this goal being moralized or trivialized. In any case it is completely clear that that the attaining of the goal can in no way be tested against some sort of learning objectives. The formulation of the goal serves only to give the sermon focus. Caemmerer, following Luther, makes a fundamental distinction between "faith goals" and love or "life goals:"[26] faith and love provide the overarching categories for formulating the goal. Even though (as Lutheran preachers certainly know) faith and love cannot be separated, and any love goal presumes faith, and the intended faith will always be active in love, I still have always found it helpful to be clear as to whether my focus will be in the area of a faith goal or a love goal.

As already indicated, "means" means nothing other than the gospel in its concrete form in the sermon lesson. Of course sniffing out this gospel in the text is a decisively important task in the preparation of a sermon. In many cases this proves very simple and obvious, but even in these instances one should lay hold of the gospel according to its unique form in the particular lesson. In other cases very close inspection is required to discern the gospel. But only by way of such discernment can a sermon, especially a sermon on a paraenetic text, be kept from slipping into legalism.

A common mistake in designating goal, malady, and means comes when goal and means are confused or each mistaken for the other. When

---

26. Caemmerer, *Preaching*, 15ff.

this happens, the goal is so formulated that the hearers would recognize or better recognize the gospel of the text. This, however, annuls the function of the goal-malady-means triad, and the sermon becomes information about something, a kind of lecture. Thus in formulating the goal, cognitive formulations such as, "The hearer should recognize," "understand," or "grasp" should be avoided. As means, the gospel is certainly expressed strongly enough in the sermon; in fact, being preached as means, it will be much more recognizable to the hearers, as it will be meaningfully applied to their lives.

Once I have formulated the goal, malady, and means in relation to the sermon's text, the general direction of the sermon is in place. I know whither I will lead the hearers thither and I how will bring up and proclaim the gospel along the way.

The next step is to set the theme of the sermon. Formulating a theme for the sermon is important; even Martin Nicol emphasizes this, albeit in a different fashion. Under the heading *"Titel und Mittel"*[27] he asserts, "The sermon's title helps to sift the material that has been gathered together. It guides decisions about what must be part of the sermon and in what form. And sometimes it forces the preacher to ask the painful question, 'What do I have to leave out?'"[28] Along these lines my honored teacher, Gerhard Aho, has the following to say in his useful work, *The Lively Skeleton*:

> Failure to articulate your theme will result in the following: (1) the loss of a unifying factor in the sermon; (2) the loss of a criterion for judging the sequence and importance of the thoughts in the sermon; (3) the loss of a sense of direction vital for maintaining continuity and achieving climactic order in the sermon.[29]

Aho himself asserts that the formulated theme should answer at least three questions, "(1) What is the preacher going to talk about? (2) What is he going to say about it? (3) What is he trying to achieve?"[30] As a young vicar or curate, preaching my first sermons in the United States, I always aimed for as trendy a formulation of the theme as I could muster, as these were printed in the congregation's Sunday bulletin. However, here in Germany, I gradually left this practice behind as only seldom do I wish to announce the sermon's theme to the congregation. As a general rule, however, I do usually close the introduction to my sermon with some sort of formulation that

27. "Title and Center."
28. Nicol, *Homiletik*, 106.
29. Coming to Concordia Theological Seminary in 1958, Aho taught homiletics and pastoral theology there until 1987.
30. Aho, *Skeleton*, 10.

answers the three questions from Aho: what I am preaching about, what I mean to say about it, and what I mean to accomplish in saying this.

As such, the formulation of a theme is indeed of the utmost importance for the success of a sermon, because the structure of the sermon is worked out from this theme. Aho mentions different ways of getting to the sermon's theme: the preacher can utilize the scope (which Aho did use); he can proceed from the goal in formulating the theme; he can put the essential statements of the text together and then ask what unifying thought holds these statements together; or he can also take a key word from the text and use it to formulate the theme.[31] Finding one's way to the theme is a very creative process that entails trial and error. Often I throw away four or five formulations of the theme that prove themselves unhelpful for the further execution of the sermon before I finally find a theme that does equal justice to the exegetical results of studying the sermon text and also to the formulation of the goal, malady, and means.

Decisive for the subsequent shaping of the sermon is then the "line of direction" that Aho mentions.[32] I wish to call special attention to this line of direction and its importance, for I think that it is here that mistakes are often made that then get in the way of a sermon being simple and targeted. To take a very simple example, if a preacher is not following a line of direction while preparing a sermon on the parable of the royal wedding feast (Matt 22:1–14) he might be tempted to preach a sermon with the following three sections: "Who are the guests?" "Why don't they want to come?" "How does God respond to this?" In this way the preacher could sort of retell the parable and perhaps even apply it to the present, but the three questions are finally aimed in three entirely different directions. The line of direction, on the other hand, sets a single subject and a uniform interrogative pronoun. In the case of the parable of the royal wedding feast this would mean that it would make sense to take God as the subject and the question, "What is God doing?" as the line of direction, which could then be answered with, "God invites; he is disappointed; he does not give up." To reiterate: in setting the line of direction for a sermon the preacher is to find a uniform grammatical or at least logical subject for the various sections of the sermon and is to develop the sermon under a unified question or problem—under "What?" or "How?" or "Why?" or "When?," but not all of them all mixed up. Otherwise we preachers lose sight of the sermon's goal, to say nothing of it being recognizable to the hearers.

---

31. Ibid., 11ff.
32. Ibid., 14ff.

With that, we come to the famously infamous three points or parts of a sermon, on which not only Nicol has especially trained his sights. To be clear: not all of my sermons have three parts. The reasons for this are various. It can happen that the presentation of a single, continuous thought so suggests itself that it would be senseless to chop it into three parts. Based on the topic and the line of thought a two-part structuring of the sermon can likewise suggest itself. And, I will admit, that not seldom do I conceive of the sermon in three parts, but in the course of its composition notice that with just two parts I have reached my length limit (five pages); then I have to see if I can let the thought of the third section fall away, or if I can somehow bring it into the sermon's closing. We dare never view the three-point-structure as a straightjacket, into which every sermon must be stuffed, whether it fits or not. If the three-point-schema is employed in this way, its critique by the so-called new homiletic as "cookie cutter" is quite justified.

As a rule, however, I still view such a three-part structuring of the sermon as helpful and sensible. It makes for clarity in the cognitive construction of the sermon. It helps the hearers to follow the sermon as it moves along and to remember the essential statements of the sermon after it is over. I find it both interesting and encouraging that time and again parishioners tell me that they find this three-part-structuring of the sermon helpful for precisely these reasons. In any case this sort of structure guards against the famously infamous "Jericho sermons," where the preacher marches around his theme seven times, making lots of noise, in the hope that the walls surrounding it will simply fall; this works in very few instances. Dividing the sermon into three parts cuts the whole of the sermon into smaller, manageable units, with which the hearers can more easily follow along as opposed to with a long sermon without a particular structure. Thus this three-part division serves not least the holding of attention. Going beyond three to four or more sections should really only happen as an exception to the rule, for in so doing the structure of a sermon most often becomes too unmanageable, and the danger of trying to pack too many different thoughts into a single sermon is very real. In my preaching I usually name the sections of my sermon at its outset, namely at the end of my introduction, so as to help the hearers follow along with the sermon as it moves along. In most cases, once a preacher has found a theme and a line of direction the sections of the sermon just unfold of their own accord. Nevertheless it is stimulating to play a bit with language and wording when formulating the captions to these three sections so as to align them with one another on a formal level. Moreover my experience with the three-point structure is that this formal schema is so unspecific that it actually leads to entirely different kinds of sermons and not at all to their being standardized. Precisely this fixed schema lends itself to being played with, shaped, and developed in very different ways.

Once captions to the three sections have been formulated, the next step is to develop the sections themselves. In doing so the preacher's problem is not usually finding enough to say to each, but rather relinquishing and sacrificing a good many ideas of which he has grown fond during his preparations. We preachers are all too happy to include this or that thought, which doesn't actually relate to the central line of thought, but is nonetheless very stimulating and important. If we succumb to the temptation to enrich our sermons with strings of excurses, they quickly lose their rigor; the hearers lose sight of the sermon's actual aim or goal; they are distracted, and we more quickly leave them behind in the course of the sermon. It is thus incumbent upon us to give serious consideration to which thoughts actually serve the formulated theme, the line of direction, and the goal of the sermon, and which do not.

In his book, *The Lively Skeleton*, Gerhard Aho then goes on to suggest that the given sections of the sermons be further outlined and filled in by preliminary drafts that grow ever more detailed so that the preacher can cross seamlessly from the final preliminary draft to writing out the sermon. For two reasons, I quickly distanced myself from this suggestion in my own practice. Firstly, it tempts the preacher to stick so many thoughts into each section that the sermon again becomes confusing. Secondly, and most importantly, I usually lack the time for such intermediate steps. When I have the three sections then I simply sketch a line of thought for each, realizing that therewith I can very quickly fill the page and a half that I have for each section. In sketching out these sections two things are important. First, that the lines of thought in the given sections actually and recognizably differentiate, so that the same thing is not just repeated three times in different ways. Sometimes, in fleshing the sections out, the preacher realizes that the general outline he has in front of him will not actually work and must itself be rewritten. Second, it is important that the line of thought in a section clearly keeps its eye on the sermon's line of direction and pulls toward its goal. To help the hearers follow along, it is advisable to furnish each of the sections with an introduction and a summary. Sometimes this feels a bit pedantic, but does at the same time make things much easier for the hearers.

The structure that the lines of thought take in the given sections can vary greatly. They can be dialogical, taking up and then refuting an objection; they can be historical, presenting first the historical situation in which the sermon lesson originally had its voice and then giving the sermon lesson voice in the present situation of the congregation. Or they may take different structures.

I offer two more practical tips for shaping the sections of the sermon. First, we need to consider that time is extremely relative and is sensed differently by the hearers at different points in the sermon. Listening to sermons, hearers often experience a phenomenon of time stretching; two minutes at the end of the sermon feel a lot longer than at the beginning. For this reason it is advisable to craft the third section shorter than the first two and quickly to get to the close. Secondly, psychological studies have shown that about two-thirds of the way through a sermon the hearers experience something of a "dead point." Thus, if possible, it is also advisable to build a wake-up into the sermon toward the end of the second section—be it a vivid striking example or a humorous quip or formulation that awakens the hearers' attention. This can't always be enforced, but I have repeatedly had good luck when I pointedly place such wake-ups in the sermon.

We have yet to consider the introduction and the close of the sermon.

As far as the sermon's introduction goes, remember that the sermon is a battle. According to my experience, even before the sermon begins the Old Adam is priming the hearer with an almost irresistible message, "What's coming now is boring. Now you'll be hearing something that you already know anyway. It's just the same old same old. So, turn on your inter-ear ventilation system; it can just go in one ear and out the other." And woe to us as preachers, when right at the beginning of the sermon we help the Old Adam by handing him more arguments for not listening! A typical example would be the popular beginning of sermons on the Sunday *Cantate*: "*Cantate*—Sing to the Lord a new song!" After the first sentence the preacher really doesn't need to say much more; in that very moment the inter-ear ventilators of many of the hearers got turn on. I thus put a lot of stock in non-religious sermon intros where the hearers do not know after the first half sentence, what the whole thing is going to be about, but are rather transferred to a world that they would not expect in a sermon. Soccer repeatedly offers nice sermon introductions.

I am aware of the objections raised against sermon introductions: they are unnecessary frill that does not even need the word of God; instead of beginning with the hearers' own experience it would be better to confront them directly with what the sermon lesson itself has to say. I grant that the introduction should in no way replace the working of the Holy Spirit or make it superfluous. On the other hand, I think it corresponds to the commandment to love one's neighbor, that preachers recognize that hearers, especially in today's media society, have a tough time just listening. It is loving to give them helps that make approaching the various statements of the biblical text easier and to place vivid models for better understanding the biblical text at their disposal. A different objection is weightier: crazy, interesting, or even shocking introductions don't bring much if they are just placed as a sort of gag or gimmick at the beginning of the sermon, but do not really relate to its further train of thought. Here a preacher really does need to think seriously about how strong the link between the introduction's beginning and the further statements of the sermons is; a good many ideas that at first appear juicy should not make the cut if they do not carry any weight for the rest of the sermon.

In addition to its rhetorical function of grabbing the hearers and getting their attention right at the beginning of the sermon, the introduction has another important function. It should also describe the background against which the theme of the sermon will be developed and made intelligible to them, and its end should lead the hearers to the naming of the sermon's theme and its outline. As far as the backdrop of the sermon, there are many different ways one can go. In some cases it makes sense to broach the malady already in the introduction, starting, optimally, with an example directly from the lives of the hearers. In other cases a preacher can clarify the historical background to the sermon lesson in the introduction, moving then to the present relevance of what it says. Or, right at the beginning, a preacher can raise what the lesson says in a broader systematic-theological context, and from there show how and where it fits in the larger whole. Important is that by the end of the introduction it is clear to the hearers why it is worthwhile to listen to the rest of the sermon.

Thinking about the length of the sermon, I am usually inclined to exceed the advice of some American homiletical literature; instead of the recommend eighth of the total length, my introduction often comes out at one-fifth. I think this is justified if the introduction does not just consist of a first hook, but leads instead directly into the theme and is itself already saying something about it.

Preachers often have greater difficulty with the sermon's close than with its introduction. Many parishioners have certainly suffered through the experience of having to watch (and listen) as their preacher attempts one landing after another, only to break them off and go into a holding pattern before finally getting his wheels to the ground with a hearty, "So let us . . ." or by reading a verse of a hymn as his runway of last resort.

Thus, as a general rule, the close should first and foremost be short and precise, and should not gainsay what has already been said in the sermon. Along with this general rule we must remember that the close is of decisive import for the overarching impression of the sermon as it hangs with the hearers as the last thing to meet their ears. Therefore, it is very important that the end of the sermon arrives at its destination and nowhere else. Here in closing the preacher should sum up exactly what he wanted to achieve in the sermon and see that it is expressed. In many cases it is both good and sensible to tie the close of the sermon to its beginning or introduction, thereby completing a bridge from beginning to end in a way that is perceptible to the hearers. Especially because the close of the sermon is strategically of such decisive importance it behooves us preachers, above all, to see that the gospel is that which is there proclaimed. C. F. W. Walther's twenty-fifth thesis in his book about the proper distinction between law and gospel applies especially to the composition of the sermon's close: "You are not rightly distinguishing Law and Gospel if you do not allow the Gospel to predominate in your teaching"[33] Even when the sermon is aiming at a love goal, the preacher must clearly highlight how this goal and its realization are anchored in the Gospel. In doing so the fundamental claim of the Apology to the Augsburg Confession is to be kept in mind, *Et haec promissio non habet conditionem* ("The promise of the Gospel includes no condition").[34] At the end of a sermon "if" clauses have no place, rather comfort, encouragement, and invitation belong there. Thus it is important that as we are writing our sermons, we think especially about their closings, and that we do so before we are exhausted or, pressured by time, just try to end them "somehow"!

In closing, two more practical tips: Many of the steps of moving from the biblical text to the written sermon, as I have presented them here (intention, kerygma, and idion; goal, malady, and means; theme and line of direction; dividing out and structuring its sections; and the formulation of introduction and close) I have now come to the point of doing simply in my head. However, I still do this in such a way, that I seek to formulate my thoughts in complete, precise sentences. I only start writing words on a scratchpad when I notice that I'm having trouble giving sensible structure to what I want to say. In this way I can write thoughts one way and re-pen them another, until they come out right. I also take some short notes in those instances where I can't write the sermon right after completing my sermon preparations. The final tip relates to the memorizing of the finished sermon. Let me be clear here: I am talking about memorizing and not learning the sermon by heart. Memorizing is not about regurgitating word for word what is written in the sermon manuscript. A preacher should commit certain central statements to memory word for word and at the same time get secure enough in his freer formulation that he does not inadvertently find himself opening all sorts of synergistic doors when he does preach the sermon. As to the importance of speaking freely when preaching,

---

33. *Law and Gospel*, 455.
34. AP IV:41 (KW 126–27 = *BSLK* 168)

Martin Nicol's book says what needs to be said. In addition to everything else, memorizing the sermon entails another great advantage: the preacher comes very quickly to recognize where things don't hang together in the sermon, be it logical discrepancies, missing transitions, or places where the hearers just plain get left behind. In memorizing the sermon the preacher steps, to a certain degree, into the shoes of the hearers, for that which lacks clarity of thought cannot easily be memorized and similarly will have a hard time sticking with the hearers. In being memorized the sermon is honed to a final sharp edge that also makes it better for the hearers to follow.

What I have presented here is a sort of handcraft, nothing more. It is not original, and artistically it certainly is of little value. But I'll be very honest: in the congregation as it actually exists, I lack both the time for and the leisure of artistic production. Producing one or more works of art each week would be asking too much of me; I am aware of that. On the other hand, the practical tools put in my hand in the USA prove themselves serviceable and helpful when it comes to composing reasonably well prepared sermons on a regular basis or, when need be, several of them one right after another. When I, after initial engagement with the sermon lessen, find a thousand different thought swirling around in my head, and I don't know how I am to master them, I repeatedly find it a very salutary experience, to come to order in this chaos with the help of the method for working through the sermon's preparation that I here present. I then know which way I am to go in the further composition of the sermon, and for this reason I can recommend these as useful tools.

THEOLOGICAL RATIONAL FOR THIS METHOD OF SERMON PREPARATION

In closing, I wish to call attention to a few experiences that one can have when using the goal-malady-means method in preparing a sermon. We preachers should never forget that any methods we use in our work must be theologically scrutinized and finally methods for which we can give theological account.

One danger of this method has to do with consequences of setting a goal for the sermon. The goal can easily be misunderstood as something to which first and foremost the imperative or linguistic forms related to it would correspond. This is not true and, in fact, poses a danger that must absolutely be avoided. Rather, indicative speech, spoken to the hearers—promise (*Zuspruch*)—correlates with the gospel as the central content of the sermon. When we preach we may do this with the confidence that through this very promise, through this indicative speaking of the gospel, the goal to which the sermon aspires will be reached with the hearers. The imperative and related linguistic forms should, on the other hand, be used very sparingly, and when then most likely in the sense of "commands of faith," as Otto Hof so wonderfully elaborated in his important article.[35]

Directly related to this issue is the next danger, namely that the goal orientation of a sermon can easily be misunderstood in a synergistic fashion, as if it were possible for us to "set hearts ablaze with the gospel," to put it the unutterable words once used on the *Ablaze!* homepage of our Lutheran sister church in the USA.[36] Faith and love cannot be methodologized by using the tool of the goal-malady-means method; we preachers should certainly not let any pressure for success be set for us, as if we could in any way tell or test whether we with our sermon reached the goal with the hearers that we set for the sermon. On the other hand, we also cannot try our best to preach sermons without goal and plan in an effort not to give the impression that we are giving the Holy Spirit a hand in his work. God himself has something in mind for those who hear his word preached; through his word he will not leave them as they were before. This very fact may and should show itself in the direction and structure of our sermons.

A further danger using goal, malady, and means consists in its being misunderstood in the sense of Tillich's method of correlation, and this possibly in its most vulgarized form, as it was presented, for example, in 1963 at the fourth plenary assembly of the Lutheran World Federation in Helsinki.[37] The sermon should not give the impression that that the Christian faith is only or even essentially about giving answers to human questions or that it holds ready the answer to the problems that befall us human beings today and at all times. Goal, malady, and means should in no way serve as a guide to fashion sermons like detergent commercials, neither in their content nor in their structure.[38] Rather, the hearers' malady is first uncovered by the word of God. How it is then treated is not simply about solving it as if it were a problem. As mentioned, when we preachers put our finger on a malady we are entering into a battle between the old and the new man. So the

---

35. "Das Gebot," 191–222.

36. *Ablaze!*™ was a evangelism initiative of The Lutheran Church—Missouri Synod that sought to reach 100 million people with the gospel by 2017. In order to measure its success, a web-based tally of "gospel-sharing events" was kept, so that members of the church could record instances in which they shared their faith with others. The webpage has, since this composition, been discontinued.

37. Cf. here my comments in *Die Rechtfertigung des Sünders*, 141–44.

38. Cf. Martens, "Glaubensgewißheit oder Daseinsgewißheit?," 171–79, esp. 173–76.

"solving" of the malady can only consist in the death of the old man and in the resurrection of the new man. Only in view of the God's judgment does the depth of a given text's and sermon's malady become clear. Already in Helsinki the cardinal sin in how justification is handled came in suppressing the context and framework of divine judgment for justification; not only did Peter Brunner suffer through this, but he also clearly elaborated the matter.[39] In the meantime, this suppression of the context and framework of divine judgment has become very normal in preaching, even when the preacher is not using the goal-malady-means method. However, using this trio should in no way help this sad trend along.

Finally, something also needs to be said of speaking of the gospel as "means." In a certain respect, speaking of the gospel in this way naturally becomes problematic if the gospel is thereby reduced to some sort of "means to an end" or to just pure "motivation." Of course if the gospel is infinitely more then it certainly may not show up in a sermon in only some instrumentalized fashion. However, when using the goal-malady-means method, the designation of the gospel as "means" can prove an important aid in drawing the gospel through the whole of the sermon instead of allocating it some particular place at the end, as happens in the classic "Prussian sermon": black and white, law and gospel. Working with the gospel as "means" constantly forces the preacher to take the gospel in the specific form presented in the given sermon lesson seriously and not just bring it at any old point with set phrases and typical verbiage, which is a quick way of checking a "gospel" box whilst ignoring the gospel in the text. With faith goals, applying the gospel as means is nothing other than unfolding this gospel as broadly as possible in the sermon, or, in the case of a penitential sermon, unfolding it as clearly as possible, in order to reach this faith goal. In the case of love goals, the gospel's designation as means assures that paranesis is evangelically anchored throughout the sermon. Understanding and working with the gospel as "means" is meant to highlight the gospel's own potency and to let the gospel come to the strongest possible expression in preaching.

This look at theological accountability in the application of homiletical method brings this essay comes to an end with the hope that what has been said of this method may prove a help and encouragement in carrying out the most wonderful service in the world!

---

39. Cf. Martens, "Die Frage," 41–71.

BIBLIOGRAPHY

Aho, Gerhard. *The Lively Skeleton: Thematic Approaches and Outlines*. Preacher's Workshop 4. St. Louis: Concordia, 1977.

Caemmerer, Richard. *Preaching for the Church*, 2nd ed. St. Louis: Concordia, 1964.

Hof, Otto. "Das Gebot des Glaubens bei Luther." In *Schriftauslegung und Rechtfertigungslehre: Aufsätze zur Theologie Luthers, mit einem Geleitwort von Edmund Schlink*, 191–222. Karlsruhe: Evangelischer Pressverband für Baden, 1982.

Martens, Gottfried. "Die Frage nach der Rettung aus dem Gericht: Der Beitrag Peter Brunners zur Behandlung der Rechtfertigungsthematik vor und bei der IV. Vollversammlung des Lutherischen Weltbundes in Helsinki 1963." LTK 13 (1989) 41–71.

———. "Glaubensgewißheit oder Daseinsgewißheit? Bemerkungen zu Auftrag und Ziel der Rechtfertigungsverkündigung der Kirche." In *Rechtfertigung und Weltverantwortung: Internationale Konsultation Neuendettelsau 9.-12. September 1991: Berichte und Referate. Herausgegeben im Auftrag der Gesellschaft für Innere und Äußere Mission im Sinne der Lutherischen Kirche*, edited by Wolfhart Schlichting, 171–79. Neuendettelsau: Freimund-Verlag, 1993.

———. *Die Rechtfertigung des Sünders—Rettungshandeln Gottes oder historisches Interpretament? Grundentscheidungen lutherischer Theologie und Kirche bei der Behandlung des Themas "Rechtfertigung" im ökumenischen Kontext*. FSÖTh 64. Göttingen: Vandenhoeck & Ruprecht, 1992.

Nicol, Martin. *Einander ins Bild Setzen: Dramturgische Homiletik*. Göttingen: Vandenhoeck & Ruprecht, 2002.

Seitz, Manfred. "Zum Problem der sogenannten Predigtmeditation." In *Praxis des Glaubens: Gottesdienst, Seelsorge und Spiritualität*, 21–32. 3rd ed. Göttingen: Vandenhoeck & Ruprecht, 1985.

Walther, C. F. W. *Law & Gospel: How to Read and Apply the Bible*. Edited by Charles P. Schaum. Translated by Christian C. Tiews. St. Louis: Concordia, 2010.

www.ingramcontent.com/pod-product-compliance
Lightning Source LLC
Chambersburg PA
CBHW050620300426
44112CB00012B/1592